SAGE was founded in 1965 by Sara Miller McCune to support the dissemination of usable knowledge by publishing innovative and high-quality research and teaching content. Today, we publish over 900 journals, including those of more than 400 learned societies, more than 800 new books per year, and a growing range of library products including archives, data, case studies, reports, and video. SAGE remains majority-owned by our founder, and after Sara's lifetime will become owned by a charitrust that secures our continued independence.

Los Angeles | London | New Delhi | Singapore | Washington DC | Melbourne

Thank you for choosing a SAGE product!
If you have any comment, observation or feedback,
I would like to personally hear from you.

Please write to me at **contactceo@sagepub.in**

Vivek Mehra, Managing Director and CEO, SAGE India.

Bulk Sales

SAGE India offers special discounts
for purchase of books in bulk.
We also make available special imprints
and excerpts from our books on demand.

For orders and enquiries, write to us at

Marketing Department
SAGE Publications India Pvt Ltd
B1/I-1, Mohan Cooperative Industrial Area
Mathura Road, Post Bag 7
New Delhi 110044, India

E-mail us at **marketing@sagepub.in**

Subscribe to our mailing list
Write to **marketing@sagepub.in**

This book is also available as an e-book.

TRENDS AND ISSUES IN DOCTORAL EDUCATION

SAGE Studies in Higher Education

Higher Education has become an important player in the global economy and has a dynamic and growing role in every society. Massification, differentiation, human resource development, knowledge development and transfer, internationalization and privatization are key characteristics of the global higher education landscape, although they manifest themselves in different ways depending on the type of institution, country and/ or region of the world. Traditional divisions—such as those between North and South, high-income and lower-middle income economies, universities and vocational schools, and so on—are no longer adequate to describe the dynamic and complex patterns of postsecondary education worldwide. *SAGE Studies in Higher Education* provides cogent discussion, analysis and debate of key themes in global higher education.

Series Editors

Philip G. Altbach
Research Professor and
Founding Director
Center for International
Higher Education
Boston College, USA

Hans de Wit
Director
Center for International
Higher Education
Boston College, USA

Laura Rumbley
Associate Director
Center for International
Higher Education
Campion Hall, Boston College,
USA

Simon Marginson
Professor of International
Higher Education
UCL Institute of Education
University College London, UK

Claire Callender
Professor of Higher Education
Studies
UCL Institute of Education and
Birkbeck University of London,
UK

SAGE Studies in Higher Education

TRENDS AND ISSUES IN DOCTORAL EDUCATION

A Global Perspective

Edited by

Maria Yudkevich
Philip G. Altbach
Hans de Wit

Los Angeles | London | New Delhi
Singapore | Washington DC | Melbourne

First published in 2020 by

SAGE Publications India Pvt Ltd
B1/I-1 Mohan Cooperative Industrial Area
Mathura Road, New Delhi 110 044, India
www.sagepub.in

SAGE Publications Inc
2455 Teller Road
Thousand Oaks, California 91320, USA

SAGE Publications Ltd
1 Oliver's Yard, 55 City Road
London EC1Y 1SP, United Kingdom

SAGE Publications Asia-Pacific Pte Ltd
18 Cross Street #10-10/11/12
China Square Central
Singapore 048423

Published by Vivek Mehra for SAGE Publications India Pvt Ltd. Typeset in 10.5/13 pt Bembo by Zaza Eunice, Hosur, Tamil Nadu, India.

Library of Congress Cataloging-in-Publication Data

Names: Yudkevich, Maria, editor. | Altbach, Philip G, editor. | de Wit,
  Hans, editor. | Sage Publications.
Title: Trends and issues in doctoral education: a global perspective/
  edited by Maria Yudkevich, Philip G. Altbach, Hans de Wit
Description: Thousand Oaks, California: SAGE Publications India Pvt Ltd,
  2020. | Includes bibliographical references and index. Identifiers: LCCN 2020008928 (print) |
LCCN 2020008929 (ebook) | ISBN
  9789353882549 (Hardback) | ISBN 9789353882556 (ePub) | ISBN
  9789353882563 (eBook)
Subjects: LCSH: Universities and colleges—Ratings and rankings—Case
  studies. | Education, Higher—Aims and objectives—Case studies. |
  Education and globalization—Case studies. | Higher education and
  state—Case studies.
Classification: LCC LB2331.62.T74 2020 (print) | LCC LB2331.62 (ebook) |
  DDC 378.1/55—dc23
LC record available at https://lccn.loc.gov/2020008928
LC ebook record available at https://lccn.loc.gov/2020008929

ISBN: 978-93-5388-254-9 (HB)

SAGE Team: Rajesh Dey, Vandana Gupta, Sonam Rana and Rajinder Kaur

Contents

List of Figures   ix
List of Tables   xi
List of Abbreviations   xiii
Preface   xv
Acknowledgements   xix

Part I: Introduction

Chapter 1   Trends and Practices: The Literature
                Concerning Doctoral Education
                *Ayenachew A. Woldegiyorgis, Victor
                Rudakov, Ksenia Rozhkova and Dara Melnyk*   3
Chapter 2   Doctoral Education Worldwide:
                Three Decades of Change
                Maresi Nerad   33

Part II: Europe

Chapter 3   Between Change and Continuity: The
                Transformation of Doctoral Education in France
                *Julien Calmand, Thierry Chevaillier and
                Jean-François Giret*   53
Chapter 4   The Past, Present and Future of Doctoral
                Education in Germany
                Barbara M. Kehm   79
Chapter 5   Poland: An Abundance of Doctoral
                Students but a Scarcity of Doctorates
                Marek Kwiek   103
Chapter 6   Russian Doctoral Education:
                Between Teaching and Research
                Elena Kobzar and Sergey Roshchin   127

Chapter 7   The UK Doctorate: History,
                   Features and Challenges
                   Rosemary Deem and Shane Dowle   152

Part III: North America

Chapter 8   Strengths, Challenges and Opportunities
                   for US Doctoral Education
                   Ann E. Austin and Emily R. Miller   181

Part IV: Africa

Chapter 9   Challenges of Development of Doctoral
                   Education in Africa
                   Ayenachew A. Woldegiyorgis   213
Chapter 10   Imperatives and Realities of Doctoral
                   Education in South Africa
                   Damtew Teferra   238

Part V: Asia

Chapter 11   Mainland China: Rapid Growth and
                   New Strategies in Doctoral Education
                   Shuhua Chen   267
Chapter 12   The Role of Doctoral Education in
                   Developing Research Capacities in India
                   N. V. Varghese   295
Chapter 13   From Quantitative Expansion to Qualitative
                   Improvement: Changes in Doctoral
                   Education in Japan
                   Futao Huang   316
Chapter 14   Development and Transformation of
                   Doctoral Education in Kazakhstan
                   Aliya Kuzhabekova   340
Chapter 15   Rapid Development and Current Rethinking
                   in Doctoral Education in South Korea
                   *HeeJin Lim, Seung Jung Kim and
                   Jung Cheol Shin*   363

Part VI: Latin America

Chapter 16   Building Research Capacity and Training:
             Brazilian Dilemmas in Doctoral Education
             Ana Maria Fonseca de Almeida,
             Mauricio Ernica and Marcelo Knobel   389
Chapter 17   Reassessing the Progress of
             Doctoral Education in Chile
             Ana Luisa Muñoz-García and
             Andrés Bernasconi   414

Part VII: Middle East

Chapter 18   United Arab Emirates:
             A Doctoral Education Start-Up
             Tatiana Karabchuk   443

Part VIII: Conclusion

Chapter 19   Doctoral Education Worldwide:
             Key Trends and Realities
             Maria Yudkevich, Philip G. Altbach,
             Hans de Wit and Victor Rudakov   467

About the Editors and Contributors   491
Index   499

List of Figures

5.1   Mean Age for Award of Doctoral and
Habilitation Degrees (1970–2016)   115

5.2   FM Ratio of Doctorates and Habilitations
Awarded (1990–2006)   118

6.1   Trends in Doctoral Training   130

6.2   System of Doctoral Training and PhD Awarding
in Russia   135

7.1   Growth in the UK Doctoral Completions   155

7.2   Enrolments by Discipline and Gender   164

8.1   Doctorate Award by Citizenship and
Major Fields of Study (1996 and 2016)   192

10.1   Headcount of the 2011 Cohort Graduating with
Doctoral Degrees in Six Years (i.e., by 2016)   242

10.2   Fields of Graduates   243

10.3   Total Doctoral Graduates per Decade
(Except for 1899–1920)   245

11.1   Numbers of Entrants, Enrolments and
Graduates (1997–2017)   269

13.1   Changes in the Numbers of Students in
Doctoral Courses   321

16.1   Number of Doctoral Programmes in
Brazil by Type of Higher Education Institution
from 1998 to 2016   398

16.2 Number of Doctoral Degrees Awarded in
Brazil by Type of Higher Education Institution
from 1998 to 2016   399
16.3 Total Number of Doctoral Degrees Awarded in
Brazil per Year from 1998 to 2016   400
16.4 Relative Percentage of Doctoral Degrees Awarded in
Brazil, by Gender, from 1996 to 2008   402

17.1 Enrolments in Higher Education in Chile (1985–2017),
by Type of Institution   417
17.2. Enrolments of Doctoral Students in Chile (1984–2017)   422

List of Tables

3.1 Unemployment Rate, Three Years After Graduation 69

3.2 Employment of PhD Graduates by Sector,
Three Years After Graduation 69

4.1 Employment Status of Doctoral Candidates in
Germany (2014–2015) 86

4.2 Doctoral Degree Awards (2007–2016) by Subject Group 93

4.3 Doctoral Degree Awards (2016) to International
Candidates by Most Represented Countries of Origin 100

5.1 Doctoral Students and Doctorates Awarded in Poland
(1990–2016) 109

5.2 Number of Doctoral Students by Major Academic
Fields (2016) 111

5.3 Number of Doctorates and Habilitations Awarded by
Gender (1990–2006) 117

7.1 UK Doctoral Students Compared to Other HE Students 162

8.1 Doctorate Recipients by Major Fields of Study 190

8.2 Doctorate Recipients by Major Fields of Study and Sex 194

12.1 PhD and MPhil Enrolment by Major Discipline and
Gender (2017, in %) 304

12.2 MPhil and Doctorate Degrees Awarded by Faculty 306

12.3 Doctoral Degrees Awarded by Faculty 308

13.1 Number of Students and Universities Offering
Doctoral Degrees as of 1 May 2017 323

13.2 Amount of Allowance for Living Expenses per Doctoral
Student (per Year)   333
13.3 Changes in the Numbers of Doctoral Students in
Total and by Discipline   334
13.4 Changes in the Numbers of Doctoral Graduates and
Awarded Doctoral Degrees   335

14.1 Enrolled PhD Students by Area of Specialization
as of 2017–2018   353

15.1 Changes in Numbers of Doctoral Students
by Discipline   367
15.2 Doctoral Degree Holders by
Categorized Universities (2017)   371

17.1 Share of Enrolments in Higher Education by
Type of Institution (1985–2017)   419
17.2 Enrolment in Doctoral Programmes
by University Type (2017)   426
17.3 Doctoral Programmes Offered by Institutions (2017)   427

18.1 Total Number of Public and Private Higher Education
Institutions in 2017 (by Emirate)   447
18.2 Total Number of Students Enrolled in Higher Education
Institutions in the UAE (2013–2017)   448
18.3 Number of Faculty Members (by Gender and Status)
in Public and Private Higher Education Institutions
in the UAE (2014–2017)   452

19.1 Statistics on Institutional Settings of Doctoral Education
in Analysed Countries   485

List of Abbreviations

AAU	Association of African Universities
ACE	Africa Centres of Excellence
ARUA	African Research Universities Alliance
BK21	Brain Korea 21
CDT–BEPS	Centre for Doctoral Training in Business, Enterprise and Professional Studies
CFT	Centros de Formación Técnica
CIRTL	Center for the Integration of Research, Teaching and Learning
CIS	Commonwealth of Independent States
CSC	China Scholarship Council
DHET	Department of Higher Education and Training
DST	Department of Science and Technology
DWC	Double-World-Class
ECRs	Early career researchers
EU	European Union
FM	Female-to-male
GDP	Gross domestic product
GER	Gross enrolment ratio
HE	Higher education
HEIs	Higher education institutions
HLC	Higher Learning Commission
IAU	International Association of Universities
IP	Institutos Profesionales
ISCED	International Standard Classification of Education
JNU	Jawaharlal Nehru University
KAIST	Korea Advanced Institute of Science and Technology
MDU	Maharshi Dayanand University

MIXT	Ministry of Education, Culture, Sports, Science and Technology
MOE	Ministry of Education
NCSES	National Center for Science and Engineering Statistics
NDP	National Development Plan
NET	National Eligibility Test
nGAP	New Generation of Academics Programme
NIH	National Institutes of Health
NISTEP	National Institute of Science and Technology Policy
NRF	National Research Foundation
NSF	National Science Foundation
NU	Nazarbayev University
ORUs	Organized Research Units
PRES	Postgraduate Research Experience Survey
R&D	Research and development
RDAPs	Research degree awarding powers
S&E	Science and engineering
SARUA	Southern African Regional Universities Association
SEH	Sciences, Engineering, and Health
SIDA	Swedish International Development Cooperation Agency
SSAUF	Staffing South Africa's Universities Framework
STEM	Science, technology, engineering and mathematics
UAE	United Arab Emirates
UAEU	United Arab Emirates University
UCAS	University of the Chinese Academy of Sciences
UCGH	University of the Cape of Good Hope
UCT	University of Cape Town
UGC	University Grants Commission
UKCGE	UK Council for Graduate Education
UNISA	University of South Africa
URM	Underrepresented minorities
USAf	Universities South Africa
USHEPiA	Universities Science, Humanities, Law and Engineering Partnerships in Africa
WU	Westlake University

Preface

Trends and Issues in Doctoral Education: A Global Perspective serves two simple yet complex purposes: to understand the present realities in doctoral education worldwide and to examine both current and proposed reforms in key countries. We link broader societal and economic issues affecting doctoral education to the realities at the universities themselves. Government policies relating to doctoral education, as well as pressures from the labour markets, both on and off campus, are also considered.

This book contains 15 case studies, 14 of which are country-based and 1 is regional. These cases analyse the range of global practice as well as the key issues facing doctoral education. The book includes a discussion of the relevant literature concerning doctoral education worldwide and an overview of the changes in it around the world over the past three decades by leading scholar Maresi Nerad. It concludes with a discussion of the broader issues and themes suggested by the case studies. Thus, this volume provides not only analysis but also suggestions for positive changes.

Doctoral education trains and nurtures new scholars, and thus is a key element for the successful future of academia. Increasingly, doctoral education provides professional qualifications for a growing number of fields outside of traditional academic professions. The future of the contemporary university and research enterprise worldwide depends on effective, imaginative and relevant doctoral education. However, in the 21st century, doctoral education faces challenges everywhere. In some countries, there are not enough doctoral degree holders graduating to respond to rapidly growing post-secondary job vacancies and to meet the demands of the knowledge economy. In others, there is an oversupply of doctoral graduates where enrolments are either flat or, in some disciplines and specializations, not in balance with the requirements of the economy or of academe. Questions about the appropriate organization and purpose of the doctorate are common. Critics challenge the very nature of the doctorate, arguing that doctoral training requires major reforms in order to meet the realities of changing labour markets and face the revolution in knowledge production and research worldwide. As universities have become globalized and borders between universities and non-university sectors have become less clear, many have argued that doctoral education needs to adjust. Despite these and other significant challenges, and the fact that there is a great variety in the organization and delivery of doctoral education among countries and universities around the world, there has been relatively little fundamental change in doctoral education. While universities have changed significantly in recent decades, doctoral education has remained more rigid. Yet, as the chapters in this book show, there is currently a good deal of discussion about both the challenges and prospects for reform and change.

Doctoral education is criticized worldwide. Some claim that traditional models are no longer relevant for the 21st century. Others point to long degree-completion times, high dropout levels, a lack of interdisciplinarity and internationality, a lack of adequate transversal skills for a more diverse labour market and poor quality of training and research due to budget cuts. There are debates concerning the two main directions in educational preparation: the European pattern of the 'research doctorate', with little coursework and a high level of dependence on a single academic advisor or laboratory, versus the North American pattern of significant coursework combined with a dissertation and a more collective advising arrangement. Patterns are adapted to national and institutional contexts, creating a great variety of realities in doctoral education as far as content, learning outcomes, length of programme, supervision and output requirements are concerned. At the same time, there has been scant discussion about how these models fit into the broader picture of the organization of academic systems, in general, and academic labour markets, in particular, or about how rigid these systems may be in their adjustment to new demands and realities. There is evidence that a number of countries and universities are moving towards a more 'American' pattern of organizing doctoral education.

There are differences in length of time to degree—in general between three and five years—although with significant variations among disciplines. There are also differences in terms of the status of doctoral candidates (in some countries they are students, while in others they are categorized as employees) and in funding (free, tuition based, with scholarships or loans, or with a salary), as well as in teaching responsibilities, supervision, requirements, outputs, and purpose and relevance. There are also differences in who awards degrees—the state or the universities themselves. Questions exist about the position of doctoral programmes within the university: Do they fall under the purview of the department or the faculty, or in one or more graduate schools within or between universities? Are they offered together with master's and continuing education programmes, or not? There is also a discussion about academic versus professional doctoral programmes, as a large proportion of doctoral graduates do not enter academia, yet remain unprepared to join the rest of the labour market. There are also wide variations (by country, discipline and individual universities) in terms of labour markets and job prospects for young doctoral degree holders in academe as well as for their career prospects in the non-university sector.

There have been some changes to the traditional dissertation, with some universities requiring published work in addition to a dissertation, or dropping the dissertation completely and replacing it with a series of related published articles. Traditional patterns of doctoral preparation have, however, proved to be highly resilient and, in general, have produced well-prepared graduates. Yet few analysts think that the current state of doctoral education is satisfactory.

Last but not least, doctoral education has become an essential component in the overall internationalization of higher education in several ways. There have been increases in the number of international doctoral students and higher student demand for access to international publications and conferences. This, however, has also resulted in more predatory journals and conferences. More international scholars are now involved in the co-supervision of students and as readers and members of defence committees. There have also been increased calls for the internationalization of the doctoral curriculum.

Doctoral education may seem to be a limited topic, but it is of great importance for the future of universities, scientific research more broadly, the knowledge economy and for the scientific and academic workforce globally. While there are statistics concerning total numbers of post-secondary students worldwide, there seem to be no easily available numbers for doctoral students, although national figures are available for many countries. It is clear that the large majority of doctorates are earned in the main research-producing countries in North America, Europe and Japan, but countries like China are rapidly expanding doctoral programmes. It is clear that many countries are experiencing major variations between the demand and production of doctorates, in terms of both specific fields and overall numbers. Rapidly expanding post-secondary systems require larger numbers of doctoral degree holders than are currently being produced, while countries with stable enrolments are in many cases producing too many doctorates for the traditional academic labour market. These and other issues are considered at length in this volume.

Acknowledgements

This book, like several other collaborative research projects between the Laboratory for Institutional Analysis at HSE University in Moscow and the Center for International Higher Education at Boston College, stems from our joint research interests. Of special importance is a concern in Russia about the future of doctoral studies. The Basic Research Program of HSE University provided the funding that made this research possible.

We are especially indebted to our authors (some of the most experienced researchers on doctoral education anywhere) for their contributions. Our research group met in Moscow in November 2019 to discuss chapter drafts, and this book is the result of our discussions and subsequent chapter revisions.

In Moscow, Vera Arbieva worked through the complexities of this research project while keeping it all together and has been central to the successful completion of our work. Our two text editors, Amsterdam-based Clark Boyd and Boston-based Hélène Bernot Ullero, are responsible for ensuring the readability of the book.

PART I

Introduction

Chapter 1

Trends and Practices
The Literature Concerning Doctoral Education

Ayenachew A. Woldegiyorgis, Victor Rudakov, Ksenia Rozhkova and Dara Melnyk

This chapter draws on literature from across different countries to paint a general picture of the state of doctoral education, and highlights major themes and common issues in different higher education systems. The review covers, and as such is limited to, literature available in English. Also, as it sets out to scan literature across common themes, the review focuses less on in-depth, country-specific case studies.

The chapter begins by elaborating the centrality of doctoral education, followed by a discussion of its purposes. Labour market conditions and quality are the next two themes that are discussed. Variations based on different considerations and major trends in contemporary doctoral education are also explored. Finally, common challenges across systems and possible prospects are discussed.

CENTRALITY OF DOCTORAL EDUCATION

Today, the once contested notion that human capital trained at a higher level makes a crucial contribution to a nation's economic development appears to be almost axiomatically accepted, particularly concerning graduate education. Doctoral-level training in particular, by fostering research and innovation, plays a unique role in human capacity development, producing the workforce fit for the knowledge- and technology-based approach to solve the multifaceted challenges of this century (Altbach 2007; Bitzer 2012; Nerad 2014a). Evidence has emerged highlighting a direct link between doctoral education and overall national development (Cloete, Sheppard, and Bailey 2015; Maheu et al. 2014).

Graduates of doctoral programmes are not only expected to have highly specialized knowledge and skills in their respective fields, but also presumed to be tomorrow's leaders (Bernstein et al. 2014)—not only in research and academe but also in other fields, as more positions demand a doctoral degree. There is a growing consensus on the overall importance of doctoral education for research productivity, and consequently for socioeconomic development (Casey 2009). Examining policy statements and practices from Europe, the United States, Canada and Australia, Bernstein et al. (2014, 6) show three major common areas regarding doctoral programmes: (a) doctoral graduates are expected to have a solid knowledge in their areas of expertise, (b) through original research, doctoral studies should contribute to knowledge and (c) doctoral-level training must incorporate the development of transferable skills and competencies. Moreover, PhD degree holders educate undergraduates, indirectly shaping the future of the whole nation (Walker et al. 2008).

In most countries, conferring a doctoral degree is a privilege limited to universities (Byrne, Jørgensen, and Loukkola 2013). For a long time, universities showed little flexibility with regard to doctoral education, relying on values and traditions from centuries ago (Salter 2013). In recent decades, though, changes in the global environment related to higher education, the labour market, the overarching move to a knowledge economy, the inevitable forces of globalization and internationalization and other factors have forced doctoral education to open up to change.

The importance of doctoral education as a central element of the research capacity of the university and as a means for knowledge

creation and innovation in the global competitive economy has made
it a prominent target of policy attention (Nerad 2014b). Nations that
aspire to become important players in the world economy, and those
who wish to maintain their position as such, rely more on doctoral
education as a source of the capacity they need. Consequently, governments around the world are expanding doctoral training and critically
examining the models of doctoral training in their higher education
systems (Nerad, Trzyna, and Higgelund 2008).

Policy attention by national governments has been influenced by
the efforts of supranational actors such as the European Union, the
OECD, the World Bank and other regional and international actors
(Nerad 2014b). These institutions use different instruments, like publication of reports and policy briefs, and exert leverage to influence
policy directions. In this respect, the most prominent among these
institutions is the European Union, which, along with other partners
and processes such as the European University Association and the
Bologna Process, has taken a series of steps towards the creation of
the European Research Area, aiming to standardize and harmonize
doctoral education throughout Europe (Fortes, Kehm, and Mayekiso
2014; Kehm 2007).

In recent decades, doctoral education has undergone a massive
expansion globally, of course, much more so in some countries than
in others. For example, right after the Cultural Revolution, China
launched what was later to become an extraordinary expansion of its
graduate education. In 2010, 49,000 doctorates were conferred, making
China second only to the United States (Yang 2012). Similarly, Chien
and Chapman (2014) noted that in the past decade, graduate enrolments in Malaysia and Thailand increased by 400 and 300 per cent,
respectively. A report covering eight flagship universities in Africa also
shows that the combined number of doctoral graduates from these
institutions has more than doubled between 2001 and 2011 (Bunting
et al. 2015). This may be the result of the emphasis that the respective
governments give to graduate education by designating certain institutions as research universities and endowing them with a substantial
boost in public funding.

International mobility in doctoral education has significantly increased since the end of the Cold War in the 1990s, with the major host countries (such as the United States, Australia, the United Kingdom, Germany and France) receiving an increasingly significant proportion of international doctoral students. These countries—with China as a recent addition to the race—are engaged in a competition to attract international students with carefully designed policies and incentive schemes.

Finally, the growing number and diversity of stakeholders in doctoral education in recent times has also contributed to changing doctoral education. What traditionally was a primary concern for the individual student and the supervising faculty has now become the direct or indirect business of university leaders, government, funding organizations, quality assurance agencies, industry and the community at large (Nerad, Trzyna, and Higgelund 2008). Similarly, with the growing recognition of the role of doctoral research in knowledge creation and its contribution to economic and social development, doctoral education and doctoral degree holders have become commodities in the global market (Evans 2014). These new and reinforced interests have triggered various changes—from structure to content—in how doctoral education is designed and managed.

PURPOSE

Despite its long history and traditionally strong association with research directed at generating new knowledge, the purpose of doctoral degree is debated across disciplines and institutions (Bitzer 2012; Cloete, Sheppard, and Bailey 2015). A doctoral degree has become a common requirement for academic positions at four-year universities and, increasingly, at junior colleges (Altbach 2007). In line with the widespread practice of doctoral training as a phase of preparation for future faculty, Bailey, Bogossian, and Akesson (2016) advocate that doctoral training has to incorporate a good amount of training in teaching skills—lesson planning, management of the classroom, grading assignments, etc.

On the other hand, doctoral graduates are sought after worldwide for their critical thinking in addressing various issues and problems, their creativity and capacity for innovation and their leadership skills (Bernstein et al. 2014). Driven in particular by the notion of the knowledge-based economy phenomenon, a growing number of doctoral graduates in high-income countries are being absorbed into the non-academic labour market. In the United States, the National Science Board (2016) reported that doctoral graduates in science and engineering who identify teaching as their primary work declined from 68 per cent to 46 per cent between 1973 and 2013. In Europe, Baschung (2010) noted similar patterns, largely driven by the reforms of the Bologna Process and the aspiration of the Lisbon Agenda to make Europe a knowledge economy.

Generally, there is a growing argument for a more diversified purpose of doctoral education. As sources of highly skilled human capital, doctoral programmes are increasingly recognized for their contributions to economic prosperity and nation building. Therefore, Maheu et al. (2014) argued that doctoral education has to be central to, and integrated with, the set-up and implementation of science, technology, innovation and overall development policy. Employers want to make sure that doctoral graduates are trained to fit their particular needs. This has resulted in the emergence of the 'fitness for purpose' notion of doctoral training (Nerad 2014b).

Nonetheless, there is a concern that because of their lengthy academic training and acculturation with the academic environment, doctoral graduates might not easily fit into the work environment of sectors other than higher education (Acosta and Celis 2014). Aware of that concern, doctoral programmes are increasingly engaging their students in practical exposures and traineeships in the work environment. Similarly, more expectations are being placed on doctoral programmes and their respective host institutions, as can be seen in the 'Salzburg Principles'—an agreement developed in 2005 (Christensen 2005).

In lower-middle income countries, as a result of the growing expansion of higher education and a continuing concern in improving quality, doctoral graduates are more likely to go into work in higher education than in industry or business (Acosta and Celis 2014). Across Asia and Africa, enrolment has significantly grown in the past few decades, leading to the expansion of graduate programmes not only to train new faculty but also to improve the qualifications of existing ones. In the Philippines, for instance, in 2002 only 8 per cent of faculty at higher education institutions had a doctoral degree. In 2012, this number increased to 13 per cent (Chien and Chapman 2014), showing that there is still much work needed in this regard. Countries such as China and Brazil are making sizable investments in training young faculty at the doctoral level. In Africa, a study of eight major flagship universities showed that only 43 per cent of their academic staff had a doctoral qualification (Cloete, Bunting, and Maassen 2015). This number is likely to be much lower for the large majority of institutions across the continent.

LABOUR MARKET CONDITIONS

A number of studies argue that the massification of higher education and the excessive growth of the number of doctoral degree holders have led to market imbalance, and an oversupply of doctoral graduates that cannot be fully absorbed—neither by academia nor by industry (Carnoy et al. 2013; Huisman, de Weert, and Bartelse 2002; Kobayashi 2011; Schwabe 2011; Trow 2007). This market imbalance has led to a decrease in the value of a doctoral degree in the labour market (Chevaillier and Duru-Bellat 2017) and raised concerns about career prospects for doctoral degree holders, triggering a broad discussion among scholars and policy-makers about reform agendas for doctoral education, along the themes listed below.

Does a Doctoral Degree Pay Off?

One of the most common indicators of the labour market value of a doctoral degree is its outcome in terms of wages and employment prospects for graduates. Results of empirical studies on the wage premium for a doctoral degree and employment opportunities vary significantly across different countries and fields of knowledge.

In the United Kingdom, a 2005 study showed that doctoral education was a worthwhile investment over and above an undergraduate degree. However, the returns to a PhD degree significantly varied according to fields of study: from a 20 per cent wage premium in business, financial studies and medicine to negative returns in arts and engineering (O'Leary and Sloane 2005). In a more recent study, Lindley and Machin (2013) obtained almost the same results. Hoeling, Gudgeon and Hagemeister (2015) found no evidence of decrease of returns to a doctoral degree, despite the significant growth of the number of doctoral degree holders. Moreover, they report that in 2013, wage premiums for doctoral degrees in the United Kingdom even rose compared to 2005.

Germany seems to be the most successful example of dealing with an oversupply of doctorates and providing different career paths for doctoral graduates. The majority of doctoral degree holders in the German labour market are employed in well-paid, full-time positions both inside and outside the academic sector (Enders 2004; Huisman, De Weert, and Bartelse 2002; Mertens and Robken 2013). Similarly, doctoral degree holders are also successful in the Swedish and Austrian labour markets (Huisman, de Weert, and Bartelse 2002; Schwabe 2011).

In contrast, a number of studies show negative or insignificant returns for doctoral degree holders compared to master's degree holders. In the Danish private sector, a doctoral degree would imply neither a wage premium (compared to a master's degree) nor a penalty. The return does not occur in the early phase of one's career either, which can be explained by the competition with 'firm-specific' or 'industry-specific' human capital—who have a master's degree but a longer work experience compared to employees with doctorates, who studied instead of working (Pedersen 2016). An analysis of the labour market in the Netherlands shows that there is a negative impact of doctoral studies compared to master's studies on male degree holders, and a positive one on female degree holders (Van der Steeg, Van der Wiel, and Wouterse 2014).

In Asia, Japan provides an example of a labour market with a negative return on doctoral studies. According to Kobayashi (2011), the excessive supply of doctoral degree holders, a lack of career opportunities in academia and the traditional preference of Japanese industry for young graduates with a bachelor's degree who can be trained on the job have weakened the position of doctoral degree holders. In contrast, in China, despite the extensive growth in doctoral education, most Chinese doctoral degree holders can easily find jobs at home, as the economy absorbs them in the workforce (Yang 2012).

Another concern about the labour market outcomes of doctoral education is connected to the long transition period from degree acquisition until a stable work position is secured. This may partly be explained by the considerable duration of doctoral training, and consequently, the age of graduates at the time they obtain the degree and start looking for a job. The possibility of unemployment in the first year after graduation is not considered to be high, but there are significant differences across disciplines. Recent doctoral degree holders rarely get permanent faculty positions, and the majority works on temporary contracts (Huisman, De Weert, and Bartelse 2002).

Academia versus Industry

Academia and industry offer the most likely career paths for doctoral degree holders. The expected earning is a major determinant of choice for employment in industry (Roach and Sauermann 2010). In the majority of cases, due to limited financial resources, academia cannot offer wages comparable to those in the private sector (Ehrenberg 2005). Still, doctoral graduates tend mostly to consider employment possibilities inside academia (Nerad 2004).

Despite this tendency, opportunities for permanent positions within academia are becoming more restricted (Huisman, de Weert, and Bartelse 2002). In most countries, the academic sector simply cannot absorb every doctoral graduate. As a result, industry's role in providing employment opportunities is increasing (Herrera and Nieto 2016). Although doctoral students go through an extensive preparation, the qualifications acquired during their studies do not necessarily match job requirements. The human capital accumulated during doctoral education can be too specific and not readily transferable to the private sector—a problem of overeducation. At the same time, firms and industry representatives claim that the professional skills provided by doctoral education are insufficient (Herrera and Nieto 2016). As a result, doctoral graduates are increasingly facing challenges when entering the labour market in terms of finding positions that correspond to their level of qualification (Boulos 2016).

Overeducation and Job: Education Mismatch among Doctoral Degree Holders

Researchers claim that overeducation is a widespread phenomenon among doctoral degree recipients. For instance, in Italy, a considerable proportion of doctoral degree holders (19%) draw no benefit from their degrees in their current job, and an even greater share (45%) do not consider the skills and competencies acquired through their doctoral training to be useful for their present job (Gaeta 2015). The situation is similar in Spain. Doctoral graduates are frequently overqualified for jobs they get in the private sector, as there is a lack of high-level positions there, compared to the increasing number of doctorate holders (Paolo and Mañé 2016). The issue of overeducation for doctoral students is significantly correlated with the field of study, international mobility during the training, channels of access to the job and residential location (Gaeta 2015).

Overeducation and mismatch between education and job requirements are country-specific. More developed economies provide a higher demand for qualified specialists, within both academic and non-academic sectors. For instance, in the United Kingdom, researchers found no evidence supporting the assumption that skills gained during doctoral studies are difficult to transfer to jobs in the private sector (Lee, Miozzo, and Laredo 2010).

The analysis of labour market conditions for doctoral graduates shows that the United Kingdom, Germany and Sweden can be described as successful cases in terms of labour market conditions and career opportunities for doctoral graduates (Hoeling, Gudgeon, and Hagemeister 2015; Huisman, de Weert, and Bartelse 2002). Despite a shrinking labour market, the United States still provides doctoral degree holders with quite optimistic job market prospects, which, however, vary significantly by field of study. In most European countries, recent doctoral graduates face difficulties finding employment in academia.

QUALITY

As with all levels of higher education, there seems to be a general agreement on the necessity to consider quality as a serious issue in doctoral education. The emergence of new routes to the doctorate, such as professional doctorates and PhD by publication (Bitzer 2012; Teferra 2015), and different national and regional contexts make the case for quality concerns. As the emphasis on doctoral education grows, policy-makers, faculty and institutional leaders are being called upon to make sure that doctoral programmes and doctoral graduates meet the expectations of current and future global challenges (Nerad 2014a).

In the United States, no quality assessment is being performed specifically for doctoral programmes at the state or national level (Altbach 2007). The closest proxy is the ranking of institutions and discipline-based programmes. In Europe, the need for quality assurance mechanisms has been a major focus of doctoral education reforms in the past decade (Byrne, Jørgensen, and Loukkola 2013). Similarly, it has been suggested that quality doctoral education is of paramount importance for lower-middle income countries. Snyder (2014) proposed that engaging with the global knowledge society would be a better way of strengthening the quality of doctoral education in South Africa, rather than attempting to address specific local issues. In some countries, the large-scale expansion in doctoral education has caused serious quality concerns. In China, a remarkable increase in the number of doctoral education enrolments, the decline in quality of doctoral training and difficulties in managing expansion have led to some serious controversies (Yang 2012). Similarly, Acosta and Celis (2014) noted that in Latin America, the quality of new graduates seems to be steadily declining, although the numbers of both doctoral degrees awarded and publications in science and engineering have increased.

One common tendency in the quality assurance of doctoral education is that it is mostly left to the responsibility of individual institutions rather than to an external quality agency. In Europe, for example, the regulatory framework for doctoral education is more relaxed, compared to the first and second cycles. It is common for institutions to have the autonomy to introduce doctoral programmes without having to fulfil prior accreditation requirements or, in some cases, only minimal restrictions apply (Byrne, Jørgensen, and Loukkola 2013).

In a more comprehensive overview, Nerad (2014b) argued that the classical input–throughput–output model of quality assurance in the business world is becoming common among universities. In doctoral education, inputs include applicants, faculty, the research infrastructure, the political context, etc. A doctoral graduate is the primary output of a doctoral programme. In itself, the number of graduates, while providing quantification for output, does not say anything about quality. On the other hand, a graduate's dissertation, which is examined for quality by internal and (sometimes) external experts, as well as publications that go through blind review processes, reflects on the quality of the work of the candidate, and hence of the programme.

VARIATIONS

A number of variations (listed below) exist with regard to how doctoral programmes are designed and implemented, and how a successful completion is evaluated. Although various procedures and standards may be established at different levels, there is no strict uniformity, even within disciplines.

Form and Assessment of the Final Product

The diverse traditions in examining doctoral dissertations are a typical example of such variations. As reported by Bernstein et al. (2014), in the United States, a candidate's dissertation committee may or may not include members who are external to the university, whereas in countries such as Canada and the United Kingdom, and elsewhere in Europe, at least one external examiner is involved. In Australia, it is a mandatory governmental requirement for evaluation to involve at least two external examiners who provide their recommendations to the thesis committee. Oral examinations are mandatory in many countries in Europe, North America and New Zealand, whereas they are optional in Australia, Brazil, India, Malaysia and South Africa.

Publication, as a requirement or as an option, is another variation. Countries differ on whether a publication is required as a doctoral output. In the United Kingdom, for instance, the Quality Assurance Agency for Higher Education recommends that a thesis submitted for doctoral fulfilment be published, though universities do not follow this as a strict requirement (Bernstein et al. 2014). In several European countries such as Denmark and the Netherlands, it is a common practice for doctoral theses to be published. Traditionally, doctoral study is expected to produce a stand-alone original research output in the form of a dissertation; yet, recently, in fields such as the biosciences and economics, publishing a specific number of peer-reviewed articles can be considered as a satisfactory fulfilment of doctoral output requirements (Nerad 2014b). Teferra (2015) offers three reasons why a PhD by publication is, and should be, a concern for global doctoral education. First, in terms of preparation, a set of publications might not match the extensive training and close mentoring required to produce graduates able to engage in research, an academic position or professional life. Second, the fact that a publication is issued in one's name does not necessarily guarantee that the work has been done by that same person, since there are entities that, for a price, provide services related to fully or partially undertaking research. Third, publishing in a journal deemed reputable does not always provide a guarantee of high quality.

Part-Time versus Full-Time Study and Duration of Doctoral Studies

Part-time doctoral programmes are increasingly considered as alternatives to full-time engagement. Archbald (2011) claims that the growth of part-time doctoral programmes is associated with the advancement of information technologies, e-learning and the expansion of adult continuing education. On the one hand, part-time studies significantly decrease the barriers, costs and risks associated with pursuing doctoral studies. Students can enter doctoral programmes without residency permissions, leaving their jobs or relocation (Archbald 2011). On the other hand, compared to full-time students, candidates who study in part-time programmes take more time to complete their degree and have a considerably lower completion rate (Gardner 2009; Watts 2008). Part-time students also have less access to university research facilities and social networks, and fewer possibilities to get employment in universities as research and teaching assistants (Niemczyk 2016). Part-time PhD students tend to be older than full-time students and need to balance a range of family and work commitments with their research, which negatively impact their productivity (Archbald 2011; Watts 2008).

The relative share of part-time students in doctoral programmes is highly differentiated per field of study. For instance, there are more part-time students in fields like education, whereas in STEM fields (science, technology, engineering and mathematics), the share of part-time students is much lower (Gardner 2009).

Another variable that determines opportunity costs is the duration of the programme. Doctoral programmes are highly differentiated in terms of duration by field of study, type of institution and mode of study (full-time or part-time; Gardner 2009; Matute 2014). The average duration of a doctorate in science, for instance, is about three to four years in Europe and five to six years in the United States for those who enrol after a bachelor's degree, or about four years after a master's degree in a related field (Gardner 2009).

Funding

The costs of higher education continue to rise across the world, including the costs of doctoral education. As a result, funding a PhD appears to be a stressful challenge for potential candidates. PhD studies can be funded by the candidate, but it is a common practice for universities to offer scholarships to doctoral students to pursue their degree. Assistantships, fellowships and student loans are three important sources of PhD funding (Mendosa, Villarreal, and Gunderson 2014).

An assistantship is a type of funding that a doctoral student receives with an obligation to work on campus for a specified number of hours, teaching or doing research. It is a form of financial aid and an effective way to facilitate scholar socialization, as a research assistantship often implies work on a project in a research group (Kim and Otts 2010). A fellowship is a different type of funding opportunity, often perceived as the most desirable as it usually covers all expenses during the study with no working obligation. The availability and size of postgraduate funding depend mostly on the discipline. Fields such as mathematics, engineering, computer science and life sciences have the largest proportions of fellowships and research assistantships due to the higher level of external funding available for these disciplines (Mendosa, Villarreal, and Gunderson 2014).

Funding has implications that carry over after graduation. Graduate merit-based scholarships are awarded to the most talented and determined students. As a result, having a funded PhD can signal the particular skills of a candidate, which may potentially influence future employment (Horta, Cattaneo, and Meoli 2016). Studies also show that fully funded students publish more and are more likely to graduate (Larivière 2013). Moreover, having a scholarship is positively related to a future tenure-track academic position (Chandler 2018).

Current trends show that self-funded schemes prevail among those pursuing a master's degree, whereas the funding sources of doctorate students are more diverse. In the United Kingdom, for instance, around 60 per cent of PhD students have external sources of funding (Higher Education Funding Council in England 2013). Elsewhere, PhD studies are encouraged by government funds. In Brazil, for example, the majority of full-time PhD students have their studies covered by full governmental scholarships (MacGregor 2013).

Candidate Status

The formal status of doctoral candidates is the object of long-standing debates. Candidates can be considered either students or employees, or both, and there is no consensus within countries or even within institutions on the issue. From one standpoint, pursuing a doctorate requires as much work as a full-time employment position, but the perception of doctoral candidates as students does not imply any labour security in return. Health insurance, parental and sick leaves and other employment benefits usually do not apply to doctoral students who do not have employee status.

Although perceiving doctoral candidates as students remains the prevailing practice, recent trends show that a growing number of institutions prefer to provide them with temporary contracts. This is mostly common in Northern and Western Europe. In Norway, for instance, doctoral candidates have the status of employees, with all corresponding rights (Thune et al. 2012). In Finland, the majority of doctoral students have employment contracts and are covered by national collective agreements. This, however, does not concern self-funded PhD candidates and candidates with fellowships (White 2015). The majority of PhD candidates in the Netherlands are employed by the universities, and are provided with salaries as staff members, as well as with legal protection and employment benefits (Waaijer, Heyer, and Kuli 2016). Still, this system remains volatile, and sometimes intentions to change their legal status from employees to students are expressed, as in the Netherlands in 2014 (Law 2016). In the United Kingdom and the United States, doctoral candidates are considered students. Yet, in both countries, there are attempts to change their status from students to employees (Else 2017). In 2007, 22 countries out of 37 participants in the Bologna Process reported a 'mixed' status for PhD candidates (European University Association 2007). Studies show that in the environment of 'mixed' status, candidates who are not employed by their institutions during their programme perceive their position as disadvantageous compared to their employed peers (Waaijer, Heyer, and Kuli 2016).

Professional Doctorate

The emergence of variations among doctoral programmes since the first half of the 20th century has challenged the traditional PhD programme. This has resulted in rethinking and reforming doctoral programmes to offer an alternative route to the doctoral degree in various fields, known mostly as professional doctorates, but also referred to as applied doctorates, practitioner doctorates or clinical doctorates (Kot and Hendel 2012). Professional doctorates try to fill the gap between academic research offered by PhD programmes that are widely criticized for their narrowness, and the need for professional orientation, as required by companies in knowledge-oriented economies (Costley and Lester 2012).

In comparison with the traditional PhD programme, professional doctorate is viewed as a more structured programme, often including more coursework and a shorter thesis, occasionally replaced by a project (Allen, Smyth, and Wahlstrom 2002; Jolley 2007; Simpson and Summer 2016). The taught components in professional doctorates lead to what is called the 'cohort effect' (Jolley 2007) and provide benefits such as social communication and networking.

As a result, professional doctorate is mostly common within areas of knowledge that can be referred to as 'practice oriented'. Examples of professional doctorates are the doctorates in education (EdD; Wildy, Peden, and Chan 2014), business administration (DBA; Simpson and Sommer 2016), nursing science (DNSc) and in clinical psychology (DClinPsy; Park 2005). Names and abbreviations, as well as content and structure, vary across countries.

Professional doctorates are often considered to have a lower status, 'cheapening the traditional doctorate degree', as Altbach (2007, 69) puts it, due to a deficiency in the rigour of scholarly research (which should be focused on the generation of theory and the development of the candidate's research capacity), as well as shortcomings in the mastery of specific disciplines (Acosta and Celis 2014). Salter (2013, 1179) argues that the common tendency to consider professional doctorates as lower-class PhDs inhibits their potential to contribute to knowledge creation, as well as their chances to improve. It would be more productive to look at professional doctorates as 'equal but different' based on the following three assumptions: (a) knowledge produced by research must be grounded in practice and application, (b) practice must be informed by knowledge provided through research and (c) both practice and research must be focused on assuring positive social change consistent with the core mission of the university.

Work-based Doctorate

What can be seen as yet another variation in doctoral education is the more recent development, mostly at Australian and British universities, of work-based or practice-based doctorates. Transdisciplinary in nature, these doctorates are centred on the candidate and based on his/her work context, combining research and development. According to Costley and Lester (2012), such programmes can be identified by the following key features. First, work-based doctorates take the individual and his/her work as the starting point—rather than a specific line of discipline or field of study. Second, their expected outcome is an original contribution to practice and the development of the individual trainee as a leader in his/her respective community of profession. Gibbs and Maguire (2012) write that 'affecting change' is the most important part of programmes of this kind. Third, the programmes are tailored to the individual's circumstances, with objectives formulated by important issues identified by the candidate in relation to his/her practice. Fourth, the articulation of and reflection on previous learning and practices by the candidate are an important basis for the doctoral endeavour and a key input in the learning agreement or the project proposal. Fifth, mentorship, rather than supervision, describes the relationship between the faculty in charge and the candidate. Sixth, in spite of the fact that the work-based doctorate is seen a disruption of well-established university structures and procedures, it constitutes a positive contribution in terms of experience and insights brought by the candidates into the learning environment.

TRENDS

Over the last few decades, there have been multiple national reforms resulting in increased international flows of students, collaborations in supervision, diversification in modes of knowledge production, the establishment of accountability mechanisms and attempts to adopt internationally acceptable methods of assessment and evaluation (Nerad 2014a). Over the years, there has been a convergence in doctoral education around the world towards adopting the basic structure of the US model (Altbach 2007). This convergence can be seen distinctly in the introduction of coursework, a set of examinations and a dissertation as requirements for the doctoral degree, as well as in the growth of institutions committed to both teaching and research, rather than keeping research and teaching separate in specialized institutions.

Internationalization and Student Mobility

Baschung (2010) sees major reforms in global doctoral education as essentially related to growing internationalization—doctoral students increasingly seeking programmes with a broad content and a structure resembling those of top American universities, increasing numbers of programmes offered exclusively in English, etc. De Rosa (2008) credits the idea of the European doctorate, the result of the combined efforts of the European Commission, the European University Association and the Bologna Process, which epitomizes the growing regional collaboration and, in effect, the internationalization of doctoral education.

Owing to this overall internationalization in the past years, there has been a significant increase in the proportion of international students enrolled in doctoral programmes in the main host countries, such as the United Kingdom and the United States (Ryan 2012). However, it is also important to note that global student flows to Europe and North America from the rest of the world have been affected by the emergence of new academic powers such as Australia (one of the major exporters of higher education in recent years), China and India. South Africa, which aspires to be a regional doctoral education hub, has seen a significant increase in doctoral enrolment. Initiatives to build world-class research universities in various countries are shaping the mobility of doctoral students by creating local strengths (Altbach 2009).

The growth in international doctoral student mobility is challenged by the growing concern and the moral dilemma associated with brain drain (Altbach 2007). However, brain circulation and strategic efforts by many lower-middle income countries to attract their citizens back after completion of their doctoral studies provide grounds for hope (Cloete, Bunting, and Maassen 2015).

Networks and Collaborations

The emphasis on doctoral education in the past decade by national and international actors has resulted in the emergence of new networks with a high level of collaboration focused on mutual goals of improving doctoral education in terms of structure, quality and outcomes (Evans 2014). Cross-border partnerships often aim to develop high standard doctoral programmes by pooling resources and positioning doctoral students in different contexts relevant to their fields. Similarly, international partnerships focus on the development of supervisory capacity, particularly in lower-middle income countries and/or in institutions with low capacity and experience in doctoral education (Bitzer, Trafford, and Leshem 2013).

University–Industry Partnerships

According to Borrell-Damian et al. (2010), collaboration takes place not only among higher education institutions but also with other stakeholders who have varying interest in the development of doctoral education. University–industry partnerships are typical collaborations that are changing traditional relationships where the university is the sole supplier of knowledge and human resources. One way such partnerships take place is through outsourcing—with a university conducting research for a partner company in an area where the latter seeks to benefit from knowledge/expertise that it does not have. Similarly, a partnership can be formed when a doctoral programme, or a large research project involving doctoral research, is designed through the combined effort of a university and a company. Such partnerships are used as a means for inter-sectoral mobility, knowledge transfer and enhancing mutual understanding.

The Growing Role of Technology

The use of technology, at the doctoral level as in other levels of education, is another emerging trend that can have a significant bearing on doctoral education. A hybrid programme that combines online and face-to-face education, for instance, is atypical example. Reflecting on such a programme in educational technology at Michigan State University, Koehler et al. (2013) conclude that hybrid doctoral programmes—if designed and implemented with a careful balance between pedagogy, technology and content—can be a positive way of engaging working professionals in doctoral studies.

CHALLENGES

The global doctoral education landscape faces a number of challenges; some are internal to institutions and the academic system, whereas others relate to broader societal forces. A common challenge in doctoral education is the issue of quality, in the absence of acceptable mechanisms to establish standards and the difficulty in measuring factors such as time management, motivation, tenacity and interaction among doctoral students as well as between current doctoral students and graduates (Acosta and Celis 2014; Bentley 2013; Bernstein et al. 2014).

As for higher education, in general, doctoral education feels the pinch of budget cuts, as government funding continues to decline and universities are required to go through tough negotiations to secure funding from external sources. These external resources often come with a certain amount of vested interest, putting universities at risk of losing their traditional independence. Similarly, in the face of austerity, governments may put stringent requirements in line with their development priorities for universities to meet specific goals, which could translate into affecting the structure and curricula of their doctoral programmes (Evans 2014).

Institutional goals of appearing in global rankings as a notable research university, and the desire to generate more income in the short term, can stand in disagreement with national goals of providing equal access to, and ensuring diversity in, doctoral education (Nerad 2014b). In this regard, Snyder (2014) noted that women and representatives of minorities are the primary victims of such policies, as these groups are challenged by multiple factors, resulting in far lower success and completion rates.

Another challenge is the question of how to reach global inclusiveness in spite of the clear imbalance between well-resourced and under-resourced countries (Evans 2014). This is exacerbated by the growing convergence of standards, which has made it easier for doctoral students to move between different countries and possibly to find jobs in countries other than their own, whereas national governments make considerable investments in the education of their citizens and expect them to return home and provide services, at least for a certain period of time (Nerad 2014b).

Unequal access for different socio-economic groups is an important challenge for modern doctoral education. For some students, pursuing a doctoral degree may be out of the question or particularly challenging, due to their gender, race, ethnicity, health issues, income, family background and/or other reasons. Some characteristics inherent to minority groups tend to overlap, multiplying the negative effect (Evans and Cokley 2008; MacLachlan 2017; Noy and Ray 2012). Although attempts to reduce these obstacles and to increase diversity among the doctoral population are evident, some minority groups remain under-represented. The higher the degree level, the lower the participation of minorities, especially within STEM disciplines (Frehill and Ivie 2013; Holmes et al. 2015).

It is not uncommon for doctoral students to face racism, sexism and classism during their studies, which affects their success, ultimately discouraging students from disadvantaged backgrounds from pursuing an academic career (Davis and Livingstone 2016; Pifer and Baker 2014; Ramirez 2017). The meagre representation of these groups in academia also deters students from those backgrounds from pursuing doctoral studies.

Multiple studies related to the problem of gender disparities show that compared to men, women experience unfavourable conditions at almost every stage of the academic ladder: enrolling in a PhD programme, studying for a PhD, right after getting a doctorate and while working in the academic sector (Auriol, Misu, and Freeman 2013; Monroe and Chiu 2010; Silander, Haake, and Lindberg 2013). There is also a gender difference by field of study: women are more likely to earn doctoral degrees in the social sciences and behavioural sciences, as well as in education, and men in STEM (Holmes et al. 2015).

PROSPECTS

There are scenarios showing positive prospects for doctoral education worldwide. The shifting focus of higher education, in many lower-middle income countries, on expanding graduate programmes is one such development. Hayward (2012) noted, for example, that for decades, African countries focused their attention on managing the massification of undergraduate education at the expense of quality and expansion of graduate education, but there is a growing consensus recently on the compelling need to improve graduate education programmes. This is backed by promising changes in the economies of some countries in the region.

Looking at developments in Australia, the United Kingdom and elsewhere, Bitzer (2012) sees that standardization in doctoral education will continue to increase across a whole range of issues, from institutional arrangements to funding models, admissions, dissertation supervision, internal and external examinations, publication of results, integration within research projects, feedback mechanisms, diversity, etc. This growing practice of benchmarking also takes place on a global scale, where smaller, less reputable institutions are trying to learn from the practice of universities identified as highly research intensive and successful in doctoral production.

The growing standardization, in turn, facilitates mobility, making it possible for knowledge and skills developed in different parts of the world to be accessible across geographic boundaries. If well utilized, these resources can enhance the quality of doctoral programmes (Maheu et al. 2014). On this specific point, Ryan (2012) notes that although international doctoral candidates bring with them different academic cultures and intellectual traditions, a lot still needs to be done in terms of recognizing the values that they contribute. The parochial view holding the Western approach to academic processes as superior to others misses out on the opportunity to generate new knowledge. Therefore, side by side with the various efforts to increase the participation of international students in doctoral studies, genuine intercultural dialogue should be fostered.

Finally, reforms on doctoral education should encourage a debate on the excessive academic orientation of traditional PhD programmes. This is a necessary condition to facilitate the transfer of scientific knowledge to the economy, and to strengthen regional innovation through collaborative university–industry relationships.

REFERENCES

Acosta, Orlando, and Jorge Celis. 2014. 'The Emergence of Doctoral Programmes in the Colombian Higher Education System: Trends and Challenges'. *Prospects* 44 (3): 463–481.

Allen, Catherine M., Elizabeth M. Smyth, and Merlin Wahlstrom. 2002. 'Responding to the Field and to the Academy: Ontario's Evolving PhD'. *Higher Education Research and Development* 21 (2): 203–214.

Altbach, Philip G. 2007. 'Doctoral Education: Present Realities and Future Trends'. In *International Handbook of Higher Education*, edited by James J. F. Forest and Philip G. Altbach, 65–81. Dordrecht: Springer.

———. 2009. 'One-third of the Globe: The Future of Higher Education in China and India'. *Prospects* 39 (1): 11–31.

Archbald, Douglas. 2011. 'The Emergence of the Nontraditional Doctorate: A Historical Overview'. *New Directions for Adult and Continuing Education* Spring 2011 (129): 7–19.

Auriol, Laudeline, Max Misu, and Rebecca A. Freeman. 2013. 'Careers of Doctorate Holders: Analysis of Labour Market and Mobility Indicators'. OECD Science, Technology and Industry Working Papers 2013/04. OECD Publishing.

Bailey, Sacha N., Aline Bogossian, and Bree Akesson. 2016. 'Starting Where We're at: Developing a Student-led Doctoral Teaching Group'. *Transformations: The Journal of Inclusive Scholarship and Pedagogy* 26 (1): 74–88.

Baschung, Lukas. 2010. 'Changes in the Management of Doctoral Education'. *European Journal of Education* 45 (1): 138–152.

Bentley, Kia J. 2013. 'Toward an Evaluation Framework for Doctoral Education in Social Work: A 10-year Retrospective of One PhD Program's Assessment Experiences'. *Journal of Social Work Education* 49 (1): 30–47.

Bernstein, Bianca L., Barbara Evans, Jeannette Fyffe, Nelofer Halai, Fred L. Hall, Hans S. Jensen, Helene March, Suzanne Ortega. 2014. 'The Continuing Evolution of the Research Doctorate'. In *Globalization and Its Impacts on the Quality of PhD Education*, edited by Maresi Nerad and Barbara Evans, 5–30. Rotterdam: Sense.

Bitzer, Eli M. 2012. 'Best Practices for the Research Doctorate? A Case for Quality and Success in Knowledge Production'. *South African Journal of Higher Education* 26 (6): 1182–1199.

Bitzer, Eli M., Vernon N. Trafford, and Shosh Leshem. 2013. '"Love It When You Speak Foreign": A Trans-national Perspective on the Professional Development of Doctoral Supervisors in South Africa'. *South African Journal of Higher Education* 27 (4): 781–796.

Borrell-Damian, Lidia, Timothy Brown, Andrew Dearing, Josep Font, Stephen Hagen, Janet Metcalfe, and John Smith. 2010. 'Collaborative Doctoral Education: University–Industry Partnerships for Enhancing Knowledge Exchange'. *Higher Education Policy* 23 (4): 493–514.

Boulos, Aurélie. 2016. 'The Labour Market Relevance of PhDs: An Issue for Academic Research and Policy-makers'. *Studies in Higher Education* 41 (5): 901–913.

Bunting, Ian, Nico Cloete, Henri L. K. Wah, and Florence Nakayiwa-Mayega. 2015. 'Assessing the Performance of African Flagship Universities'. In *Knowledge Production and Contradictory Functions in African Higher Education*, edited by Nico Cloete, Peter Maassen, and Tracy Bailey, 32–60. Cape Town: African Minds.

Byrne, Joanne, Thomas Jørgensen, and Tia Loukkola. 2013. *Quality Assurance in Doctoral Education—Results of the ARDE Project*. Brussels: European University Association. https://eua.eu/resources/publications/386:quality-assurance-in-doctoral-education-results-of-the-arde-project.html (accessed 12 December 2018).

Carnoy, Martin, Prashant Loyalka, Maria Dobryakova, Rafiq Dossani, Isak Froumin, Katherine Kuhns, Jandhyala B. G. Tilak, and Rong Wang. 2013. *University Expansion in a Changing Global Economy: Triumph of the BRICS?* Stanford: Stanford University Press.

Casey, Bernard H. 2009. 'The Eonomic Contribution of PhDs'. *Journal of Higher Education Policy and Management* 31 (3): 219–227.

Chandler, Vincent. 2018. 'Short and Long-Term Impacts of an Increase in Graduate Funding'. *Economics of Education Review* 62: 104–112.

Chevaillier, Thierry, and Marie Duru-Bellat. 2017. 'Diploma Devaluation, the Ins and Outs'. In *Encyclopedia of International Higher Education Systems and Institutions*, edited by Jung C. Shin and Pedro Teixeira, 1–5. Dordrecht: Springer.

Chien, Chiao-Ling, and David W. Chapman. 2014. 'Graduate Education in Malaysia and Thailand'. *International Higher Education* 76: 20–22.

Christensen, K. K. 2005. *Doctoral Programs for the European Knowledge Society (the 'Salzburg Principles')*. Report from Bologna Seminar. Salzburg: European University Association Council for Doctoral Education. http://www.eua.be/eua/jsp/en/upload/Salzburg_Report_final.1129817011146.pdf (accessed 12 December 2018).

Cloete, Nico, Charles Sheppard, and Tracy Bailey. 2015. 'South Africa as a PhD Hub in Africa?' In *Knowledge Production and Contradictory Functions in African*

Higher Education, edited by Nico Cloete, Peter Maassen, and Tracy Bailey, 75–108. Cape Town: African Minds.

Cloete, Nico, Ian Bunting, and Peter Maassen. 2015. 'Research Universities in Africa: An Empirical Overview of Eight Flagship Universities'. In *Knowledge Production and Contradictory Functions in African Higher Education*, edited by Nico Cloete, Peter Maassen, and Tracy Bailey, 18–31. Cape Town: African Minds.

Costley, Carol, and Stan Lester. 2012. 'Work-based Doctorates: Professional Extension at the Highest Levels'. *Studies in Higher Education* 37 (3): 257–269.

Davis, Ashley, and Allyson Livingstone. 2016. 'Sharing the Stories of Racism in Doctoral Education: The Anti-racism Project'. *Journal of Teaching in Social Work* 36 (2): 197–215.

De Rosa, Annamaria S. 2008. 'New Forms of International Cooperation in Doctoral Training: Internationalization and the International Doctorate—One Goal, Two Distinct Models'. *Higher Education in Europe* 33 (1): 3–25.

Ehrenberg, Ronald G. 2005. 'Involving Undergraduates in Research to Encourage Them to Undertake PhD Study in Economics'. *American Economic Review* 95 (2): 184–188.

Else, H. 2017. 'PhD Students: Time to Make Them University Employees?' *Times Higher Education*. https://www.timeshighereducation.com/news/phd-students-time-to-make-them-university-employees (accessed 12 December 2018).

Enders, Jurgen. 2004. 'Research Training and Careers in Transition: A European Perspective on the Many Faces of the PhD'. *Studies in Continuing Education* 26 (3): 419–429.

European University Association. 2007. *Doctoral Programs in Europe's Universities: Achievements and Challenges*. https://www.dcu.ie/sites/default/files/graduate_research/pdfs/doctoral_programmes_in_europe_s_universities.pdf (accessed 12 December 2018).

Evans, Barbara. 2014. 'Conclusion: Where Are We, and Where to Next?' In *Globalization and Its Impacts on the Quality of PhD Education*, edited by Maresi Nerad and Barbara Evans, 207–212. Rotterdam: Sense.

Evans, Gina L., and Kevin O. Cokley. 2008. 'African American Women and the Academy: Using Career Mentoring to Increase Research Productivity'. *Training and Education in Professional Psychology* 2 (1): 50–57.

Fortes, Mauricio, Barbara M. Kehm, and Tokozile Mayekiso. 2014. 'Evaluation and Quality Management in Europe, Mexico, and South Africa'. In *Globalization and Its Impacts on the Quality of PhD Education*, edited by Maresi Nerad and Barbara Evans, 81–109. Rotterdam: Sense.

Frehill, Lisa M., and Rachel Ivie. 2013. 'Increasing the Visibility of Women of Color in Academic Science and Engineering: Professional Society Data'. *New Directions for Higher Education* 163: 7–21.

Gaeta, Giuseppe L. 2015. 'Was It worth It? An Empirical Analysis of Over-Education among PhD Recipients in Italy'. *International Journal of Social Economics* 42 (3): 222–238.

Gardner, Susan K. 2009. 'The Development of Doctoral Students—Phases of Challenge and Support'. *ASHE Higher Education Report* 34 (6): 1–127.

Gibbs, Paul, and Kate Maguire. 2012. 'What Is in a Recommendation? A Perspective from Work-based Doctorates'. *Research in Post-Compulsory Education* 17 (4): 471–481.

Hayward, Fred M. 2012. 'Graduate Education in Sub-Saharan Africa: Prospects and Challenges'. *International Higher Education* 66: 21–22.

Higher Education Funding Council for England. 2013. *Postgraduate Education in England and Northern Ireland: Overview Report.* http://dera.ioe.ac.uk/id/eprint/17942 (accessed 12 December 2018).

Herrera, Liliana, and Mariano Nieto. 2016. 'PhD Careers in Spanish Industry: Job Determinants in Manufacturing versus Non-manufacturing Firms'. *Technological Forecasting and Social Change* 113: 341–351.

Hoeling, Sven, Lewis Gudgeon, and Felix Hagemeister. 2015. 'Should You Do a Doctorate? The Changing Returns to Postgraduate Qualifications'. *Undergraduate Economic Review* 11(1): 1–18.

Holmes, Barbara D., Robin Dalton, Dionne Ellis, Amanda Sargent-Lewis, Laura Scott, and Sharon Waters. 2015. 'Women—an Under-represented Population in American and International Doctoral Studies'. *American Journal of Educational Research* 3 (10): 1324–1329.

Horta, Hugo, Mattia Cattaneo, and Michele Meoli. 2018. 'PhD Funding as a Determinant of PhD and Career Research Performance'. *Studies in Higher Education* 43 (3): 542–570.

Huisman, Jeroen, Egbert De Weert, and Jeroen Bartelse. 2002. 'Academic Careers from a European Perspective: The Declining Desirability of the Faculty Position'. *The Journal of Higher Education* 73 (1): 141–160.

Jolley, Jeremy. 2007. 'Choose Your Doctorate'. *Journal of Clinical Nursing* 16 (2): 225–233.

Kehm, Barbara M. 2007. 'Doctoral Education in Europe: New Structures and Models'. In *Towards a Multiversity? Universities between Global Trends and National Traditions*, edited by Georg Kriicken, Anna Kosmiitzky, and Marc Torka, 132–153. Bielefeld: Transcript.

Kim, Dongbin, and Cindy Otts. 2010. 'The Effect of Loans on Time to Doctorate Degree: Differences by Race/Ethnicity, Field of Study, and Institutional Characteristics'. *The Journal of Higher Education* 81 (1): 1–32.

Kobayashi, Shinichi. 2011. 'The PhD as a Professional: Current Status and Issues Concerning the Early Careers of Doctorate Holders'. *Japan Labor Review* 8 (4): 46–66.

Koehler, Matthew J., Andrea L. Zellner, Cary J. Roseth, Robin K. Dickson, Patrick Dickson, and John Bell. 2013. 'Introducing the First Hybrid Doctoral Program in Educational Technology'. *TechTrends* 57 (3): 47–53.

Kot, Felly C., and Darwin D. Hendel. 2012. 'Emergence and Growth of Professional Doctorates in the United States, United Kingdom, Canada and Australia: A Comparative Analysis'. *Studies in Higher Education* 37 (3): 345–364.

Larivière, Vincent. 2013. 'PhD Students' Excellence Scholarships and Their Relationship with Research Productivity, Scientific Impact, and Degree Completion'. *Canadian Journal of Higher Education* 43 (2): 27–41.

Law, David. 2016. 'Going Dutch: Higher Education in the Netherlands'. *Perspectives: Policy and Practice in Higher Education* 20 (2–3): 99–109.

Lee, Hsing-fen, Marcela Miozzo, and Philippe Laredo. 2010. 'Career Patterns and Competences of PhDs in Science and Engineering in the Knowledge Economy: The Case of Graduates from a UK Research-based University'. *Research Policy* 39 (7): 869–881.

Lindley, J., and S. Machin. 2013. *The Postgraduate Premium: Revisiting Trends in Social Mobility and Educational Inequalities in Britain and America.* London: The Sutton Trust. http://dera.ioe.ac.uk/30284/1/Postgraduate-Premium-Report–1.pdf (accessed 12 December 2018).

MacGregor, K. 2013. 'Brazil's Doctoral Production Lessons for Africa'. *University World News.* http://www.universityworldnews.com/article. php?story=20131213152900757 (accessed 12 December 2018).

MacLachlan, A. J. 2017. 'Preservation of Educational Inequality in Doctoral Education: Tacit Knowledge, Implicit Bias and University Faculty'. Research & Occasional Paper Series: CSHE. 1.17. Berkeley, CA: Center for Studies in Higher Education, University of California. https://escholarship.org/uc/item/5zv6c3nj (accessed 12 December 2018).

Maheu, Louis, Beate Scholz, Jorge Balán, Jessica K. Graybill, and Richard Strugnell. 2014. 'Doctoral Education as an Element of Cultural and Economic Prosperity: Nation Building in the Era of Globalization'. In *Globalization and Its Impacts on the Quality of PhD Education*, edited by Maresi Nerad and Barbara Evans, 161–205. Rotterdam: Sense.

Matute, Marta Martínez. 2014. 'The Duration of the PhD at Spain from a Stochastic Frontier Perspective: Is It Really a Trick-or-Treat Issue?' *Investigaciones de Economía de la Educación* 9 (9): 545–565.

Mendosa, Pilar, Pedro Villarreal, and Alee Gunderson. 2014. 'Within-Year Retention among PhD Students: The Effect of Debt, Assistantships, and Fellowships'. *Research in Higher Education* 55 (7): 650–685.

Mertens, Anne, and Heinke Röbken. 2013. 'Does a Doctoral Degree Pay Off? An Empirical Analysis of Rates of Return of German Doctorate Holders'. *Higher Education* 66: 217–231.

Monroe, Kristen R., and William F. Chiu. 2010. 'Gender Equality in the Academy: The Pipeline Problem'. *PS: Political Science and Politics* 43 (2): 303–308.

National Science Board. 2016. Science and Engineering Indicators 2016. Arlington, VA: National Science Foundation. https://www.nsf.gov/statistics/2016/nsb20161/#/report/chapter-5/doctoral-scientists-and-engineers-in-academia (accessed 18 February 2020).

Nerad, Maresi. 2004. 'The PhD in the US: Criticisms, Facts, and Remedies'. *Higher Education Policy* 17 (2): 183–199.

————. 2014a. 'Introduction: Converging Practices in PhD Education'. In *Globalization and Its Impacts on the Quality of PhD Education*, edited by Maresi Nerad and Barbara Evans, 1–3. Rotterdam: Sense.

————. 2014b. 'Developing "Fit for Purpose" Research Doctoral Graduates: Increased Standardization of Quality Measures in PhD Education Worldwide'. In *Globalization and Its Impacts on the Quality of PhD Education*, edited by Maresi Nerad and Barbara Evans, 111–127. Rotterdam: Sense.

Nerad, Maresi, Thomas Trzyna, and Mimi Higgelund. 2008. 'Introduction'. In *Toward a Global PhD? Forces and Forms in Doctoral Education Worldwide*, edited by Maresi Nerad and Mimi Higgelund, 3–16. Seattle, WA: University of Washington Press.

Niemczyk, Ewalina K. 2016. 'Doctoral Research Education in Canada: Full-Time and Part-Time Students' Access to Research Assistantships'. *Brock Education: A Journal of Educational Research and Practice* 26 (1): 52–67.

Noy, Shiri, and Rashawn Ray. 2012. 'Graduate Students' Perceptions of Their Advisors: Is There Systematic Disadvantage in Mentorship? *Journal of Higher Education* 83 (6): 876–914.

O'Leary, Nigel C., and Peter J. Sloane. 2005. 'The Return to a University Education in Great Britain. *National Institute Economic Review* 193 (1): 75–90.

Paolo, Antonio Di, and FerranMañé. 2016. 'Misusing Our Talent? Overeducation, Overskilling and Skill Underutilisation among Spanish PhD Graduates'. *The Economic and Labour Relations Review* 27 (4): 432–452.

Park, Chris. 2005. 'New Variant PhD: The Changing Nature of the Doctorate in the UK'. *Journal of Higher Education Policy and Management* 27 (2): 189–207.

Pedersen, Heidi S. 2016. 'Are PhDs Winners or Losers? Wage Premiums for Doctoral Degrees in Private Sector Employment'. *Higher Education* 71 (2): 269–287.

Pifer, Meghan J., and Vicki L. Baker. 2014. '"It Could Be Just Because I'm Different": Otherness and Its Outcomes in Doctoral Education'. *Journal of Diversity in Higher Education* 7 (1): 14–30.

Ramirez, Elvia. 2017. 'Unequal Socialization: Interrogating the Chicano/Latino(a) Doctoral Education Experience'. *Journal of Diversity in Higher Education* 10 (1): 25–38.

Roach, Michael, and Henry Sauermann. 2010. 'A Taste for Science? PhD Scientists' Academic Orientation and Self-selection into Research Careers in Industry'. *Research Policy* 39 (3): 422–434.

Ryan, Janette. 2012. 'Internationalization of Doctoral Education: Possibilities for New Knowledge and Understandings'. *Australian Universities' Review* 54 (1): 55–63.

Salter, Daniel W. 2013. 'One University's Approach to Defining and Supporting Professional Doctorates'. *Studies in Higher Education* 38 (8): 1175–1184.

Schwabe, Markus. 2011. 'The Career Paths of Doctoral Graduates in Austria'. *European Journal of Education* 46 (1): 153–168.

Silander, Charlotte, Ulrika Haake, and Leif Lindberg. 2013. 'The Different Worlds of Academia: A Horizontal Analysis of Gender Equality in Swedish Higher Education'. *Higher Education* 66 (2): 173–188.

Simpson, Colin G., and Daniela Sommer. 2016. 'The Practice of Professional Doctorates: The Case of a UK-based Distance DBA'. *Journal of Management Education* 40 (5): 576–594.

Snyder, Cyndy R. 2014. 'A Woman's Place: Women of Color Navigating Doctoral Education in South Africa'. *International Journal of Multicultural Education* 16 (2): 15–35.

Teferra, Damtew. 2015. 'Manufacturing-and Exporting-Excellence and "mediocrity": Doctoral Education in South Africa'. *South African Journal of Higher Education* 29 (5): 8–19.

Thune, T., S. Kyvik, S. Soürlin, T. B. Olsen, A. Vabø, and C. E. Tømte. 2012. *PhD Education in a Knowledge Society. An Evaluation of PhD Education in Norway*. Oslo: Nordic Institute for Studies in Innovation, Research and Education. https:// brage.bibsys.no/xmlui/handle/11250/280895 (accessed 12 December 2018).

Trow, Martin. 2007. 'Reflections on the Transition from Elite to Mass to Universal Access: Forms and Phases of Higher Education in Modern Societies since WWII'. In *International Handbook of Higher Education*, edited by James J. F. Forest and Philip G. Altbach, 243–280. Dordrecht: Springer.

Van der Steeg, Marc, Karen van der Wiel, and Bram Wouterse. 2014. 'Individual Returns to a PhD Education in the Netherlands: Income Differences between Masters and PhDs'. CPB Discussion Paper 276. The Hague: CPB Netherlands Bureau for Economic Policy Analysis. https://www.cpb.nl/sites/default/files/ publicaties/download/cpb-discussion-paper–276-individual-returns-phd-education-netherlands.pdf (accessed 12 December 2018).

Waaijer, Cathelijn J. F., Anne Heyer, and Sara Kuli. 2016. 'Effects of Appointment Types on the Availability of Research Infrastructure, Work Pressure, Stress, and Career Attitudes of PhD Candidates of a Dutch University'. *Research Evaluation* 25 (4): 349–357.

Walker, George E., Chris M. Golde, Laura Jones, Andrea C. Bueschel, and Pat Hutchings. 2008. *The Formation of Scholars: Rethinking Doctoral Education for the Twenty-First Century*. San Francisco, CA: Jossey-Bass.

Watts, Jacqueline H. 2008. 'Challenges of Supervising Part-Time PhD Students: Towards Student-Centred Practice'. *Teaching in Higher Education* 13 (3): 369–373.

White, G. 2015. 'Supporting Early Career Researchers in Higher Education in Europe: The Role of Employers and Trade Unions'. Project Report. London: Universities and Colleges Employers Association. https://www.ucea.ac.uk/en/empres/rs/ecr.cfm (accessed 12 December 2018).

Wildy, Helen, Sanna Peden, and Karyn Chan. 2014. 'The Rise of Professional Doctorates: Case Studies of the Doctorate in Education in China, Iceland and Australia'. *Studies in Higher Education* 40 (5): 761–774.

Yang, Rui. 2012. 'Up and Coming? Doctoral Education in China'. *Australian Universities' Review* 54 (1): 64–71.

Chapter 2

Doctoral Education Worldwide
Three Decades of Change

Maresi Nerad

Doctoral education is a key element of the post-secondary landscape everywhere. With the spread of higher education massification and the rise of the global knowledge economy that began in the late 20th century and continues until today, doctoral education has expanded tremendously. Most countries have introduced reforms or changes, which have been both welcomed and criticized. Largely ignored in the previous research literature, doctoral education has recently been analysed in more detail (Gokhberg, Shmatko, and Auriol 2016; Golde and Walker 2006; Lovitts 2001; Maki and Borkowski 2006; Nerad 2004, 2010; Nerad and Cerny 1999; Nerad and Evans 2014; Nerad and Heggelund 2008; Nerad, June and Miller 1997; Posselt 2016). This book is among the latest considerations of the topic.

RELEVANT THEMES

In the late 1990s, the list of key issues for doctoral education in the United States focused on eight topics: (a) under- or overproduction of PhDs, (b) long time to doctoral degree and low completion rates, particularly in the humanities and social sciences, (c) reduction in federal and state support for research and student financial aid, (d) quality of doctoral programmes, (e) concerns about ethics in research,

(f) faculty–student relationship, (g) lack of pedagogical training for graduate student teaching assistants and (h) the increasing number and duration of post-doctoral appointments.

Four of these themes—under- and overproduction of PhDs, time to degree and attrition, reduction of federal or state money for institutional and student financial support, and the quality of doctoral education—were not new in the United States, but the institutional responses to them differed over time. What was new was that institutions started collecting comprehensive data to (re)gain a measure of institutional autonomy (a tradition in the US graduate education) and avoid constant reactions to external and internal demands. The existence of central campus graduate schools in all top American research universities was a key factor in what was a fairly swift institutional response. In short, universities wanted to become proactive at anticipating the external and internal forces impinging upon their institutions, and guide their policies and actions with readily available data.

These debates, which largely started in the United States, have gained traction globally. All eight themes outlined above are now relevant in countries around the world, and more 'hot topics' have emerged. Further, some of the recent changes in doctoral education have resulted in a convergence of doctoral education structures and requirements across countries, mainly in flagship programmes (selective, well-funded, structured, national or regional doctoral programmes) introduced and funded by new government initiatives. However, the existence of these well-funded, well-designed flagship postgraduate programmes has introduced an intensified stratification among doctoral recipients around the world, and sometimes even within the same academic department. This stratification creates a small group of excellently educated and trained students, while the rest are carried by many ordinary programmes.

GLOBALIZATION AND GOVERNMENTAL INNOVATION POLICIES

Before examining the current issues confronting doctoral education worldwide, it is useful to discuss what has happened during the past 30 years to make doctoral education a centre of attention for governmental policy groups. First, we have to remember that doctoral programmes respond to external forces such as state and national governments, as well as to the internal dynamics of their own universities. In several earlier writings, I have explained these underlying forces, as well as the connections between globalization, governmental innovation policies and postgraduate education (Nerad 1997, 2010, 2020 forthcoming). Globalization—defined as 'the intensified movement of goods, money, technology, information, people, ideas, and cultural practice across political and cultural boundaries' (Holton 2005, 14)—has likewise exerted a steady and substantial influence on doctoral education. Therefore, doctoral education and postgraduate research today can best be understood in an international context.

Motivated by the belief that more PhDs means a boost for their country's innovation potential and, in turn, economic growth, governments have established special funding models to assure increases in PhD production. On the institutional side, research universities aspire to be of world-class quality, and doctoral education plays an essential part in this. For both governments and universities, the ranking of higher education institutions worldwide (Times Higher Education World University Rankings, QS World University Rankings and Academic Ranking of World Universities) has become a notable driving force in doctoral education reforms, not only in countries of the Global North, such as the United States, Germany and the United Kingdom, but also in emerging economies such as China, Chile, Brazil and India. Doctoral education has moved beyond just one country's professorial interests and responsibilities. National policymakers are aware of, and are responding to, developments in higher education outside their national borders. The innovation policies of national governments have had impacts on doctoral education in every part of the world. These impacts have been felt at both the system (macro) level and the university and programme (micro) levels. In many cases, governments have pushed these policies even if the national infrastructure both inside and outside academia was not able to absorb newly trained doctoral recipients.

EXTERNAL CHANGES AND THEIR IMPACTS ON DOCTORAL EDUCATION

System-Level Impacts

The impacts of governmental innovation policies at the national level have six features. The first and most notable is the proliferation of doctoral programmes and the diversification of student bodies, especially with increases in the number of international doctoral students. In the United Kingdom and the United States, the number of doctoral degrees awarded doubled between 1991 and 2014 (the United Kingdom: 8,000 to 25,000; the United States: 37,000 to 67,000). In China, the number skyrocketed from 2,000 PhDs to approximately 56,000 in that same period (NSF Science Indicators 2016, 2018). Countries with low birth rates or a shrinking population—including Australia, Germany, Japan, the Scandinavian countries, and the United Kingdom—have sought to attract highly skilled workers indirectly via graduate education, particularly in science, engineering, mathematics and agriculture (Nerad 2010). Further, the global economic crisis of 2008 spurred many universities to try to make up for government funding shortfalls by recruiting more international students.

The second feature is that governmental innovation policies have contributed to a change in the mode of research. Many programmes are moving from 'Mode 1' knowledge production—the Humboldtian tradition of learning from one master scholar within one discipline—to 'Mode 2', which emphasizes the theory–practice relationship and translational research, whereby basic findings are given practical societal applications.

A third major change at the macro level is the development of competitive schemes for the allocation of government funds aimed at fostering human capital development. In addition to changes that were initiated through general reforms from ministries from the top-down, federally funded competitive research grant allocations were established that targeted professors, doctoral students and postdoctoral fellows directly. Government funding is often provided as an outcome incentive as well. The spread of these types of funding schemes is often the result of policy borrowing behaviour (Steiner-Khamsi 2016) in countries with newer doctoral programmes and in emerging economies looking to mimic the so-called top universities located mainly in the Global North.

Another impact at the macro level is the quest for greater account-ability and the increased collection of output and outcome data through accreditation schemes. In light of the rapid expansion of doctoral edu-cation and the increased mobility of doctoral candidates, governments and private agencies have established standards and designed processes to guarantee the quality of higher education, including doctoral edu-cation. Examples are the establishment of accreditation agencies in Europe, Japan and, most recently, in India (2017). These measures are intended to uphold comparable standards among doctoral programmes and theses by defining those standards externally, and then determining whether particular programmes and dissertations comply with them. Examples of standards for doctoral education include: the advice papers of the League of European Research Universities (Bogle, Shykoff, von Bülow, and Maes 2016); the many publications by individual European countries on competencies for early career research (the UK Council of Graduate Education and the German University Association of Advanced Graduate Training, to name just two); the US Council of Graduate Schools best practice publications (n.d.); and the Australian Council of Graduate Research good practice guidelines (https://www. acgr.edu.au/good-practice/best-practice/, accessed 2 March 2020).

The fifth macro factor is increased global communication driven by technological innovation. Governments and regional organizations are encouraging and funding international collaborations in research, international network building and degree offerings. Universities are actively pursuing these activities, which are now financially supported. For example, universities have established a number of joint or dual doctoral degrees.

The sixth feature is a relatively new trend in many countries. Governments have developed programmes to attract doctoral students or postdocs who studied abroad back home. For example, Germany and France sponsor get-togethers for their early career researchers (ECRs) in the United States in order to inform them of employment oppor-tunities in their home countries. China grants returning doctorates the difficult-to-get status of local residents in major cities, as well as tax and monetary incentives to start their own businesses, as enticements to reside in China. In 2013, India developed lucrative fellowships and incentives for expatriate scientists and engineers at all career levels to bring their knowledge home through year-long visits, or by returning permanently. Examples include the Ramanujan Fellowship programme for young scientists and engineers run by the Department of Science and Technology.

These system-level reforms are intended to lead to changes at national universities and in individual doctoral programmes. These governmental schemes and interventions have been introduced in both the Global North and South. They have had different effects and consequences and have produced intended and positive—but also unintended and negative—outcomes.

University- and Programme-Level Changes

At the institutional level and at the programme level, between students and supervisors, there have been a good number of changes in the past 20 years. In some countries, these changes are still happening, whereas in other countries and universities, programme-level changes have now become the norm. The most common changes are the introduction of structured programmes, the move away from a single dissertation advisor to at least two and the opening up of possibilities to study in an inter- or multi-disciplinary context. In short, it is a move away from the classical Humboldtian research model of one master professor who passes on specialized knowledge and the art of undertaking research to one student, in one discipline, in a hierarchical learning environment.

The external changes and reforms discussed above necessitate more competencies from the increasingly larger generation of doctoral candidates than were required in the past. In addition to the traditional academic competencies—critical thinking, knowing and applying research methods and design, undertaking competent data analysis, academic writing and publishing within the rules of ethical and responsible research—doctoral students are now also expected to acquire professional competencies, as well as intercultural communication understanding and skills (Nerad 2012, 2015). Professional competencies include grant writing, presenting complicated scientific concepts and results to a diverse audience, working effectively in teams, applying for professional jobs and managing people and budgets. Intercultural competency means working effectively with people from different classes, races/ethnicities, cultures, religions and perspectives (Nerad 2012). More and more structured doctoral programmes have been developed to make sure that students not only finish in a reasonable time but also receive these new types of professional development training.

Also, in many universities and programmes, supervision has moved away from a single professor to two or more. This is a paradigm shift away from the master-apprentice model to a multilevel advising and mentoring model (Nerad 2012, 2015; Rudd et al. 2008). In addition, quality assurance schemes are increasingly observed at the programme and university levels. These follow the common input, throughput and output quality assurance model used in businesses (Nerad 2014).

There are other trends worth noting. The increase in international doctoral students has spread the use of the English language in doctoral education. It is now prevalent worldwide, although it has lately come under attack in some countries such as the Netherlands and Denmark (De Groot 2019). Another trend is that there are now more defined criteria and selection mechanisms for doctoral student admissions. Further, many doctoral programmes offer three years of funding, and often financial support is cut off after the expected time to finish has been reached. Career planning has become an accepted responsibility of doctoral programmes and campus career centres.

There is also greater diversification when it comes to the accepted forms of both dissertations and doctoral degrees. Instead of a cohesive doctoral dissertation, three journal articles, or three already accepted first-author journal articles, are being accepted. Long existing professional doctoral degrees are those in business, education, medicine, clinical psychology and jurisprudence. Lately, however, new professional doctoral degrees have proliferated, especially in Australia, the United Kingdom and in the United States in fields like audiology, physical therapy and nursing.

Central campus graduate schools or graduate divisions, common in the US research universities, have become new trends in some countries. In Europe, and especially in Germany, such central organizational units have been set up to support early career researchers (ECRs). These university units provide professional competencies workshops with a strong emphasis on career development, general research skills like statistics and language courses for domestic and international doctoral and postdoctoral fellows (e.g., GRADE at the University of Frankfurt or BYRD at the University of Bremen UniWIND). These programmes also distribute travel funds, collect specialized data on their served population and generally act as advocates for ECRs, the term used in countries where doctoral candidates do not have student status, but are instead considered employees.

Finally, national doctoral flagship programmes combine many of these micro-level changes into well-structured doctoral programmes (Nerad 2020, forthcoming). These programmes are administered by national or regional research councils and are well funded, often including doctoral fellowships worth double the normal amount. The European International Training Network, the NSF National Research Training Programs in the United States and the Japan Leading Graduate School are just three examples. Their goals are to train doctoral students for employment in multiple sectors and increase student mobility. Accordingly, the grant proposals require the development of structured doctoral programmes with ample professional development opportunities. The research content and pedagogy are directed towards problem-solving approaches and often require that funded doctoral students connect with other universities, industries, businesses and local communities during their research.

Many of these recent system- and programme-level changes in doctoral education—particularly the heightened attention to the learning environment and the creation of new flagship doctoral programmes—have improved the lives of doctoral candidates and the quality of their education and training. These well-funded and well-structured doctoral programmes uniformly compare most favourably to traditional education. According to various evaluation research projects, PhD students are very satisfied with multiple supervisors, the exposure to different ways of approaching a problem, the richness of the research environment and the opportunity to study within a cohort of similarly interested peers (Manathunga et al. 2012; Morris, Pitt, and Manathunga 2012). Students say they highly value the availability of resources to attend national and international conferences and to create international collaborations along common research lines. However, only a very small number of doctoral students get the opportunity to study in these flagship programmes. The majority end up in traditional doctoral programmes in their own countries.

TODAY'S GLOBAL CHALLENGES

The key issues in the US doctoral education in the 1990s are now prevalent around the world: the increase in the production of doctoral education, the access to doctoral education for women and minorities, the quality of doctoral education, and doctoral employment, advising and mentoring. What is new, however, is that workforce preparedness now dominates the discussion, while topics like ensuring the intellectual excitement of undertaking research and creating space for intellectual risk-taking—not to mention examples in which these two conditions were successfully created, providing access and quality experiences for first-generation and non-traditional college students—get little attention.

Monetary Incentives and the Quality of Doctoral Education

The governmental competitive grant funding that directly targeted professors, doctoral students and postdoctoral fellows was intended to entice those who wanted to make changes in the structure and research approach of doctoral education. While governments hoped that these well-funded programmes would have a 'spillover effect' into all doctoral education at a given university, they have instead created a new strati-fication. On the one hand, these grant-funded initiatives have created a small group of well-funded, well-designed, project-based doctoral programmes with international components. On the other hand, there still exist many less well-funded programmes (in which students study under less favourable conditions) that carry the mass of doctoral educa-tion. This bifurcation exists now among universities across the globe, among universities in one county and even within the same department at a university. Such differences have always existed, but now a PhD awarded by one of the top 150 world-class universities is valued far more than the same degree from a good local university not ranked in the world-class university ranking system.

There has also been an unintended effect from government policies giving universities monetary incentives for every new PhD produced and every peer-reviewed publication—the rise of institutional compliance behaviour, rather than an improvement of the quality of doctoral education. In 2012, the American Society for Cell Biology passed the San Francisco Declaration on Research Assessment to stop the abuse of the academic journal impact factor by correlating this impact index to the merits of a specific scholar's contributions. A good number of European societies signed the declaration, but it has had no impact in countries like China or South Africa, where universities receive money for every peer-reviewed journal article. While positive changes may have occurred—it has certainly multiplied the number of doctorates produced—these mechanisms of quantitative monitoring have done little to encourage quality, intellectual risk-taking and true innovation.

Employment of PhD Graduates: A Shift to Postdocs

While changes at the institutional- and programme-levels have increased the number of doctoral recipients worldwide, not all countries have taken the necessary steps to provide the infrastructure needed to absorb these newly minted doctorates, who are expected to innovate in both the public and private sectors. In light of the swift increase in doctorates worldwide and the interconnectedness of labour markets, finding adequate employment has become a new, global concern for individual doctoral students and their professors. Not only have more PhDs been produced worldwide, but also many postdoc positions have been created via competitive research grants, moving completed PhDs into quasi-holding positions until more permanent employment is found. The issue of PhD employment has not been solved, but simply shifted to the postdoctoral level. A note of caution concerning differentiation: we need to understand that this 'hot' topic of PhD employment, which has caused heightened anxiety and raised issues of doctoral students' wellness in the Global North, is not yet an issue in countries where universities until recently hired university instructors without PhDs, and are now requiring all academic staff to have a doctoral degree in order to remain in their positions. Examples of this can be found in India, many African countries and in some Latin American countries.

PhD Career Path Studies

Student anxiety about the job market makes it even more important that countries regularly undertake doctorate career path studies so that current students have realistic expectations and can engage in career planning. Hence, another of today's challenges is designing PhD career path studies in order to analyse questions that are relevant to doctoral students, faculty in doctoral programmes and national agencies. Doctoral students want to learn about the career possibilities within a given field of study. They are also eager to find out how others have combined their personal and professional lives after completion of the doctorate. They want to know what the unemployment rate is for those with PhD graduates and the reasons for that unemployment. Likewise, they want to discern whether the doctorate is useful for their subsequent careers. Professors in doctoral programmes want to know what their students think about various dimensions of the programme after they have applied (or not) what they learned. In order to adjust and update programmes, department chairs like programmatic feedback from their former students after they have had some work experience. Often, national agencies collect job data on people with doctorates in order to forecast the supply and demand of highly qualified professionals. PhD career path studies are expensive, and because it is mostly governmental agencies that fund them, it is chiefly their needs that are met. However, history shows ample evidence that these 'manpower demand' studies turn out to be incorrect, because of unexpected external events like the elimination of mandatory retirement age for faculty, a surge in immigration or emigration or the effects of wars and natural disasters.

The timing of the administration of these surveys is extremely important. Surveys assessing careers immediately after degree completion are only partially useful, as many PhDs will be in postdoctoral positions or other temporary jobs. Astonishingly little knowledge exists concerning the employment of doctorate recipients five to ten years after degree completion. How can we improve doctoral education if we do not create a feedback loop from those who have applied their education, and who, from the advantage of employment experience, can evaluate the quality of their education? Although currently enrolled students can evaluate their experiences (and this is frequently done today), they cannot adequately assess the quality of their education without having had an opportunity to apply it. Simply put, we need multiple sources of evaluation.

Carefully designed doctorate career path studies can help to stop outdated assumptions about the careers of doctorates (Nerad 2009; Nerad, Rudd, Morrison and Picciano 2007). In the United States, these assumptions are: (a) most people who work towards a PhD want to become professors, (b) only the 'best' doctoral students do, in fact, become professors, (c) the career path from PhD to postdoc, then on to assistant professor, and finally to tenured professor is the dominant pattern for PhD recipients, and its primary hallmark is its linearity, (d) embedded in this linearity is the assumption that a person is able to fully optimize his or her career options and take the best job offered after PhD completion, (e) rearing children detract women from the pursuit of academic careers and (f) finally, PhDs who become professors enjoy the highest job satisfaction.

Empirical evidence from the US studies in the early 2000s found that doctoral education has been, and can be, the passport to a successful career path in many sectors outside of academia. Half of all PhDs in engineering and the biosciences do not aim for a professorial career goal. In all other fields, one-third never even had this career path in mind. The employment of a partner, the need to care for parents, geographic concerns and to a lesser degree having children are major factors that can influence PhD graduates' decisions for or against seeking an academic career. PhD graduates working in business, government and the non-profit sector are in many ways more satisfied with their jobs than those who became professors (Nerad 2009; Nerad and Cerny 2002). Such empirical information is essential in preparing doctoral students for the future. As times change, doctoral education will most likely need modifications. We will need to re-examine students' goals and motivations for getting doctorates in order to adjust curriculum, research and professional development activities around the world.

Equity of Access and Affordability

Another research and policy issue that will need global attention is a quantitative and qualitative enquiry into the participation and experience of societal groups that traditionally have not had the chance to pursue a doctorate. In this regard, it is troubling that the commitment of a university or programme to equitable access to, and affordability of, doctoral education is compromised by the wish to demonstrate world-class status. With the latter goal in mind, departments tend to admit risk-free doctoral students from other top-ranked institutions, rather than considering promising first-generation domestic students from lower-ranked universities, who will perhaps require more faculty efforts and departmental resources to be successful and to complete their studies at similar rates (Chiappa and Perez Meijas 2019; Perez Meijas, Chiappa, and Guzmán-Valenzuela 2018). It is also important to note that in many countries race, ethnicity, gender, age, class background and/or disability are seldom discussed, and relevant data collection on these topics is not done systematically. In France, for example, it is illegal to collect data on race and ethnicity.

Supervisor Training

Once a more diverse doctoral student population has been admitted (more women, minority students, older re-entry students and international students), programme and advisor behaviour will need to adjust. With the emphasis on PhD completion, and in the absence of systematically structured doctoral programmes, supervisor training has become mandatory in some countries, including Australia,

New Zealand and the United Kingdom. In a changed doctoral world, the preparation of dissertation advisors will need to be a central focus of the new professoriate.

The Decline of the Humanities and the Arts

A notably negative effect of governmental innovation policies is their focus on STEM (science, technology, engineering and mathematics) and health fields. Doctoral programmes in STEM disciplines and biomedicine are perceived as offering the strongest local and regional economic impacts. They are, therefore, the first programmes to be supported, financially and in other ways (more space, better location on campus). The humanities, the arts and the social sciences (with the exception of business administration) have received far less governmental and university funding. As a result, their status and influence within their own institutions have diminished. Not only in the United States and China, but increasingly in other countries too, doctoral programmes in the humanities and the arts are losing financial support and attention in their institutions.

Workforce Preparedness and a Lack of Intellectual Risk-Taking

The pendulum has swung too far: the overemphasis on workforce preparedness as the sole function and goal of doctoral education has resulted in a loss of intellectual curiosity, and inflamed the anxiety of current doctoral students even more. Funders and departments also put pressure on doctoral students to demonstrate efficiency by demanding the shortest possible time for degree completion. This stifles creativity and intellectual risk-taking, both necessary for innovation, which is often the emphasized goal of a research education. To be creative and innovative requires false starts and learning from experience (CIRGE 2009). If national governments truly view doctorate holders as critical for innovation and discovery, then future researchers must not only be allowed but also actively encouraged to cross disciplinary, institutional, national and cultural boundaries.

The advancement of knowledge requires the willingness on the part of some to pursue risky, but potentially transformative, research projects under the thoughtful guidance of a supervisor and a dissertation committee. Yet, in some cases, existing academic reward structures discourage both boundary-crossing and high-risk research projects. Institutions need to develop programmes to explicitly train doctoral supervisors in risk recognition and management for their students. Universities, departments and programmes need to develop a research culture that values and rewards innovation and creativity. Every doctoral curriculum needs to train students to be aware of the limits and strengths of their disciplines by exposing them to other fields through team-building opportunities (Center for Innovation and Research in Graduate Education 2009).

OUTLOOK

In view of the economic and societal changes in today's labour market for highly trained professionals, quality preparation of doctoral candidates requires coordinated efforts at many levels—within a university, among universities, between national and international funding agencies and various learning and research communities—throughout the duration of a doctoral education (Nerad 2012). It also requires creating many opportunities for doctoral candidates to build their personal and professional networks. This can be accomplished through well-structured doctoral programmes that focus on creating appropriate learning environments locally, nationally and internationally. In order to secure improvement in restructured doctoral programmes, more evaluations and research studies are needed that compare traditional doctoral education programmes with restructured ones. In short, research-based doctoral programme reviews are more necessary than ever.

Perhaps the current tensions in doctoral education can be traced back to having combined two very different concepts of the purpose of a research doctorate. On the one hand is the Humboldtian/German model of doctoral education, which had no purpose beyond the advancement of knowledge and science per se. On the other hand is the pragmatic American Progressive Era notion of using science and scholarship to eradicate poverty and illness and to solve the problems of immigration. This amalgamation of purposes has caused (and still does cause) a bifurcation with larger ramifications than we have thus far understood. Twenty years ago, there were loud complaints in the United States that doctoral students 'take too long to complete their studies, and are ill prepared for the world outside academe' (Nerad 1997). Have these valid concerns reversed themselves? Has the increase in the number of doctoral degrees brought a massification, and with it, such high costs that we only care about efficiency and workforce preparedness? Can we pull back the pendulum to the golden middle, and find a balance between doing research solely in the name of scientific curiosity and getting a degree just to secure a meaningful job?

REFERENCES

Australian Council of Graduate Research. https://www.acgr.edu.au/good-practice/best-practice/ (accessed 2 March 2020).

Bogle, D. Shykoff, J., von Bülow, I. & Maes, K. 2016. 'Maintaining a Quality Culture on Doctoral Education at Research Intensive Universities.' Advice Paper 16. Leuven: League of European Research Universities (LERU).

Center for Innovation and Graduate Education (CIRGE). 2009. The Policy Potential of Innovation & Internationalization in Doctoral Education Recommendations for Equity, Diversity and Innovations. https://www.education.uw.edu/cirge/wp-content/uploads/2013/01/Policy-Recommendations.pdf (accessed 2 March 2020).

Council of Graduate Schools. n.d. 'Best Practices'. https://cgsnet.org/best-practices (accessed 18 December 2019).

Chiappa, R., & Perez Mejias, P. 2019. Unfolding the direct and indirect effects of social class of origin on faculty income. Higher Education, 1–27. doi.org/10.1007/s10734-019-0356-4

De Groot, A. 2019. The English Trojan horse destroying Dutch universities. University World News, 27 January, Issue No. 536, p.1.

Gokhberg, D., N. Meissner, N. Shmatko, and L. Auriol, eds. 2016. The Science and Technology Labour Force: The Value of Doctorate Holders and Development of Professional Careers. Basel: Springer.

Golde, C., and G. Walker. 2006. Envisioning the Future of Graduate Education: Preparing Stewards of the Discipline. Carnegie Essays on the Doctorate. San Francisco, CA: Jossey-Bass.

Holton, R. J. 2005. Making Globalization. New York: Palgrave MacMillan.

Lovitts, B. 2001. *Leaving the Ivory Tower: The Causes and Consequences of Departure from Graduate Studies*. Lanham, MD: Rowman & Littlefield.

Maki, P., and N. Barkowski. 2006. *The Assessment of Doctoral Education: Emerging Criteria and New Models for Improving Outcomes*. Sterling, VA: Stylus.

Manathunga, C., R. Pitt, L. Cox, P. Boreham, P. Lant, and G. Mellick. 2012. 'Evaluating Industry-Based Doctoral Research Programs: Perspectives and Outcomes of Australian Cooperative Research Centre Graduates'. *Studies in Higher Education* 37 (7): 843–858.

Morris, S., R. Pitt, and C. Manathunga. 2012. 'Students' Experiences of Supervision in Academic and Industry Settings: Results of an Australian Study'. *Assessment & Evaluation in Higher Education* 37 (5): 619–636.

National Science Board. 2016. *Science and engineering indicators 2016*. Arlington, VA: National Science Foundation.

————. 2018. Science and engineering indicators 2018. Arlington, VA: National Science Foundation. https://www.nsf.gov/statistics/2018/nsb20181/assets/nsb20181.pdf (accessed 27 November 2019).

Nerad, M. 1997. The cyclical problems of graduate education: Institutional responses in the 1990s. In M. Nerad, with D. June and D. Miller (Eds), *Graduate education in the United States* (pp. vii–xiv). New York, NY: Garland Publishing.

————. 2004. 'The PhD in the US: Criticisms, Facts and Remedies'. *Higher Education Policy* 17 (2): 183–199.

————. 2008. United States of America. In M. Nerad and M. Heggelund (Eds), *Towards a global PhD? Forces and forms in doctoral education worldwide* (pp. 278–297). Seattle, WA: University of Washington Press.

————. 2009. 'Confronting Common Assumptions: Designing Future-Oriented Doctoral Education'. In R. Ehrenberg and C. Kuh (Eds), *Doctoral Education and the Faculty of the Future* (pp. 80–89). Ithaca, NY: Cornell University Press.

————. 2010. 'Globalization and the Internationalization of Graduate Education: A Macro and Micro View'. *Canadian Journal of Higher Education*, 40(1), 1–12.

————. 2012. 'Conceptual Approaches to Doctoral Education: A Community of Practice'. *Alternation* 19 (2): 57–72.

————. 2014. 'Developing "Fit for Purpose" Research Doctoral Graduates. Increased Standardization of Quality Measures in PhD Education Worldwide'. In M. Nerad and Barbara Evans (Eds), *Globalization and Its Impacts on the Quality of PhD Education Worldwide. Forces and Forms of Doctoral Education Worldwide*. Rotterdam: Sense Publishers.

————. 2015. 'Professional Development for Doctoral Students: What Is It? Why Now? Who Does It?' *Nagoya Journal of Higher Education* 15: 285–318.

Nerad, M. 1997. The cyclical problems of graduate education: Institutional responses in the 1990s. In M. Nerad, with June, D. & Miller, D. (Eds.), *Graduate education in the United States* (pp. vii–xiv). New York, NY: Garland Publishing.

————. Forthcoming 2020. 'Governmental Innovation Policies and Change in Doctoral Education Worldwide: Are Doctoral Programs Converging? Trends and Tensions'. In '*Structural and Institutional Transformations in Doctoral Education: (Mis)alignment with Doctoral Candidates*' Career Expectations (Proposed Title), edited by S. Cardoso, O. Tavares, Ch. Sin, and T. Carvalho. London: Palgrave McMillian.

Nerad, M., and J. Cerny. 1999. 'From Rumors to Facts: Career Outcomes of English Ph.D.'s Results from the Ph.D.'s—Ten Years Later Study'. *Council of Graduate Schools Communicator* 32 (7).

————. 2002. 'Postdoctoral Appointments and Employment Patterns of Science and Engineering Doctoral Recipients Ten-plus Years after Ph.D. Completion: Selected Results from the "Ph.D.s—Ten Years Later" Study'. *Council of Graduate Schools Communicator* 35 (7).

Nerad, M., and Barbara Evans, eds. 2014. *Globalization and Its Impacts on the Quality of PhD Education Worldwide. Forces and Forms of Doctoral Education Worldwide.* Rotterdam: Sense Publishers.

Nerad, M., and M. Heggelund, eds. 2008. *Towards a Global PhD? Forces and Forms in Doctoral Education Worldwide.* Seattle, WA: University of Washington Press.

Nerad, M., R. June, and D. Miller, eds. 1997. *Graduate Education in the United States.* New York: Garland Press.

Nerad, M. E., Rudd, E. Morrison, and J. Picciano. 2007. *Social Science PhDs— Five+ Years Out. A National Survey of PhDs in Six Fields.* Seattle, WA: Center for Innovation and Research in Graduate Education (CIRGE). https://www.education.uw.edu/cirge/phd-career-path-tracking/2261-2/ (accessed 27 November 2019).

Pérez Mejías, P., R. Chiappa, and C. Guzmán-Valenzuela. 2018. 'Privileging the Privileged: The Effects of International University Rankings on a Chilean Fellowship Program for Graduate Studies Abroad'. *Social Sciences* 7: 243. doi:10.3390/socsci7120243.

Posselt J. 2016. *Inside Graduate Admissions. Merit, Diversity, and Faculty Gatekeeping.* Cambridge, MA: Harvard University Press.

Rudd, E., M. Nerad, M. Emory, and J. Picciano. 2008. *CIRGE Spotlight #2 on Doctoral Education: Professional Development for PhD Student: Do they Really Need It? Findings from Social Science PhDs—Five+ Years Out.* Seattle, WA: CIRGE.

Steiner-Khansi, G. 2016. 'New Directions in Policy Borrowing Research'. *Asia Pacific Education Review* 17: 381–390. doi: 10.1007/s12564-016-9442-9.

UniWiND. https://www.uniwind.org/about-us.

PART II

Europe

Chapter 3

Between Change and Continuity
The Transformation of Doctoral Education in France

Julien Calmand, Thierry Chevaillier
and Jean-François Giret

Today, doctoral education in France consists of 'research training through research' and provides access to employment in the research sector—either academic, public or private. Historically, the role of doctoral education used to be limited to training academic personnel. Its development over time is the result of many factors such as the transformations of French higher education, the evolution of the role of universities and employment constraints for PhD graduates.

The present organization of doctoral education in France can be explained by features acquired through time in the context of a distinctive higher education system, and by a convergence process that is forced on higher education and research by increasing competition at both the European and global levels. Since the Middle Ages, the doctorate has remained the highest qualification awarded by universities and the academic requirement to teach at the university level. Over the centuries, the progress of scientific research, the increasing specialization of knowledge and the expansion of access to higher education have fostered changes in the role and organization of this degree.

The last decades of the 19th century in France were marked by an attempt to restructure higher education, after the French defeat in the 1870 war against Germany was credited to the scientific superiority of German universities. Until then, doctoral education had been limited to a loosely regulated production of academic personnel for a slowly growing higher education system.

Due to recurrent difficulties for PhD graduates to enter the labour market and a reduction of employment opportunities in universities, the end of the 20th century saw the focus start shifting towards the necessity—in a world characterized by increasing competition—of producing a highly qualified workforce. The number of students exploded and, as a result, so did the need for qualified teachers, but the doctorate was no longer seen only as the requirement for an academic career, but also as a qualification for research and development (R&D) activities in national industries.

The changes brought to French doctoral education over more than a century reflected attempts to reassign its goals and rationalize its organization. This was partly achieved by a slow process of convergence at the European level. A glance at the historical development of doctoral studies can help to understand how peculiar organizational features or practices shaped this process.

A BRIEF HISTORY OF DOCTORAL STUDIES IN FRANCE

During the Middle Ages, different regulations and organizations existed depending on the disciplines in which the doctoral degree was granted. At that time, there were four historic 'faculties' (medicine, law, theology and arts), only three of which awarded doctoral degrees according to their own specific procedures (the faculty of arts awarded only bachelor's and master's degrees). These differences in regulations by discipline have shaped the transformations in doctoral education over time.

Soon after the French Revolution abolished universities, doctoral degrees reappeared in medicine and law (in 1803 and 1804). When the 'Imperial University' was founded by Napoleon in 1808, five doctoral degrees were offered, one in each of the five faculties (the former faculty of arts was divided into two distinct institutions for sciences and humanities). Since the Napoleonic reform had created a state-controlled, centralized higher education system, the same regulations applied to each faculty across the country. Faculties were created in the main cities as branches of the 'Imperial University', with some variations among them. At that time, the doctorate was a 'state degree', awarded by universities on behalf of the state and guaranteed by it. Conditions of access, duration of preparation and examination regulations (number of theses, oral submission and composition of the examination panel) varied according to each faculty. The entrance requirement was the bachelor's degree but, through the years, additional requirements were added.

Apart from minor adjustments, this organization remained basically unchanged until the second half of the 20th century. The main changes consisted of the introduction of a series of other doctoral degrees. This created a confusing situation of several degrees called doctorate but corresponding to different levels, duration of studies or entrance requirements. In 1897, after a significant reform of higher education (recreating distinct universities across the country by splitting the former 'Imperial University'), a 'university doctorate' (*doctoratd' université*) was created, which was less demanding than the 'state doctorate'. In the first two decades of the 20th century, only 250 doctorates were awarded in France.

In 1923, an 'engineering doctorate degree' (*diplôme de docteur-ingénieur*) was introduced, specifically designed for graduates from engineering schools (which in the French higher education system are distinct from universities). In 1966, in an attempt to unify the various disciplines, a 'third cycle doctorate' (*doctorat de troisième cycle*) was introduced, based on a duration of one or two years after a specific year of preparation leading to a new degree, the 'advanced studies diploma' (*diplôme d'études approfondies*).

At that stage, the 'original 1808' doctorate (renamed 'state doctorate' [*doctoratd' état*]) coexisted with three other types of doctoral degrees of shorter duration and lesser academic value. The state doctorate remained the access requirement to full-time academic positions in universities and in national research agencies. The number of doctorates had remained fairly low during the 19th century and the first quarter of the 20th century, but exploded after the Second World War. From 10 to 20 a year in the humanities and around 20 in the sciences during the 19th century (two-thirds of them awarded in Paris), it went up to about 80 (humanities) and 300 (sciences) in the 1960s. Comparatively, the number of 'third cycle doctorates' reached more than 1,200 at the end of the 1960s.

This historical overview, however, does not include the medical doctorate. Medical studies have always been organized differently from the rest of the French higher education. There is no bachelor's or master's degree in medicine. The only degree awarded is called a 'practice doctorate' (*doctoratd' exercice*), which entitles graduates to practice medicine. This is not a research degree. Instead, it marks the end of an eight-year theoretical and practical training programme, including numerous periods of work in hospitals. The situation is similar in dentistry and pharmacy.

From the 1970s until now, there has been a massive expansion of higher education; the number of students in universities has grown rapidly. The number of PhD graduates has also risen rapidly and universities have failed to absorb them in permanent faculty positions. Over time, several reports commissioned by the French education administration revealed tensions in the academic sector linked to professional career difficulties. At the same time, the number of non-permanent staff rose rapidly, and inequalities between non-permanent and permanent faculty became more pronounced. These problems, as well as the internationalization of higher education and research, led to ministerial orders that changed doctoral education. The reform of 1984 is a milestone for the transformation of the doctorate.

TOWARDS ALIGNMENT WITH INTERNATIONAL STANDARDS

A major reform of doctoral education took place in 1984. This ministerial order was part of a wider legislative reform, the so-called 'Savary Act'. It replaced all existing doctorates with one single degree, the 'doctorate' (*doctorat*), with conditions of access, duration and type of examination that were identical for all disciplines (except medicine). The doctorate was defined as the end result of a period of 'research training through research'. Its organization was modelled on American PhD programmes, with access possible after special preparation at the master's level, and three to four years of work on a thesis—defined as a 'piece of original scientific work'—culminating with its submission. The degree was defined as a 'national' degree, meaning that it was guaranteed and recognized by the state, but it was awarded by universities under their own names. This unified organization included transitional provisions to cater to the rights of holders of former doctorates: they were granted some measure of recognition, while a new recruitment procedure for university academic personnel was devised.

The new doctorate became the requirement for recruitment of junior staff, both in universities and in national research agencies such as *Centre National de la Recherche Scientifique* (CNRS, the French National Centre for Scientific Research). To access senior positions, the 'state doctorate' was replaced by a 'habilitation to direct research' (*habilitation à diriger les recherches*, HDR), inspired by the German *habilitation*, which became a requirement for supervising PhD students. This organization has remained unchanged: the 'habilitation to direct research' is still required in order to access senior positions like 'university professor' (*professeur des universités*). During the following decades, a few adjustments were made, but the principles governing doctoral education and the recruitment of public, academic and research staff remained unchanged.

Teaching Assistantships

In 1998, teaching assistantships *(monitorats)* were created to complement the funding provided by existing doctoral grants (*allocations de recherche*) and to introduce some professional training for prospective academic staff. Among doctoral students, teaching assistants (*moniteurs*) were to be selected to teach for three years, carrying a third of the teaching load of regular university staff. Teaching assistant positions were part of the doctoral training and were offered to the more deserving students, who had been identified as capable of obtaining academic positions. Teaching assistants had to attend specific training sessions called 'introduction to higher education' in regional training centres (*centres d'initiation à l'enseignement supérieur*). These training sessions were available to students of all disciplines and addressed both teaching methodology and general research methodology.

Doctoral Contracts

This scheme was discontinued in 2009 with the introduction of doctoral contracts between universities and doctoral students. Research grants (*allocations de recherche*), initially introduced in 1931 and greatly enlarged in 1976, had been turned in 1982 into three-year contracts between the recipients and the ministry of higher education, transforming the legal status of doctoral students into that of public employees, with related rights and duties, including unemployment benefits and salaries based on legal minimum wages. The responsibility of employing state-funded doctoral students was transferred to universities in 2009. Universities were free to add a limited amount of teaching duties to doctoral contracts. Not all doctoral students benefit from such contracts, however. The share of funded students varies from almost 100 per cent in some sectors of the sciences to less than one-third in the humanities and social sciences.

Creation of Doctoral Schools

A different organization of doctoral student supervision was experimented with in the early 1990s. A ministerial order in 1992 allowed universities to create formal structures to improve research training and the supervision of doctoral students with 'doctoral schools' (*écoles doctorales*). These schools were to be organized on a voluntary basis for broad fields of research, and were recognized and funded by the ministry of higher education in the framework of a contract negotiated with the universities. In 2002, a ministerial order made doctoral schools compulsory and allowed them to be jointly organized by several universities. To be allowed to run doctoral programmes and award doctoral degrees, universities had to undergo a formal state-accreditation process. Meanwhile, two additional ministerial orders took the doctoral programme one step further by requiring each university to draw up a 'thesis charter' (*charte des thèses*) defining the rights and duties of doctoral students and organizing the 'habilitation' procedure (*Habilitation à Diriger des Recherches*, HDR), which was transferred to doctoral schools.

While French universities were free to cooperate with each other at the doctoral level by creating joint doctoral schools, there was no specific legislation for relations with foreign universities until 2002, when a ministerial order provided for 'joint supervision' (*cotutelle internationale*) of doctoral students through an agreement between two institutions located in different countries. There is no comprehensive data on the number of such agreements per year, but information available on university websites indicates that it may exceed 1,000 nationally, which corresponds to 8 per cent of PhDs overall.

The organization of doctoral studies was completed by an order in 2006, which broadened the role of doctoral schools in administrative and financial matters. It also clearly introduced, for the first time, their responsibility in facilitating the professional integration of graduates into the labour market.

PRESENT ORGANIZATION OF DOCTORAL EDUCATION

In 2016, a ministerial order defined a new national framework for doctoral studies. It was comprehensive, and in addition to confirming and clarifying the various legal adjustments that had been made since 1984, it introduced a few momentous provisions. It made it possible for universities to coordinate several doctoral schools by setting up a 'doctoral college' (*collège doctoral*). It reinforced the processes of quality assurance by enabling doctoral schools to set limits on the numbers of doctoral students a faculty member could advise, and by urging supervisors to regularly survey their students. The measure also introduced supervision committees to coordinate and supplement the duties of individual thesis advisors.

In 2016, more than 320,000 students graduated from French universities, of which 12,800 (4 %) were doctorates. Since the 2016 ministerial order, doctoral studies have been taking place in research units that are grouped in doctoral schools for this purpose. These research units (*unités d'accueil*), which are part of a university or another higher education institution,[1] are frequently associated with one of the large national research agencies[2] in what is referred to as 'joint research units' (*unités mixtes de recherche*).

Greater Role of Doctoral Schools in Doctoral Education

As mentioned above, doctoral schools were introduced in the last decade of the 20th century with the aim of organizing the training of candidates, and improving their employability and access to various careers open to researchers. They brought together a number of research units attached to one or several higher education institutions operating in a broad scientific field. As of 2018, there are more than 250 doctoral schools in France, some of them focusing on a specific scientific field, others covering broader discipline areas. Doctoral schools can be jointly operated by several higher education institutions. *Grandes écoles* (France's elite, specialized institutions of higher education up to the master's level) may take part in doctoral schools in association with at least one public higher education institution. As the training itself takes place in research units, doctoral schools have been given a central role in coordinating doctoral education in French universities. They are incharge of selecting candidates for the doctoral programmes, giving them the grants made available by their university, and designing and implementing courses and training activities to help them acquire

---

[1] Among the *grandes écoles*, there are several institutions with a very high research profile. They operate by themselves or in association with national research agencies, research centres or units that may be grouped to form their own doctoral schools, or joint doctoral schools with universities. Although they are not formally universities, they are very similar to American research universities. The most prestigious are: École Normale Supérieure in Paris and Lyons; École Polytechnique; Institut d'Etudes Politiques de Paris.

[2] There is one large multidisciplinary agency, the Centre National de la Recherche Scientifique (CNRS), and a dozen of smaller specialised agencies in health, agronomy, informatics, etc.

research skills, scientific culture and knowledge of both scientific ethics and of the economic impact and organization of research. Although there is no administrative data available to confirm this, there is definitely an increase in the weight of courses in doctoral programmes, with significant differences between disciplines and doctoral schools. There is no documentation on student attendance or on their levels of satisfaction with the courses. However, in some doctoral schools, proof of attendance is required for the candidates to be allowed to defend their theses. As doctoral schools are completely free to determine the necessary conditions to obtain a doctoral degree, there are no common rules relative to course attendance in the overall system.

Doctoral schools are accredited for a period of five years by the Ministry of Higher Education, Research and Innovation, after an evaluation by the Higher Council for Evaluation of Higher Education and Research (HCERES), an independent state agency responsible for quality assurance in higher education. The schools are governed by a council elected by the members of the constituent research units, and a director appointed by the president of the university. They are expected to monitor the quality of doctoral work supervision and ensure that students have the materials and administrative support they need. Along with employers, organizations and specialized agencies, doctoral schools collect and distribute information on employment prospects and conduct surveys to monitor the employment of graduates.

Access and Registration

Students may apply for doctoral studies if they hold a national or foreign master's degree or an equivalent postgraduate diploma or qualification. When their degree qualification is not a 'research master', candidates need to obtain a specific authorization after examination of their records by the school council and the scientific council of the university to ensure that they have the necessary preparation for research. The director of the doctoral school decides on admission based on reports from the prospective supervisor or supervisory team and the head of the research unit in which the doctoral work will take place. Admission is officially pronounced by the president of the university.

In 2017, about 75,000 students were enrolled as PhD students in French doctoral schools, and a little fewer than 15,000 graduated. As many as 40 per cent may be considered international students, which can be explained, to a certain extent, by the internationalization of higher education in Europe, but mainly by France's colonial history. In fact, African students are overrepresented in the share of international PhD students, and most of them are funded by their own country.

Subject Selection

Traditionally, the subject of the thesis was chosen by a candidate in agreement with a supervisor. Once the subject was identified, the candidate would write a research proposal that would be submitted to the supervisor and the research unit. Funding was allocated based on merit—the students' results at the master's level. Over the last two decades, this procedure has evolved towards a more competitive alloca- tion of subjects linked with changes in funding allocations for doctoral students. In the majority of cases, the subjects and the funding that goes with them are advertised by research units, and candidates apply by submitting a detailed research proposal. A university panel set up by the doctoral school selects the candidates who seem best prepared to deal with each subject. Once the candidate is selected and the exact subject is specified, the candidate is allowed to enrol in the doctoral programme and the subject is recorded in a national registry. (The national registry of theses was created in order to give the doctoral student rights of intellectual property and avoid the duplication of research projects.)

Duration of Study

The regulations of doctoral studies set a duration of three years for the completion of the thesis by a full-time doctoral student. For part- time studies, the maximum duration is six years. Students may apply for a one-year extension granted by the head of their doctoral school, subject to the approval of the thesis committee, their thesis supervisor and the head of their research unit. Whatever their status, all doctoral students must enrol and pay a yearly 'registration fee' (presently under EUR 400). In late 2018, the government suggested an increase in PhD tuition fees for international candidates in order to improve the global attractiveness of French doctoral programmes, since low fees seemed to signal low quality. Doctoral schools have great autonomy in defining mandatory courses for doctoral students, either subject focused or more broadly relating to methods and skills. They may also require candidates to publish before graduation, with wide variations between the natural and the social sciences.

Supervision

The tradition of individual supervision of doctoral students by a single supervisor (*directeur de thèse*), in an exclusive and somewhat private relationship, has lost ground recently in favour of a more collective and structured supervision. Initiated in the sciences, 'thesis committees', comprising several researchers to whom the doctoral student reports periodically, have been made compulsory by the 2016 order in all scientific fields, including the social sciences and the humanities, where it used to be rather unusual. Doctoral schools organize regular public presentations by doctoral students on progress and results.

Dual supervision is explicitly mentioned in the case of joint doctoral programmes organized with a foreign university (*cotutelle de thèse*). Dual supervision is also used to enable junior researchers to gain supervising experience and prepare for the *habilitation*. The scientific committee of the university senate may exceptionally allow researchers without *habilitation* to take part in thesis supervision. Upon proposals from doctoral schools, scientific committees may set a limit to the number of doctoral students a thesis director is allowed to supervise.

Completion of Doctoral Studies

Once the thesis is completed, the director of the doctoral school submits it to two experts external to the university. If these experts report favourably, the director authorizes the oral presentation and defence (*soutenance*) of the dissertation. An examination panel (*jury*) of three to eight members is selected and appointed by the president of the university. At least half of the members of this panel should be from outside of the university. Each doctoral school has its own rules. Some universities require a balanced gender representation, but this is not mandatory.

After the oral defence, the panel assesses the thesis and the defence. If successful, the candidate is declared admitted to the grade of doctor of the university. A report (*rapport de soutenance*) is then written by the panel. Since 2016, the supervisor, who used to be a full member of the panel, no longer takes part in the assessment of the thesis.

Funding of Doctoral Studies

There is a final point worth mentioning in this historical survey, since it contributes to shaping the working conditions of doctoral students. Heads of institutions where doctoral education takes place are responsible for the material condition of doctoral students during their thesis. Access to doctoral programmes frequently depends on the availability of sufficient resources for the candidates. The way public research is funded in France has undergone dramatic changes in recent decades, with an impact on the way doctoral studies are financed. Since 2005, recurrent funding of university research has been reduced in favour of competitive funding. An increasing proportion of research funds now comes from new agencies, set up to allocate resources to research projects for which research units submit bids. It is a new way of channelling research money to 'research operators'. Such competitive funds are granted for a limited period of time (two to four years) and tend to be used for hiring postdoctoral researchers on contract and doctoral students. Increasingly, the funding of doctoral students is therefore linked to contractual arrangements entered into by universities. This, in turn, leads universities to treat doctoral students as contractual partners, with a specific type of employment contract similar to that of postdocs or other non-permanent research staff.

The development of research contracts between universities and various partners, research agencies and private firms has led to a diversification of funding channels for doctoral studies. In the past, a majority of 'funded' doctoral students received three-year doctoral grants from the Ministry of Higher Education, Research and Innovation. Some were on paid training leave from their employers. Thanks to a scheme named CIFRE (*convention industrielle de formation par la recherche* or Industrial Conventions Training by Research), a growing number of doctoral students were jointly funded by the state and by companies in which they worked on research projects that had contracted with universities. Others relied on grants from local or regional authorities, foreign governments or international organizations. Still others received donations from charities and foundations in a form that was legally undetermined, known as 'liberalities' (*libéralités*).

This variety of sources meant large differences with respect to amounts and conditions of funding. This is the reason why new regulations on doctoral student funding, passed in 2009, state that irrespective of the source of funding, research students should sign contracts with the universities in which they are preparing their degrees. Universities collect the various funds and channel them along the same contractual conditions to all funded students, in order to increase equity and security. In a way, this new legislation has turned universities into employers and funded students into employees (e.g., as is formally the case in Nordic countries).

As mentioned earlier, the funding of doctoral studies may come from various sources: public subsidies (from national or local authorities), participation in research contracts, partial funding by industry like the CIFRE scheme, etc. Funded doctoral studies both improve the working conditions of the students and enhance the image of PhD graduates on the labour market. Beyond being a research experience, doctoral studies become a work experience that is valued by potential employers. Similarly, the transformation of research grants into doctoral contracts has greatly contributed to clarifying the status of doctoral students, who are regarded as salaried employees rather than students, transforming their studies into a valuable salaried work experience and changing the perception of companies likely to hire them.

In the humanities and the social sciences, the share of students who do not get funded is much higher than in other disciplines. The number has remained stagnant between 2009 and 2016. The CIFRE funding scheme, which aims to support the integration of PhD graduates in private companies, finds it hard to expand outside of the engineering sector. Students who are not funded by public or private research grants are either self-funded or employed. Self-funded students, which make up 27 per cent of all PhD students, must cover their living expenses in addition to (limited) registration fees. They also pay the expenses related to their doctoral work that are not covered by the research unit or the doctoral school to which they belong. When they have the necessary financial resources (assistance from their family, their own savings or a bank loan), they may study full time. If they are employed, they may ask for part-time status, which enables them to complete their doctoral studies in six years.

One may question the efficiency of the reforms introduced since 2006. Not all are innovative, since many of them only generalized existing practices, especially in the formal and natural sciences. In those sectors, the prescription of funded doctoral studies and the collective management of thesis supervision existed long before 2006. The CIFRE scheme, which facilitated the integration of PhD candidates into the private sector, was introduced back in 1980 and was limited in scope. The 2006 reform was intended to homogenize doctoral programmes across the whole academic spectrum, but some sectors of the arts and humanities have found it hard to adopt practices that have originated in the formal and natural sciences, in particular the prescription of funded doctoral studies, for which one finds a very low proportion of doctoral contracts.

EMPLOYABILITY AND LABOUR MARKET PERSPECTIVES FOR PhD STUDENTS
Growing Attention to Preparation for Employment

In the last two decades, growing attention has been given in France to preparing doctoral students for various employment perspectives, in the both public and private sectors. Several events are organized locally or nationally, such as specific training sessions where researchers and managers of companies, administrations and research agencies present their work and working conditions to doctoral students. Such events, known as *doctoriales*, are organized across the country with financial aid from the Ministry of Higher Education, Research and Innovation. The state also subsidizes organizations dedicated to supporting doctoral students and graduates in their search for employment. The best known among these organizations is the Association Bernard Gregory. It manages a website called 'scientific employment in France' (*Emploi Scientifique en France*), which has been created and is operated with public financial support and is meant to centralize and disseminate information useful to doctoral students and graduates in search of a job. The doctorate students' guild (*guilde des doctorants*) and the confederation of young researchers (*Confédération des Jeunes Chercheurs*) are similarly active in providing information on work opportunities. Several discipline-based graduate associations cater more specialized services to new graduates within their field of research.

Recruiting to the Professoriate: Changes in the Academic Career

In France, access to a permanent job in the academic sector takes place early in one's career, even if, in some scientific fields, the development of postdoctoral fellowships has lengthened the transition period from finishing the PhD to stable employment. Most academic staff are employed as permanent employees of the state (*fonctionnaires titulaires*) and benefit from civil service status (*statut de la fonction publique*), which provides for lifetime employment. This concerns staff employed in universities with teaching and research duties, as well as those employed by public research agencies in research-only careers, with possible, although not frequent, transfers between the two. As mentioned above, research agencies operate joint research units with universities so that very often both types of permanent employees work together.

In the early 2000s, the average recruitment age for a permanent position as lecturer (*maître de conférences*) was 31, which was also the age limit to apply for a position as a junior research officer (*chargé de recherche*). By 2015, the average age had increased to 34 for lecturers;

the age limit has been abolished for junior researchers. In parallel, the share of non-permanent staff has increased in universities, partly because of the development of postdoctoral fellowships. In 2015, every third lecturer was recruited after a postdoc.

High Unemployment of PhD Graduates in France

For the past three decades, youth unemployment has been a major issue in France. According to a survey from CEREQ (*Centre d'Études et de Recherche sur les Qualifications*, the French Centre for Research on Education, Training and Employment), in 2013, 20 per cent of young people were still unemployed three years after graduation. PhD holders face difficulties in the labour market, as do those with only bachelor's and master's degrees. In recent years, the transition to the labour market for PhD graduates, compared to that of master's degree graduates, has improved but remains difficult. Three years after graduation, 10 per cent of young doctoral degree holders aged 35 or younger and living in France at the time of the survey were unemployed, a share that is higher than that of graduates of '*grandes écoles*' of engineering and business (the elite sector of French higher education), who graduate at the master's level (Table 3.1). Their employment conditions vary according to field of study and type of financial support enjoyed during doctoral studies. The situation is particularly worrying for earth and life sciences graduates, where unemployment reaches 14 per cent. It is much better in computer science and engineering, where graduates have more opportunities in the private sector (Table 3.2). In the humanities and social sciences, the situation is improving, as PhD graduates can be recruited as teachers in secondary education institutions. However, compared to a master's-level degree graduate, the wage premium of a PhD graduate is generally low, except in engineering.

A distinctive feature in the early careers of PhD graduates is the relatively limited share of employment in the private research sector, especially in R&D activities (Table 3.2). Although doctoral studies are supposed to foster innovation and economic growth through transfers of skills and knowledge from the academic world to industry,

Table 3.1 *Unemployment Rate, Three Years After Graduation*

Degree	2004 (%)	2007 (%)	2010 (%)	2013 (%)	2016 (%)
PhD *of which*	11	10	10	9	10
Combined engineering and PhD	5	5	–	5	8
PhD in engineering	11	10	–	12	11
PhD in other fields	16	10	–	9	11
Engineering degree (master level)	6	4	5	4	7
Master	9	7	12	12	11

Source: French national surveys of graduates three years after graduation (Cereq Generations surveys 1998, 2001, 2004, 2007, 2010 and 2013).

Table 3.2 *Employment of PhD Graduates by Sector, Three Years After Graduation*

	2001 (%)	2004 (%)	2007 (%)	2010 (%)	2013 (%)	2016 (%)
Public research (universities, CNRS and other research agencies)	43	49	49	49	49	39
Public non-research sector	17	14	16	15	15	16
Private sector R&D	19	18	17	17	17	22
Private non-research sector	21	19	18	19	19	24

Source: French national surveys of graduates three years after graduation (Céreq Generations surveys 1998, 2001, 2004, 2007, 2010 and 2013).

the private research sector in France relies heavily on graduates of *grandes écoles*, where research is generally weaker than in universities. Even if their research production has improved under the pressure of international academic standards, the role of research in the training of *grandes écoles* students is rather limited, especially in their last year. Only a small proportion of *grandes écoles* graduates enter PhD programmes, a choice that is not likely to improve their conditions on the labour market (Bonnal, Bourdon, and Paul 2011).

However, when we consider the whole population of PhD graduates, as opposed to just recent graduates, their employment situation is roughly similar to that of graduates from engineering schools (Vourc'h and Inan 2017), and sometimes even better, depending on the discipline.

Competition between Engineers and PhD Graduates in R&D

The French higher education system is defined as a dual system. As described above, alongside universities, *grandes écoles* award engineering and business degrees at the master's level. Traditionally, employment in private R&D has been the territory of engineering schools graduates. There are many explanations for why the private research sector favours engineering school graduates. First, alumni networks have an impact on access to employment, especially in manufacturing industries where engineers are preferentially recruited for most functions, including R&D (Beltramo, Paul, and Perret 2001). Hiring often happens by replicating past practices. Also, a majority of vacancies are first channelled to schools through alumni networks. Through frequent and lengthy industrial placements, engineering graduates have a particularly good understanding of how companies and factories operate, which gives them a comparative advantage. The career structure of private companies also plays a part, as it encourages mobility among various functions: R&D is likely to be only one stage in the career of an employee, and therefore preference is given to applicants with more versatile profiles, which is a strength of French engineering graduates. Finally, there is a perception that doctoral education is too abstract and remote from business concerns, when compared to the training of engineers at the master's level (Duhaubois and Maublanc 2005; Grivilliers and Cassette

2014). Despite a clear government policy in favour of increasing the presence of PhD graduates in the private R&D sector, until 2013 their share remained below 20 per cent. However, the most recent tracking study (of 2013 graduates surveyed in 2016) reveals a sharp increase of the share of PhD graduates in the private sector, as well as in R&D jobs (5%) and in other private sector employment (5%).

THE ROLE OF DOCTORAL EDUCATION IN SOCIETY AND ITS CHALLENGES

Fostering the Employment of PhD Graduates through a Tax Credit Scheme for Research

In order to promote innovation and employment in the private sector, a tax credit scheme for research, 'CIR', was introduced in 1983. As the basic purpose of the scheme was to prompt investment in R&D, a component called 'young doctors', focusing on scientific employment and specifically on the employment of PhD graduates in the private sector, was added in 1999 and strengthened in 2006 and 2008. The efficiency of the scheme is debated and some consider it responsible for cuts in the funding of public research (Guyon 2012). In 2013, more than 1,500 companies received tax credits for hiring young PhD graduates, compared to 700 in 2008. As of 2008, companies were able to increase their tax credit from 30 per cent to 60 per cent of the salary cost when they offered a PhD graduate his or her first permanent employment in R&D. A report shows the positive impact of CIR on permanent employment in R&D (Margolis and Miotti 2017). Before 2008, CIR used to favour the employment of engineers rather than PhD graduates. After 2008, it showed a slight advantage for PhD graduates, especially in large companies.

Career Diversification and Professionalization of the Doctorate

Doctoral education reforms received a new impetus between the mid-2000s and 2016. In August 2006, a ministerial order marked a turning point in the history of doctoral education in France. First, it explicitly made access of PhD graduates to the labour market a central issue of doctoral education. That point had never been mentioned in any of the numerous regulations passed since the 1970s. Second, it stated clearly that doctoral programmes do not prepare students exclusively for careers in the public sector of academic research, as was traditionally the case, but also for employment in the private sector. Consequently, doctoral schools were assigned a new mission of fostering the access of new PhD graduates to the labour market. They were asked to take steps to improve the employability of doctoral students and inform them about labour market outcomes on the basis of graduate tracking surveys. Such momentous changes were not specific to doctoral education, since the whole of higher education had been subjected to a long-term process of 'professionalization' that aimed at making programmes more relevant to the needs of the labour market (Rose 2014; Verdier 2001). The process took multiple forms, ranging from the creation or expansion of existing vocational tracks (higher technician diplomas, short technology programmes or bachelor's programmes) to the introduction into the curriculum of labour-related activities like sandwich courses, industrial placements or sessions on preparing to enter the labour market. The 2007 Law on Liberties and Responsibilities of Universities ratified this trend by making professional integration one of the missions of universities. In this general framework, the drive of doctoral programmes to include professional integration relied on a wide set of tools, some common to the whole of higher education, others specific to the PhD.

Tools common to all programmes are those providing students with information on labour outcomes for graduates, such as tracking surveys (Calmand 2016a) and job fairs; those improving the transition from graduation to employment, such as training for job interviews and assistance in writing resumes; and those easing integration into the labour market, like improving students' understanding of business or developing transferable skills. Tools that are specific to doctoral programmes focus on turning training into real work experience. The students' professionalization is supported by better supervision and guidance during their thesis writing, the monitoring of their progress by committees and contracts to fund their doctoral studies. The injunction of academic authorities to give priority to studies funded through doctoral contracts has been a major step, since it has been clearly demonstrated that the material conditions of doctoral students is a determining factor of their professional success (Bonnal and Giret 2010; Bonnard, Calmand and Giret 2016).

Transformation of Doctoral Education

A succession of legal regulations reforming doctoral education has deeply affected doctoral schools in their mission, organization and operation. Nowadays, they have become much larger through mergers, and they are responsible for the whole curriculum of doctoral studies and professional integration of their students. In their application of the principles of new public management, universities and their doctoral schools are assessed based on indicators such as supervision, scientific production and the professional integration of their students.

Since 2006, doctoral schools play an essential part in doctoral education, owing to certification criteria for the doctoral degree and tighter supervision of students. The writing of the thesis is monitored in a more collegial fashion. In contrast to the personal nature that once marked the relationship between the supervisor and the supervisee, which was similar to that of craftsman and apprentice, doctoral supervision has turned into a process of collective management (Musselin 2009). This makes it possible for the student to escape painful situations like professional or sexual harassment, and to avoid loneliness and anxiety when supervision is inadequate or lacking. But it may also create tensions inside research laboratories, which explains why it is opposed by a fraction of the academic community.

As shown by a number of qualitative research papers, this new organization of doctoral education impacts the academic profession. Supervisors experience tensions between contradictory instructions: preparing doctoral students for academic careers and preparing them for the labour market, especially for employment in the private sector. Supervisors feel diverted from their initial function of training students for the practice of scientific research, and deprived of their professional identity (Dahan 2007). Collegial management of thesis monitoring, which is the norm in many countries, is seen as a break from the tradition of individual supervision and a restriction of scientific autonomy.

Moreover, these reforms do not appear very successful in terms of harmonizing the conditions of doctoral education across disciplines. Based on '"Generation', a large survey on graduate integration into the labour market, one may observe that reforms have in fact reinforced a long-standing segmentation of doctoral studies and the differentiation of graduates' careers according to discipline (Calmand, Prieur, and Wolber 2017).

Beyond the increased segmentation of doctoral studies and the remaining differentiation of practices according to discipline, some members of the academic community are concerned with a change in the nature of the doctorate. Since 2016, there has been increasing support for the possibility of obtaining a doctorate degree through recognition of previous professional experience (*validation des acquis de l'expérience*, VAE). This new pathway to the doctorate makes it possible for high-level professionals to build on experience acquired in their occupations and improve their employment perspectives, either with their own employer or on the labour market in general. In the early 2010s, only 15 PhD degrees on average had been awarded this way each year by French universities. The concept behind it being rather recent, it still appears to be an experiment, and raises concerns among the academic community about the potential of increasing the heterogeneity of quality criteria, and of lowering the conditions of access to the highest positions of academia and public research.

Similar concerns fuel the debate on the introduction of professional doctorates in the French higher education system, which will further increase fragmentation. Professional doctorates already exist in France in the health care sector. Medicine, pharmacy, dentistry and veterinary medicine are professions that require a doctoral degree, but as explained above, this degree is clearly distinct from the PhD. It is called a 'practice doctorate' (*doctorate' exercice*). Professional organizations are trying to push for something similar in nursing and psychology, highlighting the need for recognition of a level higher than the master's degree. A university with a focus on business administration, Université Paris–Dauphine offers a programme entitled 'Executive Doctorate in Business Administration'. Within some disciplines (education, law, business administration and others), there is a perception that the meaning of a doctorate differs according to its use and that it does not necessarily have to prepare for a research career.

CONCLUDING REMARKS

In 2018, doctoral studies, traditionally understood in France as writing a thesis, do not have much to do with what they were in the 1980s. After a long period of status quo, a new curriculum has been introduced and demands for scientific production have been raised. Before entering doctoral studies, students must secure funding. Once enrolled, they must anticipate their future professional life and train for an array of jobs while carrying on with their basic duty of producing a piece of original research. The impact of the transformation on doctoral education is difficult to measure, especially because it does not have the same intensity in every discipline. Fields with historical links to companies have been able to adapt doctoral education programmes more rapidly, in line with new state recommendations. At the individual level, these changes also have an impact on the activities of teaching staff, who have to organize doctoral courses on top of their research and teaching duties. In some ways, the differentiation between activities segments academic staff between those who have mainly research duties and those who do not. Notably, investing in teaching is not valued as much as scientific production. As for the students, there is no information on their degree of satisfaction about coursework implementation. However, access to these classes is uneven, depending on disciplines, universities and doctoral schools.

More importantly, doctoral education in France bears the impact of the dual structure of higher education with, on the one hand, universities and, on the other, the *grandes écoles*. *Grandes écoles* are the most selective segment of higher education and attract the brightest students, yet they rarely drive them towards doctoral programmes, which are only offered by research departments at universities. In recent times, a government policy of driving institutions to merge or associate has increased the cooperation between universities and *grandes écoles* (Van Zanten and Maxwell 2015) and widened the access of graduates to doctoral studies. Still, cooperation structures are limited and their governance fragile.

This partly explains why the integration of doctoral graduates into the labour market is problematic. Despite data comparability problems, the comparison of French tracking studies with international statistics clearly shows that in this country, access to the labour market is harder for PhD graduates (Auriol 2010; Harfi and Auriol 2010). Moreover, labour market integration continues to be more difficult for doctoral graduates than for *grandes écoles* graduates, especially from engineering schools, despite the fact that the level of the *grandes écoles* degree (a master's) is lower. For the latter group, there is no obvious benefit of studying further and therefore little incentive to enter doctoral programmes.

The difficult integration of PhD graduates into academic research in France has urged public authorities and representative bodies of doctoral students to look for employment possibilities in other sectors. It looks as if efforts to increase the employability of PhD graduates in the R&D sector are beginning to deliver results. Other steps have been taken to widen the spectrum of employment by ensuring recognition of the doctorate degree in all sectors.

The Law on Higher Education and Research of July 2013 aims at improving the professional integration of PhD graduates by setting two objectives: easing the recruitment of PhD graduates in public administration and obtaining recognition for the doctorate as a professional qualification in collective employment agreements with the private sector. In the public sector, access to about 50 different occupations has been facilitated, mostly through the adaptation of competitive entrance examinations. In 2018, after negotiations between doctoral student associations and the ministry of labour, the doctorate was finally recorded in the National Register of Professional Certifications, which was created in 2002 as a directory of all professional qualifications recognized by the state. Recognition in collective employment agreements has not yet been entirely achieved, owing to the opposition of employers' unions. Yet a few companies have individually signed agreements with some universities.

REFERENCES

Auriol, L. 2010. 'Careers of Doctorate Holders: Employment and Mobility Patterns'. OECD Science, Technology and Industry Working Papers No. 2010/04. OECD Publishing.

Beltramo, J. P., J. J. Paul, and C. Perret. 2001. 'The Recruitment of Researchers and the Organization of Scientific Activity in Industry'. *International Journal of Technology Management* 22 (7/8): 811–834.

Bonnal, L., and J. F. Giret. 2010. 'Determinants of Access to Academic Careers in France'. *Economics of Innovation and New Technology* 19 (5): 437–458.

Bonnard, C., Bourdon, J., & Paul, J. J. (2011). *Travailler dans la recherche privée au sortir d'une école d'ingénieur: est-ce la bonne stratégie?* [Is it a good strategy to work in research and development after graduating from an engineering school]. *Revue d'économie industrielle* (133), 9–30.

Bonnard, C., J. Calmand, and J. F. Giret. 2016. *Devenir chercheur ou enseignant chercheur: le goût pour la recherche des doctorants à l'épreuve du marché du travail* [Becoming a researcher or a university lecturer, the interest of doctoral candidates for doing research rather than for the labour market]. *Recherches en Education* 25: 157–173.

Bonnard, C., J. Calmand, and J. F. Giret. 2016. 'Becoming a researcher or a university lecturer'.

Calmand, J. 2016a. 'Les enquêtes sur le devenir professionnel des docteurs, État des lieux et usages' [Surveys on PhDs careers: status and purposes]. In *Étudier Le Devenir Professionnel Des Docteurs*, edited by S. Jaoul-Grammare and S. Macaire. Groupe de Travail Sur l'enseignement Supérieur, Céreq. Céreq Echanges 2.

Calmand, J., M. H. Prieur, and O. Wolber. 2017, June. 'PhDs' Early Career Trajectories Strongly Differentiated'. *Training and Employment* 127: 4.

Dahan, A. 2007. 'Supervision and Schizophrenia: The Professional Identity of Ph.D Supervisors and the Mission of Students' Professionalisation'. *European Journal of Education* 42 (3): 335–349.

Duhautbois, R. & Maublanc, S. (2005). *Les carrières des chercheurs dans les entreprises privées* [The careers of researchers in private industry], Rapport du Centre d'études de l'Emploi, 25, 72 p.

Grivillers E., Cassette M. (2014). Quelle employabilité pour les docteurs dans le secteur privé? Une analyse des discours des recruteurs. In Bonnard C., Giret J.F. (ed.) *Quelle attractivité pour les études scientifiques dans une société de la connaissance?* [Attractivity of scientific studies in the knowledge society] (pp. 143–165). Paris: L'Harmattan.

Harfi, M., L. Auriol. 2010. 'Les difficultés d'insertion professionnelle des docteurs' [Challenges of access to employment of PhD graduates]. *Note d'analyse du Conseil d'Analyse Stratégique* (189).

Margolis, D., and Miotti L. 2017. 'Why Do French Engineers Find Stable Jobs Faster than PhDs?' IZA DP No. 11197. IZA Institute of Labor Economics.

Musselin, C. 2009. *The Markets for Academics*. New York, NY: Routledge.

Rose, J. 2014. *Mission Insertion: Un Défi Pour Les Universités* [Employability, a challenging mission for universities]. Rennes: PUR.

Van Zanten, A., and C. Maxwell. 2015. 'Elite Education and the State in France: Durable Ties and New Challenges'. *British Journal of Sociology of Education* 36 (1): 71–94.

Verdier, E. 2001. 'La France A-t-Elle Changé de Régime d'Educationet de Formation' [Has France changed its education and training regime?]. *Formation Emploi* 76: 11–34.

Vourc'h, R. & Inan, C. 2017. *La situation des docteurs sur le marché du travail* [Researchers' employment situation on the labour market] Note, Note d'information Enseignement Supérieur- Recherche, SIES. 17.03, 8 p.

Chapter 4

The Past, Present and Future of Doctoral Education in Germany

Barbara M. Kehm

In recent years, many higher education reforms and policy initiatives around the world have focused on doctoral education. Most high-income and upper middle-income countries see themselves as knowledge societies and economies, for which a highly qualified workforce is deemed increasingly important. Accordingly, doctoral education has become a focus, but not without doubts concerning quality of supervision, time to degree and qualification for non-academic jobs, to name only a few (Shin, Kehm, and Jones 2018). In fact, new approaches are sometimes strongly resisted by those academics who educate, train and supervise doctoral students. This chapter explores how these tensions are playing out in Germany, where doctoral education and training have drawn the attention of both policymakers and institutional leaders, but where many professors insist that the highest academic standards and values must continue to apply (Kehm 2009, 2015).

THE NATURE AND MAGNITUDE OF DOCTORAL EDUCATION IN GERMANY

Historical Roots

In medieval times, some European universities such as the University of Bologna did award doctoral degrees. In many other universities, however, the highest degree was the master's. Until the second half of the 18th century, procedures for awarding a master's or doctoral degree were quite different from what was required after the establishment of the research-based doctorate. First, a doctoral candidate was vetted in terms of morality and previous studies. This was followed by a disputation over a theme 'which was drawn by lot the previous evening or in the morning' (Verger 1992, 145). Finally, there was a public examination on a theme of the candidate's choice. A written dissertation demonstrating mastery of a subject was not introduced until the 18th century. However, the dissertation was generally not based on original research, and in many cases was written by a professor. The candidate then had to defend the professor's ideas in public (Bogle 2017, 1; Wollgast 1998).

The modern research-based doctorate emerged with the founding of the University of Berlin in 1810. That is when the faculty of philosophy established the doctor of philosophy—still known as PhD or DPhil—as the highest academic degree, officially giving it more value than the master's. Thus, the PhD became closely linked with the Humboldtian idea of the research university, and was intended to produce original and creative research (Park 2005). Furthermore, the University of Berlin issued new regulations on the successful attendance of seminars, the submission of a dissertation based on original research and the passing of an oral examination. An emphasis was put on the production of new knowledge. Throughout the 19th century, the PhD was adopted in a number of other European countries, including France, the Netherlands and Switzerland. The University of Oxford awarded the United Kingdom's first research-based PhD degree in 1919 (Aldrich 2006; Bogle 2017). In the United States, the research-based doctoral degree was first introduced by Yale University in 1861 (Park 2005, 192).

Although the processes and requirements for being awarded a doctoral degree have changed somewhat over time, the main principles have not. A doctoral degree candidate has to prove his or her ability to carry out scholarly or scientific work by submitting a dissertation— a piece of written work that the candidate has produced without the help of others. Candidates also have to pass an oral examination, which nowadays is usually a defence of the main theses of the dissertation. Upon successful defence, the examiners can give permission for the dissertation to be published, but this may be made dependent on revisions. Only after the dissertation's publication are candidates allowed to carry their doctoral degrees as part of their names. In Germany, as in other continental European countries, the doctoral degree includes grades that are still issued in Latin.

Magnitude of PhD Production

All 113 German universities have the right to award doctoral degrees. The number of PhDs awarded is an important performance indicator, and many universities try to improve the number to increase their reputation. All university professors (33,154 in 2014) have the right to recruit and supervise doctoral candidates (Statistisches Bundesamt 2014, 22), and very few professors choose to oversee no one at all. In 2016, German universities awarded 29,303 doctoral degrees. The percentage of master's students who proceed into doctoral work is about 20 per cent, but the figures vary greatly from subject to subject. In 2014–2015, the federal office of statistics estimated the number of doctoral candidates in the process of completing their degree to be around 196,200. Of these, 56 per cent were men and 44 per cent were women. The proportion of international doctoral students was 14.6 per cent (28,700), and the majority of them were from either Europe or Asia (Statistisches Bundesamt 2016, 24–28).

These rather high figures stem from the fact that the German non-academic labour market has traditionally been very open to hiring doctoral degree holders. In fact, a 2017 federal report on junior academic staff stated that 73 per cent of all doctoral degree holders who were employed had jobs in the private sector, while 12 per cent were employed in public service and 15 per cent in higher education institutions. This indicates the importance of doctoral degrees for non-academic careers (BuWiN 2017, 186). In fact, in some sectors a doctoral degree is almost required to become eligible for an adequate job. This is the case in medicine and chemistry, as well as in mathematics (around 40%) and other natural sciences (Mayer 2018).

Recruitment and Status of Doctoral Candidates

As a rule, in Germany, eligibility for embarking on a doctoral degree requires a master's. In addition, the grade point average linked to the master's degree should be either 'very good' or 'good', serving as an indicator of academic talent. The master's is proof that the potential doctoral candidate has already acquired an in-depth knowledge of his or her discipline, including related knowledge of the methodology, and has developed some kind of specialization, which has been successfully proven by completing a master's thesis and passing an oral examination. After a master's degree, the years of study are considered finished, and independent research can begin under the supervision and mentorship of a professor.

In contrast to most Anglo-American countries, doctoral candidates are not students in Germany. More than 60 per cent of them (in some subjects the percentage is even higher) are employed by their universities as research and teaching assistants, and thus regarded as junior academic staff. Germany has neither a two-phase graduate qualification period uniting the master's and doctoral-level coursework with ensuing research nor 'graduate studies' in the Anglo-American sense of the term. In fact, until Germany adopted the Bologna reforms in 1999, there were no bachelor's degrees awarded by German universities. All first degrees were essentially at the master's level, and could be followed by research work leading to the doctorate.

Germany is known for its clientelism in doctoral candidate recruitment (Mayer 2018), which can basically take three different forms. The first is that either a professor offers a student within the same university the opportunity to work towards a doctoral degree or a student approaches a professor with a proposal for doctoral work. The person being approached is free to accept or decline. If an agreement is reached, the student continues at the same university. However, if the professor moves to a new institution, the student will typically go as well. Most professors who want to recruit doctoral candidates can offer them part-time contracts as junior teaching or research assistants, or will promise to help students find funding through scholarships. The second pattern entails research projects funded by third parties.

In such cases, even if the professor has a candidate in mind, the job still must be publicly advertised so that those from other universities may apply. The third form consists of a potential candidate who wants to write a dissertation on a topic for which there is no proper expertise available at the same university. In this case, the candidate will find a professor with the required expertise and ask for supervision. If an agreement is reached, the student typically moves to the professor's institution.

These patterns might seem informal and prone to academic inbreeding. The informality is indeed a concern, and policies are being developed to establish a registration system. Inbreeding, in contrast, is not seen as an issue because all junior research and teaching positions will typically be advertised, and recruitment procedures are linked to quality and equality regulations. Furthermore, professors are generally trusted to select only those students who have demonstrated a high level of performance. Institutions are only involved insofar as they issue contracts for junior staff. Scholarship holders typically have no formal relationship with the institution at all.

In Germany, students interested in doing doctoral work do not always search for the best programme or supervisor. Some might, but the rule is that the student either searches for a supervisor whose field of expertise fits the prospective dissertation topic, or a professor offers a dissertation topic—often linked to a junior position—and attracts the interest of a particular student. Thus, moving into doctoral work is more related to field of expertise rather than a search for 'the best'. The same holds true for doctoral degree holders moving into the non-academic labour market. The reputation of the university awarding the degree plays a lesser role than the student's own specialization and how the candidate potentially fits into a company's culture. International students who wish to come to Germany for doctoral work often contact a variety of universities and professors to try to secure a place, while those already in Germany might apply for an advertised position or approach a professor they know.

With the exception of a handful of graduate schools supported by special government funding through a programme called the German

Excellence Initiative, there are no regulated structures of recruitment, or integration of doctoral candidates, into doctoral programmes at German universities. Instead, the master–apprentice model still prevails. In short, the German doctoral degree is currently a hybrid model. It is shifting from a research-only degree to one still largely focused on research, but sometimes complemented by course offerings in which student participation is voluntary.

Doctoral research is usually carried out in the supervisor's field of expertise, which leads to the question of funding. Each full professor, also called a chair holder (more on this below), has a negotiated number of positions for doctoral candidates that are funded by the university. These jobs are typically part-time (between 50% and 60% of the regular working hours per week). In the case of third-party-funded research projects, the number of doctoral candidates increases. A research project privately funded for three or four years might yield another one or two positions in addition to those associated with the chair. In such cases, doctoral candidates will work as junior researchers and write their dissertations on topics closely related to the research projects. Still, they remain employed by the university, and their work and dissertations are supervised by their professors.

A professor might also decide to supervise one or more doctoral students, but without proper funding already in place. In this case, the professor will encourage the candidate to apply for a doctoral scholarship at any of the numerous public or private foundations and will write a letter of recommendation. Even if the application is successful, the doctoral candidate has no official status at the university, only a relationship to the supervising professor. The same is true for another group of the so-called 'external' doctoral candidates. These candidates have a job outside the university and do their dissertations in their spare time. However, they need to find a professor who will agree to supervise them. This professor will also act as the main reviewer of the dissertation, choose a second reviewer and chair the defence committee. In Germany, this high dependence of doctoral candidates on their supervisors has been heavily criticized.

The fact that Germany has statistics on the number of doctoral degrees awarded, but not on the number of doctoral candidates in the process of getting degrees, is strongly related to the recruitment patterns described above. Of the four groups of doctoral candidates mentioned, the first two—junior researchers who are part of the chair infrastructure and junior researchers engaged in third-party-funded research projects—are employed by the university as junior academic staff. Almost 60 per cent (in some disciplines more than 80%) of all doctoral candidates are part of this group, called *wissenschaftlicher Mitarbeiter*, or 'academic co-workers'. Until recently, official statistics have not differentiated between those *wissenschaftlicher Mitarbeiter* who have a doctoral degree and those who do not. The other two groups, scholarship holders and externals, have no status in relation to the university, and might only become known to the administration when beginning the doctoral examination process. As there is no official status of doctoral candidates within universities, scholarship holders frequently remain enrolled as students in order to get access to the lab or library. Finally, there is also a group of doctoral candidates who work on their dissertation while they are still studying. This is typical in the field of medicine (Statistisches Bundesamt 2016, 35–38).

Independent of the distinction between 'internal' and 'external', about 83 per cent of all doctoral candidates (162,900) have some form of employment. The overview provided by the federal office of statistics is shown in Table 4.1.

One can clearly see the difference between employment status (fixed-term versus permanent contract) in the public and private sectors. However, public institutions outside of the higher education and research sector also show a better balance in favour of permanent contracts.

Supervisors and Supervision

Most German full professors are so-called chair holders, a term originating from the raised chair or lectern from which a medieval professor gave lectures. Today, chair holders negotiate not only their own salaries with the university but also the resources that will be associated with the chair. A chair's typical infrastructure consists of a few elements: a full- or part-time secretary; between one and five positions for junior

Table 4.1 *Employment Status of Doctoral Candidates in Germany (2014–2015)*

Institution/ Organization	Fixed-Term Contract (%)	Permanent Contract (%)	Total in Figures (%)
Higher education institution	96	4	124,900 (64)
Non-university research institute	92	8	10,600 (5)
Other institution	49	51	10,200 (5)
Private economic sector	41	59	17,200 (9)
Total	88	12	162,900 (100)

Source: Statistisches Bundesamt 2016, 39f.

researchers (doctoral candidates) and possibly one postdoc position; budgets for travel, a library, computers and information technology; and, in the natural and engineering sciences, access to a laboratory (or even one's own lab), including the necessary technical staff. These additional costs are paid for by the university. The junior researchers and the postdoc are expected to support the chair holder's research and teaching while working towards their own qualifications. The professor was and still is relatively free to recruit suitable persons for these junior positions. If the professor comes from another university, he or she will often bring junior researchers and postdocs along to the new university. This kind of clientelism is embodied in the way PhD candidates often refer to their supervisors as 'doctor father' or 'doctor mother'.

Doctoral education in Germany was, and to a considerable extent still is, considered a purely academic affair. Only university professors are allowed to supervise doctoral candidates, and only universities are allowed to award doctoral degrees. This means that universities of applied sciences and extra-university research institutes, for example, the Max Planck Society or the Fraunhofer Society, do not have this right. Furthermore, university professors are free to recruit as many doctoral candidates as they want, but this varies according to discipline. An active professor in the humanities or social sciences might supervise between one and eight doctoral candidates. In the laboratory sciences with large amounts of third-party-funded research, the number of doctoral candidates supervised by one professor might be 20 or even more. A recent survey conducted by the federal office of statistics calculated the following figures. In 2016, there were 33,154 professors in Germany who had the right to be doctoral supervisors. Where 50 per cent oversaw 1–5 doctoral candidates, 11 per cent chose to supervise no one at all; 24 per cent supervised 6–10 doctoral candidates; 9 per cent supervised 11–15 doctoral candidates; 3 per cent supervised 16–20 doctoral candidates and 3 per cent supervised 21 or more doctoral candidates.

The average number of supervisions was 6, but varied between an average of 11 in engineering and 5 in the humanities and medicine/ health care (Statistisches Bundesamt 2016, 22). For a professor, there are no particular personal incentives for supervising a larger number of doctoral candidates, except maybe boosting an academic reputation. However, having many doctoral candidates can be a sign that a professor has a big lab to run and is able to generate high levels of third-party research funding. In such cases, the doctoral candidates and postdocs carry out the actual research work, while the professor focuses on managing the projects and writing applications for more funding.

Traditionally, German universities do not require doctoral candidates to do any coursework. As eligibility for doctoral work is constituted by a master's degree with a reasonably good grade point average, candidates are expected to already have a solid knowledge of their fields and research methods. Supervision of a doctoral candidate typically consists of two elements. The first is that a doctoral candidate submits draft chapters, or parts of the dissertation, to his or her supervisor. The student then asks for a meeting and receives critical comments and feedback from the supervisor. The frequency of these meetings is left to the candidate. The second element is research colloquia offered by the supervising professor every two to four weeks. All of the professor's doctoral candidates are expected to participate by presenting aspects of their research, while in turn receiving comments and feedback from the other participants and the supervisor.

Procedures for Awarding the Doctoral Degree

Once a supervision agreement between a potential candidate and a professor has been made, the candidate can start the research work. In doctoral schools, programmes and graduate colleges, the supervision agreement is increasingly a written one, outlining the rights and obligations of both parties. Often, a second supervisor is also added. Those candidates working as junior researchers and teaching assistants for a chair holder, or in the framework of a third-party-funded project, are typically supervised by the professor for whom they work. In programmes, schools or colleges, supervision is more distributed and is mostly related to the expertise of the professors involved. The dissertation will first be submitted to the professor, who acts as the main supervisor, for approval. It will then go to the relevant administrative unit of the department with a request to set in motion the doctoral examination procedure.

The main supervisor takes the lead in reviewing the dissertation. However, all dissertations are required to be reviewed by a second person, who might be from the same department, from another department within the same university or from another university in Germany or abroad. Once the two reviewers have submitted their assessments of the dissertation, an ad hoc examination committee is formed consisting of the two reviewers, a person who takes the minutes and two or three more examiners. These extra examiners are often from another university department, but have some expertise on the topic. They might also be from another German university or from a university abroad. Overall, the composition of the examination committee tends to be flexible.

A date for an oral defence of the dissertation is then fixed and publically announced, so that all interested parties can attend. Typically, some members of department staff, and perhaps family and friends of the candidate, choose to be there. During the defence, the candidate will present a summary of his or her findings, emphasizing any newly generated knowledge and insights. This presentation is typically restricted to 30 minutes, which is then followed by another 30 minutes of questions from the examination committee. After this, the candidate and the audience are sent outside the room while the committee deliberates the grade and possible stipulations for publication. Candidate and audience are then called back into the room for the results. Grades are issued in Latin and apart from *insufficienter* (failed), which happens very rarely, there are four different grades, from *summa cum laude* to *rite* (sufficient/ passed). Stipulations for publication tend to be related to the grade. A *summa cum laude* result means that few, if any, revisions are needed, while a lower grade may call for more.

Dissertation publication varies according to disciplinary culture. In the humanities and social sciences, it takes the form of a book, while in the natural sciences and in engineering, publication tends to be in the form of a journal article. Electronic publications have also become frequent in recent years. There is a rather strict rule that no part of the dissertation should be published before the award of the title. This rule, however, excludes publications on other topics and nowadays, doctoral candidates frequently have some publications in their portfolio. In cases of PhD by published work, the department itself decides whether a student has the option to complete the degree in this fashion.

With the increasing internationalization of German universities, the role of the English language has become more pronounced. International doctoral candidates will typically submit their dissertations in English and defend them in English as well. In quite a number of doctoral schools, programmes and graduate colleges, the working language is English. Other languages are only used in subjects related to the respective country and its culture, language and literature.

Relationship between the Doctoral Degree and the Habilitation

In order to successfully embark on an academic career in Germany, a doctoral degree is necessary but no longer sufficient. Like some other continental European countries, Germany requires a *Habilitation*, sometimes called a 'second doctorate', to become eligible for a professorship. The process is generally undertaken by someone while working for a chair holder (full professor). A *Habilitation* is an independent piece of written research that goes beyond the doctoral dissertation, delving deeper into a particular topic or specialization. It is submitted to a university department, which then selects two or three reviewers. Upon acceptance of the written research, the candidate will be invited to give a public lecture. All professors on the faculty then decide if the lecture is worthy of an award called *venia legendi* (Latin for the right to give public lectures). The title attached to this is *Privatdozent* (Dr. habil.; literally 'private lecturer'), and it constitutes eligibility to apply for a professorship. The professorial title can only be carried once the candidate has managed to actually become a professor and, in contrast to the doctoral degree, it is not officially part of the name, but merely an indication of status. In Germany, only professors are allowed to give lectures, while junior academics do their teaching in seminars and tutorials.

Earning a *Habilitation* usually takes five to eight years, and is usually done in the framework of fixed-term employment (part-time or full-time) at a university. In Germany, this long path to a professorship has been criticized for quite a while, and some ministers of education have attempted to abolish it. One such attempt has been the creation of a new position called junior professor in 2002, which so far has been less successful than anticipated. Another attempt has grown from a more grassroots level, with an increasing number of departments accepting applications for a professorship from candidates without a *Habilitation*, but with equivalent experience and achievements. This does not happen in all subjects, however. More conservative disciplines like law and economics continue to require a *Habilitation*, while more liberal disciplines such as sociology accept '*Habilitation* adequate' scholars. In contrast to Anglo-American countries, Germany, like most other continental European countries, does not really have a concept of a postdoc. Some universities, however, have tried to import the idea, and it has been frequently used to indicate the phase between completion of a doctoral degree and getting a professorship. So far, though, it has not really taken shape in any way. Academic positions associated with this phase of qualification are instead called assistantships, junior professorships or simply *wissenschaftlicher Mitarbeiter*.

Despite the fact that the junior professorship has not taken off, it is becoming more popular and accepted. The number of *Habilitations* has decreased from 2,128 in 2000 to 1,627 in 2014, while the number of junior professorships has increased from 102 in 2002 to 1,613 in 2014 (BuWin 2017, 110–115). It is difficult to say whether or not the *Habilitation* will eventually disappear. In the foreseeable future, it will likely continue to exist alongside the junior professorship.

It is also necessary to emphasize here that all *wissenschaftlicher Mitarbeiter* positions are fixed-term. They can be held up to six years before the doctoral degree, and up to six years after it. The principle is 'up or out'. Tenured positions are only available at the professorial level, although there are some rare exceptions. But even an initial professorial position is nowadays mostly a fixed-term position for six years, after which the person has to apply elsewhere in order to move into a tenured position.

With eight to ten hours of classroom time per week, professors carry the heaviest teaching load among all academic staff at German universities. It is important to note that there are no teaching-only universities in Germany. All universities are considered to be research-driven institutions. Teaching-only institutions are called *Fachhochschulen* or 'universities of applied sciences'. However, in the German context, these teaching-only institutions would never be allowed to call themselves universities.

RECENT REFORMS AND NEW DEVELOPMENTS

As is the case in most other European countries, doctoral education in Germany has seen two major developments in recent years. The first is a shift from product (dissertation) to process (supervision). The second is the increased focus of national and supranational policymakers, as well as university management, on doctoral education, because it is deemed too valuable a resource in knowledge societies to be left exclusively in the hands of academics (Bao, Kehm, and Ma 2016; Kehm 2015).

Germany adopted the Bologna Process reforms by introducing a two-tiered system of studies and degrees (bachelor and master). However, there are currently heated debates about adopting the idea of doctoral education as a third cycle of studies. Given the fact that

60–70 per cent of all doctoral candidates are employed by universities as junior research assistants, treating them as students goes against the grain of the German research and innovation system. However, the combination of a commitment to the Bologna reforms plus growing criticism of the traditional system of doctoral education, be it individual supervision or the master-apprentice model, has led to a number of new developments that make German doctoral education a hybrid between the Anglo-American model and the continental European master–apprentice model (Kehm et al. 2018). These new developments and reforms, as well as lingering traditions, will be discussed next.

The Importance of Disciplinary Cultures

The continuation of the traditional forms of doctoral education in Germany is related to the important role of disciplinary or subject 'cultures' (Becher and Trowler 2001). These cultures are reflected in the differences in the proportions of doctoral degree awards to master degrees (see Table 4.2). High proportions of doctoral degree awards can be found in medicine, chemistry, physics and biology, but low proportions in German language and literature, as well as in economics (Burkhardt 2008, 12).

Disciplinary differences are also seen at the postdoc level and the level of junior professorships. The humanities (25%), the social sciences including law (26%) and mathematics/natural sciences (27%) had the highest proportions of junior professors, while medicine had the highest level of *Habilitations* (51% of all *Habilitations* in 2014; BuWin 2017, 110–115). The *Habilitation* in medicine also has an important role for careers within hospitals (BuWin 2017, 109). In medicine, only 4 per cent of doctoral degree holders stay in academia, while in the humanities it is 40 per cent (BuWiN 2013, 290).

These disciplinary differences also affect recruitment to professorial positions. More than half of all new professors in the humanities, and almost two-thirds of all new professors in medicine, had a *Habilitation*. New professors in mathematics and natural sciences were more often '*Habilitation* adequate', and junior professors could also be found more

Table 4.2 Doctoral Degree Awards (2007–2016) by Subject Group

	Humanities	Sports	Law, Economics, Social Sciences	Mathematics, Natural Sciences	Medicine, Health Care	Agro Sciences, Forestry, Food Sciences, Veterinary Medicine	Engineering	Art, Art Sciences	Total
2007	2,649	110	3,368	6,863	7,222	1,074	2,247	262	23,843
2008	2,679	110	3,769	7,303	7,352	1,011	2,541	323	25,190
2009	2,625	101	3,549	7,425	7,700	994	2,340	258	25,084
2010	2,760	115	3,534	8,092	7,287	1,019	2,561	261	25,629
2011	2,711	138	3,761	8,460	7,771	1,027	2,833	248	26,981
2012	2,890	129	3,509	8,718	7,350	1,065	2,860	256	26,807
2013	2,997	128	3,746	9,560	7,003	897	3,119	255	27,707
2014	3,015	157	3,646	9,521	7,326	969	3,187	306	28,147
2015	3,036	148	3,692	9,950	7,322	1,016	3,736	318	29,218
2016	2,175	105	4,794	8,782	7,414	1,008	4,719	302	29,303

Source: Statistisches Bundesamt 2017, 11 and 13f.

frequently in these subjects (BuWiN 2017, 192). In engineering subjects, one in four doctoral degree holders aspired to an academic career, while in the humanities the figure was nine out of ten (BuWiN 2017, 180). These are only a few of the striking examples of the complex effects disciplinary cultures have on career choice in Germany.

Structuring the Doctoral Phase

Most universities have created some kind of structured doctoral programme—sometimes a graduate school for the university as a whole, sometimes a disciplinary or interdisciplinary graduate college—to offer courses to doctoral candidates. Such courses cover a broad spectrum of topics (theory, methodology, transferable skills, etc.), but are typically not obligatory in terms of participation. Doctoral candidates usually pick and choose courses in areas in which they feel weak, or in which they could use a bit more knowledge. It is important to note here that the term 'graduate' has been adopted from the Anglo-American programme model for doctoral education. It does not mean that bachelor degree holders are accepted into such a school, college or programme. A master's degree continues to be the rule when it comes to eligibility as a doctoral candidate. There are a few rare exceptions to this, as some programmes offering a 'fast-track PhD' for particularly talented bachelor graduates. A recent survey by the federal office of statistics that tried to calculate the number of doctoral candidates in the process of getting their degrees came up with the following figures for structured doctoral programmes: altogether, about 23 per cent of all doctoral candidates participate in such programmes. However, this varies according to subject: for example, 33 per cent in mathematics and natural sciences, and 14 per cent in medicine and health care (Statistisches Bundesamt 2016, 33).

Shared Supervision of Doctoral Candidates

Supervision is increasingly shared. Many doctoral candidates now have two supervisors in order to not only reduce dependency on the main supervisor but also to increase the quality of supervision. Increasingly, the candidate and supervisor sign a written agreement. Almost 60 per cent of all supervisions now include such a document, but the number does vary considerably among disciplines, from 70 per cent in mathematics and natural sciences to 50 per cent in social sciences, economics and law (Statistisches Bundesamt 2016, 32).

Reducing Time to Degree

There are efforts to reduce time to degree. According to the Bologna reforms, a doctoral education should take no longer than three years. In Germany, it is now closer to four years, but it frequently used to take much longer. However, as doctoral education, like all university studies, is free from tuition fees (for domestic as well as international students), there is no fixed deadline regulating submission. Reducing time to degree is related more to the duration of contracts and scholarships, as well as improving the quality of supervision.

Provision of Transferable Skills

The acquisition of transferable skills has also become more important in Germany. There is now considerable awareness and acceptance among professors and university leaders that the overwhelming majority of doctoral degree holders will not stay in academia, and thus have to be prepared for jobs in the non-academic labour market. Graduates need presentation, networking and communication skills, and need to be able to work as part of a team. Seminars and workshops in acquiring these kinds of transferable skills are mostly organized and offered in the framework of doctoral schools, colleges or programmes.

Internationalization and Network Building

Internationalization and network building have received more attention in recent years. For domestic doctoral candidates, this means attending international conferences and presenting their work in English. It might also entail shorter research periods at a partner university abroad. These activities contribute to the ability of doctoral candidates to build up and sustain their own networks. Other forms of internationalization have also become more common. International experts might be invited to Germany to give lectures or workshops for doctoral candidates, and most universities are making an effort to recruit more international students into doctoral work in Germany. Some universities make use of the European Erasmus+ programme, which provides funding for the establishment of doctoral programmes linking two or more universities from different European countries. Finally, there are an increasing number of doctoral schools or programmes that are international, in so far as they have a good mix of domestic and international doctoral candidates and use English as the language of communication.

Registering Doctoral Candidates

There is cause for concern among policymakers about the fact that Germany does not have a registration system for doctoral candidates, and thus has no idea how many candidates are engaged in getting a doctoral degree, or how many students who drop out along the way. Three policy initiatives have been developed to remedy this situation. First, universities are encouraged to officially register doctoral candidates. The difficulty here is that universities have to create a status for doctoral candidates in order to establish an appropriate registration system. They also have to convince supervisors to register their external candidates and scholarship holders. Second, a national reporting system has been established (The Federal Report on Young Academics or BuWiN). It is produced every four years by an independent academic consortium in order to provide more relevant information to policymakers about doctoral candidates. Third, the federal office of statistics has made an effort to gather more and better data about doctoral candidates in the process of getting degrees.

Eroding the Monopoly of Universities to Award Doctoral Degrees

In recent years, the monopoly of universities to award doctoral degrees has come under considerable pressure from two sides—the universities of applied sciences on one, and research institutes, especially those of the Max Planck Society, on the other. There are a number of universities of applied sciences in Germany that have developed a considerable reputation, in particular for applied research carried out in cooperation with industry. In the framework of these activities, the number of doctoral candidates being trained at universities of applied sciences has increased. As these institutions cannot award doctoral degrees, and the idea of a professional doctorate is still contested, universities of applied sciences have had to form cooperation agreements with universities in order to secure doctoral degree awards for their candidates. In 2015, the German state of Hesse gave all its universities of applied sciences the possibility to award doctoral degrees under certain conditions. One of these conditions is that the right to award the degree is not given to the institution as a whole, but instead to individual departments with strong research portfolios. There is also an application procedure. Another condition is that the committee awarding the degree must include at least one university professor.

To some extent, this policy shift grew out of the criticism of the 45 graduate schools funded by the German Excellence Initiative mentioned above. These schools increased the number of doctoral candidates considerably, but tended to be oriented towards basic research, and were criticized for not providing the kind of practical training that would help doctoral degree holders find jobs in the non-academic labour market. The institutes of the Max Planck Society also brought pressure to bear on the issue, because many of them had established schools or programmes over the years that educated and trained many scholars. The institutes argued that although their levels of doctoral-level training were frequently better than those at universities, they still were not allowed to award doctoral degrees. The solution was to make the director of a Max Planck institute, which is a position commensurate with a full university professor, an honorary professor at a university. In this way, the university could award the doctoral degree to the candidate coming from a Max Planck Institute. Given these developments, it can be said that the monopoly of universities in awarding doctoral degrees is eroding, but only at the margins.

THE ROLE OF DOCTORAL EDUCATION IN AND FOR SOCIETY

The German policy response to the realization the country was becoming a knowledge society was twofold. First, the number of doctoral degree awards was increased, while knowing that most recipients would eventually enter the non-academic labour market. Second, the government tried to open up more flexible pathways to the doctorate. Kehm (2009) has identified nine different models of doctoral education in Europe, most of which are common in Germany as well. Most universities now offer courses for their doctoral candidates to acquire transferable skills. Closer relationships between doctoral education and the non-academic labour market have been created by the fact that many subjects in the natural sciences and engineering have professional doctoral degrees in place through cooperation with industry or through cooperation between universities and universities of applied sciences.

As indicated above, the German non-academic labour market has always been very open to those holding a doctoral degree. In fact, there are disciplines—chemistry is a particularly good example—in which a doctorate is essentially a must in order to get a job, especially in the pharmaceutical industry. This is also common in the field of medicine. In many companies, especially those with research and development units, highly qualified people with research training are wanted and needed. The same is true in parts of the public sector, for example, in the legal system (Gokhberg, Shmatko, and Auriol 2016).

The overproduction of PhDs was a common topic of discussion in Germany during the 1970s and 1980s, but is no longer an issue. The general view is that there should be many pathways to the doctorate, and that Germany can be proud of its high number of doctoral degree holders. Statistics support this view. A special report by the Federal Office of Statistics (2016) showed that in 2015, of a total of 604,000 doctoral degree holders, about 15 per cent were employed in higher education institutions, 12 per cent in other public services and 73 per cent in the private sector. Unemployment among doctoral degree holders (between 0% and 2%) is the lowest compared to those with other qualifications. Job satisfaction for those with doctorates is also relatively high, as well as the feeling that their skills and job tasks are well matched. This seems to suggest that the effort in recent years to help doctoral degree holders get the skills they need to transition into non-academic labour markets is paying off.

One aspect that is worrying, however, is the bottleneck at the postdoc stage for academic jobs. Many more doctoral degree holders and postdocs want to stay in academia than there are jobs available, particularly in the humanities and some of the social sciences. It is important to note here that almost all academic jobs at or below the position of associate professor are fixed-term positions. Therefore, many doctoral degree holders who try to stay in academia and fail end up looking for jobs elsewhere in their mid-to-late 30s. Vis-à-vis almost 30,000 doctoral degree awards per year, there are at most 1,000 first-time professorships available. Thus, it can be estimated that only around 3 per cent of all doctoral degree holders eventually become professors (Mayer 2018, 122; Statistisches Bundesamt 2016).

International Doctoral Candidates

Over the years, the number of international doctoral candidates in Germany has gradually increased due to various methods of recruitment and support. In 2016, the proportion of all doctoral degrees awarded to international students was 17.3 per cent. Table 4.3 shows the number and proportion of doctoral degree awards to international students in 2016, and gives the most common countries of origin. No tuition fees are charged to international doctoral candidates, and there are a variety of scholarships available to them, especially through the German Academic Exchange Service or through scholarships attached to international graduate schools funded by the German Excellence Initiative. A lack of German language skills is often not a problem, because practically all academic staff at German universities speaks English reasonably well. There are quite a number of doctoral programmes, schools and graduate colleges that have an explicit international dimension. As a rule, they recruit doctoral candidates internationally, the language of instruction is English, and they frequently offer lectures or seminars by scholars or scientists invited from abroad.

Table 4.3 *Doctoral Degree Awards (2016) to International Candidates by Most Represented Countries of Origin*

China	770 (15.2%)
India	328 (6.5%)
Italy	304 (6.0%)
Iran	214 (4.2%)
Russian Federation	188 (3.7%)
Austria	159 (3.1%)
Poland	152 (3.0%)
Turkey	146 (2.9%)
Greece	134 (2.7%)
France	110 (2.2%)
Ukraine	104 (2.1%)

Source: Statistisches Bundesamt 2016, 31.
Note: No information available per discipline.

CONCLUSIONS

This chapter explored recent developments and ongoing changes in doctoral education and training in Germany. Since the release of the Federal Reports on Young Academic Staff (BuWiN 2008, 2013, 2017), German policymakers have become more aware of the challenges facing doctoral degree holders and the reforms needed to help them succeed both inside and outside of academia. Increasingly, policies are being developed to find ways to move forward.

One problem is the lack of a registration system for doctoral candidates in the process of getting their degrees. Although universities are being encouraged to develop such a system, a real solution to the problem has not yet been found. This might mean creating a distinctive status for doctoral degree candidates that goes beyond remaining enrolled as a student, being employed as a junior research or teaching assistant or having no formal relationship to the university at all (scholarship holders outside of graduate schools or doctoral programmes and external candidates). However, if such a registration system were linked to formal procedures of selection and recruitment by, for example, departmental or institutional committees, many professors would see it as an unwanted interference in their academic freedom.

A second challenge is structuring academic career pathways for doctoral graduates that reduce the role of clientelism and create opportunities for tenured academic employment below the level of the professorship. Currently, the tenure track option as it exists in the United States is being widely discussed in Germany, and there are policy intentions to implement it. Yet there is also hesitation, because moving up the career ladder within an institution is often regarded as a form of unwanted inbreeding. When the junior professorship was introduced in 2002, it was hoped this policy would provide enough incentives to universities to attach a tenure track to each of these positions. However, many departments resisted and it rarely happened. Still, there are exceptions. For example, the Ludwig Maximilian University of Munich, one of the winners of the German Excellence Initiative, has decided to attach a tenure track to all its junior professorships.

The introduction of the junior professorship was an explicit attempt to reduce the length of time it took for doctoral graduates to reach a professorship. It was also an implicit criticism of the *Habilitation*. Apart from the junior professorship, there is also an ongoing discussion about a postdoc stage in German higher education, modelled on the Anglo-American system. However, this remains relatively shapeless and undefined, both in terms of the criteria for moving up the academic career ladder and in terms of status and funding. It is a situation still looking for a solution.

REFERENCES

Aldrich, J. 2006. 'The Mathematics PhD in the United Kingdom'. http://www.economics.soton.ac.uk/staff/aldrich/Doc1.htm (accessed 14 January 2019).

Bao, Y., Barbara M. Kehm, and Y. Ma. 2016. 'From Product to Process: The Reform of Doctoral Education in Europe and China'. *Studies in Higher Education* 41 (9): 1–18. doi:10.1080/03075079.2016.1182481.

Becher, T., and Paul R. Trowler. 2001. *Academic Tribes and Territories*. 2nd ed. Buckingham and Philadelphia: SSRHE and Open University Press.

Bogle, D. 2017. '100 Years of the PhD in the UK'. https://www.vitae.ac.uk/news/vitae-blog/100-years-of-the-phd-by-prof-david-bogle (accessed 29 November 2019).

Burkhardt, A., ed. 2008. *Wagnis Wissenschaft. Akademische Karrierewege und das Fördersystem in Deutschland* (Venture Science and Scholarship. Academic Career

Paths and the German Support and Funding System.) Leipzig: Akademische Verlagsanstalt.

BuWiN. 2013. *Bundesbericht Wissenschaftlicher Nachwuchs 2013: Statistische Daten und Forschungsbefunde zu Promovierenden und Promovierten in Deutschland* [Federal Report on Doctoral Candidates and Early Career Researchers]. Bielefeld: Bertelsmann Verlag.

————. 2017. *Bundesbericht Wissenschaftlicher Nachwuchs 2017: Statistische Daten und Forschungsbefunde zu Promovierenden und Promovierten in Deutschland* [Federal Report on Doctoral Candidates and Early-Career Researchers]. Bielefeld: Bertelsmann Verlag.

Gokhberg, L., Natalia Shmatko, and Laudeline Auriol, eds. 2016. *The Science and Technology Labor Force: The Value of Doctorate Holders and Development of Professional Careers*. Cham: Springer.

Kehm, B. M. 2009. 'New Forms of Doctoral Education and Training in the European Higher Education Area'. In *The European Higher Education Area: Perspectives on a Moving Target*, edited by B. M. Kehm, Jeroen Huisman, and Bjørn Stensaker, 223–241. Rotterdam, Taipei: Sense.

————. 2015. 'Entering Academia: Realities for New Faculty in German Higher Education'. In *Young Faculty in the Twenty-First Century: International Perspectives*, edited by M. Yudkevich, Philip G. Altbach, and Laura E. Rumbley, 111–139. Albany, NY: State University of New York Press.

Kehm, B.M., Shin, J.C., Jones, G.A. (2018). Conclusion: Doctoral Education and Training – A Global Convergence? In: Shin, J.C., Kehm, B.M., Jones, G.A. (Eds.). Doctoral Education for the Knowledge Society. Convergence or Divergence in National Approaches. Cham: Springer, p. 237–255.

Mayer, K. U. 2018. 'Wissenschaft: Weder Berufung noch Beruf?' [Science and Scholarship: Neither Vocation nor Profession?] *Denkströme: Journal der Sächsischen Akademie der Wissenschaften* 19: 115–123.

Park, C. 2005. 'New Variant PhD: The Changing Nature of the Doctorate in the UK'. *Journal of Higher Education Management* 27 (2): 189–207.

Shin, J. C., Barbara M. Kehm, and Glen A. Jones, eds. 2018. *Doctoral Education for the Knowledge Society: Convergence or Divergence in National Approaches?* Dordrecht: Springer.

Statistisches Bundesamt. 2014. *Personal an Hochschulen*. Fachserie 11, Reihe 4.4. Wiesbaden: Statistisches Bundesamt. [Federal Office of Statistics: *Staff at Higher Education Institutions*. Subject Series 11, Sequence 4.4]

————, ed. 2016. *Promovierende in Deutschland*. [Doctoral Candidates in Germany] *Wintersemester 2014/15*. Wiesbaden: Statistisches Bundesamt.

————. 2017. *Prüfungen an Hochschulen* [Examinations at Higher Education Institutions]. Fachserie 11, Reihe 4.2. Wiesbaden: Statistisches Bundesamt.

Verger, R. 1992. 'Teachers'. In *A History of the University in Europe*, vol. 1, edited by Hilde De Ridder-Simoens, 144–169. Cambridge: Cambridge University Press.

Wollgast, S. 1998. 'Zur Geschichte des Dissertationswesens in Deutschland im Mittelalter und in der Frühen Neuzeit' [On the History of Doctoral Dissertations in Medieval Germany]. *Leibniz Sozietät*. https://leibnizsozietaet.de/wp-content/uploads/2012/10/01_wollgast2.pdf (accessed 29 August 2018).

Chapter 5

Poland
An Abundance of Doctoral Students but a Scarcity of Doctorates

Marek Kwiek

The massification of doctoral studies in Poland has not led to an equivalent increase in doctoral degrees. While the number of doctoral students increased steadily through the 1990s and 2000s, the number of doctorates awarded did not follow suit. Many students entered doctoral programmes, but only a minority were awarded degrees. Most either dropped out or completed the programme but did not defend their dissertations. This disparity between entrants and doctoral degrees awarded is central to understanding emergent tensions around doctoral education in the Polish context. Based on international comparative statistics, the current intake of 43,000 doctoral students (GUS 2017; OECD 2017) represents an overproduction of doctoral students but a scarcity of doctorates.

HISTORY OF DOCTORAL EDUCATION IN POLAND

Traditionally, as in other European systems, the number of doctoral students in Poland was low and completion rates were high. There were a limited number of available places and doctorates were awarded upon completion of a highly competitive programme and dissertation defence, or by dissertation defence only if the candidate was already employed as an assistant in a degree-awarding institution. The proportion of new entrants to the academic profession through doctoral studies and assistantships has varied over time. At present, a doctoral degree is required for all new academic posts. Prior to 1989, the Polish higher education system was elitist and competitive. The number of academics increased slowly, from 22,523 in 1965 to 61,400 in 1989—an almost threefold increase within a quarter of a century. During that period, 1,700–3,700 doctoral degrees were awarded annually.

After 1989, the delayed massification of higher education changed the landscape beyond recognition. By 2016, there were four times as many students and sixteen times as many doctoral students, but the number of academics only increased by about 50 per cent (Białecki and Dąbrowa-Szefler 2009; Siemieńska and Walczak 2012). In other words, the dramatic expansion in student numbers, which stopped in 2006 (Kwiek 2013; Kwiek and Szadkowski 2018), was not accompanied by a corresponding expansion in the academic profession. One consequence of this disparity was that academic employment opportunities for new doctoral graduates shrank in the post-1989 period, which largely explains why the increasing number of doctoral students did not lead to a proportionate increase in doctorates awarded. Because the chances of academic employment were very low, the motivation to pursue or complete a doctoral degree was also low.

Prior to the end of communist rule in 1989, the basic rationale behind Polish doctoral education was to provide highly trained personnel to higher education institutions. After 1989, doctoral education was extended to those who wished to continue in higher education without necessarily considering academic jobs. These new 'third-cycle students' (as they were called following the Bologna Process) qualified for benefits such as scholarships and health care provisions. The traditional rationale of intensive training in research and research methods for a small number of future academics was turned upside down, and in most academic fields and institutions, the traditional Humboldtian bond between pupil and master was broken. Among the exceptions were some research-intensive faculties in elite universities, especially in the hard sciences. Massified, underfunded, organizationally uncoordinated—and most of all, perhaps, devoid of a clear purpose—Polish doctoral education has drifted into the unknown, and most doctoral students now combine doctoral studies with non-academic work rather than being socialized to academic norms.

This drift can be explained by a combination of several factors. Perhaps the most important of these was a failure to understand why the country needed doctoral studies on such a massive scale. It was also unclear what kind of professional life doctoral students might pursue if, as was already clear by about 2005, they were unlikely to secure academic jobs. Until recently, there was little debate about these issues, either in the public domain or among political parties. After two decades of failure, a new law passed in July of 2018 introduced fundamental changes, including a focus on research-intensive institutions and making scholarships available only for those enrolled in newly created doctoral schools.

DOCTORAL EDUCATION AND SOCIETY

The status of doctoral students in the higher education sector is unclear (Szadkowski 2014), as is the overall status of doctoral education in society. Are doctoral studies expected to produce national elites, or are they merely expanding the pool of highly qualified personnel in the labour market? Are universities more interested in the quantity or the quality of doctoral studies and, by extension, of doctoral degrees? When the Bologna Process was introduced about a decade and a half ago, the traditionally elite status of doctoral studies disappeared as higher education massified and programmes became largely non-selective. In Poland, the whole system of doctoral education had traditionally focused on producing future university professors; with massification, the question was where these future university professors were to be employed. In terms of non-academic employment for doctoral graduates, there is a vast difference between the needs of industry (where those with degrees in technical disciplines might find employment) and of business enterprises and public administration (for those with degrees in social sciences and economics).

Given the scarcity of new academic posts and the large number of doctoral students, the decision not to complete one's studies, or to even engage in research activities, can be seen as a rational strategy at the individual level. If only about 10 per cent of this population can reasonably expect to find employment in the academic sector, there seems little point in pursuing an education that prioritizes academic research and publications. Ninety per cent of doctoral students will never find their way to higher education employment. In a heavily declining higher education system (Kwiek 2013), with decreasing numbers of students and academics, the pool of new academic posts is very limited. For purely demographic reasons, the number of students declined by about one third in the last decade, and the number of academics, with a delay, followed suit. This disinterest in academic employment among doctoral students was matched by the frustration of doctoral supervisors, who saw no point in supervising students who showed little interest in research. However, the new law of 2018, if skilfully implemented and backed by new funding for doctoral schools, may bring much-needed change.

ORGANIZATION, PROCEDURES, FUNDING AND INTERNATIONALIZATION

While doctoral students are predominantly enrolled in higher education institutions (94.23% of candidates), data from 2016 indicate that some can also be found in the Polish Academy of Sciences (4.72%) and research institutes (0.95%). All higher education institutions, including those specializing in one discipline such as agriculture, economics, education, technology or medicine, offer doctoral programmes. About half of these students (48.25%) are enrolled in universities and about one fifth (18.05%) in universities of technology. In organizational terms, doctoral education is provided at the faculty level. Faculties are the main organizational units within academic institutions and, in most cases, they comprise several departments and are headed by a dean. In 2018, almost 90 per cent of about 1,000 faculties (880) were eligible to provide doctoral education (POLON 2018). Doctoral education is located almost exclusively in the public sector. The number of doctoral students (and doctoral degrees awarded) in the private sector is marginal. In 2016, the private sector accounted for just 3,418 doctoral students (7.9%), while only 122 doctoral degrees (2.8%) and 17 *Habilitation* degrees (0.9%) were awarded (GUS 2017). The demand–driven nature of the private sector largely accounts for this low level of participation (Antonowicz, Kwiek, and Westerheijden 2017; Kwiek 2018b).

Doctoral education in Poland is currently provided through a combination of structured teaching (lectures, classes, laboratory hours) at the faculty level and individual collaboration with academic supervisors. One main supervisor is responsible for the student's academic development and progress. In 2016, almost 90 per cent of doctoral students failed to specify their dissertation themes and titles, which are required for the so-called opening procedure. The number of doctoral students who passed the opening procedure is very low (5,209 of 43,181 doctoral students, or just 12.1%). In all other cases, official supervisors had not even been assigned.

The criteria for doctoral programme providers are strictly defined. According to the Law on Higher Education (LHE 2011), an academic institution must be authorized to confer the PhD degree in at least two different disciplines before being allowed to provide doctoral programmes in those disciplines. In practice, only faculties or departments that employ at least eight full-time senior academics in a given discipline may confer doctoral degrees.

Entry to doctoral studies is offered to top graduates as a continuation of their master's-level studies. There is a required minimum average grade (usually 4.0 on the Polish scale, in which 2.0 is a fail and 5.0 is the maximum). Because the number of candidates usually exceeds places available, oral entrance exams are commonplace. Admissions committees comprising professors from the given faculty organize these exams and evaluate candidates partly on the basis of their academic accomplishments to date, and partly on their project proposals. Doctoral studies take four years, and scholarships may be provided for that entire duration. Most universities will agree to extend the period of study by one year, with all privileges maintained (including coverage of costs for the doctorate defence procedure, which all part-time candidates or those not enrolled in a doctoral programme must pay themselves), but with no scholarship. Doctoral programmes may be full-time or part-time. In public higher education institutions, no tuition fees are charged for full-time programmes, but there may be fees for part-time studies, especially in law, business and economics.

Although this chapter addresses doctoral education, it is important not to disregard the specific structure of academic degrees in Poland. One feature that the Polish higher education system shares with countries such as Austria, Finland, France, Germany, Russia and Switzerland is the postdoctoral degree (or *Habilitation*), which can be granted by about two-thirds (647) of all Polish faculties (POLON 2018). While a doctoral degree opens the door to junior positions, the *Habilitation* is the first step in a senior academic career. The powerful gatekeeper status of the *Habilitation* as a prerequisite for university professorship, and ultimately full professorship, means that the doctoral degree becomes less important. It is merely the entry ticket on the long journey to academic seniority.

The changing proportion of doctoral students to degrees awarded has important policy implications. Other than Russia, Poland is the largest producer of doctorates in Central and Eastern Europe. In 2016, there were 43,181 Polish doctoral students, and 5,999 doctoral degrees were awarded. Since the collapse of communism in 1989, about 117,000 new doctorates have been awarded. The number of those completing a *Habilitation* degree has been much smaller, as they are awarded to those already employed in the academic sector (in 2016, for instance, 1,848 were awarded). While the number of doctoral students grew roughly by a factor of 10 between 1990 and 2000, and a factor of about 16 by 2016, the number of doctorates awarded in the same period increased by no more than a factor of 2 or 3, depending on the year. The period of greatest expansion was the 1990s. The number of doctoral students increased from 2,695 in 1990 to 25,622 by 2000. Following an increase to 37,492 by 2010, the number has remained in the 40,000–43,000 range for the last three years (Table 5.1).

These data can be analysed along several dimensions, including academic field, institutional type, gender and regional concentration.

Table 5.1 *Doctoral Students and Doctorates Awarded in Poland (1990–2016)*

Year	Total	Full-Time	Part-Time	Doctorates Awarded
1990	2,695	1,926	769	2,324
1995	10,482	6,779	3,703	2,300
2000	25,622	18,882	6,740	4,400
2005	32,725	23,169	9,556	5,917
2010	37,492	27,066	10,426	4,815
2015	43,177	37,101	6,076	5,956
2016	43,181	37,548	5,633	5,999

Source: Author's analysis based on GUS (Central Statistical Office) data.

While the number of men pursuing a doctoral degree increased by 5,445 in the period 2000–2016, the number of women increased by almost double that figure (12,548). This is a strong trend. While a majority of doctoral students in 2000 were men (55.44%), they were in the minority (44.95%) by 2016. This change may be attributed to the decreasing attractiveness of the academic profession (Kwiek 2017), especially in the context of low entry salaries in the higher education sector in Poland and elsewhere, and also relatively low salaries for senior academics (Kwiek 2019; Yudkevich, Altbach, and Rumbley 2015). Poland clearly represents the feminization of academe, which may further diminish its financial attractiveness, as a growing number of women enter doctoral studies and move on to junior positions in higher education.

While the growth of doctoral education in the university sector has been remarkable, it has been less dramatic in universities of technology, which are focused on both teaching and research. For the period studied, the number of doctoral students increased by 61.24 per cent in universities, but only 27.02 per cent in universities of technology. This, in part, explains the increasing numbers of women doctoral students, as new opportunities have appeared predominantly in the university sector. In 2016, women accounted for two-thirds of all students at the master's level (67.19%). It is hardly surprising, then, that the number of women doctoral students in universities increased by about 5,000 (79.06%) in the period 2000–2016.

In 2016, there were 8,106 doctoral students in the humanities and 4,674 in the social sciences. With 3,728 in economics and 3,860 in law, the total in 'soft fields' was 20,368 (47.17 %); in other words, about half of all doctoral students that year were enrolled in fields unrelated to STEM (science, technology, engineering and mathematics). The proportion of women is higher in these non–STEM fields, totalling 62.05 per cent in the humanities, 62.84 per cent in the social sciences, 51.52 per cent in economics and 54.72 per cent in law, which are all well above the proportion of women in the doctoral population as a whole. The number of doctoral students in technical sciences is widely considered too low at 15.75 per cent (6,802), 36.64 per cent of which are women. In international terms, STEM fields are underrepresented in Polish doctoral education, while non–STEM fields are overrepresented (see Table 5.2).

In terms of regional concentration, 40.93 per cent of doctoral students are located in Warsaw and Krakow, the two largest academic centres. A further 38.70 per cent are located in five smaller academic centres. Warsaw's dominance is strong, with one in four doctoral students in Poland enrolled in Warsaw-based institutions. Similarly, one third of research funding from the National Research Council goes to the two national flagship universities, the University of Warsaw and the Jagiellonian University in Krakow (Kwiek 2018b).

The distribution of doctorates by academic field reveals the tension between high numbers of doctoral students and low numbers of doctorates awarded. In 2016, the largest numbers of doctorates were awarded in medicine and technical sciences, followed by the humanities and social sciences. In all other fields, the number was considerably smaller. In the case of *Habilitations*, these four fields also dominated, accounting for 51.35 per cent of all Polish postdoctoral degrees. Of 5,999 doctorates awarded in 2016, 91.13 per cent were awarded by higher education institutions (predominantly universities and universities of technology), with 4.96 per cent (297) awarded by the various institutes of the Polish Academy of Sciences, 3.23 per cent (194) by

Table 5.2 *Number of Doctoral Students by Major Academic Fields (2016)*

| | Total | | Doctoral Students | | | |
| | | | Full-Time | | Part-Time | |
	Total	Female	Total	Female	Total	Female
Total	43,181	23,772	37,548	20,931	5,633	2,841
Humanities	8,106	5,030	7,811	4,815	295	215
Religious studies	1,720	422	1,492	395	228	27
Social sciences	4,674	2,937	3,900	2,585	774	352
Economics	3,728	1,921	2,444	1,295	1,284	626
Law	3,860	2,112	1,724	891	2,136	1,221
Mathematics	541	144	537	142	4	2
Physics	1,202	471	1,192	468	10	3
Chemistry	1,763	1,160	1,755	1,155	8	5
Biology	1,991	1,381	1,991	1,381	0	0
Earth sciences	946	497	939	494	7	3
Technical sciences	6,802	2,492	6,543	2,448	259	44
Agriculture	1,585	1,066	1,492	1,017	93	49
Forestry	178	65	106	48	72	17
Medicine	3,183	2,143	2,967	2,022	216	121
Health sciences	677	557	639	529	38	28

Source: Author's analysis based on GUS (Central Statistical Office) data (2017).

research institutes and 0.68 per cent (41) by ecclesiastical higher education institutions (GUS 2017).

From October 2019 onwards, it is expected that the newly created doctoral schools required by the 2018 law will lead to further regional concentration. The data for 2000–2016 shows that the academic peripheries (in terms of the 16 Polish administrative units) have not been developing as rapidly as Warsaw and Krakow, and in some cases, the number of doctoral students in 2016 was the same as in 2000. Detailed analysis of the regional concentration of doctoral students over time confirms this skewed pattern of expansion. The two major academic centres differ substantially from the rest of the country, making them natural candidates for flagship status as 'research universities' under the 2018 law (Kwiek 2018a).

Doctoral studies in Poland are funded by the public budget (included in ministerial subsidies for teaching) and by fees (for part-timers in public universities and for all doctoral students in private ones). Public and private institutions each have separate funding streams for doctoral studies, and the funding is included as part of the general financial support for students. In 2016, about 40 per cent of doctoral students received financial support—one in five (19.9%) received doctoral scholarships and one in five (21.20%) got social scholarships or need-based support related to family income (GUS 2017, 158–159).

The number of international students enrolled in doctoral studies in Poland is the lowest across all OECD countries. In 2015, it was 1.9 per cent (OECD average=25.7%; EU22 average=21.7%). In Europe, only Hungary (7.2%), Latvia (8.8%), Slovenia (8.5%) and Germany (9.1%) had a share of international students lower than 10 per cent (OECD 2017, 300). This is perhaps the most worrying indicator, suggesting that the Polish doctoral system as a whole is uncompetitive and unable to attract international talent. Despite its relatively large size, the system is focused almost exclusively on Polish students, and predominantly uses the Polish language for instruction.

POLISH DOCTORAL EDUCATION: AN INTERNATIONAL COMPARATIVE PERSPECTIVE

To assess Poland's international standing in this context, the most meaningful comparison is with other OECD economies (OECD 2017). The number of doctorate holders in Poland's working age population (ages 25–64) is one of the lowest in Europe. At fewer than 5 doctorates per 1,000 people, Poland is most similar to post-communist countries such as Russia, Estonia, Slovakia and Latvia, as well as Portugal and

Italy. In contrast, 10 OECD countries achieve figures of 10 or more doctorates per 1,000 (OECD 2015, 102).

Polish doctoral recipients are relatively young, with a median age at graduation of 32 years. That is one of the lowest in the OECD area. Cross-disciplinary differences are relatively small, with the median age being 31 in the natural and agricultural sciences and 33 in the medical sciences and humanities. In Europe, the median age is lower only in the Netherlands and Switzerland (29–31; OECD 2010). The typical age of entry to doctoral education in Poland is 24–26, which is among the lowest in the OECD area (OECD 2017, 420). The age structure of Polish doctoral holders indicates that they are a relatively homogeneous population group, with the highest share below 45 years old (68.7% for men; 70.8% for women). This is the highest rate across all OECD countries, with most European countries at 40–50 per cent.

In Poland, the structure of doctorate holders by employment sector differs radically from all other countries for which data are available. The most recent data (2016; GUS 2017) show that 213,971 people in the Polish labour force are involved in research and development, and that 87,027 of them hold doctoral degrees. Using the OECD classification of research and development personnel, 87.39 per cent of Polish doctoral holders are employed in the higher education sector (including the Polish Academy of Sciences), with 8.71 per cent in the business enterprise sector and 3.90 per cent in the government and private non-commercial sectors combined (GUS 2017, 42). Poland is one of several countries in which the business enterprise sector accounts for less than 10 per cent of the pool of doctorate holders. The picture that emerges is one of a Polish higher education and science system that produces doctorates for academia, and then keeps them there.

Distribution of Doctorates Awarded

In the Polish context, only one in four doctoral students is ultimately awarded a doctoral degree (NIK 2015, 6). It follows that the processes affecting the distribution of doctoral education differ from those that determine the distribution of doctorates. The emergent tensions reveal the fundamental difference between the changing higher education system in terms of teaching, which is where the Bologna Process places doctoral education, and research, in which doctorates awarded belong. In Poland, there is a further difference in national statistics, as the fields of study used to report doctoral student numbers differ from those used to report doctorates awarded.

While the rise in the number of doctoral students can be linked to financial mechanisms (e.g., more doctoral students per institution means higher public subsidies), the rise in the number of doctorates awarded can be linked to factors such as internal academic promotion procedures and doctoral supervision as a formal requirement in applying for full professorship. While doctoral education is therefore undertaken for reasons other than the award of a doctorate (e.g., to prolong the period of study), doctorates awarded signal a new stage, leading predominantly to employment in the academic sector. Measuring the changing distribution of doctorates awarded over time by academic field reveals shifts in the academic sector better than changes in doctoral education, as a high proportion of doctoral students are academically inactive. More doctorates are reported in academic fields that either afford more employment opportunities in the academic sector or—as in medicine and law—lead to new opportunities in non-academic sectors of the economy.

From a historical perspective, the number of doctorates (and *Habilitations*) awarded was relatively stable in the period prior to the regime change (1970–1990), and so too was the gender distribution of both types of degrees. Women were awarded about one-third of all doctoral degrees (27–32%), and about one-fifth (20–21%) of *Habilitations*.

It is useful to view Polish doctorates and *Habilitations* in the context of academic careers and how they relate to age. In the last half century, the average age range for doctorates was 30–35 years; over the last 15 years, this has remained stable at 32–33 years. In the case of *Habilitations*, the average age increased until 2008, peaking at 47 and then decreasing slowly to about 45 by 2016 (Figure 5.1). What is especially important in both academic and policy contexts is the time lapse between

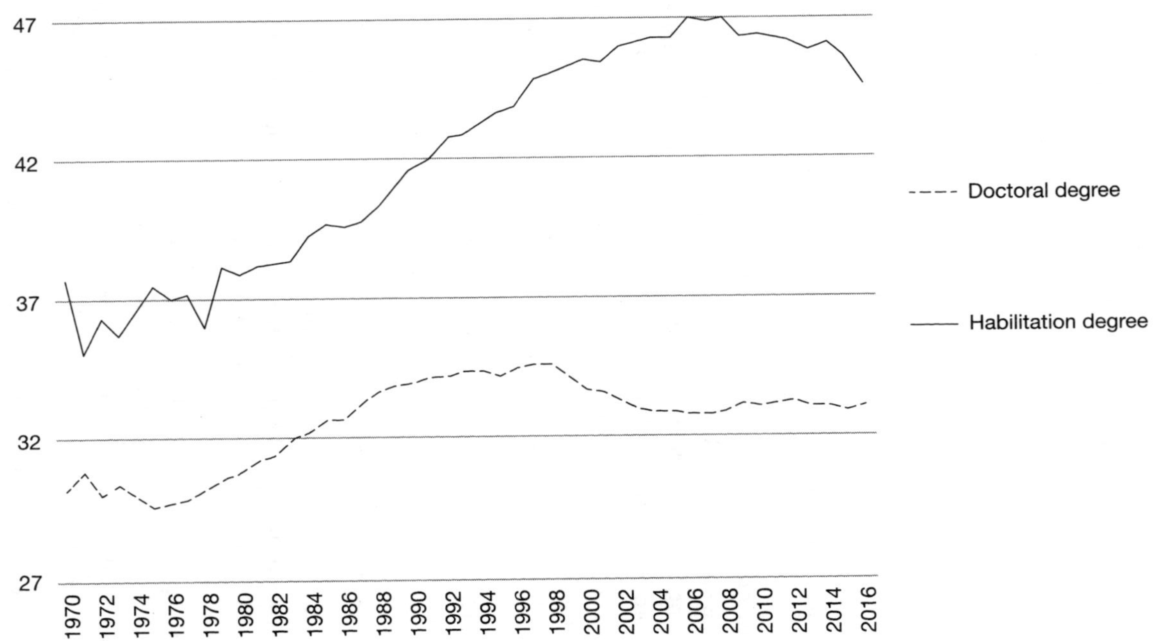

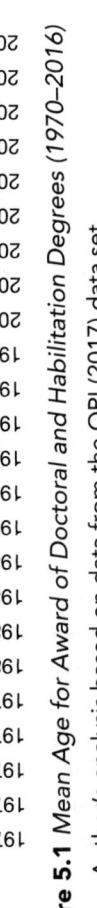

Figure 5.1 *Mean Age for Award of Doctoral and Habilitation Degrees (1970–2016)*

Source: Author's analysis based on data from the OPI (2017) data set.

the two degrees. In the 1980s, this averaged 7–9 years, increasing in the mid–1990s to an average of 12–13 years, where it remains today. This means that junior-level academic careers are very long in Poland compared to other countries. As mentioned earlier, the second degree is just the entry ticket to academic seniority. The full professorhip is not reached, on average, until academics are in their 50s. In the case of the *Habilitation*, the age factor has major policy implications, and its possible abolition has been at the centre of the academic reform debate over the last quarter of the century.

During the period studied (1990–2016), the number of doctorates awarded annually increased by 158 per cent (from 2,324 to 5,999). A total of 92,993 new doctorates have been awarded since 2000. This increase is not impressive when compared to the fourfold increase in the number of students, and the huge increase (×16) in the number of doctoral students in the same period. Rather, the limited expansion of doctorates during the period from 1990 to 2016 reflects the limited growth of the academic profession (Kwiek 2015b, 2017). There is a clear connection here; while doctoral education witnessed phenomenal growth (as did higher education in general), the growth in doctorates awarded reflects the emergent opportunities in the academic sector. From a European perspective, employment opportunities for doctoral holders in Poland are almost exclusively academic. As the academic sector did not grow quickly enough, the growth in the number of doctorates was therefore modest. During the expansion period of doctoral education (2000–2016), the number of doctorates was stable at about 5,000–6,000 per year.

What did change fundamentally during this time, however, was the gender composition of doctorate holders, with a gradually increasing share of women receiving doctorates. While 31 per cent of doctorates in 1990 were awarded to women, the percentage rose to 42 per cent in 2000, and 53 per cent by 2010. From a gender perspective, the turning point came in 2008. This is when, for the first time in the history of Polish science, the number of women exceeded the number of men receiving doctorates (Table 5.3).

The female-to-male (FM) ratio is a useful tool for studying gender differentiation in doctorates (and *Habilitations*), and reveals dramatic changes in the gender composition of doctorates in Poland. This ratio

Table 5.3 Number of Doctorates and Habilitations Awarded by Gender (1990–2006)

	Doctorates						Habilitations					
	Total	Male	Female	FM Ratio	% Male	% Female	Total	Male	Female	FM Ratio	% Male	% Female
1990	2,324	1,607	717	0.45	69	31	973	765	208	0.27	79	21
1995	2,300	1,537	763	0.50	67	33	628	457	171	0.37	73	27
2000	4,400	2,568	1,832	0.71	58	42	829	589	240	0.41	71	29
2005	5,917	2,986	2,931	0.98	50	50	955	611	344	0.56	64	36
2010	4,815	2,260	2,555	1.13	47	53	960	610	350	0.57	64	36
2015	5,956	2,787	3,169	1.14	47	53	1,643	921	722	0.78	56	44
2016	5,999	2,817	3,182	1.13	47	53	1,848	1,047	801	0.77	57	43

Source: Author's analysis based on GUS (Central Statistical Office) data.

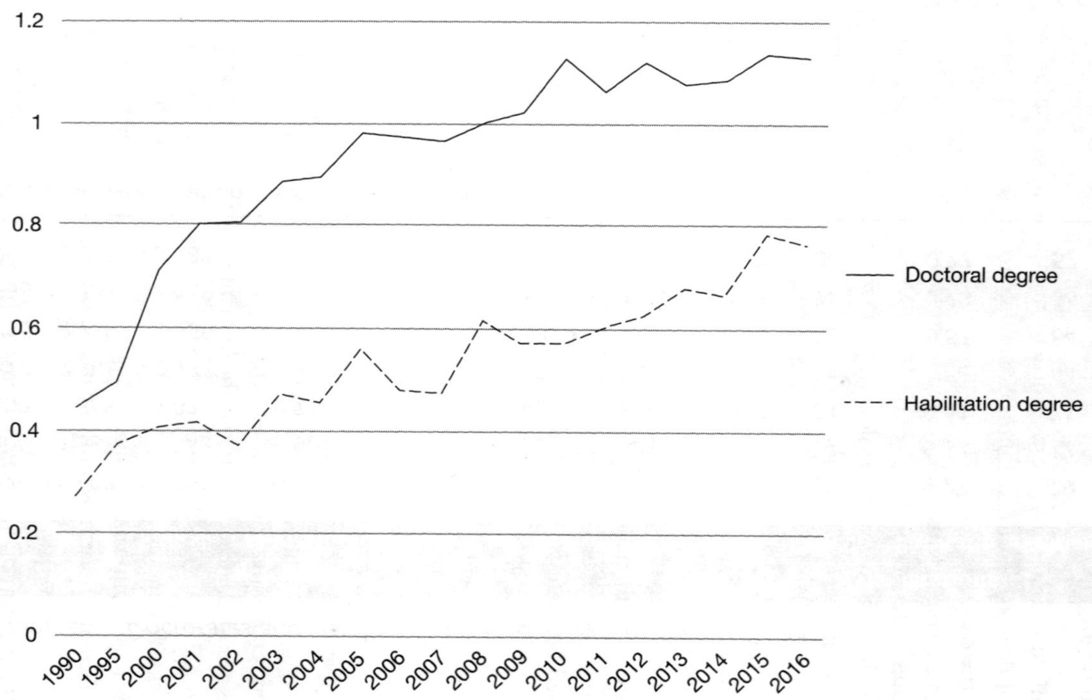

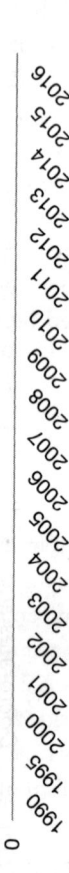

Figure 5.2 *FM Ratio of Doctorates and Habilitations Awarded (1990–2006)*

Source: Author's analysis based on data from OPI (2017).

was 0.45 in 1990; it increased steadily, reaching 1.00 in 2008 (a turning point, with an equal number of male and female doctorates) and 1.13 in 2016 (Figure 5.2).

While doctorates may be awarded to non-academics, the post-doctoral degree is awarded almost exclusively to academics. In other words, the changing gender composition of the *Habilitation* over time highlights changes within the academic profession. The FM ratio for doctorates differs considerably from the FM ratio for *Habilitations*, although both show a substantial increase in women receiving degrees. In the case of the *Habilitation*, the gender factor is very clear. In the same period (1990–2016), the FM ratio increased from 0.27 in 1990, to 0.41 in 2000, to 0.57 in 2010, and reached 0.77 in 2016. The gender gap is also evident in the number of *Habilitations* awarded (1,047 men and 801 women in 2016; see Table 5.3). While the share of women with doctorates increased from 31 per cent in 1990 to 53 per cent in 2016, the share of women awarded *Habilitations* increased from 21 per cent to 44 per cent over that same period. One further dynamic—not addressed here but worthy of attention—is the slowly changing low share of female professorships over time.

A detailed analysis of the changing composition of doctorates awarded in Poland from 2006 to 2016 reveals stability in all major academic fields. While in some cases there has been a slight decrease in the number of doctoral degrees awarded (biology, economics, physics, medical sciences, technical sciences), there have been slight increases in others (chemistry). Other fields (law) have shown substantial increases, although overall numbers remain low. The only academic field in which the number of degrees awarded exceeded 1,000 is the humanities, with 1,349 degrees in 2016 (22.49%). This has important policy implications, as the state may decide to limit the number of places available in these fields through the new organizational mechanism of doctoral schools and the financial mechanism of scholarships for those in doctoral schools only.

REFORM DEBATES: ACADEMIC DEGREES AND ACADEMIC CAREERS

In terms of funding and governance, Polish universities remained largely unreformed until 2009–2012 (Kwiek 2016). Prior to 2009, the higher education system was governed by two laws: a 1990 law granting academic freedom and institutional autonomy, and a 2005 law, which sought to adapt the system as a whole to Bologna Process requirements (including the introduction of a three-cycle model of higher education studies). Throughout this period, however, the system was based on non-competitive funding modes and excessively powerful collegial governance (Kwiek 2015a). The next set of reforms (from 2009 to the present) aimed to reinstitutionalize the research mission (Kwiek 2012) and to reorient Polish universities towards research activities and closer cooperation with wider socio-economic interests. As of 1 October 2018, another new wave of reforms has taken the same direction, with internationalization of research as one of the major goals (Antonowicz, Kwiek, and Westerheijden 2017; LHE 2018).

Since 2010, doctoral education in Poland has attracted severe public and academic criticism, following Bologna-related changes in the law on higher education introduced in 2005. The major lines of criticism include: lax selection criteria that allow the inflow of large numbers of doctoral students (selection and size), declining quality of doctoral education and doctoral dissertations (quality), narrow choice of courses for doctoral students (educational offerings), low numbers of doctoral scholarships (incentives), and the inability of Polish institutions to attract international doctoral students (internationalization).

As in a number of other European countries, the legal and academic status of Polish doctoral students remains unclear. The key question is whether they are young academics (as was traditionally the case in Poland) or third-level students (in the spirit of the Bologna Process). The young academic/older student distinction has a number of practical implications, including access to national-level research funding and access to institution- and faculty-level research infrastructures. Doctoral students in the humanities and social sciences report the lowest levels of access to funding; more than 40 per cent of the former and 35 per cent of the latter report no access to funding at all (Bień 2016, 261). Reported reasons for pursuing doctoral studies are as follows: self-development (90%), influencing research in one's academic discipline (49.7%), professional career (40.3%), social advancement (28.9%) and access to scholarships (20%; Bień 2016, 266).

In the debate around Polish higher education reforms from 1999 to 2018, three questions related to doctoral education figure prominently. First, how is doctoral education to be linked to the research status of degree-awarding institutions (or their academic units, predominantly faculties)? In other words, how can it be ensured that doctorates are produced only in research-intensive academic environments? Second, how can it be ensured that doctoral students are fully focused on their dissertations rather than on outside jobs? And finally, how can doctoral education be linked to the labour market and/or social needs? These three issues reflect the three major lines of criticism of doctoral education: the declining quality of doctoral dissertations, doctoral students' declining interest in research, and the mismatch between scientific fields in which dissertations are awarded and available employment opportunities inside and outside the university sector.

The new law on higher education advances a comprehensive solution to these three issues (Antonowicz, Kwiek, and Westerheijden 2017; LHE 2018). From October 2019 onwards, the right to award doctoral degrees is granted only to institutions of at least middle ranking in the periodic national research assessment exercise known as the 'national research evaluation' (Kulczycki 2017). In a national ranking system for 47 academic fields, only institutions with middle and high marks are able to award doctoral degrees in a given academic field. The new requirement brings an end to the earlier situation, which granted this right to 88 per cent of academic units.

The new law on higher education also introduces the concept of doctoral schools, which are to be located exclusively in institutions that are highly ranked for research performance. A new geography of doctoral education will gradually be introduced, with all full-time doctoral students concentrated in doctoral schools and a limited number of part-time doctoral students still scattered across the system. As mentioned earlier, all full-time students in doctoral schools will be entitled to relatively generous scholarships, which will be accompanied by a ban on non-academic outside work. The idea of these schools is to confine doctoral education to research-focused institutions and to keep doctoral students focused on their dissertations.

At the same time, Polish doctoral education has been experimenting with an entirely new type of doctorate: the so-called 'implementation doctorate', which is similar to the professional doctorate. Although the number of such doctorates is limited (500 new doctoral student per year as of 2017), it warrants mention as a new idea. Under this new ministerial scheme, doctoral students are entitled to receive a relatively generous doctoral scholarship, as well as a salary, from any enterprise that employs them. Both doctoral education and dissertations will be undertaken in partnerships between higher education institutions and enterprises. Only the highest ranking institutions (according to the national research exercise) are eligible to offer this new type of doctoral education. Agreements are signed between the ministry, the higher education institution and the enterprise. Dissertation themes are proposed by enterprise partners rather than by academic institutions or doctoral students. This measure is meant to address the criticisms that doctoral education is unrelated to business sector needs. In the first round of the programme in 2017, 54 institutions were awarded ministerial funding, including major universities of technology and several medical universities.

However, the debate around Polish doctoral education has mostly concerned another issue: the complicated, three-degree structure within university authority and prestige systems. The doctoral degree marks entry into the junior ranks of an academic career, the post-doctoral degree (*Habilitation*) marks entry into the lower senior ranks and full professorship marks real academic seniority and is considered the pinnacle of the academic profession (as in several other Central European systems). This three-degree system has frequently been criticized by reform-minded academics and policymakers as obsolete, complicated and energy-wasting, as academics must struggle to finish degrees rather than solving problems and publishing research. The number of full professorships—based on individual research achievements assessed by the Central Committee for Academic Degrees and Titles rather than academic posts granted by institutions as in most European systems—is small, but not limited by the state or institutions. In 2016, there were 10,988 academics with the full professorship title (11.99%; GUS 2017).

Every round of debate about the complicated structure of academic degrees inevitably includes the criticism that the doctoral degree is academically weak and that it is a necessary, but somehow insignificant step on the ladder of academic prestige. By abolishing the title of full professor, or by abolishing both full professorships and *Habilitations*, the role of the doctoral degree in higher education and in the national system of science would be substantially strengthened. The key problem has always been the structural position of the *Habilitation* in the academic career. Its abolition has always been linked to potentially increased requirements, and higher prestige, for the doctoral degree.

In the 2009–2012 wave of reforms in Poland, the role of the *Habilitation* degree was fundamentally weakened, but still remained mandatory. Under the new law of 2018, however, this is no longer the case. Also, all three degrees have been internationalized, in that proof of international publications and international research cooperation are now entry requirements. From the perspective of doctoral education, its concentration in doctoral schools over the next few years represents a major change, and this is where major public research funding seems likely to be invested in all academic fields (Kwiek and Szadkowski 2018).

CONCLUSIONS AND FUTURE CHALLENGES

Polish doctoral education, along with the entire higher education sector, is clearly in need of reform. However, both the feasibility and affordability of the current reforms remain unclear. During extensive preparations in 2016–2018, doctoral education and doctoral degrees were at the centre of public and academic debates about the organizational and financial changes to doctoral education. The decision was made to form doctoral schools from scratch. The success of this effort will depend on the overall success of the imminent, larger-scale higher education reforms. The complicated structure of academic degrees in Poland—with doctorates, *Habilitations* and professorships awarded on the basis of research achievements—clearly needs to be simplified. However, abolition of the *Habilitation* degree will entail giving higher academic status to, and more internationalized requirements for, the doctoral degree, a move that is always at the centre of the controversy surrounding academic careers.

Whatever the future structure of Polish academia, it is essential to improve the quality of doctoral education and the quality of doctoral dissertations in the interest of international competitiveness. The ability to bring the 'best and brightest' into doctoral education is one thing, the ability to retain them in the university sector after graduation is quite another. Both recruitment and retention are key elements in enhancing the attractiveness of an academic career, and both require increased public funding, which has not been guaranteed in the current reform package. Initially, university governance reforms were supposed to be combined with increased, albeit selective, public funding. Currently, reforms are accelerating and the expectation is that public funding for both higher education and academic research will be higher. At the centre of this reform package is the concept of increased competition among existing research teams, academic units and institutions, with a new model of academic research assessment to be applied in 2021. The concept also includes new doctoral schools competing for public subsidies and top minds.

REFERENCES

Antonowicz, D., M. Kwiek, and D. Westerheijden. 2017. 'The Government Response to the Private Sector Expansion in Poland'. In *Policy Analysis of Structural Reforms in Higher Education*, edited by H. de Boer, J. File, J. Huisman, M. Seeber, M. Vukasovic, and D. Westerheijden, 119–38. New York, NY: Palgrave.

Bień, D. 2016. 'Studia trzeciego stopnia w polskich uczelniach - funkcjonowanie, diagnoza, rekomendacje' [Third-Cycle Studies in Polish Universities – Organization, Diagnosis, and Recommendations]. *Nauka i Szkolnictwo Wyższe.* 1(47): 247–277.

Białecki, I., and M. Dąbrowa-Szefler. 2009. 'Polish Higher Education in Transition: Between Policy Making and Autonomy'. In *Structuring Mass Higher Education: The Role of Elite Institutions*, edited by D. Palfreyman and D. T. Tapper, 183–199. London: Routledge.

GUS. 2017. 'Higher Education Institutions and Their Finances in 2016'. Warsaw: GUS (Central Statistical Office).

Kulczycki, E. 2017. 'Assessing Publications through a Bibliometric Indicator: The Case of Comprehensive Evaluation of Scientific Units in Poland'. *Research Evaluation* 16 (1): 41–52.

Kwiek, M. 2012. 'Changing Higher Education Policies: From the Deinstitutionalization to the Reinstitutionalization of the Research Mission in Polish Universities'. *Science and Public Policy* 39: 641–654.

———. 2013. 'From System Expansion to System Contraction: Access to Higher Education in Poland'. *Comparative Education Review* 57 (3, Fall): 553–576.

———. 2015a. 'The Unfading Power of Collegiality? University Governance in Poland in a European Comparative and Quantitative Perspective'. *International Journal of Educational Development* 43: 77–89.

———. 2015b. 'Academic Generations and Academic Work: Patterns of Attitudes, Behaviors and Research Productivity of Polish Academics after 1989'. *Studies in Higher Education* 40 (8): 1354–1376.

———. 2016. 'Constructing Universities as Organizations. University Reforms in Poland in the Light of Institutional Theory'. In *Ideologies in Educational Administration and Leadership*, edited by E. Samier, 193–216. New York, NY: Routledge.

———. 2017. 'A Generational Divide in the Polish Academic Profession. A Mixed Quantitative and Qualitative Approach'. *European Educational Research Journal* 17: 1–26.

———. 2018a. 'High Research Productivity in Vertically Undifferentiated Higher Education Systems: Who Are the Top Performers?' *Scientometrics* 115 (1): 415–462.

———. 2018b. 'The Robust Privateness and Publicness of Higher Education: Expansion through Privatization in Poland'. In *Towards the Private Funding of Higher Education. Ideological and Political Struggles*, edited by D. Palfreyman, T. Tapper, and S. Thomas, 90–111. New York, NY: Routledge.

———. 2019. *Changing European Academics: A Comparative Study of Social Stratification, Work Patterns and Research Productivity*. London and New York, NY: Routledge.

Kwiek, M., and K. Szadkowski. 2018. 'Higher Education Systems and Institutions: Poland'. In *International Encyclopedia of Higher Education Systems*, edited by Pedro N. Texeira and J. C. Shin, 1–20. Cham: Springer.

LHE. 2011. 'Law on Higher Education'. http://prawo.sejm.gov.pl/isap.nsf/DocDetails.xsp?id=wdu20110840455 (accessed 12 December 2018).

———. 'Law on Higher Education'. http://prawo.sejm.gov.pl/isap.nsf/DocDetails.xsp?id=WDU20180001668 (accessed 12 December 2018).

NIK. 2015. *Informacja o wynikach kontroli. Kształcenie na studiach doktoranckich* [*Information about Control: Teaching in Doctoral Studies*]. Warsaw: NIK (Supreme Court of Audit).

OECD. 2010. *Careers of Doctoral Holders Indicators—2010*. Paris: OECD.

————. 2015. *OECD Science, Technology and Industry Scoreboard 2015*. Paris: OECD.

————. 2017. *Education at a Glance 2017: OECD Indicators*. Paris: OECD.

OPI. 2017. 'OPI (National Information Processing Institute) Database'. https://polon.nauka.gov.pl/ (accessed 12 December 2018).

POLON. 2018. 'The Integrated System of Information on Science and Higher Education'. https://polon.nauka.gov.pl/en/index.html (accessed 12 December 2018).

Siemieńska, R., and D. Walczak. 2012. 'Polish Higher Education: From State toward Market, from Elite to Mass Education'. *Advances in Education in Diverse Communities: Research, Policy, and Praxis* 7: 197–224.

Szadkowski, K. 2014. 'The Long Shadow of Doctoral Candidate Status. Case Study—Poland'. *Social Work and Society* 12 (2): 1–17.

Yudkevich, M., P. G. Altbach, and L. E. Rumbley. 2015. *Young Faculty in the Twenty-First Century. International Perspectives*. Albany, NY: SUNY Press.

Chapter 6

Russian Doctoral Education
Between Teaching and Research

Elena Kobzar and Sergey Roshchin

Doctoral education in Russia has a long history, with the first PhD degree being awarded more than 200 years ago. The modern Russian model of doctoral education and the models in those countries that are part of the Commonwealth of Independent States (CIS) go back to Soviet times. Doctoral education reform in Russia began later than in other CIS countries. The current state of doctoral training in CIS countries represents a diverse set of approaches, but in most of them, the European model prevails. Meanwhile, five years ago, Russia switched to a US model with structured programmes. Despite this transition, Russian doctoral training essentially maintains some of the main features of the Soviet system.

A distinctive feature of the Soviet system of training researchers was the two-level system of scientific degrees: the candidate of sciences and the doctor of sciences. Russia is one of only a few countries that does this (Zavgorodnyaya 2016). The Russian system follows the structure of the German system. The candidate of sciences degree, equivalent to a PhD, is usually considered the top achievement in the Western scientific hierarchy. According to the International Standard Classification of Education or ISCED (2011), the candidate of sciences belongs in ISCED level 8—'doctoral or equivalent', together with the PhD, DPhil, DSc, LLD, doctorate or similar. The doctor of sciences degree is considered more valuable, equivalent to the DSc (doctor of natural sciences), DLitt (doctor of humanities), DSocsc (doctor of social science) or doctor habilitatus. The candidate of sciences degree allows holders to reach the level of associate professor, while the doctor of sciences opens the way to the level of full professor. In this chapter, our focus will be on candidate of sciences degrees, and when we use the phrases 'doctoral training' and 'doctoral education', we are referring to that degree.

The key features of the modern system of Russian doctoral education had remained largely unchanged since the Soviet era, and by the beginning of the 21st century, there were many problems. Low success rates of doctoral programmes have continued for four decades, with fewer than 30 per cent of enrolled students receiving their degrees. Against the backdrop of a significant increase in the number of doctoral students who studied primarily with government funding, the quality of dissertations also declined. These days, young PhD holders prefer to explore the corporate labour market rather than the academic sector due to the significant wage gap. In addition, the low return on government investment in doctoral education has worsened the success rate of doctoral programmes, and led to fewer PhD holders going into the sciences. In fact, the declining quality of dissertations has been at the centre of debates in Russian political and academic communities for the past two decades (Maloshonok 2016).

During the 2010s, Russia carried out large-scale reforms of doctoral education. The government sought to improve the quality of doctoral training by strengthening its control over universities. This meant detailed regulation of all processes and procedures. For example, the requirements for PhD dissertation defence procedures were significantly tightened. In another bid to improve the quality of doctoral training and spread innovative approaches, the government also took control of the university evaluation process and began either defunding low-performing universities or removing them from the doctoral education system entirely. The side effect of this measure, aimed at improvement of the quality of doctoral education, was a significant reduction in the

total number of doctoral students. There have been some small devia-
tions from this push for stricter governmental control, such as allowing
universities more autonomy in the admission process, but these are
exceptions and not the rule.

Two more government reform measures are worth noting. The first
pushed universities to transition to structured doctoral programmes.
Under an education law passed in 2012, the framework for doctoral
studies changed to adhere to the Bologna Process. Starting in 2014,
Russian doctoral programmes became the third level of education after
the bachelor's and master's degrees. Second, in 2017, the government
also tried to make it easier to apply to Russian doctoral programmes
by allowing online applications.

This chapter will focus on the key features of the Russian model of
doctoral education, including its scale and the ways it is funded. Next,
we will give an overview of the most ambitious recent reforms and
changes. Finally, we will analyse the main challenges faced by Russian
doctoral education, including funding, quality, government regulation
and the relationship between doctoral education and the labour market.

DOCTORAL EDUCATION IN MODERN RUSSIA

The number of doctoral students in Russia remained stable during
the second half of the 20th century (60,000 students per year). Then,
starting in the 1990s and 2000s, the number began to steadily grow,
reaching 157,000 in 2010. By 2016, it had dropped again to 98,000
(Figure 6.1).

The increase in the number of doctoral students in the period from
1990 to 2010 was due to both the widening of the number of doctoral
programmes at existing institutions and the emergence of new universities, both public and private. There was growing demand for academic
degrees, particularly from those who did not wish to pursue careers
in research, but rather saw the doctorate as a status symbol. However,
beginning in 2010, shrinking government funding meant an overall
decline in the numbers of doctoral students. Until 2014, the share of
part-time doctoral students was 30–40 per cent of the total. But those

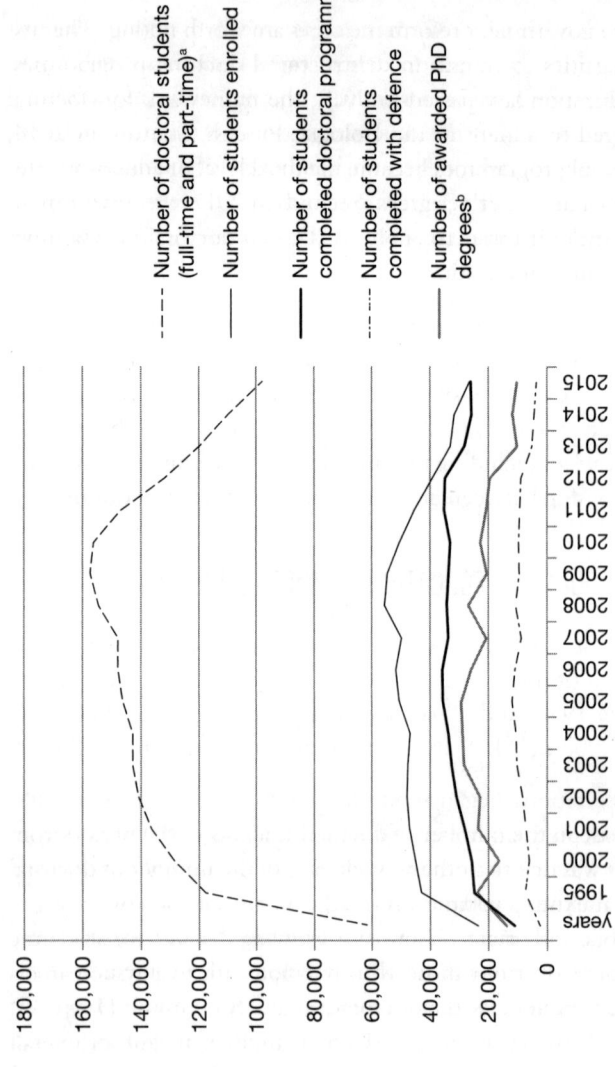

Figure 6.1 *Trends in Doctoral Training*

Source: Federal State Statistics Service (2017).

Notes: [a] Students' training on 'candidate of sciences' programmes.

[b] By doctoral students and by external doctoral candidates.

Legend:

- - - - Number of doctoral students (full-time and part-time)[a]

——— Number of students enrolled

——— Number of students completed doctoral programme

—·—· Number of students completed with defence

——— Number of awarded PhD degrees[b]

numbers have also decreased, because the government has ceased to fund part-time doctoral training.

Foreign doctoral students account for less than 4 per cent of all doctoral students in Russia. A significant number of those doctoral students come from other CIS countries, and are mostly Russian speakers. Due to the legal requirements to defend one's PhD thesis in Russia, doctoral programmes have been relatively uncompetitive in recruiting top foreign graduates. On the other hand, some Russians do attend foreign universities for doctoral training, and many of them stay abroad after obtaining a degree. There are no statistics on the number of such students, or their distribution by country. Despite the fact that the flow of students leaving for doctoral studies abroad is a small fraction of the total number of Russian doctoral students, brain drain is a concern for both society and politicians. In the past 10 years, the government has made efforts to get Russian scientists who have earned PhD degrees abroad to return. In addition, young Russian researchers with degrees from leading foreign universities are participating in joint projects with universities back home.

The Dynamics of Awarding PhDs

Until the end of the 1990s, the number of new PhD holders remained at a level of 15,000–16,000 annually. But in the late 1990s, the number of PhD degrees awarded began to grow along with the increase in the number of doctoral students. The number reached a peak in 2006, when 30,000 PhD dissertations were defended. Then the number of defended dissertations began to decline, and by 2016, had reached 10,000 defences per year. Meanwhile, the success rate (the ratio of completed doctoral defences to the number of doctoral students enrolled) has been running below 30 per cent, and is the result of a combination of many factors. The main reason is that by the end of the doctorate, the vast majority of students are already employed outside academia, and the lack of a degree does not interfere with their career prospects. They simply choose not to defend and complete their degrees. An additional reason for the decline in the absolute number of new PhD holders and the success rate over the past four years is that significant changes were made to the system of awarding PhDs in order to improve the quality of the dissertations. The requirements for PhD candidates have been toughened, and defence procedures have become longer and more complex.

Doctoral Programmes in Universities versus Research Institutes

In Russia, doctoral programmes are carried out by three types of organizations: universities, research institutes and organizations that provide programmes for additional vocational training. The latter are about 1 per cent of the total number of all organizations providing doctoral programmes. The overwhelming majority of doctoral students (more than 85%) study at state universities.

Research institutes are the part of the Russian Academy of Sciences system, and focus on fundamental and applied research in all fields of science. With few exceptions, research institutes do not provide bachelor's and master's programmes, and staff are not involved in the teaching of students. Many of the research institutes of the Russian Academy of Sciences do, however, provide doctoral training. The majority focus primarily on STEM (science, technology, engineering and mathematics) disciplines, and the usual practice is to have students work in large laboratory teams or research groups. This is recognized as a successful form of doctoral training. By law, coursework is now an obligatory part of the doctoral programmes in research institutes, but the truth is that they can barely cope with organizing it for doctoral students due to a lack of staff. Research institutes are trying to attract more university teachers to address this issue, and are also working to reduce the amount of coursework required. Universities, on the other hand, are more likely to involve doctoral students in teaching and have greater opportunities for providing coursework. The downside is that universities provide fewer opportunities to include doctoral students in research projects.

According to the law, universities and research institutes must provide the same type of doctoral programmes, with a combination of coursework and research, plus equal conditions of admission and graduation. During the Soviet era, around 40 per cent of doctoral students studied in research institutions and 60 per cent in universities. Since 1990, the situation has changed dramatically. In the post-Soviet period, the number of universities has grown, as has the number of doctoral programmes those universities provide. In the meantime, the number of researchers who are able to serve as potential scientific supervisors and doctoral team leaders in research institutes has declined. Still, in 2016, doctoral programmes were provided by 730 research institutes and 610 universities, and in the public debates about doctoral education, the positions of research institutes and the Russian Academy of Sciences still carry a lot of weight.

The average admission to university doctoral programmes is 40 students per year, and the average number of doctoral students at universities is 140. At the same time, the differentiation among universities is significant. Breaking it down by discipline, one finds that the largest number of students specialize in engineering (28%), while those focusing on economics, management and medical sciences make up about 10 per cent each. The highest quality standards for doctoral training remain primarily in the STEM disciplines. At the core of the system are approximately 25 leading universities, including the two largest universities in Russia, which are located in Moscow and St. Petersburg. These 25 universities admit between 100 and 1,200 graduate students per year. There is a further group of top universities in terms of the quality of education, the scale and quality of research, and the ability to attract public and private funding. These universities are granted more autonomy than others when it comes to determining the rules for the implementation of educational programmes and research. These universities also have the right to establish certain requirements regarding learning outcomes for students and to determine part of the curricula. They can also recognize diplomas and degrees awarded abroad—which greatly facilitates the possibility of accepting foreign students as well as hire foreign researchers. A number of such universities have been granted the right to determine their own rules and procedures for the conferring of PhD degrees.

In all, a little fewer than 4 per cent of universities account for the preparation of almost a quarter of the doctoral students in Russia. Other universities usually open one to three doctoral programmes with small number of students (less than 10). This makes it costly for smaller universities and programmes to offer and implement structured programmes, particularly the coursework requirements. Leading universities, on the other hand, surpass other institutions in the scale of doctoral training, the amount of research, financial capabilities, the number of qualified academic supervisors and in appropriate infrastructure. These top universities contribute to the development of doctoral education, attracting students of other universities to their doctoral programmes. In general, these are the centres of excellence in terms of new, productive models of doctoral training in Russia.

The Rules of the Game

A distinctive feature of the modern Russian doctoral education system is a set of uniform conditions and requirements for the implementation of doctoral programmes for all universities and doctoral students. As mentioned above, only a few leading universities are excluded from this. In recent years, steps have been taken to differentiate these 'rules of the game' for various universities and doctoral students, and to provide universities with greater autonomy to establish and implement doctoral programmes.

In accordance with the Bologna reforms, doctoral programmes in Russia now constitute the third level of higher education after bachelor's and master's programmes. But, in Russia, doctoral programmes are formally separated from the system of awarding the PhD degree. There are actually two methods for getting the degree—the first through a doctoral programme and the second via a system for external doctoral candidates (Figure 6.2).

We look first at the external doctoral candidate category, which was inherited from the Soviet Union. It has been designed for those who have not attended classes, but have, under supervision, prepared a dissertation. There are a set of academic jobs for faculty without

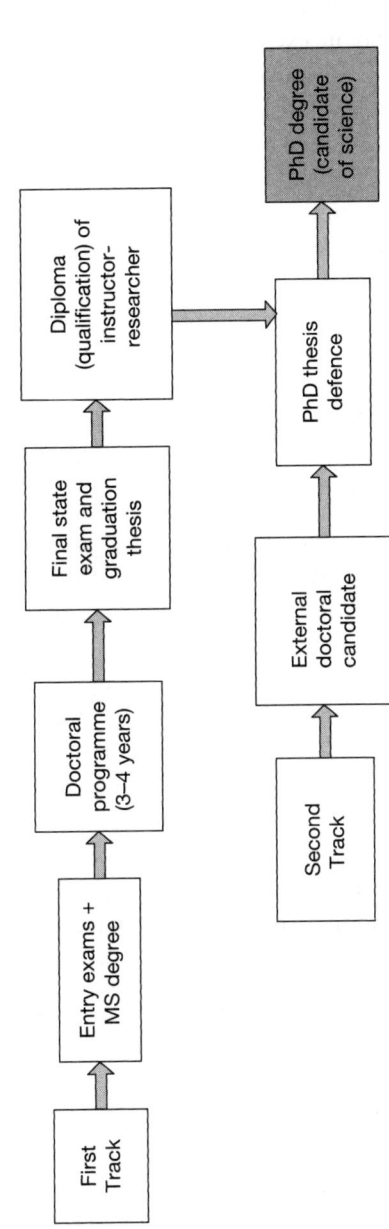

Figure 6.2 *System of Doctoral Training and PhD Awarding in Russia*

degrees, but a career in the academy can really only develop through obtaining the degree. So the external doctoral candidacy is commonly used by junior scholars in universities and research institutes who already have some research skills. It should be noted here that the state does not fund external doctoral candidates, and in contradiction to its approach to doctoral programmes, the state does not control or regulate the recruitment or training of external doctoral candidates. As a rule, for admission to a university as an external doctoral candidate, it is enough to submit a research proposal and find a supervisor. It is not required to pass exams, which are mandatory for admission to doctoral programmes. In recent decades, this track has been in higher demand for employees in the non-university sector, who considered external candidacy as a less time-intensive way to get a degree. External doctoral candidates now make up approximately 25 per cent of the total number of PhDs awarded annually.

Now, let us look at the first track (see Figure 6.2) for obtaining a PhD—the doctoral programme. As we have noted, Russia switched to the preparation of doctoral students on the basis of structured programmes in 2014 (Popova and Biricheva 2017). The first important change to the system was that the educational component (coursework) became compulsory. Also, to complete the programme, students must now pass a final state exam and defend a graduation thesis. After completing these steps, students receive a diploma and the qualification 'researcher-instructor'. After graduation, students may complete and defend their PhD dissertations, although, paradoxically, according to the new Russian legislation, it is no longer mandatory for graduates to defend (Zavgorodnyaya 2016). However, universities continue to encourage students to do so.

The duration of doctoral training is three years for full-time programmes and four years for part-time programmes. In 2012, the duration of study for a number of fields (in engineering and mathematics) was increased to four years for full-time and five years for part-time. In Russia, doctoral and master's programmes are separated (the duration of master's programmes is two years), and for admission to a doctoral programme, a student must pass entry exams. Until 2017, the rules for selecting applicants for doctoral programmes were set by legislation and were the same for all universities and institutes. The main criteria for admission were the results of entry exams in philosophy, a foreign language and the chosen discipline. All examinations were in Russian.

Since 2017, universities have been given more autonomy in setting the admission rules for doctoral programmes. Faculties (schools) take an active part in the selection of doctoral students, but the final decision on admission is taken by the university. Universities now have the right to establish procedures and conditions for admission. Most of the leading universities dropped the philosophy exam, began to accept certificates of language proficiency and started to select applicants by portfolio instead of oral exam. Also, examinations can now be passed in either Russian or English, and applicants may take distance (online) exams. In general, admission procedures have become more like those at foreign universities. This modernization has contributed to attracting the best Russian students, who used to be more attracted to foreign doctoral programmes after completion of a master's.

The structure of doctoral programmes is fixed by the federal higher education standard, and is the same for all universities and research institutes across all fields of research. The programme entails six months to one full year of coursework, with compulsory attendance at lectures or seminars and an interim assessment. Approximately one-third of the coursework is taken up with foreign language courses (research writing in English), courses on the history and philosophy of science and on the techniques and methods of teaching. The other two-thirds of the coursework are comprised of field courses. The remaining time includes research related activities and teaching: preparation of publications and dissertations, conference participation and teaching internships.

Doctoral students prepare for their dissertations under the supervision of one professor. This generally occurs while the student is completing the coursework component, which is a peculiarity of the Russian doctoral programme. The obligation to combine coursework and research activities means that students have a rather intensive schedule. In just two to three months after enrolment, a student has to choose a thesis topic and a supervisor. During the first six months to a year, students are completing coursework while also preparing a research proposal for the dissertation.

In general, doctoral students must publish the main results of their research in no fewer than two or three articles. In order to successfully complete the programme, students must pass three qualification exams (on the history and philosophy of science, foreign language and special discipline). At the end of the course, students must pass state exams and defend their graduation thesis. When all the above requirements are fulfilled, graduates can complete their PhD dissertation and submit it to the committee for defence.

The Russian Model of PhD Conferral

The Russian model of PhD conferral is country-specific, and under-standing the circumstances is crucial for comprehending the problems currently faced by doctoral education in the country. There are three specific features of the Russian system of awarding academic degrees: a two-level system of degree conferral, the separation of doctoral edu-cation from the conferral system and unified requirements for PhD candidates, with some exceptions as discussed below.

The requirements for awarding PhDs are fixed by the ministry of education and science (Zavgorodnyaya 2016). Dissertation com-mittees are opened at universities and research institutes. To open a dissertation committee or change its composition, it is necessary to obtain a permit from the ministry. The dissertation committee consists of 20–25 scholars. The committee is not specially created for each doctoral candidate, but rather is a standing committee that oversees all dissertation defences in a particular discipline, such as labour economics or psychophysiology. As a rule, each dissertation committee is responsible for several years of dissertation defences and therefore several cohorts of doctoral students. Dissertation defences are public, and are conducted in Russian. The thesis of the disserta-tion defence should also be presented in Russian. After the defence, the documents, including a video recording of the meeting of the committee, are sent to the ministry. After the ministry confirms the decision of the dissertation committee, the student receives the diploma.

To get permission for doctoral training, a university or research institute must get a licence and accreditation from the ministry. There are very detailed requirements, and tough state control over their implementation makes doctoral training highly bureaucratized. We should also note here that the criteria for getting permission for dissertation committees differ from the criteria for permission to offer doctoral training. For example, to open a doctoral programme, it is sufficient for the university to have 3–5 researchers in a particular discipline. However, for opening a dissertation committee, 7–10 researchers are required. So it is quite often the case that universities that provide doctoral programmes have no dissertation committees. This means that it is not unusual when doctoral students who graduate from one university are forced to look for another in order to defend their dissertations. The 'network' of doctoral programmes and dissertation committees does not coincide, and this mismatch may arise even in large universities with a wide range of doctoral programmes. For PhD candidates, the search for the closest university with dissertation committees can impose substantial, sometimes even prohibitive, financial and time expenses. These expenses are most often imposed on PhD candidates, not on universities.

Between 2016 and 2018, 28 leading universities and research institutes were granted the right to award their own academic degrees. These universities and institutes can now independently establish rules of PhD conferral, including the requirements for applicants and dissertation committee members. The first defences under the new rules have already taken place at five universities. Thus, some institutions have been able to remove a large number of bureaucratic barriers that exist in the traditional Russian system of PhD conferral. Such innovations make the doctoral training system more attractive to students.

Funding for Doctoral Training

Doctoral training has been funded primarily by the Russian state, with the amount of funding dependent on the number of students at the particular university or research institute. As during the Soviet period, the number of doctoral students to be enrolled and the structure of enrolment by respective fields are still determined annually by the state. The government compiles a doctoral programme admission plan for each university and research institute and issues appropriate licences on an annual basis; the allocation of state funding depends on this plan. State funds are spent primarily on teacher and supervisor salaries and on building and maintaining infrastructure. Additionally, universities and research institutes with licences for training can accept doctoral students on a fee (self-funded) basis. The share of fee-paying doctoral students in the post-Soviet period has reached 30 per cent.

The majority of doctoral students receive a state stipend worth less than $50 per month. For students who specialize in disciplines considered priorities by the state (mathematics, engineering and computer sciences), the monthly stipend is doubled to $100, which is 10–20 per cent of the average monthly salary in Russia. The size of the stipends is tiny and insufficient to cover living expenses. Due to insufficient support, 90 per cent of doctoral students are forced to combine research training with work. Fifty per cent of them work full-time. The majority of doctoral students (56%) are employed outside their universities or institutes. Full-time doctoral programmes are, therefore, actually part-time.

In addition to these regular stipends, the state also funds a limited number of additional stipends and grants for internships. A number of non-state sources also fund doctoral students. However, the density of 'coverage' of doctoral students with such additional funding programmes is low. Leading universities have their own stipend programmes for attracting the best students and supporting them. A vast majority of students do not receive financial support for academic mobility, and lack opportunities to connect with research networks outside of their university. This lack of academic mobility reinforces the regionalization of Russian science.

DOCTORAL EDUCATION REFORMS

In Russia, both the doctoral education and the system of awarding PhDs have changed remarkably during the last five years. The two main driving factors have been the low success rate of doctoral programmes and the low quality of dissertations. While the number of doctoral students has grown (and, correspondingly, the amount of state funding for doctoral study), the success rate has stayed consistently low, sparking sharp discussions over the last 10 years about the poor performance of the doctoral training system. These discussions became even more heated when cases of plagiarism in PhD dissertations became public, making it a main topic in the debate about the devaluation of academic degrees and, more broadly, the poor quality of doctoral training and the system of awarding PhDs. Meanwhile, there have been efforts to improve the quality of dissertations. The most important measures include a reform of the way PhDs are awarded and a push to remove low-ranking universities and research institutes from the system.

Ranking of Universities

The ministry has reduced the number of universities receiving state funding for doctoral programmes. There are now approximately 300 universities and research institutes with doctoral training licences and the ability to award PhD degrees. This is down from 1,550 in 2013 to 1,250 in 2018. Admission rates have also reduced, falling from 50,000 students in 2011 to 26,000 students in 2016. These moves have hit universities, especially with low research performance hard, while the situation in leading universities and research institutes remains almost unchanged.

In fact, leading institutions have received additional funding in a bid to improve the quality of training and research. Some of this additional funding has gone to doctoral programmes to help promote academic mobility, fund stipends, engage students in research projects and recruit international faculty. These faculty members have become involved in the preparation of doctoral students. However, the impact of additional support for doctoral training has not been so high in terms of numbers of students trained via these advanced programmes. It is difficult, however, to overestimate the value of these experiences from the viewpoint of spreading innovative patterns of training.

Reforming the System of PhD Conferral

The main ambition for reforming the system of PhD conferral has been to ensure higher quality PhD dissertations via tougher regulation of almost all of the procedures that accompany the process. Procedures and requirements are now, for the most part, unified for all universities and applicants for PhD degrees, with small variations among different disciplines. Only the 28 leading universities that were granted the right to award their own academic degrees in 2016–2018 are excluded from these regulations.

One example of reform is the attempt to introduce and streamline publication requirements for PhD degree applicants. It is quite a new tradition in Russia to require PhD candidates to publish in peer-reviewed journals before the end of their training. However, this has now become compulsory for the PhD defence. The idea has been to try to better control the quality of dissertations by stipulating the quality of the journals in which PhD degree candidates must publish. In 2006, the ministry established the requirement that those defending a thesis had to publish in a peer-reviewed journals selected by the ministry itself, which chooses the publications based on the following criteria: articles must be peer-reviewed, publication must be free of charge for authors, online versions of the publications must exist and so on. Currently, in addition to publications included in international indexes, this list contains about 2,300 journals. It should be noted that most journals on this list are not international, and the language of publication is predominantly Russian. In fact, this list is an attempt to create a domestic bibliographic database in response to the fact that the overwhelming majority of doctoral students find it difficult to publish in international, peer-reviewed journals. In 2013, the minimum requirements for publications were doubled, or even tripled, depending on the discipline.

The criteria for dissertation committees have also been adjusted, including the requirements for the composition of the committee and the scientific and publication activity of its members, and for the defence procedure itself. Committee meetings and defence procedures are strictly regulated, and the fulfilment of these requirements is confirmed by video recordings and a set of documents drawn up according to rules set out by the ministry. The government regularly revises the requirements for dissertation committees and reassesses their performance. The last large-scale assessment of dissertation committees in 2013 found that over a five-year period, the total number of committees decreased by 30 per cent (to 2,230).

Unfortunately, state regulations on PhD degree conferral and doctoral training itself are mismatched. For example, a decision to close a dissertation committee may not take into account the fact that there is a doctoral programme in that subject at the university. In other words, dissertation committees have been closed in universities with doctoral programmes that need the committees in order to confer degrees. The shrinking number of dissertation committees has also exacerbated the disparity between universities with doctoral programmes and ones with dissertation committees.

The result of these changes in the requirements for applicants and dissertation committees was a sharp and significant decrease in the total number of dissertations defended; within two years (2013–2014), the number was cut in half. However, it is difficult to speak about significant changes in the quality of these dissertations. The techniques, methods and openness to information that were implemented did manage to reduce the flow of plagiarized dissertations. However, plagiarism is not the only issue. Many dissertations simply do not contribute any added value to the science.

As noted above, leading universities are granted the right to award their own academic degrees and set more flexible rules. They have been moving towards a system of defending dissertations more similar to that in Europe, in which dissertation committees are created temporarily for one dissertation defence and consist of specialists on the dissertation topic, rather than on a broad discipline. Another important change has been the possibility of defending a thesis in a foreign language. Previously, Russian was the compulsory language for the defence, and if the dissertation was not in Russian, it had to be translated into Russian. Making it possible to both write and defend a dissertation in English contributes to the internationalization of the Russian system of awarding PhDs and increases the motivation of foreign (primarily, English-speaking) applicants to enter doctoral programmes at leading Russian universities.

Results of Reforms: Conflicts and Contradictions

The reforms of the system for awarding degrees have not been synchronized with the transformation of doctoral education. The changes outlined above have led to many students making a cost-benefit assessment of preparing a PhD dissertation, and as a result, have contributed significantly to the sharp decrease in the total number of defences and the success rate of doctoral training. Doctoral students (and their institutions) are under pressure to defend a PhD thesis within three to four years. How are the new requirements for defences compatible with the requirements to complete the thesis on time? As mentioned above, in order to defend a PhD thesis, a student must publish two or three articles in journals from a special list made by the ministry. Add to that the writing of the dissertation: taking publishing lags into account, it is necessary to have articles ready for submission as early as the second year of study. Doctoral students are faced with the choice of publishing articles of inferior quality, shortening the period for their preparation and submitting them to low-demand journals, or focusing on the quality of their dissertation, but going beyond the allowed time. For students in STEM disciplines, who often prepare dissertations and publications as part of large research teams, such requirements are more realistic, but not for those who study the social sciences and humanities. The lack of linkages between the requirements and criteria for defence on the one hand and the preparation of the dissertation on the other, shows that these requirements are counterproductive and work against both quality and success rates.

The most urgent task in this regard is therefore to eliminate such mismatches and better synchronize the requirements for the preparation of doctoral students and the awarding of PhD degrees. The model of degree conferral created over the last two years by leading universities, which tries to better balance time, quality and quantity when it comes to dissertation preparation, will be a testing ground for revising the general requirements for all PhD candidates.

MODERN CHALLENGES TO RUSSIAN DOCTORAL EDUCATION

Recent reforms have not solved the most important problems facing doctoral training in Russia. The most significant challenges are persisting problems with the quality of both dissertations and doctoral programmes, and the fact that recent changes in the model of doctoral training in Russia have proven counterproductive. The response to both of these challenges requires reflection on global changes in the essence and boundaries of research work (Popova and Biricheva 2017). Ideas about what research is have blurred, fuelled by the expanded demand for PhD degrees from those working outside of academia like managers or state employees. At the same time, many non-academic professions and activities now demand research skills. Such significant changes in the labour market require the need to discuss the overall mission of doctoral training.

Research and Science: The Erosion of Boundaries

The substantial decline in the quality of defended dissertations over the past 20 years has resulted not only in the erosion of ethical principles in academic behaviour, the increase in plagiarism, for example, but also in the fact that in a number of areas the entire concept of science has become blurred. In many cases, the results of dissertations are very difficult to correlate with research activities. The line between scientific knowledge and technological achievements is very subtle, and often technological improvements are presented as scientific knowledge. In short, large-scale demand for doctoral training for non-academic careers contributes to the erosion of standards when it comes to the preparation of the dissertation. The reforms carried out, focused on combating opportunistic behaviour (for instance, plagiarism), have failed to solve this problem of demand for academic degrees from those who do not plan to work in the academy. This pseudo demand has arisen in the absence of professional degrees, which would have allowed for the recognition of professional achievements of a non-academic nature. One way to stop this erosion would be the creation of a system of professional degrees in Russia (Bednyi 2017).

Purpose of Doctoral Education

While politicians and scientists are discussing the purpose and outcomes of doctoral training (Bednyi, Rybakov, and Sapunov 2017; Gokhberg, Meissner, and Shmatko 2017; Shmatko 2016), there remains great inertia when it comes to public expectations regarding the purpose of doctoral training. It still retains the features of the Soviet system, in which doctoral training was considered a path to academia and alternative career tracks in the non-academic labour market were not considered appropriate. This ignores the fact that in the past 20–30 years, the corporate sector has created a huge number of jobs that require research skills. Many people still perceive researchers as a homogeneous socio-professional group of scientists engaged exclusively in the academic sector by teaching or by research, but this is clearly no longer the case.

The purpose shared by most universities and research institutes offering doctoral programmes has remained practically unchanged since Soviet times. The common idea is that the main function of doctoral education is replenishing academia with new faculty (Maloshonok 2016). Doctoral programmes remain the main source of new faculty, but the outflow of researchers from the academy is not being replenished by new PhD holders. The main reason for pursuing careers outside academia is that job conditions there, including salaries, are more attractive. The rigidity in the interpretation of the purpose of doctoral training contradicts the actual differentiation of career paths for PhD holders (Roshchina 2016). Likewise, the motivation of doctoral students and their actual professional career tracks in occupations outside the academia have diversified (Rybakov 2018). Only 53 per cent of doctoral students report that their plans are to pursue careers in the academic labour market as teachers or researchers. Another 13 per cent intend to do research in the corporate sector. Two other career tracks, in public administration and entrepreneurship, attract 10 per cent each. The remaining 14 per cent state they would like to get a position in the corporate sector, but not related to research (Bekova et al. 2017). These intentions are reinforced by the fact that the majority of doctoral students are already employed while studying, usually in the same sector in which they plan to continue their careers after graduation.

In conclusion, the expansion of demand for doctoral training in the last 20–25 years has been caused by a wide range of factors (Bednyi 2017), chief among them are the emergence and expansion of the corporate labour market and the knowledge economy. But the shared purpose of doctoral programmes at Russian universities remains, in their own eyes, the development of the skills necessary to work only in the academic labour market (Bednyi 2017; Gruzdev and Terentev 2017). PhD degrees in Russia are not divided into academic and professional ones (Gruzdev and Terentev 2017). There are also few differences in the content of Russian doctoral programmes. The European trend is focused on developing transferrable skills within the framework of doctoral programmes, but in Russia, programmes are not aimed at developing such skills.

Quality of Russian Doctoral Programmes

Currently, the overall quality of doctoral programmes is one of the most pressing issues. A conjunction of factors—the low academic mobility of doctoral students and faculty, and the peculiarities of the Russian model of doctoral training, with its high dependence on mentorship—has led to the production of new researchers who are largely copying the skills of their supervisors. The spread of new methods and techniques of research work has been significantly hampered.

The current model presupposes that the training of core research skills comes through communication with a supervisor. The main flaw in this 'learning by doing' model is poor supervision. A lack of qualified faculty, able to train researchers in accordance with modern global standards, the low replenishment of scientific supervisors and the low quality of supervision remain major challenges for doctoral education in Russia. Many supervisors have a very poor knowledge of English, have not published in international peer-reviewed journals and remain far from the modern research agenda. In fact, most new PhD holders inherit these shortcomings from their supervisors. The problem of non-competitiveness of supervisors is exacerbated by the fact that the structured doctoral programmes de facto still reproduce the model in which the doctoral student is locked to the supervisor (Maloshonok and Terentev 2018). The low quality of supervision is made worse by the fact that doctoral students are insufficiently involved in their training, as they have to work during their study.

Mobility and integration in doctoral programmes are crucial ways to improve the quality of programmes and students, and to overcome the problem of poor supervision and inbreeding mentioned above. This is all the more important as 85 per cent of doctoral students graduating with master's degrees complete their doctorates in the same university (Bekova et al. 2017). There is some financial support for the academic mobility of doctoral students: government grants for graduate students, grants from international programmes (for instance, Erasmus) and institutional funding allocated by some universities. However, the number of students involved in these various forms of mobility is relatively small.

Promoting academic mobility is an urgent task for leading universities. For their students, mobility gives an opportunity to enter the international academic market, and for the universities themselves, it represents an opportunity to hire international faculty. Challenges with regard to quality are less acute among leading universities. They are able to involve doctoral students in research collaborations, including international ones. Doctoral students from these universities are more often published in international peer-reviewed journals, and after graduation, they can compete in both national and international labour markets.

Insufficient Funding of Doctoral Education

The development of doctoral programmes and the successful preparation of doctoral candidates require adequate and stable funding. Sufficient funding is a pledge to fulfil the conditions of the Salzburg Agreement of 2005, which also stipulates that sufficient time should be provided for students to complete full-time doctoral programmes. One of the most acute problems in Russian doctoral education is the small state stipends to students (Rybakov 2018). Only a limited number of leading universities fund additional stipends on their own budget. Insufficient financial support means that students are not allowed to focus on training and pushed into employment. This is how full-time programmes are essentially transformed into part-time ones.

Previously, doctoral students were on unstructured programmes (without coursework), and had an opportunity to combine work and study. The transition to structured programmes has made doctoral training more intensive for them (Gruzdev and Terentev 2017). The new requirements have reduced the amount of time available to prepare a dissertation, and so the motivation for doctoral students to carry on with their study, especially those who are employed, has become less strong. Students wishing to focus on their doctoral training may have to quit their job. Some students see attending classes as an additional and unproductive burden, and the need for employment as an imposition. Thus, the involvement of the students in their own thesis work is inadequate, the programme dropout rate is high and the degree completion rate remains low. This is why there is a tendency among many universities and students to reduce the amount of required coursework.

EVALUATION OF RECENT REFORMS AND PROSPECTS FOR THE FUTURE

The response of Russian doctoral students to the transition to a structured training model has not been universally positive. Likewise, universities and research institutes feel ambiguous about the results of these reforms, and find the government rules more fitted for regulating education, not science. One of the side effects of the reforms has been the emergence of a large number of bureaucratic barriers for universities and research institutes. These barriers hamper both academic network interaction and mobility. In general, the regulation of doctoral programmes has become increasingly tougher (Bednyi 2017; Bednyi, Rybakov, and Sapunov 2017). The new model has transferred substantial burdens to students, universities and research institutes, but has not created the prerequisites for significant improvements in doctoral training. There is no reason to assert that the transition to structured

programmes has led to improvements in the quality of doctoral training, and there are many voices in favour of a return to the previous
model (Bednyi, Rybakov, and Sapunov 2017). Upcoming changes
focus on weakening the effects of the unintended consequences of
recent reforms.

At the same time, other reforms have had positive effects: the
improvement of the application procedures, for example, and the provision of greater freedom to the best-ranked universities. The strongest
students now have increased incentives to apply to doctoral programmes.
New forms of doctoral training are emerging, such as joint (network)
programmes, blended forms of instruction (via Coursera) and other
advanced and innovative methods. State reforms in the field of general
education have had an impact on doctoral programmes. As a result of
investments over the past 10 years, a number of leading universities
and research organizations have created and maintained strong research
infrastructures. This has had a positive effect on doctoral training.

Leading universities and research institutes will remain central for
Russian doctoral education in the future. They will serve as the largest
national centres for training researchers and for the transfer of modern
technologies needed for that training. For the entire system of Russian
doctoral education, the experience of leading universities in establishing
their own systems of awarding academic degrees is extremely important.
This is an attempt to build a system of expertise through dissertations
and based on academic reputation. Finally, we should note that at the
beginning of 2019, the government initiated a national project called
'Science', which provides for strengthening the financial support for
doctoral students. Along with funding from universities, this will significantly expand opportunities for talented students to make a choice
in favour of a career in research.

REFERENCES

Bekova, S., I. Gruzdev, Z. Dzafarova, and N. Maloshonok. 2017. 'Portrait of a
Russian Doctoral Student'. *Contemporary Analytics of Education* 7 (15): 1–60.
Bednyi, B. 2017. 'A New Postgraduate School Model: Pro et Contra'. *Higher
Education in Russia* 4: 5–16.

Bednyi, B., N. Rybakov, and M. Sapunov. 2017. 'Doctoral Education in Russia in the Educational Field: An Interdisciplinary Discourse'. *Sociological Studies* 9: 125–134.

Federal State Statistics Service. http://www.gks.ru (accessed 6 December 2019).

Gokhberg, L., D. Meissner, and N. A. Shmatko. 2017. 'Myths and Realities of Highly Qualified Labor and What It Means for PhDs'. *Journal of the Knowledge Economy* 8 (22): 758–767.

Gruzdev, I., and E. Terentev. 2017. 'Data against Myths: Evidence from the Survey of PhD Students in Leading Russian Universities'. *Higher Education in Russia* 7: 89–97.

International Standard Classification of education (ISCED). 2011, 2012. *UNESCO Institute for Statistics*: 1–84

Maloshonok, N. 2016. 'Doctoral Students' Reasons to Pursue a PhD as a Cause of Low Completion Rate of Russian PhD Programs'. *Higher Education in Russia and Beyond* 3 (9): 18–20.

Maloshonok, N., and E. Terentev. 2018. 'National Barriers to the Completion of Doctoral Programs at Russian Universities'. *Higher Education* 77 (2): 195–211.

Popova, N., and E. Biricheva. 2017. 'Training Young Researchers at the Postgraduate Level: In Search of a Goal'. *Higher Education in Russia* 1: 5–14.

Roshchina, Y. 2016. 'What Determines Students' Intentions to Pursue a PhD in Russia?' *Higher Education in Russia and Beyond* 3 (99): 16–17.

Rybakov, N. 2018. 'A New Model of Russian Postgraduate Education: Pilot Study of the First Graduation of PhD Students'. *Higher Education in Russia* 7: 86–95.

Shmatko, N. 2016. 'PhDs within and outside of the National Labor Market'. *Higher Education in Russia and Beyond* 3 (9): 9–11.

Zavgorodnyaya, O. 2016. 'The Institute of PhD Awarding in Russia and Doctoral Education: Convergence and Divergence'. *Higher Education in Russia and Beyond* 3 (9): 7–9.

Chapter 7

The UK Doctorate
History, Features and Challenges

Rosemary Deem and Shane Dowle

The 21st-century UK doctorate has a relatively short history, but provides a quality-assured and varied system of doctoral degrees, ranging from research doctorates by monograph or article to professional, performance and practice-based arts doctorates. There are diverse student cohorts, multiple study modes (full-time, part-time and distance learning) and access to an extensive range of research and generic skills training, as well as supervisor development. In recent decades, students are increasingly paying for their doctoral education. More and more of the programmes themselves are located within doctoral colleges, graduate schools or other multidisciplinary, collaborative and inter-institutional settings. Doctoral graduates now find employment in many fields, not just academe. Unlike many other countries, the UK doctoral assessment uses a non-public examination of the final dissertation, with both external and internal examiners (sometimes with an independent chair). Supervisors are present only as observers, if at all. This chapter will explore all of this in some depth, beginning with some background.

A SHORT HISTORY OF THE UK DOCTORATE

The first UK doctorate was awarded at the University of Oxford in 1917, at a time when potential American applicants were enquiring about what the university could offer compared with Germany's already existing doctorate (*Oxford Today* 2017). Other universities quickly followed Oxford's lead. The initial Oxford doctorate allowed graduates from the university to submit a dissertation in five terms, while graduates of other universities were allowed eight terms. Until well after the Second World War, doctoral candidates in the United Kingdom were not supervised. In the 1970s and 1980s, the doctorate gradually became important for academic employment (Bogle 2017).

The UK doctorate evolved very slowly (Simpson 1983, 2009). For many decades, the degree was regarded as a magnum opus. Finishing it could take many years, and some candidates never completed it at all. There was minimal supervision and little training when it came to research methods and other research training. Bogle (2017) notes four stages in the development of the UK PhD. From 1917 to 1945, the doctorate was an elite pursuit. During the Second World War, unsurprisingly, doctoral numbers declined. In period two, from 1945 to the 1970s, there was some growth in numbers, and the University Grants Committee (founded in 1918 and reconstituted after the Second World War) gave financial support to research as well as teaching. The first UK research funding council, the Medical Research Council, started in 1920. Others followed, with social sciences in 1965, and arts and humanities in 2005. These councils funded doctoral study as well as research projects. The 1960s saw much growth in the higher education (HE) sector, including the establishment of 'new' universities such as Lancaster and Sussex, and the acquisition of university status by former colleges of advanced technology like Aston and Salford. In 1964, the Council for National Academic Awards was established, which made it possible for polytechnics to award degrees, including research degrees.

Bogle's third period runs from the 1970s to 2003. During the 1980s, the UK research funding councils examined doctoral completion rates. The 1987 Winfield Report to the Economic and Social Science Research Council noted two distinct routes to the degree—the knowledge PhD and the training PhD. The former focused on making a major contribution to new knowledge and could take many years to complete. The training route concentrated on supporting the development of research skills and the dissertation, though expected to be original and to contain work worthy of publication, only had to demonstrate that the writer was capable of future independent research. Although Winfield did not recommend ending the knowledge route, from the early 1990s, many universities, trying to improve completion rates, changed their regulations to reflect the fact that a doctoral dissertation could be accomplished in three to four years of full-time study, or the part-time equivalent of six to eight years. The 1990s saw a rapid development of research methods training for doctoral students and the growth of professional doctorates, which included taught units plus a shorter, practice-focused dissertation aimed at professionals studying alongside a full-time job. In 1992, many polytechnics in England were transformed into universities (Pratt 1997). Over time, many of these institutions acquired their own research degree awarding powers (RDAPs).

Bogle's final period, 2003 to the present, dates from the year when a report to the UK research councils on the employment prospects of research students (Roberts 2002) recommended the provision of short courses and workshops on transferable skills, such as media training, project management and research ethics. By the late 2000s, research councils and charities such as Wellcome were developing new funding models for doctoral training. These were often multidisciplinary partnerships and many involved more than one university. It should be noted here that multi-site partnership has often proved challenging (Deem, Barnes, and Clarke 2015). The case for collaborative, inter-institutional training in the United Kingdom has not yet been fully demonstrated outside STEM (science, technology, engineering and mathematics) disciplines (Bartholomew et al. 2015; Budd et al. 2018). Typically, doctoral collaborations are aimed at full-time students and do not include those registered for professional doctorates, except in the field of engineering (Figure 7.1).

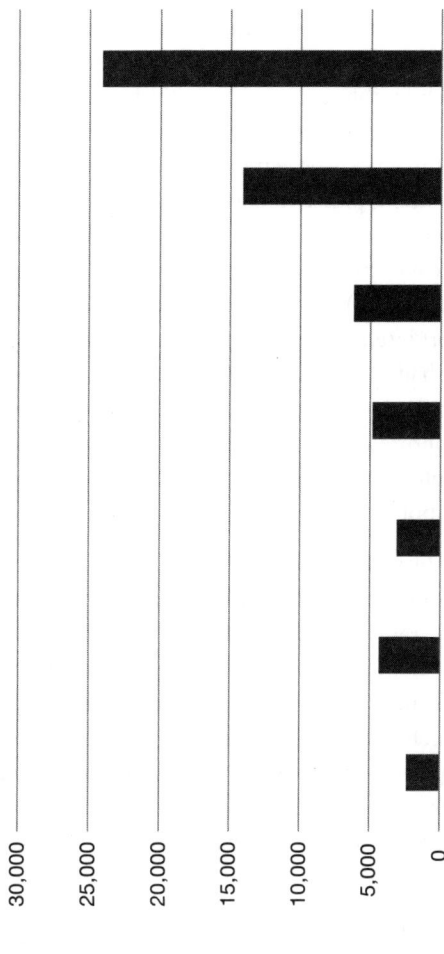

Figure 7.1 *Growth in the UK Doctoral Completions*
Source: Higher Education Statistics Agency (HESA).

TYPES OF DOCTORATES IN THE UNITED KINGDOM

Kehm and others have examined doctoral types in Europe, most recently in comparison with those in China (Bao, Kehm, and Ma 2018; Kehm 2009). These authors outline the following types of doctorates relevant to the United Kingdom: the research doctorate; the professional doctorate, with a shorter dissertation aimed at mid-career professionals who want their research studies to reflect on their professional practice; a doctorate by publication; an arts and humanities practice/performance doctorate; and an integrated doctorate. The UK professional doctorate varies from extensive modules on research methods and substantive subject content, plus a 40,000–60,000 word dissertation, to portfolios of work supplemented by a project report (Mellors-Bourne, Robinson, and Metcalfe 2016; Robinson 2018). The integrated or 'new route' PhD (Park 2005) was developed in the United Kingdom in the 1990s to support international students, typically from the Middle East, whose degrees had not equipped them to cope with a standard research doctorate and who needed modules with substantive subject content. This was supported by the Higher Education Funding Council for England and adopted by several research-intensive universities, but has now declined in popularity.

The PhD by publication (Powell 2004) has two forms. One is a doctorate by prior publication, in which a candidate with existing research publications registers for the degree and then produces an essay tying together that research. The essay is meant to explain the methodology, significance and coherence of the work in the relevant field, and where it includes joint publications, the candidate's contribution to those outputs (Powell 2004). Candidates undergo a period of supervision to help them shape the submission, and then defend it orally. Prior publication doctorates may be restricted to the awarding institution's staff and alumni (the latter after a qualifying period, subject to previous good degree grades). These type of degrees are popular with academic staff who do not have a doctorate (often having arrived late to academe from a professional background in, for example, social work, law or teaching), and those working in research and development in the private sector. There is also a higher doctorate with a somewhat similar format offered by some research-intensive universities, but in this case, the candidate already has a research doctorate, and so the higher award must use different publications, reach a higher standard and provide evidence of external impact. This latter route, however, seems to be in decline according to a recent survey (Barnes 2013).

By contrast, a doctorate by concurrent publication, whereby candidates produce articles from their research in their dissertations, is simply a regulatory variant of the research doctorate, which permits the submission of what is sometimes called an 'alternative thesis format'. This is written in the form of articles (some university regulations do not require these to have been submitted or accepted for publication) plus other supporting written materials, which replaces a monograph-style dissertation. Supervision, research, generic skills training and the examination process are the same as for the monograph. In some disciplines like economics and earth sciences, the alternative format is particularly favoured. It is helpful in cases where journal papers are the preferred format for outputs, whereas the prior publication doctorate suits those who have academic publications, but no doctorate.

Finally, the practice or performance-based doctorate is another regulatory variant of the standard research doctorate, but has been adapted for the arts and humanities. Research outputs can take a variety of forms: sculpture or paintings as well as musical, drama or media performances (Nilsson, Dunin-Woyseth, and Janssens 2017; Schwarzenbach and Hackett 2016). Bao, Kehm, and Ma (2018) suggest that this doctorate came about as arts colleges merged with universities, but it also happened as some colleges obtained university status and RDAPs. Also critical here was the transition of the UK Arts and Humanities Research Board into a research council in 2005, and the development of a greater understanding of how to support arts/ humanities disciplines in formats suited to the kinds of research outputs produced in those fields.

OTHER FEATURES OF THE UK DOCTORATE

There are several features of the UK doctorate that are important to highlight in order to gain a full understanding of the national context. These include the status of doctoral students, coursework requirements and supervision, funding arrangements, the organization of doctoral education at the institutional level, research degree regulations, quality assurance and the availability of support and resources at the national level. The UK doctoral candidates have definitive status as students, unless they are also full-time research assistants or studying part-time while already working as an academic or administrator in the same institution. Staff and students have different conditions and statuses, so the two are never combined, even for those who have both affiliations.

It is now a standard UK practice for doctoral students to have at least two supervisors, one being the main supervisor. In some institutions, they may also have a pastoral advisor. For projects shared with and/or partly sponsored by outside organizations, there may be an external supervisor as well. It is usual to offer training to both new and experienced supervisors, rather than rely on their innate sense of how supervision works (Duke and Denicolo 2017). The first year of full-time study (or first two years of part-time study) generally includes research methods training, which may involve taking taught master's degree modules, perhaps leading to a postgraduate certificate or diploma. There is also generic skills training, typically provided as a series of voluntary workshops. These are available in any year of study, but are emphasized in the first year. Some part-time students may study via distance learning, which is now a common mode for doctoral education in many countries (Erichsen, Bolliger, and Halupa 2014; Nasiri and Mafakheri 2015). Supervisions may be done via Skype or email, perhaps with short blocks of time spent at the institution itself. Supervision frequency varies by stage and mode of study, from weekly or fortnightly for first-year full-time students to once a fortnight or month for second and subsequent years. Part-time students may be supervised less frequently. Publications are not required for the standard monograph dissertation, although some of the work must be of a publishable standard. Publication is required, though, for some alternative formats and for degrees by prior publication. Interdisciplinarity is an increasing feature, with supervisors coming from different disciplines within the same or even another university—though this can pose challenges in supervision—and in relation to where students publish their work (Strengers 2014).

Typically, a successful doctoral applicant needs a first or high second-class degree, a distinction or merit in a master's (it depends on the discipline whether a master's is needed), and either a good project outline (arts/humanities and social sciences) or a good fit with a project that a supervisor has identified (STEM). Prospective doctoral candidates are interviewed but are often expected to contact potential supervisors beforehand. The UK doctoral candidates also pay fees, although they are lower than those for domestic undergraduates; doctoral students from abroad are charged more. While full-time domestic students may receive financial help from a UK funding council, a major charity like Wellcome or Leverhulme, or by a university scholarship, these funding sources are in decline. The UK government has recently introduced a doctoral loan scheme with income-contingent repayments, but it would be almost impossible for a full-time student to live on this after paying fees. For their part, European Union (EU) students can access a variety of funding sources, ranging from national research councils to the European Commission's Marie Skłodowska-Curie Actions and other co-funding schemes. Non-EU international students in the United Kingdom rely mostly on self-funding or help from their own governments or employers.

There are detailed regulations for doctoral study, including for the standard PhD/DPhil (including variants such as performance) and professional doctorates, and also for doctorates by prior publication. Maximum dissertation length varies by institution, but is typically between 80,000 and 100,000 words. Only universities that have successfully applied for RADPs may award doctorates. RDAPs used to be awarded by independent quality assurance agencies after a complex process of paperwork, some years of awarding doctoral degrees via another university with RDAPs and an institutional visit. Since 2018, RDAPs in England are now overseen by a newly established regulator, the Office for Students, which has no expertise in relation to doctoral degrees. At present, it is unclear which new process will replace the old one.

Quality assurance of doctoral degree programmes is also complex, and in recent years, it has drawn heavily on the UK Quality Code for Higher Education. The experience for doctoral students is evaluated annually via internal, institutionally run surveys and annual monitoring exercises. But there is no publicly available national survey of doctoral students comparable with the final year undergraduate National Student Survey, which feeds into UK-wide rankings. The UK Higher Education Academy (now part of a new organization called Advance HE) runs the Postgraduate Research Experience Survey (PRES), which is now sent annually to all registered research students at participating universities. The results of PRES lead to the publication of aggregate outcomes (Higher Education Academy 2017), but not results for individual institutions. The latter are made available to the institutions for internal use and are benchmarked against the whole sector. Typical areas of concern include: the lack of integration of doctoral candidates into the research cultures of their academic unit; failure of institutions to act on feedback from students; lack of preparation for incorporating innovation and creativity into research degree work; and inadequate support to help develop professional networks. Student communities/cohorts and inclusiveness are still issues for most institutions, with full-time, part-time and distance students posing different challenges (Pilbeam and Denyer 2009; Pilbeam, Lloyd-Jones, and Denyer 2013; Thomas 2015).

Surveys apart, other quality assurance measures for doctoral programmes rely on the annual monitoring of supervisors and the outcomes of dissertation defences (pass, minor changes, moderate changes and resubmission) at the institutional level. Until very recently, the Quality Assurance Agency (England, Wales and Northern Ireland) and the Quality Assurance Agency (Scotland) used periodic institutional visits to audit programmes and quality assurance mechanisms, including those associated with research degrees. Also, institutions themselves have typically held periodic internal reviews of academic departments. These can last from two to four days, and involve a panel of internal and external experts. Data from departments and from focus groups with staff and students (including research degree students and supervisors), is also included. However, the institutional audits for England have now gone, as has the requirement for institutions to report annually on quality enhancement to governing bodies that in turn reported the findings to the Higher Education Funding Council for England, which ceased to exist in early 2018. Following the establishment of the Office for Students in England, student progression and outcome metrics are now the main means of monitoring quality assurance in all degree programmes, including research degrees.

Due to the rising number of students, as well as the complexity of types of degrees and modes of study, doctoral education itself has been forced to become much more organized at the institutional level (Smith McGloin and Wynne 2015). Graduate schools (with academic and administrative leads and sometimes also taught master's students) first became popular at research-intensive universities in the mid-1990s, as research councils applied pressure on completion rates and encouraged a research-training curriculum for students in the early stages of their studies. More recently, there has been a trend towards the creation of doctoral schools, which exclude taught master's students. This development coincides with the decision of the UK research councils to encourage intra-institutional and cross-institutional collaboration in doctoral education (Lunt, McAlpine, and Mills 2013).

Finally, at the national level, the United Kingdom has a non-profit organization entirely focused on supporting postgraduate education, the UK Council for Graduate Education (UKCGE), formed in 1994. The majority of UK HE institutions with postgraduate provision belong to this organization. The UKCGE runs workshops and conferences and produces a range of resources to help academics and administrators who work in postgraduate education. There are also UKCGE networks for directors, managers and supervisors of graduate and doctoral schools.

PARTICIPATION, COMPLETION AND GRADUATE DESTINATIONS IN THE UK DOCTORAL PROGRAMMES

Doctoral students are the smallest cohort within the UK HE student population. The most recent figures, presented in Table 7.1, show

Table 7.1 *UK Doctoral Students Compared to Other HE Students*

Academic Level	Number of Students (% of Overall Population)
Undergraduate (bachelor's degrees)	1,597,825 (68.9)
Other undergraduate (sub-degree qualifications, for example, diploma or certificate of higher education)	168,460 (7.3)
Postgraduate taught (taught master's degrees or postgraduate certificates/diplomas)	439,075 (18.9)
Postgraduate research (doctoral research degrees)	112,520 (4.9)

Source: Higher Education Statistics Agency (HESA).

that they comprise around 5 per cent (112,520) of the overall student body. (All figures in this section are taken from the Higher Education Statistics Agency (HESA). The most recent figures available are for the 2016–2017 academic year.)

Seventy-five per cent (84,630) of doctoral students in the United Kingdom are full-time, compared with 25 per cent (27,895) researching part-time. Non-science subjects see the largest cohort of part-time students (16,225), compared to science disciplines (11,670). As regards country of origin, 58 per cent (65,125) of registered doctoral students are from the United Kingdom, 13 per cent (14,985) are from the EU and 29 per cent (32,410) are from non-EU countries. While cohorts are typically a mix of nationalities, tensions between international and other students are not common, though the former may not always feel fully integrated (Deem and Brehony 2000); a phenomenon also found in other countries (Laufer and Gorup 2018). The United Kingdom formally left the European Union on 31 January 2020, though for one year nothing much will change except that there will be no UK members in the European Parliament. After that, there will certainly be fewer European doctoral candidates at UK universities (as except in Scotland, they will have to pay international fees, which are much higher) and fewer, if any, opportunities for UK doctoral researchers to spend time in Europe as part of their studies, since UK citizens will have no automatic right to study or live in any EU country. For international doctoral applicants in STEM fields, the United Kingdom losing access to EU and European Research Council funding may make the United Kingdom a less popular destination.

Although doctoral researchers account for only 5 per cent of the total student population in the United Kingdom, the number of students entering doctoral programmes has risen steadily over the last decade, from 28,905 in 2007–2008 to 35,340 in 2016–2017. Consequently, the number of doctoral degrees awarded in that same period rose from 19,470 to 28,155.

As Figure 7.2 shows, science subjects attract the largest proportions of doctoral researchers. Engineering and technology, biological sciences and physical sciences have the highest student numbers, possibly as a result of more funding for doctoral research being channelled into these subject areas. Outside of scientific disciplines, social studies, historical and philosophical studies, business and administration, and education also attract significant numbers of doctoral researchers.

At the national level, there is a gender imbalance in enrolments in doctoral degrees, with men accounting for 52 per cent (58,150) of the total doctoral student population and women accounting for 48 per cent (54,285). Individuals who do not identify as male or female account for 0.07 per cent of the population (85). However, the data masks starker male/female imbalances in specific subject areas. In engineering and technology, for example, women account for just 25 per cent (3,540) of total doctoral enrolments. Physics and computer science fare equally badly, with women accounting for just 37 per cent (4,705) and 27 per cent (1,305), respectively. This is concerning, because it likely means fewer women going on to prestigious and lucrative careers in science and technology. Fortunately, nationwide HE accreditation initiatives such as Athena SWAN (once just for STEM, but now for all disciplines), which are assessed on the opportunities and achievements of female academics and students, and campaign groups such as Women In Science and Engineering (WISE) are beginning to address the lack of gender parity in science, engineering and technology. Despite this excellent work, there is still some way to go to address the gender imbalances in engineering, technology, physics and computer science. Conversely, in the biological sciences and education,

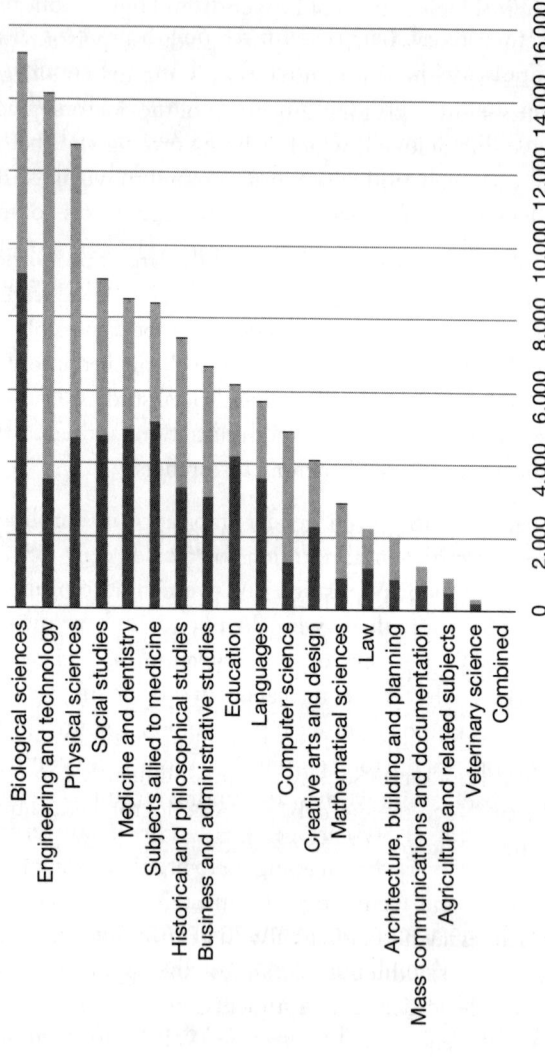

Figure 7.2 *Enrolments by Discipline and Gender*
Source: Higher Education Statistics Agency (HESA).

men account for a much smaller proportion of the total doctoral student enrolments—40 per cent (6,055) and 32 per cent (1,975), respectively.

According to a report by VITAE (2013) that examined national data from the Longitudinal Destinations of Leavers from Higher Education (DLHE) surveys in 2008 and 2010, doctoral graduates perform well on the labour market compared with bachelor's and master's degree holders. The figures showed that just 2 per cent of the doctoral graduates surveyed were unemployed, which is noteworthy given that the United Kingdom was in a period of economic downturn when the data was collected. The report also showed that doctoral graduates go on to work in a variety of sectors, including HE research (16.7%), non-HE research (12.2%), teaching in HE (21.4%), school and further education teaching (7.3%), health, engineering, information technology, business and finance (23.2%) and other occupations such as technical roles, public services and service industries (19.2%). The report also identified a wage premium associated with holding a doctoral degree compared to a bachelor's or master's.

THE ROLE OF THE DOCTORATE IN SOCIETY

Doctoral education in the United Kingdom has undergone a radical transformation during the last three decades. Policy interventions have attempted to move the doctorate away from its purely epistemic role and recreate it for the knowledge-based economy. These developments have radically altered the purpose, form and organization of doctoral education, so that it now serves society in a predominantly economic and marketized way. Nevertheless, debates about doctoral education's contribution to the public good have not entirely disappeared.

From the Servant of Academia to Driving the Knowledge Economy

Doctoral education in the United Kingdom was strongly influenced by the German Humboldtian model, when it was introduced over a century ago (Simpson 1983). The doctorate's role in society was to train a small elite of researchers engaged in the quest for pure knowledge and fundamental truth (Taylor 2012). The doctorate was meant to be of service to the academic discipline, with doctoral students responsible for carrying out research projects to enrich and develop their fields of study. During this period, it was assumed that all doctoral researchers would go on to pursue academic careers and would serve as 'stewards of the discipline' (Jackson 2003).

Today, those epistemic roots and core structure are still recognizable. The doctorate remains a research project conducted under the supervision of academic experts, culminating in the production of a written dissertation that is examined in a closed *viva voce*. Recipients of a doctoral degree have to first demonstrate the capacity to make an original contribution to knowledge. Similarly, the doctorate could still be seen as producing stewards of the discipline, but with a greater emphasis now on shaping future leaders (Balaban 2016). The doctorate still provides universities with their future academic workforce, but it is now clear that many graduates will not get, or do not even want, a permanent academic job.

Since the 1990s, the successive UK governments have prioritized scientific and industrial innovation and encouraged partnerships between universities and industry, in order to strengthen the United Kingdom's competitiveness in global markets (Hancock, Hughes, and Walsh 2015). The influence of the knowledge economy on universities is a continuous process, exemplified by a recent government white paper entitled 'Success as a Knowledge Economy' (Department for Business Innovation and Skills 2016) that underpinned the English Higher Education and Research Act of 2017.

Because of high enrolments, the UK doctorate has come under increasing external scrutiny. It has been subject to policy interventions challenging universities to better service the global knowledge economy (Duke and Denicolo 2017; John and Denicolo 2013), and has led to some consolidation of its main components (Quality Assurance Agency 2015). The policy imperative is to reposition the doctorate as a motor of the economy (European Universities Association 2009). The outputs of doctoral programmes have become more focused on: (a) research skills and methods of training, (b) generating applied knowledge and knowledge translation and (c) training research students for jobs outside academe as well. Sponsorship by outside organizations is encouraged by research councils. There is also considerable interest in placements and internships for research students, encouraged by the research councils that allow funded students to interrupt their studies for two to three months to accommodate this.

There has also been a transformation in what is considered legitimate knowledge production. According to Green and Usher (2003), knowledge has become legitimized by its performative capacity and bears a closer resemblance to Mode 2 knowledge production (Gibbons et al. 1994). In other words, the knowledge produced during a doctorate has expanded beyond pure, theoretical thinking to encompass real-world applications (Green and Usher 2003; Usher 2002). This has been actively encouraged by UK Research and Innovation, a newly formed body that now directs government investment in research. Doctoral researchers are encouraged to develop non-academic impact pathways for their research from the outset (Engineering and Physical Sciences Research Council 2018). These measures have been introduced to more closely align research projects with the needs of industry as well as public, charitable and third-sector organizations. It also seeks to secure those organizations' commitment to doctoral education by turning them into funders. This is not confined to STEM disciplines. Doctoral programmes in the social sciences, arts and humanities are increasingly designed to generate knowledge that addresses real-world issues in the workplace. This has been partly achieved through the creation of more professional doctoral programmes (Bourne, Robinson and Metcalfe 2016), such as the DClinPsy, the doctor of education (EdD) and the doctor of business administration (DBA). Some commentators argue that the future lies with these kinds of professional doctorates, rather than research doctorates (Blackman 2016).

Development of human capital has also become a much stronger feature of the UK doctorate. The most important product of the doctorate is no longer the dissertation, but the individual. The traditional model of the doctorate has been criticized for its narrow academic focus (Roberts 2002). There has been concern that it is not preparing doctoral researchers for diverse career trajectories (Department for Business Innovation and Skills 2016). There is also some anxiety that recruitment to strategically important subject areas in STEM has been tailing off (Higher Education Commission 2012).

As numbers of doctoral students rose, graduates began to move into sectors outside of traditional academe, which demand skill sets beyond the PhD. The knowledge economy created the need for a new kind of doctoral graduate—one capable of generating new knowledge, but also with the ability to competently use that knowledge and translate it into a commercially or socially viable enterprise (Hancock, Hughes, and Walsh 2015). Doctoral graduates needed to use 'transferable skills' to help improve productivity, economic growth and stability (Neumann and Tan 2011). To address these concerns, additional funding was provided to universities that held research council grant awards, the so-called 'Roberts' funding', to develop a broader suite of skills training for doctoral researchers. Although the Roberts' funding disappeared in 2012, almost all UK HE institutions with RDAPs now provide research development skills courses.

The reframing of doctoral education has extended to doctoral researchers themselves. Although they were once thought of as academics-in-the-making and future 'stewards of the discipline', policy documents have tended to conceptualize them as neoliberal agents—self-interested, economically motivated individuals. Balaban (2016) suggests that research students are emerging as entrepreneurial leaders. The UK doctoral education policy shifts have pressured universities to publish data on dissertation completion rates, satisfaction levels, average earnings and careers of graduates in order to help students make informed choices about where to do their doctoral degree and maximize their future earning potential.

The Doctorate as a Force for Social and Public Good

There is still some recognition, however, of the role that doctoral education plays in nurturing a fair and just society. A growing concern in the United Kingdom is that skewed participation in postgraduate education has been identified as a problem for social mobility. Research has provided compelling evidence that when access issues are addressed at the undergraduate level, those inequalities are pushed up to higher educational levels, including the doctorate (Wakeling and Hampden-Thompson 2013; Wakeling and Laurison 2017). The risk is that doctoral education remains the preserve of the privileged and that barriers to access serve to reproduce unequal access to certain professions because, unlike at the undergraduate level, no allowance is made for those from disadvantaged backgrounds, who may take longer to display their academic potential than their more fortunate peers. Although funding is available for research students, competition for research council and other awards is significant and the stipends that accompany fee payments are often barely adequate for students. This may help explain why mental health problems in research students are rising fast (Bothwell 2017; Levecque et al. 2017), as a recent Higher Education Funding Council for England catalyst funding initiative recognized. Mental health problems among research student populations are, of course, not specific to the United Kingdom and are found in many systems, including in the United States (Thomas 2015).

In addition, some UK policy documents still acknowledge that doctoral education can contribute towards a more open, intelligent and just society that values debate. The widening of the impact agenda to encompass social benefits is an important step, because it formally recognizes that the benefits of doctoral research are not restricted to economics alone.

CURRENT DEBATES ABOUT THE UK DOCTORAL EDUCATION

The preceding section has shown that the doctorate is being pulled in several different directions. While there is pressure from the government to repurpose the doctorate for the knowledge economy, the degree remains a pipeline for the academic workforce, albeit in much smaller proportions. These days, well under 10 per cent of all doctoral graduates find a permanent academic post. There is also ongoing recognition of the good that doctoral graduates and their research do for society more broadly. So it is perhaps more accurate to think of the modern doctorate as a contested space, where neoliberal notions of economically motivated doctoral candidates and economically driven research compete against the idea of the doctorate as part of universities' contribution to the public good, a concept previously applied mainly to first degrees (Calhoun 2006; Marginson 2018; McCowan and Deem 2018). The multiple purposes of the UK doctoral education have sparked debates on the existential nature and meaning of the doctorate and on more pragmatic considerations concerning the evolving form of doctoral education, in particular the fitness-for-purpose of the closed viva voce assessment process.

Denicolo and Park (2013) draw our attention to the difficulty faced when trying to define the essence of the doctorate—those qualities that all doctoral programmes and graduates should possess. Advances have been made in the United Kingdom in codifying standards for doctoral awards (through Level 8 of the Quality Assurance Agency framework for HE) and for the broader skill set that successful researchers should possess (the VITAE Researcher Development Framework; VITAE 2009–2018). Nevertheless, as Denicolo and Park (2013) point out, it is not always straightforward to evidence and document these skills. Also, such documents do not necessarily reach down into the different way of thinking that the doctoral experience must necessarily engender. Thus, 'doctorateness' remains a slippery and elusive concept that defies definition because of the rich mixture of qualities involved.

Debate about the purpose and nature of doctoral degrees has sparked further deliberation about the form doctoral education should take. Although Roberts' funding has facilitated the embedding of skills development in most doctoral provisions across the United Kingdom, McAlpine (2017) has criticized this model for inadequately integrating skills development components into the curriculum. Instead, she argues, skills training occupies peripheral territory, having been tacked on to the main business of carrying out an academically rigorous research project and producing a dissertation. However, Soubes' research (2017) on the challenges of running generic skills training in a large science faculty suggests that research grant principal investigators are one of the groups that actively stop this from happening to its full extent. Hancock and Walsh (2014) concur with McAlpine, arguing that the current model of doctoral education fails to offer sufficient time and space for doctoral researchers to develop the entrepreneurial and transferable skills required in the knowledge economy. While there is evidence that doctoral graduates enjoy a salary premium (VITAE 2013) and employers clearly value the contribution doctoral degree holders make to their organizations (Diamond et al. 2014), these employability gains may not be solely attributable to the current model of doctoral education.

As mentioned, a controversial aspect of the UK doctorate is the final *viva voce* examination. All UK doctoral candidates submit a written dissertation and are then examined in a secret *viva voce* by academic experts. The closed nature of the UK system, in contrast to the public defence more common in continental Europe and the United States, has led to mechanisms that allow regulation of the viva voce and provide evidence in the event of appeals against 'fail' or 'resubmission' verdicts. Such mechanisms include independent chairs and audio recordings. With the growing emphasis on training and skills development in contemporary doctoral programmes, the continued narrowness of the examination has been critiqued (Denicolo and Park 2013; Hancock and Walsh 2014). There is growing concern that an increasingly important aspect of the doctorate—the researcher's own development—is not formally assessed as a part of the normal doctoral process, though some universities do accredit both subject-specific and generic training with a postgraduate certificate or diploma.

The heightened focus on ensuring the efficiency of doctoral programmes might be complicit in squeezing the time and space required for an accurate assessment of researcher skills. Doctoral researchers are confronted by the challenge of ensuring that they reach the standard of intellectual rigour required for the doctorate, while also broadening their skills to encompass a variety of possible career trajectories. This is a daunting prospect and places enormous pressure on doctoral researchers, who are required to do more on a compressed timescale (Duke and Denicolo 2017; McAlpine 2017). Currently, the debate over appropriate timeframes for doing a doctorate has reawakened, and some funders are showing more willingness to assist doctoral researchers for more than three years in some circumstances (Arts and Humanities Research Council 2018; Natural Environment Research Council 2018).

In summary, the UK doctorate retains links with its epistemic origins and the degree remains rooted in the production of new knowledge. Nevertheless, the advent of the knowledge economy and resulting policy interventions have reformed the contemporary doctorate. Greater emphasis is now placed on applicable, impactful knowledge and multi-skilled PhDs as desirable outcomes of a doctoral education. Against this economic imperative, there is recognition that the doctorate provides for the public good, particularly in regard to social mobility and its contribution to a just society.

SOME CONCLUDING THOUGHTS

In this chapter, we have explored the historical development of the doctorate in the United Kingdom and taken a look at its main features and infrastructure. Critical periods in the 20th and 21st centuries have seen significant changes to accepted practice: the introduction of structured training in research methods and generic skills; the growth of professional doctorates alongside the standard research doctorate; the development of supervisor training; the expansion of graduate schools and doctoral colleges; a shift to collaborative, cross-institutional doctoral training partnerships; systematic evaluation of the student experience; a greater emphasis on preparation for non-academic jobs through placements; and outside organizations co-sponsoring and supporting students. Since the late 1980s, the focus has been on prompt completion of the dissertation and away from the knowledge and magnum opus model towards a training model of the PhD. Professional doctorates have helped those in mid-career capitalize on their own practice while studying. Increased PhD enrolments and a decline in the number of permanent academic posts are turning attention away from the research doctorate as preparation solely for a career in academe, and towards the many non-academic jobs that PhD graduates can do. Supervision has been the subject of greater surveillance and support, and joint supervision is now much more common, as is group supervision in both the research PhD and professional doctorates. The Internet allows supervision and research training to take place at a distance when required. The final dissertation defence, however, remains a private affair; there have been few innovations in dissertation assessment in the United Kingdom in recent decades.

There are big question marks on the horizon for the UK PhD. One is money, as research councils reduce their funding and many doctoral programmes barely break even financially. Other challenges include: developing fully integrated training programmes, not just add-ons; improving the student experience; working out the future societal contribution and employment of doctoral students; and considering how to ensure positive student mental health. Furthermore, the question of how to motivate supervisors is still to be fully resolved, as overseeing doctoral students becomes yet another burdensome task for overworked academics. The future recruitment of research students from outside the United Kingdom may also need to be reviewed in light of Brexit.

Finally, the increasing role of artificial intelligence in carrying out literature reviews and data scraping/analysis will bring up questions about what exactly constitutes an original contribution to knowledge and the part that universities will play in the future as arbiters and certifiers of that knowledge (Deem and Eggins 2017). In light of the growing importance of educational technology, organizations such as Coursera (Thomas and Nedeva 2018) will in time move the doctorate in fresh directions. The PhD will almost certainly survive, but it may no longer look like it does today.

REFERENCES

Arts and Humanities Research Council. 2018. *AHRC Doctoral Training Partnership.* https://ahrc.ukri.org/documents/calls/dtp2-application-guidance (accessed 9 December 2019).

Balaban, Corina. 2016. 'From Steward to Leader: A Decade of Shifting Roles for the PhD Student'. *Learning and Teaching: The International Journal of Higher Education in the Social Sciences* 9 (1): 90–100.

Bao, Y., Barbara Kehm, and Yonghong Ma. 2018. 'From Product to Process. The Reform of Doctoral Education in Europe and China'. *Studies in Higher Education* 43 (3): 524–542. doi:10.1080/03075079.2016.1182481.

Barnes, Tina. 2013. *Higher Doctorates in the UK.* Lichfield: UK Council for Graduate Education.

Bartholomew, R., Richard Disney, Joe Eyerman, Jennifer Mason, Steve Newstead, Harry Torrance, and Rebekah Widdowfield. 2015. *Review of the ESRC Doctoral Training Centres Network*. Swindon: Economic and Social Research Council. https://esrc.ukri.org/files/skills-and-careers/studentships/full-report-review-of-the-esrc-doctoral-training-centres-network/ (accessed 9 December 2019).

Blackman, Tim. 2016. 'The Professional Doctorate and the 21st Century University'. *Work Based Learning E-Journal* 6 (1). https://wblearning-ejournal.com/currentIssue/1_Tim_Blackman_Professional_Doctorates.pdf (accessed 9 December 2019).

Bogle, David. 2017. '100 Years of the PhD in the UK'. Leuven League of European Research Universities. https://www.vitae.ac.uk/news/vitae-blog/100-years-of-the-phd-by-prof-david-bogle (accessed 9 December 2019).

Bothwell, Ellie. 2017. 'Universities Urged to Tackle PhD Mental Health Crisis: Institutions Told They Have a "Culture of Excluding Postgraduates" in Wake of Damning Study'. *Times Higher Education*, 13 April. https://www.timeshighereducation.com/news/universities-urged-tackle-phd-mental-health-crisis (accessed 9 December 2019).

Bourne, Robin Mellors, Carol Robinson, and Janet Metcalfe. 2016. *Provision of Professional Doctorates in English HE Institutions*. Bristol: Higher Education Funding Council for England, Vitae/Crac.

Budd, Richard, Catherine O'Connell, Olga Ververi, and Ting TingYuan. 2018. *The DTC Effect: ESRC Doctoral Training Centres and the UK Social Science Doctoral Training Landscape*. Liverpool: Liverpool Hope University.

Calhoun, C. 2006. 'The University and the Public Good'. *Thesis Eleven* 84: 7–43.

Deem, Rosemary, Sally Barnes, and Gill Clarke. 2015. 'Social Science Doctoral Training Policies and Institutional Responses: Three Narrative Perspectives on Recent Developments in and Consequences of the UK Transition to Collaborative Doctoral Training'. In *Universities in Transition: Shifting Institutional and Organisational Boundaries*, edited by Emanuela Reale and Emilia Primeri, 137–162. Rotterdam: Sense Publishers.

Deem, Rosemary, and Heather Eggins, eds. 2017. *The University as a Critical Institution?* Rotterdam: Sense Publishers.

Deem, Rosemary, and Kevin Joseph Brehony. 2000. 'Doctoral Students' Access to Research Cultures—Are Some More Equal than Others?' *Studies in Higher Education* 25, (2): 149–165.

Denicolo, Pam, and Chris Park. 2013. 'Doctorateness—an Elusive Concept?' In *Critical Issues in Higher Education*, edited by Michael Kompf and Pam Denicolo, 191–198. Rotterdam: Sense Publishers.

Department for Business Innovation and Skills. 2016. *Success as a Knowledge Economy: Teaching Excellence, Social Mobility and Student Choice*. London: Department for Business Innovation and Skills.

Diamond, Abigail, Charlie Ball, Tim Vorley, Tristam Hughes, Rachel Moreton, Peter Howe, and Tej Nathwani. 2014. *The Impact of Doctoral Careers: Final Report*. Swindon: Research Councils UK (now UK Research and Innovation).

https://www.ukri.org/files/skills/Summaryidc-pdf/ (accessed 9 December 2019).

Duke, Dawn C., and Pam M. Denicolo. 2017. 'What Supervisors and Universities Can Do to Enhance Doctoral Student Experience (and How They Can Help Themselves)'. *FEMS Microbiology Letters* 364 (9). doi:10.1093/femsle/fnx090.

Engineering and Physical Sciences Research Council. 2018. 'EPSRC 2018 Centres for Doctoral Training'. https://epsrc.ukri.org/files/funding/calls/2018/2018 cdtsoutlinescall/ (13 April 2018).

Erichsen, Elizabeth, Doris Bolliger, and Colleen Halupa. 2014. 'Student Satisfaction with Graduate Supervision in Doctoral Programs Primarily Delivered in Distance Education Settings'. *Studies in Higher Education* 39 (2): 321–338. doi:10.1080/03075079.2012.709496.

European Universities Association. 2009. *European Universities—Looking Forward with Confidence. Prague Declaration 2009.* Brussels: European Universities Association.

Gibbons, Michael, Camille Limgoges, Helga Nowotny, Simon Schwartzman, Peter Scott, and Martin Trow. 1994. *The New Production of Knowledge: The Dynamics of Science and Research in Contemporary Societies.* London: SAGE Publications.

Green, Pam, and Robin Usher. 2003. 'Fast Supervision: Changing Supervisory Practice in Changing Times'. *Studies in Continuing Education* 25 (1): 37–50.

Hancock, Sally, Gwyneth Hughes, and Elaine Walsh. 2015. 'Purist or Pragmatist? UK Doctoral Scientists' Moral Positions on the Knowledge Economy'. *Studies in Higher Education* 42 (7): 1244–1258. doi: 10.1080/03075079.2015.1087994.

Hancock, Sally, and Elaine Walsh. 2014. 'Beyond Knowledge and Skills: Rethinking the Development of Professional Identity during the STEM Doctorate'. *Studies in Higher Education* 41 (1): 37–50.

Higher Education Academy. 2017. 'Postgraduate Research Student Experience Survey'. UK Higher Education Academy.

Higher Education Commission. 2012. 'Postgraduate Education: An Independent Inquiry by the Higher Education Commission'. Policy Connect. http://www.policyconnect.org.uk/hec/sites/pol1-006/files/he_commission_-_postgraduate_education_2012.pdf (accessed June 2018).

Jackson, Allyn. 2003. 'Carnegie Initiative on the Doctorate'. *Notices of the American Mathematical Society* 50: 566–568.

John, Tomasz, and Pam Denicolo. 2013. 'Doctoral Education: A Review of the Literature Monitoring the Doctoral Student Experience in Selected OECD Countries (Mainly UK)'. *Springer Science Reviews* 1 (1–2): 41–49.

Kehm, Barbara. 2009. 'New Forms of Doctoral Education in the European Higher Education Area'. In *The European Higher Education Area: Perspectives on a Moving Target*, edited by Barbara M. Kehm, Jeroen Huisman, and B. Stensaker, 223–241. Rotterdam: Sense Publishers.

Laufer, Mellisa, and Meta Gorup. 2018. 'The Invisible Others: Stories of International Doctoral Student Dropout'. *Higher Education.* doi:10.1007/s10734-018-0337-z.

Levecque, Katia, Frederik Anseel, AlainDe Beuckelaer, Johan Van der Heyden, and Lydia Gislef. 2017. 'Work Organization and Mental Health Problems in PhD Students'. *Research Policy* 46: 868–879.

Lunt, Ingrid, Lynn McAlpine, and David Mills. 2013. 'Lively Bureaucracy? The ESRC's Doctoral Training Centres and UK Universities'. *Oxford Review of Education* 40 (2): 151–169.

Marginson, Simon. 2018. 'Public/Private in Higher Education: A Synthesis of Economic and Political Approaches'. *Studies in Higher Education* 43 (2): 322–337. doi:10.1080/03075079.2016.1168797.

McAlpine, Lynn. 2017. 'Building on Success? Future Challenges for Doctoral Education Globally'. *Studies in Graduate and Postdoctoral Education* 8 (2): 66–77. doi:10.1108/sgpe-d–17-00035.

McCowan, Tristan, and Rosemary Deem. 2018. 'Understanding the Role of University Graduates in Society: Which Conception of Public Good?' In *Pathways to the Public Good: Access, Experiences and Outcomes of South African Undergraduate Education*, edited by Paul Ashwin and Jenni Case, 61–77. Cape Town: African Minds.

Mellors-Bourne, Robin, Carol Robinson, and Janet Metcalfe. 2016. *Provision of Professional Doctorates in English Higher Education Institutions*. Bristol: HEFCE & Careers Reaearch and Advisory Centre.

Nasiri, Fuzhan, and Fereshteh Mafakheri. 2015. 'Postgraduate Research Supervision at a Distance: A Review of Challenges and Strategies'. *Studies in Higher Education* 40 (10): 1962–1969.

Natural Environment Research Council. 2018. 'Natural Environment Research Council Doctoral Training Partnerships 2018'. Swindon: Natural Environment Research Council.

Neumann, Ruth, and Kim Khim Tan. 2011. 'From PhD to Initial Employment: The Doctorate in a Knowledge Economy'. *Studies in Higher Education* 36 (5): 601–614.

Nilsson, Fredrik, Halina Dunin-Woyseth, and Nel Janssens, eds. 2017. *Perspectives on Research Assessment in Architecture, Music and the Arts: Discussing Doctorateness*. London: Routledge.

Oxford Today. 2017. '100 Years of the DPhil'. 28 November.

Park, Chris. 2005. 'New Variant PhD: The Changing Nature of the Doctorate in the UK'. *Journal of Higher Education Policy and Management* 27 (2): 189–208.

Pilbeam, Colin, and David Denyer. 2009. 'Lone Scholar or Community Member? The Role of Student Networks in Doctoral Education in a UK Management School'. *Studies in Higher Education* 34 (3): 301–318.

Pilbeam, Colin, Gaynor Lloyd-Jones, and David Denyer. 2013. 'Leveraging Value in Doctoral Student Networks through Social Capital'. *Studies in Higher Education* 38 (10): 1472–1489. doi:10.1080/03075079.2011.636800.

Powell, Stuart. 2004. 'The Award of PhD by Published Work in the UK'. UK Council for Graduate Education. http://www.ukcge.ac.uk/

NR/rdonlyres/F3EFEA04-C6E1-4B16-A1CD–19DEF22AF3AD/0/
PhDbyPublishedWork2004.pdf (accessed July 2007).

Pratt, John. 1997. *The Polytechnic Experiment 1965–1992, SRHE*. Buckingham: Open University.

Quality Assurance Agency. 2015. 'Characteristics Statement: Doctoral Degree'. Gloucester: Quality Assurance Agency.

Roberts, Gareth. 2002. 'SET for Success: A Review'. Department for Trade and Industry and Department for Education and Skills. http://webarchive. nationalarchives.gov.uk/+/http://www.hm-treasury.gov.uk/ent_res_roberts. htm (accessed October 2018).

Robinson, Carol. 2018. 'The Landscape of Professional Doctorate Provision in English Higher Education Institutions: Inconsistencies, Tensions and Unsustainability'. *London Review of Education* 16 (1): 90–103. doi:10.18546/ LRE.16.1.09.

Schwarzenbach, Jessica, and PaulHackett, eds. 2016. *Transatlantic Reflections on the Practice-Based PhD in Fine Art*. New York, NY and London: Routledge.

Simpson, Renate. 1983. *How the PhD Came to Britain: A Century of Struggle for Postgraduate Education*. Guildford: Society for Research into Higher Education.

———. 2009. *The Development of the PhD Degree in Britain, 1917–1959 and Since: An Evolutionary and Statistical History in Higher Education*. New York, NY: Edward Mellon.

Smith McGloin, Rebekah, and Carolyn Wynne. 2015. *Structural Changes in Doctoral Education in the UK: A Review of Graduate Schools and the Development of Doctoral Colleges*. Lichfield: UK Council for Graduate Education. http://www.ukcge. ac.uk/Search/Default.aspx?q=Structural+Changes+in++Doctoral+Educatio n+in+the+UK%3A+A+Review+of+Graduate+Schools+and+the+Developm ent+of+Doctoral+Colleges (accessed 9 December 2019).

Soubes, Sandrine. 2017. 'Postdoctoral Research Development in the Sciences: A Bourdieusian Analysis'. EdD dissertation. Sheffield: The University of Sheffield.

Strengers, Yolande Amy-Adeline. 2014. 'Interdisciplinarity and Industry Collaboration in Doctoral Candidature: Tensions within and between Discourses'. *Studies in Higher Education* 39 (4): 546–559. doi:10.1080/03075 079.2012.709498.

Taylor, Stan. 2012. 'Changes in Doctoral Education'. *International Journal for Researcher Development* 3 (2): 118–138. doi:10.1108/17597511311316973.

Thomas, Duncan, and Maria Nedeva. 2018. 'Broad Online Learning EdTech and USA Universities: Symbiotic Relationships in a Post-MOOC World'. *Studies in Higher Education* 43 (10). doi:10.1080/03075079.2018.1520415.

Thomas, Scott. 2015. 'Academic Socialization and Social Support at the Postgraduate Level'. UK Council for Graduate Education. http://www.ukcge. ac.uk/events/documents/Presentations-53.aspx (accessed 9 December 2019).

Usher, Robin. 2002. 'A Diversity of Doctorates: Fitness for the Knowledge Economy'. *Higher Education Research & Development* 21: 143–153. doi:10.1080/07294360220144060.

VITAE. 2009–2018. 'Researcher Development Framework'. https://www.vitae. ac.uk/researchers-professional-development/about-the-vitae-researcher-development-framework (accessed 17 July 2018).

———. 2013. *What Do Researchers Do? Early Career Progression of Doctoral Graduates*. London: VITAE.

Wakeling, Paul, and Gill Hampden-Thompson. 2013. 'Transition to Higher Degrees across the UK: An Analysis of National, Institutional and Individual Differences'. Higher Education Academy. http://www.heacademy.ac.uk/assets/documents/research/Transition_to_higher_degree_across_the_UK.pdf (accessed August 2018).

Wakeling, Paul, and Daniel Laurison. 2017. 'Are Postgraduate Qualifications the 'New Frontier of Social Mobility?' *British Journal of Sociology* 68 (3): 533–555. doi:10.1111/1468–4446.12277.

Winfield, Graham. 1987. *The Social Science PhD: The Economic and Social Research Council Enquiry on Submission Rates*. Swindon: Economic and Social Research Council.

PART III

North America

Chapter 8

Strengths, Challenges and Opportunities for US Doctoral Education

Ann E. Austin and Emily R. Miller

Doctoral education in the United States is respected and emulated by higher education leaders across the globe. Its history and design serve to advance several purposes simultaneously. Doctoral education produces faculty members for higher education institutions of all kinds across the world; the research done by doctoral students contributes directly to research discoveries across fields and fuels national goals for economic advances, health improvements and overall societal well-being. At the same time, the structure of doctoral education and the efforts of doctoral students ensure high-quality learning experiences for undergraduates working towards bachelor's degrees in the US system.

This chapter begins by explaining the historical context that has been critically important in shaping the defining features of doctoral education in the United States. It delineates specific characteristics and features that define the US model of doctoral education, and then provides a picture of recent trends and key elements of the doctoral landscape today. While US doctoral education serves as an exemplar and benchmark in the global context, it simultaneously faces important challenges and critiques. Thus, the remainder of the chapter discusses the major challenges facing US doctoral education today, followed by a review of the reforms underway or proposed. The chapter concludes with examples of current initiatives designed to respond to concerns and critiques. Maintaining the elements that have brought recognition to US doctoral education, while also recognizing and addressing substantive concerns, constitutes the agenda confronting US doctoral education at this time.

A BRIEF HISTORY OF DOCTORAL EDUCATION IN THE UNITED STATES

Doctoral education in the United States dates back to the establishment of the first doctoral degree at Yale University in 1860, with the first doctoral degree awarded in 1861. However, histories of doctoral education typically note the establishment of Johns Hopkins University in 1876 as the first university to focus on doctoral education. Informed by the experiences of groups of American scholars who visited research-oriented German universities during the mid and later 1800s, the founders of Johns Hopkins University saw the PhD as an opportunity for novices to work with experienced researchers in focused research as preparation for becoming part of the guild of scholars (Brubacher and Rudy 1997; Rudolph 1990). By 1900, 14 higher education institutions offered PhDs, with 300 doctoral degrees awarded that year. The American Association of Universities (AAU), established in 1900, created a set of elite institutions (both public and private) respected for the research and graduate education they offered; the prestige of the AAU helped establish criteria of excellence and a degree of homogeneity across the emerging graduate programmes (Gumport 2005).

The growth of doctoral education in the United States was aided by funding initiatives from outside higher education institutions. Beginning in the later decades of the 19th century, some philanthropic organizations, such as the Carnegie Foundation and the Rockefeller Foundation, provided support for research and fellowships. However, it was the US federal government's investment in research and research training that has been a seminal force shaping the nature of doctoral education in the United States. After each World War, government investment in research and research training increased.

The major involvement of the federal government in supporting research and research training emerged, however, in the years after the Second World War. A key event occurred in 1945, when Vannevar Bush proposed to President Roosevelt a federal agency to advance science as 'an endless frontier' (Gumport 2005). The establishment of the National Science Foundation, resulting from Bush's proposal, increased federal support for the training of scientists and engineers and solidified the relationship between research funding and doctoral education in the United States, thus advancing the quality and scope of US doctoral education. Reaction to the launch of the Russian satellite Sputnik in 1957 ignited much concern about the quality of scientific work in the United States and led to increased federal funding for research, including more support for doctoral students. This support took the form of fellowships (which provided direct aid to students), traineeships (which provided funding to higher education institutions to be used to support graduate students) and direct funding for projects (which indirectly supported doctoral education through funding for research assistants). At the same time, enrolment of undergraduates was rising, as veterans utilized federal support to pursue undergraduate education. This trend meant universities needed graduate students to help teach undergraduate courses.

In response to these factors, PhD production increased dramatically in the post-Second World War decades (Thelin 2011). In 1950, about 6,000 doctoral degrees were awarded; in 1960, 10,000 and in 1970, 30,000 doctoral degrees (Gumport 2005). Most of these degrees were in the life sciences, physical sciences and engineering, with far fewer awarded in the social sciences and humanities. In addition to the Doctor of Philosophy, doctoral degrees emerged in many professional areas, such as education, business, theology and art. The majority of degrees awarded after the Second World War were from the top-tier public and private universities, where research resources were extensive, and those were most often in the sciences and engineering. The less elite institutions tended to focus on a fewer range of degrees, often in the professional fields that did not require expensive instruments, laboratories and equipment.

In the 1970s, fiscal constraints led to less federal money to support research and doctoral students. At the same time, the government saw a shift from interest in basic research towards greater interest in initiatives that would enhance national economic competitiveness (Gumport 2005). Funding for doctoral fellowships declined and research grant budgets became leaner, with less support for doctoral student traineeships. Student funding shifted to assistantships and taxable institutional stipends. As discussed later in the chapter, as funding patterns changed and the job market for PhD graduates tightened, a range of stakeholders raised concerns about aspects of the doctoral experience and offered ideas for improvement.

DEFINING FEATURES OF THE US MODEL OF DOCTORAL EDUCATION

The defining features of the US model of doctoral education can be organized into four categories: (a) structural dimensions of the doctoral experience; (b) connections between federal research goals, institutional missions and doctoral education; (c) socialization processes and the role of disciplinary cultures and (d) the location of doctoral education in academic departments.

Structural Dimensions of Doctoral Work

The structure of doctoral programs in US universities is quite consistent across institutions. Perhaps the most well-known aspect of the US doctoral degree is its course-based feature. Virtually all doctoral programmes in US universities require students to complete a certain number of courses (or credits, which is the currency in the US higher education system). Often some courses are prescribed, with others either required to be selected from specified course groupings or allowed as open-choice electives. After completing coursework, students typically take an exam, which upon successful completion allows them to use the designated term 'candidate'. The exam may be comprehensive, drawing on all the coursework the student has taken, or it may be more forward-looking (such as a paper that frames a research question and proposes a research direction to address the question). Exams also may vary in length required for the answer, amount of time needed (e.g., a few days, a month, a semester) and format (e.g., take-home or a formal sitting to write the exam). Once students are candidates (having successfully completed the exam), they work on the dissertation, although in some fields that work has already begun. The dissertation is required for all doctoral degrees, but it may take a variety of forms, based on the norms and expectations of the particular department and field. Typically, a student frames a problem in the field, collects and analyses data, writes a description of the findings and offers an interpretation of the importance and contribution provided by the study and its findings. The length of the dissertation varies by discipline (e.g., math dissertations may be a problem solution and require relatively few pages; a dissertation in humanities fields may involve hundreds of pages). The common theme, however, is that all dissertations require original work by the candidate.

Throughout the doctoral experience, a student is guided by a faculty mentor who, ideally, discusses the students' goals and offers advice about course selection. The initial advisor often becomes the dissertation chairperson, but sometimes students may select a chairperson other than the advisor. The relationship of the student with the advisor and dissertation chairperson will vary depending on disciplinary traditions. In the sciences, for example, the doctoral student may be working in the advisor's research team. All candidates experience a dissertation defence in which they present, discuss, explain and answer questions about the completed dissertation with a committee of, typically, four or five scholars (often called the dissertation committee). This panel usually involves the faculty advisor, other faculty members who know the discipline or field and one or two faculty members from outside the candidate's primary field. In general, all committee members are from the candidate's home university.

Connections between Federal Research Goals, Institutional Missions and Graduate Education

As discussed earlier, the expansion and nature of American doctoral education has been directly connected with the role of US universities in responding to federal research priorities, with implications primarily for the sciences, technology fields, engineering and mathematics (STEM). One sociologist explained the relationship as one of 'interdependence' (Gumport 2005, 427). Universities need research money to fulfil their missions; faculty members need doctoral students to help conduct their research; students need opportunities to learn, be mentored and earn financial support. In this complex interrelationship, research pressures—and the accompanying roles that doctoral students play in labs and as research assistants—can challenge, undermine or thwart consistent attention to developing students' teaching skills or other career-related skills. In recent decades, with less robust federal financial support, some universities have established Organized Research Units (ORUs), usually related to STEM fields, that receive funding outside departmental structures, often for interdisciplinary or applied work. For doctoral students, an advantage of ORUs is that they offer opportunities to engage in applied research on current topics, use cutting-edge equipment and create relationships with potential employers. However, work in an ORU may diminish the nature of the student experience, as the doctoral candidate is treated as an employee rather than a mentored novice learner. Additionally, issues of privacy that benefit the funders may interfere with traditional norms of autonomy, peer review and open publishing that, within the traditional university context, protect doctoral students as well as faculty researchers (Gumport 2005).

Doctoral Education as a Socialization Process to the Scholarly Profession and the Discipline

A key function of doctoral education in US higher education is to provide a socialization process in which doctoral students learn the norms, traditions, expectations, attitudes, habits, knowledge and skills associated with being a member of the scholarly profession, and, specifically, of the profession as it is enacted in their specific discipline or field (Austin 2002; Weidman, Twale, and Stein 2001). The socialization process occurs through multiple experiences that involve formal, planned and structured processes in classrooms, laboratories and advising sessions as well as informal interactions and unscripted experiences during daily interactions and conversations on and off campus. Interactions with faculty members, student peers, potential employers and others in the field all play their roles. The current thinking is that socialization involves not only the process through which the doctoral experience teaches newcomers about their responsibilities, the expectations they face, and the disciplinary and scholarly traditions of which they will be a part, but it also involves a bidirectional process in which the newcomers impact the organization that they are joining (Tierney and Rhoads 1994). This process is illustrated in the history of doctoral education in the United States, in which the interests, values and expectations of doctoral students have played a role in shaping the nature of doctoral education. For example, the increasing diversity of those entering doctoral education in recent years, including women and people of colour, has introduced expectations for a doctoral experience that honours more fully the range of interests, backgrounds and aspirations of participants (Antony 2002; Austin 2006; NASEM 2018).

Location of Doctoral Education in Academic Departments

Doctoral education in the US context has historically been located within university academic departments, an organizational characteristic with two important implications. First, over the past century, academic departments within US universities have developed considerable control over curricular decisions, policies and practices (Veysey 1965). Thus, while institutional graduate schools have been instituting more policies and exercising greater controls over graduate processes in the past decade (such as length of time allowed for degree completion), the faculty members in individual departments and the programmes within those departments typically have had considerable influence over the content of the doctoral experience and the curriculum, including the course requirements for degree completion. The second implication of situating doctoral programmes within departments is that graduate and undergraduate education are closely intertwined (Gumport 2005). Since academic departments are responsible for offering courses for undergraduates, they have turned to doctoral students to teach undergraduate courses, especially over recent decades as student enrolments have increased. Teaching assistantships provide professional experience for doctoral students, while also placing them in the role of being university employees, a situation that has led to concerns about the potential for institutional needs to take precedence over doctoral students' learning needs. Such issues, often played out in regard to the time spent on teaching assistantships and the level of stipends for teaching assistants, have contributed to graduate student unionization at some universities.

While departments have been the home for graduate education, shifts are occurring. In the sciences, faculty members are highly dependent on doctoral students to have productive research laboratories, so doctoral students often hold research assistantships. However, as 'team science' promises to address complex scientific questions, collaborative research that is multidisciplinary or transdisciplinary is producing new opportunities for scholars, while at the same time also challenging university practices and policies governing graduate education that have historically been situated within an academic department or college (National Research Council 2015).

PORTRAIT OF US DOCTORAL EDUCATION AND RECIPIENTS

Data on doctoral recipients and trends and patterns in doctoral education by major disciplinary fields provide a portrait of doctoral education in the United States. This section draws upon the National Center for Science and Engineering Statistics (NCSES) data that includes the Survey of Earned Doctorates (SED; NSF, NCSES 2018). SED is an annual census conducted since 1957 of all individuals receiving a research doctorate from an accredited US institution in a given academic year. The survey is sponsored by six federal agencies: the National Science Foundation (NSF), the National Institutes of Health

(NIH), the Department of Education, the National Endowment for the Humanities, the Department of Agriculture and the National Aeronautics and Space Administration. The survey collects information on educational history, demographics and postgraduation plans. The most recent report provides data on doctoral recipients up to 2016 (NSF, NCSES 2018).

US Doctorates Awarded by Field of Study

The total number of research doctorate degrees awarded by US institutions in 2016 was 54,904 (NSF, NCSES 2018). Over time, the number of doctorates awarded across all fields of study shows a strong upward trend—an average annual growth of 3.3 per cent—although there have been periods of slow growth and even declines in some major fields of study (Table 8.1).

Doctorates in science and engineering (S&E) fields are a growing share of all doctorates awarded. Overall, S&E doctorates accounted for 75 per cent of all doctorates awarded in 2016, a substantially larger share than 10–20 years earlier (69% and 67%, respectively). Every broad S&E field except for psychology and social sciences increased both their number and share of doctorates over the past two decades. Psychology and social sciences increased in the number of doctorate recipients, but their share of all doctorates stayed about the same. Mathematics and computer sciences, with the smallest number of doctorates awarded among the S&E fields, almost doubled the number of doctorates awarded over the past 20 years, from 2,042 in 1996 to 3,957 in 2016 (NSF, NCSES 2018).

Despite an increase in the number of humanities and arts doctorates, the relative share of doctorates awarded in these fields fell by 2 per cent from 1996 to 2016. The share of doctorates in other non-S&E fields, like business management, has remained fairly stable over the past two decades. The number of doctorates awarded in education has declined over the past two decades, leading to a large, steady drop in the relative share of doctorates in that field from 16 per cent in 1996 to 9 per cent in 2016 (NSF, NCSES 2018).

Table 8.1 *Doctorate Recipients by Major Fields of Study*

Fields of Study	1996		2001		2006		2011		2016	
	42,437		40,744		45,620		48,911		54,904	
Life sciences	8,337	19.6%	8,369	20.5%	9,703	21.3%	11,535	23.6%	12,568	22.9%
Physical sciences and earth sciences	4,550	10.7%	4,024	9.9%	4,686	10.3%	5,271	10.8%	6,252	11.4%
Mathematics and computer sciences	2,042	4.8%	1,840	4.5%	2,778	6.1%	3,273	6.7%	3,957	7.2%
Psychology and social sciences	7,167	16.9%	7,151	17.6%	7,231	15.9%	8,221	16.8%	9,078	16.5%
Engineering	6,309	14.9%	5,512	13.5%	7,186	15.8%	8,032	16.4%	9,469	17.2%
Education	6,785	16.0%	6,356	15.6%	6,122	13.4%	4,670	9.5%	5,153	9.4%
Humanities and arts	4,982	11.7%	5,430	13.3%	5,332	11.7%	5,226	10.7%	5,484	10.0%
Other	2,265	5.3%	2,062	5.1%	2,582	5.7%	2,683	5.5%	2,943	5.4%

Source: National Science Foundation, National Center for Science and Engineering Statistics (2018).

Citizenship, Race and Ethnicity of Doctoral Recipients

An important feature of US doctoral education is that it attracts large numbers of international students. It is argued that the US national interests are best served when the world's top students, scientists, researchers and engineers live and work in the United States. (The current discussion of immigration issues in the United States could lead to shifts in the numbers of international students who choose to study or remain in the United States after earning their degrees.)

As presented in Figure 8.1, in every broad field of study, the share of doctorates awarded to temporary visa holders has increased over the past 20 years. The total number of doctorates awarded to temporary visa holders grew to 16,489 in 2016, up by 69 per cent since 1996. Of significance was the dramatic increase in temporary visa holders receiving doctorates in the field of mathematics and computer sciences, where a 148 per cent growth occurred between 1996 and 2016 (NSF, NCSES 2018).

Over the past two decades, the number of doctoral awards to temporary visa holders has been highly concentrated among a few nationalities— Chinese (including Hong Kong), Indians and South Koreans. In 2016, citizens from these three countries accounted for 54 per cent of all temporary visa holders' doctoral awards (NSF, NCSES 2018).

To maintain high-quality graduate education programmes, it is also critically important to find ways to increase participation in doctoral education by minority US citizens. Participation in doctoral education by underrepresented minorities (URM) who are US citizens or permanent residents is increasing; however, the proportion of doctorates earned remains staggeringly low. The proportion of doctorates earned by African Americans has only risen slightly from 6 per cent in 2006 to 7 per cent in 2016, and the proportion awarded to Hispanics or Latinos has only grown from 5 per cent to 7 per cent over the same time period. The proportion earned by American Indians or Alaska Natives has remained under 1 per cent from 2006 to 2016 (NSF, NCSES 2018).

Among minority US citizens and permanent residents, doctorate recipients of different racial or ethnic backgrounds are more heavily

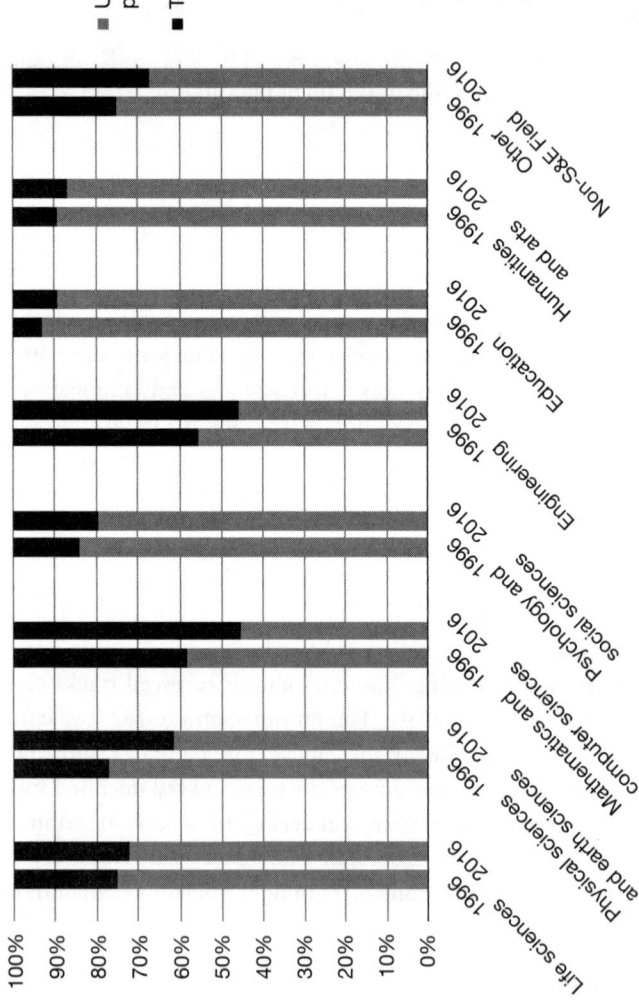

Figure 8.1 *Doctorate Award by Citizenship and Major Fields of Study (1996 and 2016)*
Source: NSF, NCSES (2018).

represented in some fields of study than others. In 2016, Asians earned more doctorates than other racial and ethnic minority groups in life sciences (11%), physical sciences and earth sciences (8%), mathematics and computer sciences (13%) and engineering (15%). African Americans were the largest US minority population in the field of education. Hispanics or Latinos earned a larger share of doctorates in psychology and social sciences and in humanities and arts than did any other minority group (NSF, NCSES 2018).

Sex and Age of Doctoral Recipients

Considerable discussion has occurred in recent years about the representation of women in doctoral education overall, and in certain fields in particular. As represented in Table 8.2, women's share of doctorates awarded has grown over the past two decades in all fields of study. In 2016, women earned the majority of doctorates awarded in life sciences (55%), psychology and social sciences (59%), education (70%) and humanities and arts (52%). While the majority of recipients of doctorates in physical sciences, earth sciences and engineering are men, women's relative shares of doctorates awarded in those fields has been growing rapidly. From 1996 to 2016, the share of doctorates in physical sciences and earth sciences awarded to women increased from 22 per cent to 31 per cent, and in engineering grew from 12 per cent to 23 per cent. The share of female doctorate recipients in mathematics and computer sciences grew, although more modestly, from 18 per cent to 24 per cent during this period (NSF, NCSES 2018).

The median age at which the doctorate is received tracks closely for men and women. In 2016, women's median age (32.0 years) was only slightly higher than men's median age (31.3 years). From 1996 to 2016, the median age at the time of doctorate award declined for US citizens by 2.9 years to 31.9 years and declined 1.4 years for temporary visa holders to 31.0 years. Doctorate recipients with temporary visas consistently received doctorates at a younger median age than did US citizens and non-US citizen permanent residents (NSF, NCSES 2018).

Fields of study also impact the age distributions at the time of degree completion. In 2016, at least one-half of the doctorate recipients in

Table 8.2 *Doctorate Recipients by Major Fields of Study and Sex*

All fields of study	1996 (%)	2001 (%)	2006 (%)	2011 (%)	2016 (%)
Male	59.9	56.0	54.9	53.6	54.0
Female	40.1	44.0	45.1	46.4	46.0
Life sciences					
Male	56.5	52.9	48.4	45.5	44.9
Female	43.5	47.1	51.6	54.5	55.1
Physical sciences and earth sciences					
Male	78.1	74.5	70.9	68.9	68.6
Female	21.9	25.5	29.1	31.1	31.4
Mathematics and computer sciences					
Male	81.7	76.6	74.7	75.1	75.8
Female	18.3	23.4	25.3	24.9	24.2
Psychology and social sciences					
Male	48.3	45.3	42.5	40.5	41.3
Female	51.7	54.7	57.5	59.5	58.7
Engineering					
Male	87.6	83.1	79.8	77.8	76.9
Female	12.4	16.9	20.2	22.2	23.1
Education					
Male	38.1	35.4	34.8	30.7	30.1
Female	61.9	64.6	65.2	69.3	69.9
Humanities and arts					
Male	51.6	51.2	50.3	49.2	48.1
Female	48.4	48.8	49.7	50.8	51.9
Other					
Male	59.4	55.2	51.4	47.8	50.1
Female	40.6	44.8	48.6	52.2	49.9

Source: NSF, NCSES (2018).

Note: Excludes respondents who did not report sex: 193 in 1996, 77 in 2001, 41 in 2006, 22 in 2011 and 10 in 2016.

life sciences, physical sciences and earth sciences, mathematics and computer sciences, and engineering completed their degrees at age 30 or younger. The majority of doctorate recipients in humanities and arts (61%) and other non-science and engineering fields (52%) earned their degrees between the ages of 31 and 40. Education doctorate recipients were more likely than recipients in other fields to be older: 40 per cent earned doctorates at age 41 or older and only 12 per cent received doctorates at age 30 or younger (NSF, NCSES 2018).

Primary Sources of Financial Support for Doctoral Recipients

The patterns of financial support for doctoral education vary by discipline and institution. Overall, among US citizens and permanent residents, the primary sources of support for doctoral education are teaching assistantships (for 20.4% of US citizens and residents), research assistantships or traineeships (for 23.5%), fellowships or grants (for 31.0%), students' own resources (for 20.5%), employers (for 4.4%) and other sources (for 0.2%). In contrast, for those with temporary visas, almost half (46.9%) had their primary support from research assistantships and traineeships, 23.6 per cent from teaching assistantships, 20.4 per cent from fellowships or grants, 3.2 per cent from their own resources, 0.4 per cent from employers and 5.5 per cent from other sources (NSF, NCSES 2018). International graduate students are typically supported by some form of funding (which is a different pattern than for undergraduates, who usually pay full tuition).

Large federal grants that provide research assistantships or trainee fellowships are typical in most science and engineering fields. These funding sources cover not only tuition and fees but also provide stipends. In 2016, 41 per cent of doctoral students in life sciences received fellowships or grants. Research assistantships were the leading source of support in physical sciences and earth sciences (49%), mathematics and computer sciences (37%) and engineering (57%). Teaching assistantships were the most common source for doctoral students in humanities and arts (40%). Doctoral students in education were the most likely to rely on their own resources, with 46 per cent reporting this as their primary source of support (NSF, NCSES 2018).

DOCTORAL EDUCATION IN SOCIETY: CONCERNS AND CRITIQUES

Over the past three decades, concern has been increasing about doctoral education in the United States. Much of this concern relates to the relationship—indeed, the perceived mismatch—between the needs of society, the interests of doctoral students, and the knowledge, skills and abilities provided by doctoral education as preparation for a career after graduate school. A statement by Golde and Dore (2001), in their report on doctoral education entitled *At Cross Purposes*, captured this: 'There is a three-way mismatch.... The training doctoral students receive is not what they want, nor does it prepare them for the jobs they take' (2001, 4–5). Those concerns have only gained momentum in the decade and a half since the publication of their report.

By the mid–1990s, a tight labour market had resulted in concern about doctoral students finding positions in basic research. Various national reports in the 1990s and then in the new century created a chorus of questions about the outcomes of doctoral education (Association of American Universities 1998; COSEPUP 1995; National Science Board 1997, 2003). These reports questioned whether graduate education in the United States was meeting national needs for scientific excellence and discovery, innovation, and national security and prosperity, and whether it was preparing students sufficiently for the demands of a changing societal context. Additionally, concerns about the quality of undergraduate education and its role in preparing engaged citizens and competent employees raised questions about the lack of preparation that doctoral students received as future teachers. Overall, discussion across institutions and at the national level argued that graduate education should prepare doctoral students for the actual landscape they would enter, a perspective leading to consideration of the range of skills needed for a variety of career pathways (American Chemical Society 2012; COSEPUP 1995, 2018; NIH 2012). At the same time as employers, governmental leaders and funders were raising such concerns, doctoral students themselves were expressing discontent with the nature of the graduate experience, including problems such as insufficient mentoring and inadequate information and guidance about career options and preparation (Austin 2006; Golde and Dore 2001; Wulff and Austin 2004). A closer analysis follows below of the specific critiques facing doctoral education in the United States.

Alignment with Career Pathways

A central question in doctoral education has been whether it is aligned with the realities of the labour market and adequately prepares students for the employment needs of the nation. A number of projects organized by national organizations, as well as initiatives at some universities, seek to document career outcomes, although efforts that involve one-time surveys, rather than longitudinal designs, are usually limited by not capturing shifts in careers over time. At present, however, detailed, reliable national information about the jobs obtained by PhD graduates is not available. Traditionally, doctoral education emphasized preparation for academic careers. In actuality, however, doctoral graduates enter a wide variety of careers, with academic work being just one option. Many doctoral graduates enter work in government, industry and non-profits, as well as academe. According to a recent report from the National Research Council (2012), more than 50 per cent of new doctoral recipients work outside academe. The most current data show that in 2015, 56 per cent of employed humanities PhDs were teaching at the postsecondary level as their principal job (AAA&S 2018, Indicator III–7a). According to the recent National Science Board report entitled *Embracing the Breadth of Career Opportunities for Sciences, Engineering, and Health (SEH) Doctorates*, across SEH fields, 57 per cent of graduates are employed outside the four-year academic institution (typically in business, industry and government) 10 to 14 years after receiving the doctorate (National Science Board 2013). Furthermore, just 18 per cent of employed STEM doctoral degree recipients were in tenure-track faculty positions within five years of graduation (NASEM 2018, 97). Overall, there has been a continuous decline in the percentage of doctoral recipients entering the professoriate since the 1970s. In fact, academic careers are becoming less attractive to many doctoral students, as they observe that permanent faculty positions are difficult to obtain. A steady shift away from tenure track to fixed term and part-time academic positions (Gappa, Austin, and Trice 2007) is occurring across the United States, so that even those who enter academe are likely to get less secure academic positions than in past decades. Firm figures on actual unemployment of PhDs are not available, but many of those not working in academe may be underemployed (i.e., not fully using their academic preparation).

Even for those specifically preparing for academic positions, that preparation typically is not fully aligned with the needs of current scholarly work or with the various teaching and research missions across the range of US universities and colleges. Historically, doctoral education has been designed to guide students to become deeply familiar with the scholarly traditions of their fields. They are supported in identifying specific questions not yet fully answered and in developing specialized skills and abilities needed to advance their fields. However, overspecialization can limit researchers' creativity in their research contributions, especially as interdisciplinarity becomes a key element of much groundbreaking scholarly work (COSEPUP 1995; NASEM 2018). Furthermore, moving into new areas or new kinds of employment over the years of a career can be challenging if the scholar is highly specialized.

Given the range of career paths that doctoral graduates will enter, the lack of attention to helping students develop the range of skills and abilities they will need has become a major concern (NASEM 2018). Typically, US doctoral education has emphasized the development of research skills, and until quite recently, most universities did not provide explicit career preparation around additional skills and abilities. Furthermore, faculty members sometimes have discouraged their doctoral advisees from explicitly preparing for teaching responsibilities or other career options. Fortunately, on many campuses, graduate deans and faculty members are becoming more aware of the importance of supporting students in examining a range of career options and highlighting ways to apply research-specific skills in other workplace situations.

Length of Time to Degree and Attrition

Students, higher education leaders and governmental leaders have been concerned about the length of time to complete a doctoral degree. Nettles and Miller (2006) reported that the mean time to completion in sciences, mathematics and social sciences is 5.75 years; in engineering, 4.74 and in humanities, 6.75. Particularly in the sciences and social sciences, additional time is required to complete a postdoctoral experience, lengthening even further the number of years of overall preparation, during which individuals are not fully employed in the workplace.

Attrition is a related concern, and over the past decade, it has been a high priority for deans of graduate schools. The overall figure for attrition from doctoral education is usually cited around 45–50 per cent (Levine 2000), although the figure is closer to 27–30 per cent for those who have completed coursework (Bowen and Rudenstine 1992). It is probably best for those who recognize, soon after the start of a doctoral programme, that their interests do not align with the programme and start making alternative plans. However, when a graduate student invests considerable time and resources into the doctoral experience, and then does not attain the degree, there are considerable negative consequences for the individual student, the institution and those who have provided funding. Possible reasons for attrition are discussed below.

Extent of 'Student-Centredness': Advising, Mentoring and Sense of Community

With its heavy emphasis on research productivity, doctoral education has been critiqued for providing insufficient attention to student needs (NASEM 2018). Regular and informed advising and mentoring are critical elements of meaningful and productive doctoral experiences. However, doctoral students have reported concerns about inconsistent advising practices, which can interfere with their satisfactory progress (Austin 2002; Austin and McDaniels 2006; NASEM 2018). When ineffective advising hampers degree progress or appropriate decisions about preparation experiences, it also contributes to concerns about adequate preparation and timely degree completion.

Doctoral students also have reported perceptions of a lack of community and support as they traverse the doctoral experience (Austin 2002; Lovitts 2004). Feeling a sense of isolation can thwart progress towards the degree and overall commitment to completing the degree process. Concerns about isolation can be especially strong for those in under-represented groups and for international students, for whom language differences may constitute a barrier to feeling part of a community. Both men and women in the current generation of doctoral students, overall, report interest in creating lives in which professional and personal responsibilities are experienced with a degree of balance. Observing their faculty members negotiate the pressures of busy academic careers can undermine the enthusiasm of doctoral students hoping to include both family responsibilities and active careers in their life plans (Mason, Goulden, and Frasch 2009).

A compelling critique of doctoral education is that it provides little opportunity for students to reflect on and discuss such issues. Of note also, in both research and teaching, doctoral students constitute critical components of the academic labour force. Doctoral students work as research assistants to advance the research mission and spur productivity, especially in the sciences and social sciences. In the humanities, doctoral students are the core of the professional staff who teach undergraduates. Thus, initiatives to address students' personal concerns have the possibility of running counter to an institution's immediate research productivity or teaching efforts. Institutional economic forces may supersede commitment to the professional development of doctoral students.

Challenges in Recruiting and Retaining a Talented and Diverse Student Body

Successful recruiting and retention of a highly able graduate student body is essential to maintaining the stature and reputation of US doctoral education. National organizations, such as NSF and many scholarly societies, emphasize that recruitment of highly talented doctoral students, characterized by intellectual vitality and creativity, requires explicit attention to recruiting and retaining women and members of URM groups. Yet the critiques of doctoral education, particularly questions about the viability of employment paths, may deter some talented individuals. In particular, aspects of the culture of doctoral education, especially in STEM fields that have only small percentages of women and URM faculty and graduate students, serve to undermine the ability to attract and retain women and those from historically URM groups (Antony and Taylor 2004; Taylor and Antony 2003; NASEM 2011). International graduate students also bring interesting and valued perspectives, but, as already discussed, may be at particular risk of feeling isolated in the graduate school environment. Thus, finding ways to ensure that US universities are safe, welcoming and supportive environments that attract a full array of highly talented students has been a major concern and commitment for institutional leaders.

RECENT RECOMMENDATIONS AND NEW DIRECTIONS

In response to these critiques of US doctoral education, institutional leaders, national organizations, professional societies and funders have been active in designing reforms, developing programmes and initiating changes. While the basic model for doctoral education continues, several key trends are apparent within universities and at the national level, as presented below.

Programmatic Changes to Prepare Doctoral Students for Multiple Career Options

As doctoral education in the United States is critiqued for not preparing students for the full array of career options they may undertake and the many abilities and skills they will need (even in the traditional academic role), national leaders, researchers, institutional leaders and faculty members are developing clearer ideas of what the learning outcomes of graduate education should include (Austin and McDaniels 2006; NASEM 2018; Weisbuch and Cassuto 2016). Concept papers are quite consistent in the abilities and skills that they identify: deep disciplinary knowledge; ability to work in interdisciplinary contexts; so-called 'soft skills' in communication, teamwork, conflict resolution, project management, ethics, entrepreneurial skills and leadership; teaching skills; and analytical skills and familiarity with new technologies, analytics and the implications of 'big data'.

Due to concerns about the time to degree completion, plans for ensuring a fuller range of learning outcomes usually avoid lengthening programme duration and emphasize clear communication to students about career options available to them (NASEM 2018; NIH 2012; Weisbuch and Cassuto 2016). Along with emphasizing opportunities for the development of transferrable skills, reformers encourage graduate programmes to make available to prospective students explicit information about the career pathways that graduates can consider, with attention to the range of roles and sectors, including academe, government, industry and corporations, and non-profits, where they might use the abilities and skills they develop. Similarly, interest is increasing in integrating internships and other applied experiences into doctoral programme curricula.

Other developments include the establishment of a variety of professional doctorates, such as in business administration, education, public health and social work. These degrees differ from traditional PhDs in their explicit focus on aligning areas of study with industry and workforce needs. Another difference is that these degrees usually focus on addressing real-world problems and give credit for work experience. A few universities, such as Georgetown University, offer a Doctor of Liberal Studies, featuring an interdisciplinary focus and attracting working professionals. In 2010, the Higher Learning Commission (HLC), one of six regional accreditors for higher education institutions in the United States, approved seven professional doctorate programmes. By 2015, the HLC approved 31 (CGS 2016). There has also been some growth of accredited online doctoral education programmes, which usually include a residency requirement (making them not exclusively online).

Increased Attention to Creating More 'Student-Centred' Learning Environments

The concerns of doctoral students, chronicled in research about their experiences, have been consistent for several decades: inadequate advising, perceptions of too little sense of community and worries about the feasibility of a realistic work-life balance (Austin 2002, 2006, 2010). The heavy emphasis on research productivity has typically left little opportunity for systematic preparation for teaching, and ignored the possible career interests of those not envisioning careers in a prestigious research university. At the national level, the National Academies have produced a report on *Graduate STEM Education for the 21st Century* that urges a shift away from emphasis primarily on the needs of universities and the research enterprise to 'one that is student centred, placing greater emphasis and focus on graduate students as individuals with diverse needs and challenges' (NASEM 2018, 3).

The tide has turned, however, and many universities are now taking proactive approaches to providing teaching preparation, developing institutional strategies to support students in managing stress and creating personally meaningful lives, and providing opportunities for students to explore a range of career options. At the heart of such a shift is growing attention to creating more inclusive and supportive higher education environments that welcome and support women and men who bring a range of personal characteristics, backgrounds, educational and professional goals, interests and needs. Specific plans, called for in the National Academies report and already underway at many universities, include opportunities for better mentoring (often with the use of multiple mentors to meet an individual's various needs), more regular and documented feedback from faculty to students, clearer paths to degree completion, explicit policies addressing harassment and inappropriate behaviour and provision of support for mental health issues (NASEM 2018). Evidence of university commitment to student well-being and success is becoming an important part of institutional excellence, and a key element as universities seek to attract and retain 'the best and the brightest' doctoral students.

Emergence of a Systems Approach to Strengthening Doctoral Education

While the basic structure of doctoral education is likely to continue, some changes are underway. The National Academies report asserts that changes 'will only be accomplished with a consistent and robust commitment from all stakeholders in the nation's scientific enterprise and in its STEM graduate education system' (NASEM 2018, 2). Consideration of who is involved in graduate education reform suggests that such system-wide reform is in process (although certainly not fully accomplished). The National Academies (2018) are using their stature to call for change, or, in the case of the NSF, to fund grants that address key challenges in doctoral education. Disciplinary communities, such as the American Sociological Association, the American Historical Association, the American Chemical Association and the Modern Languages Association, organize sessions on 'alternative' career paths at their scholarly meetings, discuss issues related to graduate education in their journals and have issued reports on doctoral education (MLA 2014). The chief academic officers of leading research universities have issued a statement urging greater doctoral education data transparency (Association of American Universities 2017). University graduate deans and their association, the Council of Graduate Schools, encourage innovation pertaining to career guidance, clarity of expectations and feedback, and assessment of learning outcomes (CGS 2010). Chairpersons encourage departmental curricular responsibility for students to develop diverse skills appropriate for their work-related goals. Researchers examine the experiences of doctoral students, the factors impacting their development and learning and the paths they follow into careers. While the reform movement is arguably still gaining momentum, with more time needed to know the outcomes, the key players in the overall system of graduate education are involved.

Examples of Reform Efforts

Over the past two decades, a number of initiatives have developed, often supported by funding from government agencies or private foundations, to support universities in implementing efforts to strengthen doctoral education. Such initiatives often address several reform goals simultaneously. This section highlights a few of the initiatives as examples of the considerable attention that funding agencies, higher education institutions and higher education leaders are directing towards improvements in US doctoral education. The first example illustrates efforts to support doctoral students' career development both within and beyond academe. Recognizing that the doctoral experience seldom includes systematic preparation for teaching responsibilities, the Center for the Integration of Research, Teaching and Learning (CIRTL) began 15 years ago with support from NSF. CIRTL's goal is to prepare STEM doctoral students to be not only strong researchers, but also excellent teachers. Participants learn to use research skills to improve their teaching, as well as how to implement evidence-based teaching practices. NIH has expectations for individual development plans for funded doctoral students (myIDP) and finances the Broadening Experiences in Scientific Training (BEST) consortium to support innovative approaches in biomedical doctoral education to prepare graduates for the robust biomedical, behavioural, social and clinical research enterprise. Career-focused initiatives have also developed in the humanities. The Responsive PhD programme of the Woodrow Wilson Foundation has encouraged doctoral programmes in the humanities to prepare participants for various career options beyond academe. The Mellon Foundation is using its influence to encourage new directions in graduate humanities education. Foundation-supported initiatives address pedagogical preparation, new approaches to interdisciplinary study, the use of media and other new tools in research, and opportunities in doctoral education for public engagement. While addressing career development goals, these and other programmes have addressed the needs of doctoral students for community and support. Additional targeted efforts, such as the Southern Regional Education Board (SREB)–State Doctoral Scholars Program, are dedicated to increasing the number of URM obtaining STEM doctoral degrees and preparing graduates to be successful university faculty members.

Other initiatives have focused on PhD programme tracking strategies and career outcomes data. For example, the Council of Graduate Schools, supported by funding from a national agency and a private foundation, has a project designed to help universities gather data on the career pathways of PhDs in STEM and the humanities (CGS 2015). The Coalition for Next Generation Life Sciences involves a group of nine leading research universities committed to adopting common reporting standards for doctoral students and postdoctoral researchers in the life sciences (Blank et al. 2017). The Association of American Universities Data Exchange facilitates the institutional exchange of data to support institutional decision-making. One of their projects has fostered the exchange of information related to PhD programmes and career outcomes. Collectively, these initiatives bring together a range of stakeholders and exemplify the growing commitment to strengthen the graduate experience. Of course, change is challenging and not always successful or sustainable—as illustrated by the short-lived effort to implement the Doctor of Arts degree, a teaching-focused graduate degree, back in the later decades of the 20th century.

LOOKING FORWARD

Even as doctoral education in the United States serves as a model for other nations, it is facing critiques and calls for reform at home. While commitment to preparing future scholars within deep disciplinary traditions and creating conditions for high-level research training are hallmarks of the US model, several issues are likely to remain at the forefront of national discussion for some time to come. First, consideration will continue to focus on approaches to doctoral education that will help students prepare for the full array of employment options in the academy and beyond. Such preparation needs to include both depth in areas of expertise and breadth in competencies needed in a constantly changing work environment. For example, the increasing role of technology must be factored into doctoral preparation; doctoral students should also become aware of the growing trend towards interdisciplinarity and team science and the need for flexibility, innovation and creativity.

Second, finding ways to attract, welcome and support highly able students, including women, domestic students from underrepresented groups and international students, will continue to be an important goal as universities strive to tap into a wide reservoir of talent to achieve the purposes of higher education. Efforts to support student well-being are likely to stay on the agenda also, including strategies to ensure that doctoral students have the mentoring and communities of support they need to succeed in their goals. Third, funding has become one of the greatest challenges for individual doctoral students and for the institutions offering doctoral programmes. The complex relationship between federal and private funding for research, institutional missions to teach undergraduates and priorities within doctoral education promises to remain a central and changing theme within the US doctoral context. Disciplinary differences in funding possibilities will continue to shape very different experiences and career choices for doctoral students, depending on their areas of study. Fourth, the importance of creating supportive environments where students receive clear mentoring, regular feedback and support for the personal and professional rigours of participating in doctoral work is reflected in innovative programmes and strategies emerging in a number of graduate schools. A key part of developing such supportive environments will mean preparing faculty for expanded roles as mentors and guides to career pathways. Aligning the faculty reward system so that these roles are valued will be a related challenge to instantiating a more 'student-centred approach' (NASEM 2018).

In addition to these policy and institutional initiatives, the quality of doctoral education in the US context will also benefit from robust research. Important questions will probe how students experience doctoral education as reform efforts gain momentum, the impact of explicit attention to career options during the graduate school experience and the nature of the doctoral experience for students from different identity groups. Additionally, supplementing some of the national databases with institutionally gathered information on the career paths of doctoral graduates will provide more nuanced understandings of the relationships between educational experience and employment outcomes. Doctoral education within the United States has earned the respect and admiration it receives. Yet the changing characteristics and expectations of the students, new advances in the sciences as well as in other disciplines, and the pressing needs of the nation and the broader society require a commitment to assessing strengths and identifying concerns. History provides a base, but continuing excellence demands adaptation and innovation.

REFERENCES

AAA&S. 2018. 'Humanities Indicators: Occupations of Humanities Ph.D.'s'. https://humanitiesindicators.org/content/indicatordoc.aspx?i=69 (accessed 10 December 2019).

Antony, J. S. 2002. 'Reexamining Doctoral Student Socialization and Professional Development: Moving Beyond Congruence and Assimilation Orientation'. In *Higher education: Handbook of Theory and Research*, Vol. XVII, edited by J. S. Smart, pp. 349–380). New York: Agathon Press.

Association of American Universities. 1998. 'Committee on Graduate Education: Report and Recommendations'. Washington, DC: Association of American Universities. https://www.aau.edu/key-issues/committee-graduate-education-reports-and-recommendations (accessed 10 December 2019).

————. 2017. 'Statement by AAU Chief Academic Officers on Doctoral Education Data Transparency'. Washington, DC. https://www.aau.edu/key-issues/statement-aau-chief-academic-officers-doctoral-education-data-transparency (accessed 10 December 2019).

American Chemical Society. 2012. 'Advancing Graduate Education in the Chemical Sciences'. https://www.acs.org/content/dam/acsorg/about/governance/acs-presidential-graduate-education-commission-full-report.pdf (accessed 10 December 2019).

Antony, James S., and Edward Taylor. 2004. 'Theories and Strategies of Academic Career Socialization: Improving Paths to the Professoriate for Black Graduate Students'. In *Paths to the Professoriate: Strategies for Enriching the Preparation of Future Faculty*, edited by Don H. Wulff and Ann E. Austin, 92–114. San Francisco, CA: Jossey-Bass.

Austin, Ann E. 2002. 'Preparing the Next Generation of Faculty: Graduate School as Socialization to the Academic Career'. *Journal of Higher Education* 73 (1): 94–122.

————. 2006. 'Preparing the Professoriate of the Future: Graduate Student Socialization for Faculty Roles'. In *Higher Education: Handbook of Theory and Research*, Vol. XXI, edited by John C. Smart, 397–456. Dordrecht: Springer.

————. 2010. 'Reform Efforts in STEM Doctoral Education: Strengthening Preparation for Scholarly Careers'. In *Higher Education: Handbook of Theory and Research*, edited by John C. Smart, 91–128. London: Springer.

Austin, Ann E., and Melissa McDaniels. 2006. 'Preparing the Professoriate of the Future: Graduate Student Socialization for Faculty Roles'. In *Higher Education: Handbook of Theory and Research*, Vol. XXI, edited by John C. Smart, 397–456. Dordrecht: Springer.

Blank, Rebecca, Ronald J. Daniels, Gary Gilliand, Amy Gutman, Samuel Hawgood, Freeman A. Hrabowski, Martha E. Pollack, Vincent Price, L. Rafael Reif, and Mark S. Schlissel. 2017. 'A New Data Effort to Inform Career Choices in Biomedicine'. *Science* 358 (6369): 1388–1389.

Bowen, William G., and Neil L. Rudenstine. 1992. *In Pursuit of the Ph.D.* Princeton, NJ: Princeton University Press.

Brubacher, John S., and Willis Rudy. 1990. *Higher Education in Transition: A History of American Colleges and Universities*. 4th ed. New York, NY: Routledge.

Committee on Science, Engineering, and Public Policy (COSEPUP). 1995. *Reshaping the Graduate Education of Scientists and Engineers*. Washington, DC: National Academies of Sciences, National Academy of Engineering, and Institute of Medicine, National Academy Press. http://www.nap.edu/read/4935/chapter/1 (accessed 19 February 2020).

Council of Graduate Schools and Educational Testing Service (CGS). 2010. *The Path Forward: The Future of Graduate Education in the United States*. Report from the Commission on the Future of Graduate Education in the United States. Princeton, NJ: Educational Testing Service. http://www.fgereport.org/rsc/pdf/CFGE_report.pdf (accessed 10 December 2019).

CGS. 2015. *Understanding PhD Career Pathways for Program Improvement.* Washington, DC. https://cgsnet.org/understanding-phd-career-pathways-program-improvement-0 (accessed 17 February 2020).

———. 2016. *Tenth Annual Strategic Leaders Global Summit on Graduate Education.* Washington, DC. https://cgsnet.org/ckfinder/userfiles/files/2016%20Global%20Summit%20BookletFinal.pdf (accessed 10 December 2019).

Gappa, Judith M., Ann E. Austin, and Andrea G. Trice. 2007. *Rethinking Faculty Work: Higher Education's Strategic Imperative.* San Francisco, CA: Jossey-Bass.

Golde, Chris M., and Tim M. Dore. 2001. *At Cross Purposes: What the Experiences of Today's Doctoral Students Reveal about Doctoral Education.* Philadelphia: Pew Charitable Trusts.

Gumport, Patricia J. 2005. 'Graduate Education and Research: Interdependence and Strain'. In *American Higher Education in the Twenty-First Century: Social, Political, and Economic Challenges,* edited by Philip G. Altbach, Robert O. Berdahl, and Patricia J. Gumport, 425–461. 2nd ed. Baltimore, MD: The Johns Hopkins University Press.

Levine, Arthur A. 2000. *Higher Education at a Crossroads.* Earl Pullias Lecture in Higher Education. Los Angeles, CA: Center for Higher Education Policy Analysis, Rossier School of Education, University of Southern California.

Lovitts, Barbara E. 2004. 'Research on the Structure and Process of Graduate Education: Retaining Students'. In *Paths to the Professoriate: Strategies for Enriching the Preparation of Future Faculty,* edited by Don H. Wulff and Ann E. Austin, 115–136. San Francisco, CA: Jossey-Bass.

Mason, Mary Ann, Marc Goulden, and K. Frasch. 2009. 'Why Graduate Students Reject the Fast Track'. *Academe* 95 (1): 11–17.

Modern Language Association of American (MLA). *Report of the MLA Task Force on Doctoral Study in Modern Language and Literature.* https://www.mla.org/content/download/25437/1164354/taskforcedocstudy2014.pdf (accessed 19 February 2020).

National Academies of Sciences, National Academy of Engineering, and Institute of Medicine (NASEM). 2011. *Expanding Underrepresented Minority Participation: America's Science and Technology Talent at the Crossroads.* Washington, DC. The National Academies Press. Doi: 10.17226/12984. https://sites.nationalacademies.org/PGA/PGA_084658 (accessed 19 February 2020).

———. 2018. *Graduate STEM education for the 21st Century.* Washington, DC: The National Academies Press. doi:10.17226/25038.

National Institutes of Health (NIH). 2012. *Biomedical Research Workforce Working Group Report.* https://acd.od.nih.gov/documents/reports/Biomedical_research_wgreport.pdf (accessed 17 February 2020).

National Research Council. 2012. *Research Universities and the Future of America: Ten Breakthrough Actions Vital to Our Nation's Prosperity and Security.* Washington, DC: The National Academies Press. doi:10.17226/13396.

———. 2015. *Enhancing the Effectiveness of Team Science.* Washington, DC: The National Academies Press. doi:10.17226/19007.

National Science Board. 1997. *The Federal Role in Science and Engineering Graduate and Postdoctoral Education* (NSB 97–235). https://www.nsf.gov/nsb/documents/1997/nsb97235/nsb97235.pdf (accessed 10 December 2019).

National Science Board. 2003. *The Science and Engineering Workforce: Realizing America's Potential*. https://www.nsf.gov/nsb/documents/2003/nsb0369/nsb0369.pdf (accessed 10 December 2019).

———. 2013. *Embracing the Breadth of Career Opportunities for Sciences, Engineering, and Health (SEH) Doctorates*. https://www.nsf.gov/nsb/sei/infographic2/?yr=2013&fd=All%20SEH%20Fields&cs=None#main (accessed 10 December 2019).

National Science Foundation, National Center for Science and Engineering Statistics (NSF, NCSES). 2018. *Doctorate Recipients from U.S. Universities: 2016*. Special Report NSF 18–304. Alexandria, VA. https://www.nsf.gov/statistics/2018/nsf18304/static/report/nsf18304-report.pdf (accessed 17 February 2020).

Nettles, Michael T., and Catherine M. Millett. 2006. *Three Magic Letters: Getting to Ph.D.* Baltimore, MD: The Johns Hopkins University Press.

Rudolph, Frederick. 1990. *The American College and University: A History*. Athens: University of Georgia Press.

Taylor, Edward, and James S. Antony. 2003. 'Stereotype Threat Reduction and Wise Schooling: Towards Successful Socialization of African American Doctoral Students in Education'. *Journal of Negro Education* 69 (3): 184–198.

Thelin, John R. 2011. *A History of American Higher Education*. 2nd ed. Baltimore, MD: The Johns Hopkins University Press.

The Modern Language Association of America. 2014. *Report of the MLA Task Force on Doctoral Study in Modern Language and Literature*. https://www.mla.org/content/download/25438/1164362/execsumtaskforcedocstudy.pdf (accessed 10 December 2019).

Tierney, William G., and Robert A. Rhoads. 1994. *Enhancing Promotion, Tenure and Beyond: Faculty Socialization as a Cultural Process*. ASHE-ERIC Higher Education Report No. 6. Washington, DC: The George Washington University, School of Education and Human Development.

Veysey, Laurence R. 1965. *The Emergence of the American University*. Chicago, IL: The University of Chicago Press.

Weidman, John C., D. J. Twale, and E. L. Stein. 2001. *Socialization of Graduate and Professional Students in Higher Education—A Perilous Passage?* ASHE-ERIC Higher Education Report No. 28 (3). Washington, DC: The George Washington University, School of Education and Human Development.

Wulff, Donald H., and Ann E. Austin, eds. 2004. *Paths to the Professoriate: Strategies for Enriching the Preparation of Future Faculty*. San Francisco, CA: Jossey-Bass.

Weisbuch, R., and Cassuto, L. 2016. 'Reforming Doctoral Education, 1990–2015: Recent Initiatives and Future Prospects'. A Report Submitted to the Andrew W. Mellon Foundation. https://mellon.org/media/filer_public/35/32/3532f16c-20c4-4213-805d-356f85251a98/report-on-doctoral-education-reform_june-2016.pdf (accessed 17 February 2020).

PART IV

Africa

Chapter 9

Challenges of Development of Doctoral Education in Africa

Ayenachew A. Woldegiyorgis

Although it is fair to say that Africa is a latecomer to the world of modern higher education (Hayward and Ncayiyana 2014), not to mention the competitive arenas of the global knowledge economy, the continent is increasingly focused on developing, expanding and improving doctoral education (Harle 2013a). This stems from the growing realization that countries with a better stock of highly educated people can achieve faster economic growth, become more competitive and better sustain socio-economic development (World Bank 2012). Doctoral education pushes the frontiers of human thinking through research and scientific enquiry, and thus is central to this endeavour (Golde and Walker 2006).

In Africa, higher education enrolment is far behind the world average, and the numbers are even worse when it comes to graduate programmes. Hayward and Ncayiyana (2014, 183) describe the state of African graduate education as 'continuing to be in crisis'. This is compounded by the absence of complete data on key indicators in doctoral education (Obamba 2017). Hayward and Ncayiyana (2014) did manage to collect data on doctoral enrolment in 19 Sub-Saharan African countries in 2013. They estimated the total number of doctoral students in those countries to be 18,872. However, one country alone, South Africa, accounted for 68 per cent of that enrolment.

At a 2012 conference, experts from English, French and Portuguese-speaking African countries noted considerable overlaps in the aspirations of academic institutions across the region, and the challenges they face in providing doctoral education. Stark differences also exist, owing to each African country's own colonial history and each educational institution's roots (IAU and ACUP 2012). Therefore, research on doctoral education in Africa should look at both regional factors and factors affecting specific countries.

This chapter will focus on Sub-Saharan Africa, with the exception of South Africa, which is discussed in a separate chapter of this book. It will use examples from across the region to explore major trends affecting the development of doctoral education across the continent. Capacity gaps will be noted, as will the contributions and limitations of donor-driven collaborations as a way of addressing those gaps. The chapter will also look at the viability of regional collaborations in addressing common challenges and looking ahead to the future.

A BRIEF HISTORICAL CONTEXT

Africa's colonial and postcolonial relationships with European countries have, in the words of Lulat (2005, 42), 'marked a permanent rupture' on the content, organization and management of higher education in Africa. Graduate education is one of the areas where this is strongly evident (Quintana and Calvet 2012), both explicitly and implicitly. Many Sub-Saharan African countries created their first universities as European colonial rule dwindled after the Second World War. Many of these institutions were originally established as extensions of universities in the colonizing countries (Obanya 1999). Gradually these institutions gained more autonomy, finally achieving full university status after independence. Although modelled after their European counterparts, the institutions focused initially on vocational and clerical training, and later on professional training for teachers, lawyers, doctors, engineers, etc. (Lulat 2005). Graduate education was peripheral.

From the beginning, African universities were constrained by the lack of a critical mass of home-grown scholars, and so were forced to rely on expatriate faculty primarily from former colonial countries (Hayward and Ncayiyana 2014). As African universities emerged and grew, the effort to meet faculty requirements, both in number and in qualifications, continued for decades. Mkandawire (1995) captured this process by identifying three generations of African academics. The first generation are those who were sent abroad to be educated, mainly in universities in Europe and the United States. The impetus was twofold. Newly independent African nations needed help with capacity building, and the West, spurred in large part by Cold War competition, wanted to create strong relationships within Africa. Most of this first generation returned home to take key teaching and administrative positions that pushed institutional expansion and furthered efforts at capacity building.

The second generation of scholars obtained their undergraduate education at national universities in Africa, and then pursued graduate education abroad. Most of them, however, did not return to their respective countries. As a result, the expansion of African universities, and especially the effort to find qualified faculty, met with serious challenges. The third generation of scholars was trained at both the undergraduate and graduate levels in African universities. The circumstances, however, were difficult. From the 1970s through the 1990s, repressive regimes and political instability exacerbated brain drain (Mkandawire 1995), while economic crises and the deprioritization of higher education in resource allocation resulted in the dilapidation of universities across Africa. Therefore, the later two generations of academics were forced to study and work under extremely difficult circumstances (Akuffo et al. 2014), which ultimately resulted in severely depleted institutional capacity.

These historical developments have had major consequences on the development of graduate education and research, and hence on doctoral education. Despite modest success in 'Africanizing' themselves (Obanya 1999), universities remain challenged in establishing themselves as institutions that research African problems and generate African knowledge. One main reason for this is that they were established by Europeans and modelled on European institutions. As such, their vision and mission were set to match those of European institutions and had little to do with African realities (Hayward and Ncayiyana 2014). Second, fledgling African universities were staffed mainly by European expatriates, and Africans educated abroad, meaning curricula and institutional traditions were inspired by European universities instead of being home grown. Third, African universities have traditionally focused on vocational and professional training at the expense of a deeper engagement with, and systematic interrogation of, African knowledge.

African scholarly perceptions about knowledge—what is valuable and should be the subject of research—have been shaped by the forces discussed above. It is not unheard of for African scholars to write their PhD dissertations on topics of European history, literature and the like, although Szanton and Manyika (2002) observed that is more common in francophone Africa. The attempt to develop and teach African knowledge in African ways is outweighed by the desire to meet 'global standards'. As Backhouse (2009, 31) puts it: 'the need for validation by the metropoles persists and is supported by higher education policies that insist on publication in "overseas" journals, the use of "overseas" examiners and the benchmarking of institutions against those in Europe'.

Historical factors have also constrained the institutional capacity of African universities to offer doctoral education. Graduate studies were not considered important in the early development of African universities. When graduate education was deemed necessary, African students were sent abroad for training, and then returned to a small number of jobs in the public sector. African governments, as well as higher education institutions, failed to foresee the need and value of research (Hayward and Ncayiyana 2014). Add to this decades of political instability, economic crises, hostile relations between academia and political power (Mkandawire 1995), and the lack of an industrial base that could support commercial research. The result was a dearth of resources for African higher education in general and graduate research in particular. Discussions about doctoral education in Africa have tended to take place 'within a discourse of crisis, deficit and uncertainty' (Obamba 2017, 13).

A NEW DAWN FOR DOCTORAL EDUCATION IN AFRICA

In the past two decades, there have been signs of positive change. Increasingly, internal and external stakeholders have become more interested in the development of doctoral education in Africa. As a result, there have been changes in the design, resourcing and management of doctoral education. Viewed within the context of broader global changes, the following major trends can help explain these developments.

Impetus of the Knowledge Economy

Despite their levels of development, many countries around the world have come to see knowledge and innovation as paths to economic and social development (Jørgensen 2012). African countries are no different, and in fact, for the past 20 years, the continent has seen some of the fastest growing economies in the world. This growth, however, has mainly been achieved through increased exports of natural resources, which hardly translates into commensurate social development (Hayward and Ncayiyana 2014).

Against this backdrop, African countries are realizing that doctoral-level academic research and professional training are vital. In its 'Agenda 2063', the African Union acknowledged the importance of a strategy focused on the advancement of knowledge, innovation and technology, particularly in certain priority areas (Friesenhahn 2014). Doctoral education and research are gaining traction as the means to ensure the development of human capital in agriculture, health, information technology, energy, etc. African countries are increasing investment and committing themselves to reforming and expanding doctoral programmes as a way of carrying themselves forward in global knowledge economy.

Massification of Higher Education

Following global trends, African higher education has been expanding in the past few decades. A growing middle class, success in expanding lower level education and the notion that tertiary education is a requirement for personal development have, along with other factors, contributed to a considerable increase in higher education enrolment (Harle 2013b). African universities are trying to keep up with this increased demand. The overwhelming growth has resulted in a higher ratio of students to faculty, which jeopardizes quality, overburdens academics and ultimately exacerbates brain drain (Tettey 2009). In short, African universities need more well-qualified faculty and staff, and that means expanding graduate education. Many countries are trying. Ethiopia, for instance, has set a target of producing 5,000 PhD graduates as part of a five-year plan ending in 2020 (Desie and Tefera 2017). The country hopes to achieve this not only through expanding doctoral programmes, but through scholarships for study abroad and distance education as well.

In a study looking at eight flagship universities across Africa, Bunting, Cloete, and van Schalkwyk (2014) noted that enrolment in doctoral programmes has increased at an average annual rate of 8 per cent between 2001 and 2011. The growth was considerably higher in some institutions. The University of Ghana and Makerere University in Uganda had 472 per cent and 2,165 per cent increases, respectively. However, the starting point for these institutions was very low, with only 67 and 26 doctoral students, respectively, in 2001.

Need for Capacity-building

Doctoral education is expected to train not only future academics but also public policy experts, entrepreneurs, business leaders, technocrats and other key players in economic and social development (Friesenhahn 2014). Universities are also increasingly absorbing doctoral graduates into senior research and management positions in order to strengthen their own capacity. For instance, Akuffo et al. (2014) have noted how graduates from a collaborative doctoral programme between Makerere

University and the Swedish International Development Cooperation Agency (SIDA) have taken key leadership positions in the university as well as in the Ugandan ministry of health. Cross and Backhouse (2014) found similar developments in South Africa.

Growing Focus on the Labour Market

Universities in Africa have traditionally trained graduates for work in the public sector, giving little attention to private sector needs in determining the content of their programmes and the method of delivery. This disengagement with the employment market, Friesenhahn (2014) has claimed, extends to graduate programmes. Indeed, doctoral education in Africa is predominantly for those who are in, or seek to join, the academic world as a career. Stackhouse and Harle (2014), for example, found that 71 per cent of African doctoral students studying on the continent had aspirations of working in academic and research positions after completing their programmes. However, there is a growing realization that doctoral graduates have to be prepared for work outside of academia as well. In an International Association of Universities (IAU) study (2011), Kenya's Kenyatta University is singled out for its exceptional record in placing top graduates in jobs outside of the academy. This, along with the recent launch of a professional doctoral programme in Ghana (Owusu-Manu et al. 2015), demonstrates that labour market conditions will be, if they are not already, a driving force in the development of doctoral education on the continent.

VARIATIONS IN DOCTORAL EDUCATION

Across countries and institutions, African doctoral programmes vary in several respects. These include duration of the programme, level of formal structure in course offerings and research, requirements for graduation, forms of evaluation, arrangements for supervision and organization in cohorts (Backhouse 2009; IAU 2011). Historical factors play a major role in these differences, but so do resource availability, size of enrolment and supervisory capacity. Institutions also have different views on the purpose of doctoral education (Backhouse 2009).

The IAU's 2011 study looked, in part, at the duration of doctoral programmes at prominent universities in six African countries. Four universities in the study—Université de Douala (Cameroon), Université Gaston Berger de Saint-Louis (Sénégal), University of Ilorin (Nigeria) and Université des Sciences et Technologies du Bénin—require at least three years to complete a doctoral degree, while the National University of Rwanda and Kenyatta University require minimum of four and two years, respectively. While independent research is always central to the doctoral programme, the required duration of the research period varies from one semester to two years, depending on whether the doctoral programme is by research only or if it involves coursework (IAU 2011).

Besides producing a thesis or dissertation, the requirements for graduation also vary to a certain extent. Ayiro and Sang (2011) reported that the University of Cape Town (UCT; South Africa), Université des Sciences et Technologies du Bénin and Addis Ababa University (Ethiopia) require an oral defence of the thesis before a doctoral degree is awarded. Makerere University and Dar-es-Salaam University (Tanzania) put emphasis on both the thesis and viva voce. The University of Ghana requires candidates to pass a qualifying examination as well as an oral examination of the thesis. At the National University of Rwanda, the thesis has to be published.

A study by the British Council and German Academic Exchange (DAAD; 2018) that covered six countries across Africa—Ethiopia, Ghana, Kenya, Nigeria, Senegal and South Africa—concluded that the typical structure of a doctoral programme reflects the doctorate-by-research model, rather than the taught doctorate model common in North America. Doctoral research training courses mainly focus on methodological preparations aimed at enabling the candidate to undertake independent research (IAU 2011). Nonetheless, this structure is seen to have limitations, and there are moves to incorporate more coursework into African doctoral programmes.

One development that speaks to the efforts of universities to respond to market demands is the emergence of profession-oriented doctoral programmes. While it is increasingly a popular model elsewhere, professional doctoral training is uncommon in Africa. One rare example is the Centre for Doctoral Training in Business, Enterprise and Professional Studies (CDT–BEPS) at Kwame Nkrumah University of Science and Technology (KNUST) in Ghana. Documenting the case of CDT–BEPS, Owusu-Manu et al. (2015) have highlighted the five areas of skills development that make the programme distinct from the taught or by-research models: business, research, creativity, transferability and evidential learning (an industry-oriented research approach that culminates in the production of a thesis).

Another ongoing discussion with respect to the organization of doctoral education in Africa is the use of the PhD-by-publication model. Although it varies by discipline and by institution, this model requires the production of published or publishable articles based on the doctoral research of the candidate as the requirement for graduation (Robins and Kanowski 2008). Limiting their argument to doctoral degrees in science and technology, Asongu and Nwachukwu (2018) make the case that the PhD by publication is of considerable advantage in the African context. The authors claim that if PhD by publication is viewed as a means for innovation and technology transfer, it is a far more suitable vehicle than the traditional thesis in promoting knowledge exchange between industrial and academic researchers and in facilitating the conversion of scientific know-how into economically sound innovation.

Teferra (2015), on the other hand, is sceptical about the PhD-by-publication model. Although he focuses on South Africa, his arguments can be applied more broadly. First, he says, the importance of engaging a student in a rigorous research process resulting in a PhD dissertation should not be downplayed. It is, in fact, critical to nurturing a capable academic researcher or professional. Second, the mere publication of an article does not prove that the work was indeed undertaken by the author, nor does it guarantee the quality of the work. There are service providers who, for a fee, will do everything a doctoral student is expected to do. There are also predatory journals that, for a fee, will publish a manuscript regardless of its quality.

One variant of doctoral education that is particularly pertinent to the African context is what is called the 'sandwich model'. Due to limitations in both resources and supervisory capacity at African universities, many students travelled to high-income countries to undertake their doctoral studies. This was unsustainable, not only because it was expensive but also because an increasing number of students opted not to return after completing their programmes (Sadlak 2004). The sandwich model—so called because the training is 'sandwiched' between the home institution and a partner abroad (Fallenius 1996, 102)—is a response to this problem. The student does his/her fieldwork in the home country, while the partner institution arranges for the use of libraries and other scientific facilities. The coursework and supervision are done jointly at both institutions (Akuffo et al. 2014; Fallenius 1996). Besides its overall advantages for creating in-house research capacity at African institutions, the sandwich model is especially suitable for developing junior faculty. Students doing fieldwork can teach while they are at their home institution, thus reducing the burden on other faculty. Moreover, sandwich programmes, compared with full-time study abroad programmes, are more suitable for older African doctoral students with family commitments (Stackhouse and Harle 2014). Szanton and Manyika (2002) have also noted that sandwich programmes offer opportunities for African scholars to meet potential future collaborators as well as the chance for students to bring back new ideas to their home institutions, thereby reducing intellectual inbreeding. Sandwich programmes are not without issues, however. They are often donor-financed, and therefore tend to be driven by the interests of the better-resourced partner institution and/or donor (Gaillard 1994). This power imbalance can be seen most clearly in the social sciences, where African doctoral students become mere data collectors, rather than partners who meaningfully participate in the conceptualization and analysis of research projects (Szanton and Manyika 2002). Nonetheless, the sandwich model continues to be widely utilized. (Akuffo et al. 2014; Cross and Backhouse 2014; Kassam et al. 2009; Manabe et al. 2011).

COLLABORATION IN DOCTORAL EDUCATION

The number of international collaborations between African universities and their counterparts around the world has increased since the start of the century. International organizations such as the World Bank and the United Nations have helped spur this, although they were late to recognize the potential of higher education and graduate studies in accelerating economic development in African countries (Teferra 2016; Woldegiyorgis 2014). As part of this shift, collaborations in doctoral education are now being pursued and supported by national governments, development agencies, supranational organizations, non-profit organizations, private foundations and higher education institutions.

Collaborations and external funding for doctoral education in Africa often take the form of joint research and training. The idea is to increase the stock of doctoral graduates, which in turn improves the institutional capacity of African universities (British Academy and the Association of Commonwealth Universities [ACU] 2011). This may take the form of fully funded scholarships at African or foreign universities, split-site or sandwich programmes, collaborative doctoral programmes, sponsoring doctoral students/projects within a broader aid programme, direct support to doctoral students or small grants for either fieldwork or some other component of doctoral study.

Enhancing the quality of doctoral education is another common focus, although it is not equally emphasized. Support of this type can include increasing access to facilities, exchange of subject experts or students, conducting research training, joint workshops, collaborative research projects and training on dissertation supervision. The Carnegie Corporation's Next Generation of African Academics is one example that focuses on strengthening the quality of doctoral supervision. Other examples include capacity-building training programmes for mid-career researchers led by Nuffic, the Dutch organization for international education, and the aforementioned SIDA (British Council and DAAD 2018).

International collaborations and external support have contributed in different ways to the development of doctoral education on the African continent. Beyond the overarching capacity development for research and doctoral education, specific areas of improvement include: increased enrolment, improved capacity and quality in research skills and management, formation of lasting networks of experts across countries, increased dissemination of research results, introduction and cultivation of innovative approaches in the design and management of doctoral programmes, improved collaboration among African institutions and researchers, and the showcasing of innovative approaches to create a set of best practices (Jones, Bailey, and Lyytikainen 2007; Molla and Cuthbert 2016).

Meanwhile, there are limitations to such collaborations. The inequality in terms of resources and expertise often creates a power imbalance that gives the upper hand to non-African partners in determining the research agenda and the details of management (Akuffo et al. 2014). Collaborations started with insufficient understanding of the research capacity gap at African universities can undermine the possibility for any meaningful effect on the improvement of doctoral education (Bates et al. 2011). Other limitations include: too much focus on the operation of programmes, rather than on the generation of knowledge or creation of capacity; shallow connections between projects to improve doctoral programmes and existing research centres; inefficiency in knowledge transfer; less emphasis on collaborative teaching and weaknesses in monitoring and evaluation (Akuffo et al. 2014; Harle 2010; Jones, Bailey, and Lyytikainen 2007; Quintana and Calvet 2012).

Even with the caveats mentioned above, collaboration in research and graduate education is mutually beneficial overall. As Jørgensen (2012) noted, European universities engage in collaborations in other regions to further their own research agendas; they gain access to certain geographic features, populations or biodiversity that they otherwise could not have. In so doing, they also acknowledge the need for helping their African partners, if for no other reason than the sustainability of their own research.

REGIONAL COLLABORATION

Partnerships between African universities is an emerging trend that deserves recognition. Often financed by external sources or involving universities from other parts of the globe, such collaborations often take the form of North–South–South partnerships. There are also cases of South–South partnerships, although they are limited in number and often restricted to clusters, such as former French colonies, former

British colonies or predominantly Arab countries in North Africa (Quintana and Calvet 2012).

African universities are acknowledging that they lack the capacity to individually develop expertise, leading them to forge regional and sub-regional partnerships aimed at strengthening capacity in research and training (Cross and Backhouse 2014; Tettey 2009). In a study conducted by the Southern African Regional Universities Association (SARUA), 90 per cent of the institutions involved said they were interested in regional capacity-building initiatives in doctoral training and supervision (MacGregor 2013a). Across the continent, there are numerous examples of successful regional and sub-regional collaborations. Established in 1995, the Universities Science, Humanities, Law and Engineering Partnerships in Africa (USHEPiA) at UCT is a collaborative teaching programme targeting junior staff members at participating universities, namely the universities of Botswana, Dar es Salaam, Nairobi, Zambia, Zimbabwe, Makerere University and Kenyatta University. USHEPiA not only allows students from these universities to earn joint degrees with UCT, but also supports UCT faculty wishing to spend time at partner universities developing supervisory skills (Backhouse 2009).

Another example is the arrangement between the University of South Africa (UNISA) and the government of Ethiopia. In 2008, in order to meet the demands of its rapidly expanding higher education sector, the Ethiopian government entered into an agreement with UNISA, which allowed the latter to launch its distance learning graduate programme. UNISA also runs face-to-face research workshops for graduate students, training hundreds of junior university teachers (Molla and Cuthbert 2016). Obamba (2017) has also documented other prominent initiatives that support doctoral education, including the African Economic Research Consortium (AERC), the Consortium for Advanced Research Training in Africa (CARTA), the Regional Universities Forum for Capacity Building in Agriculture (RUFORUM), the African Centers of Excellence Program II (ACE II) and the Regional Initiative for Science and Education (RISE).

Referring specifically to the case of USHEPiA, Mouton (2010) noted that one critical factor in the programme's success was the consultations that took place before the initiative began. This enabled the identification of common interests among the participating institutions and led to the development of a memorandum of understanding that guided the work to come. Good planning also helped the Promoting Excellence in PhD Research Programmes in East Africa project. Three universities in East Africa and the University of Copenhagen in Denmark began by outlining the five common features of doctoral programmes in the East African universities as the basis for the subsequent action plan (Timm 2011). The project succeeded in developing rules and regulations for doctoral programmes, updating training manuals for courses and training hundreds of supervisors. In general, though, financial, administrative, supervisory and institutional challenges are to be expected in such collaborations. That is why close monitoring and evaluation procedures, not to mention continuous consultations, are required to effectively address those challenges (Jones, Bailey, and Lyytikainen 2007; Mouton 2010).

University associations, whether regional or thematic, also need due acknowledgement. As shown above, thematic consortiums and sub-regional university associations, such as SARUA in Southern Africa, the Inter-University Council for East Africa (IUCEA) and the Association of West Africa Universities (AWAU), as well as the continental body, the Association of African Universities (AAU), are instrumental in facilitating collaborations, and need to be central to this discussion. A promising development in this regard is the emergence of the African Research Universities Alliance (ARUA). Established in 2015, and currently constituting 16 top-tier universities from 9 countries across the continent, ARUA aims to harness the comparative strengths of its member institutions towards the goal of integrating Africa into the competitive global knowledge economy, as stipulated in the African Union's 'Agenda 2063' (Obamba 2017). ARUA pursues that mission by supporting capacity building in research and doctoral education and promoting collaboration among partner universities and their global counterparts (McGregor 2015). As of 2018, it has also organized centres of excellence in seven thematic areas.

Another innovative approach in structuring collaborations, the 'hub-and-spokes' model, is also sparking interest across the continent. Each hub is a university with demonstrated strength in a particular field, while the spokes attached to it are institutions that could use more support and training (MacGregor 2013a; Obamba 2017). Depending on the relative strengths of the institutions involved, a university that is a hub for one subject area may be a spoke in another. This arrangement requires distinguishing the roles of participating institutions, creating mechanisms for the exchange of expertise and students and sharing resources in order to build each institution's capacity. An example of this model is the Africa Centres of Excellence (ACE) programme funded by the World Bank. Facilitated by AAU, ACE supports regional centres of excellence at different institutions in participating countries. The second phase of ACE, for instance, involves the establishment of 23 centres of excellence in 15 universities across 8 countries in Eastern and Southern Africa (World Bank 2015). This model is advantageous because it provides students easier access to a centre of excellence in their own region. It also improves resource efficiency through economies of scale and the reduction of redundancy, particularly for expensive facilities and equipment (MacGregor 2013a). On the other hand, institutional differences among participants, in terms of governance, culture, the gathering and processing of information, etc., could pose difficulties in making the 'hub-and-spokes' model work effectively.

CHALLENGES

Doctoral programmes in Africa share similar challenges to those in other parts of the world (Mutula 2009). It is also true that many of those challenges are shared by institutions across the African continent. While the specifics may vary, the following outline some of the commonalities.

Quality

The overall quality of education in Africa is a major issue, but the quality of doctoral education is particularly problematic and poses a serious challenge for at least two reasons. First, problems with the quality of doctoral education have not been given the same attention as problems at other educational levels. As graduate education rapidly expanded, the concern for quality was not equally pursued (Desie and Tefera 2017), allowing the problems to grow deeper and wider. Second, because doctoral education is a more flexible and personalized learning process, the absence of formal standards such as criteria for grading, benchmarks for becoming an independent researcher and guidelines from quality assurance agencies makes it difficult to measure success (Ayiro and Sang 2011; Khodabocus 2016).

Multiple factors are reported as causes for the poor quality of doctoral education in Africa. These include: students who are juggling their studies with full-time jobs and families, poorly prepared students, weak research practices of supervisors, limitations in the selection processes and the political motives for programme expansion that often undermine sufficient preparation. Poor scientific facilities and the absence of clear institutional quality guidelines have also been cited (Ayiro and Sang 2011; Desie and Tefera 2017; Friesenhahn 2014; IAU 2011; Muriisa 2015; Stackhouse and Harle 2014).

Institutional Capacity

Jones, Bailey, and Lyytikainen (2007) argue that limited capacity is a standing problem inhibiting research and graduate education. For their part, Colenbrander et al. (2015) note that institutional shortcomings can be explained by over centralization, low accountability (particularly for supervisors), poor infrastructure and low-impact research engagement.

Numerous authors have shown challenges related to capacity (Ayiro and Sang 2011; Garwe 2015; Molla and Cuthbert 2016; Obamba 2017; Stackhouse and Harle 2014; Tettey 2010). The findings are perhaps best captured by Bates et al. (2011, 5) in their summary of capacity gaps in African doctoral programmes. These include: incomplete supporting documentation such as policies, regulations and handbooks; lack of suitably qualified academic faculty with experience in supervising doctoral students; inadequate resources (such as books, journals, computers and Internet access) to support doctoral programmes; lack of dedicated desk space for doctoral students and very little formal opportunity for mutual support; lack of a formal induction programme to make students aware of requirements or the availability of resources; lack of a systematic skills development programme within the institution for either supervisors or students; unclear mechanisms for identifying and managing students who are failing to progress or who have missed their completion dates; excessive time taken to complete the final examination process; students being unaware of appeal processes that are independent of their supervisor(s); and lack of mechanisms for soliciting feedback from students and staff or for routinely using such feedback to enhance the programme.

Resources, Facilities and Funding

Insufficient funding, resources and facilities pose major challenges to doctoral education in Africa. Most African universities lack proper research infrastructure. There is little consistency in the power supply and not enough libraries, laboratories, ICT services, seminar facilities, Internet access, workshop equipment, etc. (Friesenhahn 2014; Hayward 2012; IAU 2011; Quintana and Calvet 2012). Limited funding handicaps universities in addressing these issues (Garwe 2015; Harle 2010). Money for doctoral education comes predominantly from public sources, and there is limited private sector engagement with universities in research and innovation (IAU 2011). Doctoral education, therefore, is reliant on external funding. Scholarships for doctoral students are very limited, as is support for students to participate in international conferences and doctoral summer schools (British Council and DAAD 2018; Stackhouse and Harle 2014).

Supervision

In the countries covered in the recent study by the British Council and DAAD (2018), serious concerns were raised about the adequacy and quality of supervision in African doctoral education. This is consistent with other Africa-wide studies that have found inadequate numbers of supervisors and poor relationships between supervisors and students. Moreover, institutional systems are not in place to proactively prevent these problems from happening.

The availability of qualified staff to supervise doctoral students is a common problem as well. Bunting, Cloete, and van Schalkwyk (2014), for instance, reported that seven of the eight flagship universities covered in their study had less than 25 per cent senior academic staff (full professors and associate professors). The problem is even more serious for newer, less established institutions (Harle 2010). Budget cuts, hiring freezes, low salaries, poor working conditions and brain drain have exacerbated the situation (Hayward and Ncayiyana 2014). Therefore, either senior faculty members take up the bulk of the supervising duties or junior professors, despite their lack of qualifications, end up directing doctoral students. Both result in compromised quality.

Institutional circumstances add to the problem as well. For instance, low salaries push faculty members to moonlight, which means they have less time to invest in their students. Some institutions offer financial incentives to encourage senior staff to take more supervisory work. In some cases, however, this has resulted in faculty taking on too much and failing to offer adequate supervision. Absence of explicit policy on the supervisor–supervisee ratio and failure to correlate admission with supervisory capacity, amplify the problem (IAU 2011; Obamba 2017). Muriisa (2015) has documented cases of students who had no advisor until their last year of study or who were forced to change advisors repeatedly. Other students had supervision only by email. The predicament is best captured in the statement of MacGregor (2013b, paragraph 2): 'In order to produce more doctoral graduates, more PhD supervisors are needed', she writes. 'But in order to have more supervisors, more PhDs are needed'.

Gender Gap

Reflective of the overall higher education landscape in Africa, enrolment at the doctoral level shows considerable gender inequity. Although the number of women has been rising (Tettey 2009), the problem remains serious at the doctoral level. Bunting, Cloete, and van Schalkwyk (2014) looked at doctoral programmes at eight universities in their study. They found that the average proportion of women in those programmes was 37 per cent. The University of Botswana was the only institution in the study with a rate above 50 per cent. Another study (British Council and DAAD 2018) highlighted one of the worst cases, showing that the gender disparity in Ethiopian doctoral programmes is particularly low. In 2015, women comprised a mere 12 per cent of enrolments and 6.3 per cent of graduates.

This gender gap extends to faculty and staffing at African universities, which can lead to a vicious circle. Without a representative number of women among staff, female students may not feel encouraged or supported enough to finish their advanced studies. If fewer women complete doctoral degrees, then the number rising through the ranks of the academic community will also be limited (British Academy and ACU 2011).

Williamson (2016) notes that not enough research has been done on the experiences of African women going through doctoral studies. Available data, however, shows that the doctoral journey is particularly difficult for women due to numerous social and economic circumstances, as well as institutional impediments. Synthesizing the literature, Bireda (2015) identifies some major factors: multiple roles in family and society, lack of support structure, sexual relationships, stress, low self-expectation and overall underrepresentation of women in the academic environment. Responding to these circumstances requires specific strategies to improve participation at the doctoral level, and those strategies need to be line with getting more women to participate at lower levels (Stackhouse and Harle 2014).

PROSPECTS AND FUTURE DIRECTIONS

The case for expanding doctoral education is clear. Trends show that national governments are committed to improving graduate education and research in a bid to become more globally competitive. The African Union, for example, is pushing for each of its member states to spend 1 per cent of GDP specifically on research and development (Akuffo et al. 2014). Governments are particularly interested in supporting science, technology, engineering and mathematics (STEM); the British Council and DAAD (2018) note that STEM fields are prominent in national policy documents. Non-governmental sources of funding will also be of increasing importance. Notwithstanding the political nature of charging tuition, Hayward and Ncayiyana (2014) have predicted that institutions will increasingly ask students to pay for certain services and create additional places for self-paying students. The question remains whether any of these efforts will be enough to significantly impact budgets and improve research conditions.

One can also expect to see more collaborations between African institutions. As the interests of international actors shift, there will be more space for players on the continent to address their issues collectively. The traditional North–South collaboration will gradually be overtaken by North–South–South and South–South partnerships. Better information and communication technologies, as well as data-driven projects like IAU's doctoral education database, are already facilitating such projects. Emerging initiatives in building communities of learning (Van de Laar, Rehm, and Achrekar 2017) and in using the 'cohort model' (Samuel and Mariaye 2014) will also push in this direction.

African universities will need to focus on finding ways to effectively supervise doctoral students. Some new approaches already being considered include using a mix of local, national, regional and/ or international supervisors for a single student. Other remedies may include: the development of codes of practice for supervisors, linking recruitment to supervision capacity, e-supervision and professional development for supervisors (IAU 2011; Obamba 2017). Furthermore, universities need to find ways to support and retain more women in doctoral programmes, and help them move through the academic ranks after graduation.

Finally, the African intellectual diaspora will be another force for change in the years ahead. National governments, as well as regional organizations like the African Union, want to better engage the diaspora (Adisa 2017). With heightened interest at the national and regional levels, initiatives such as those of the Carnegie Corporation—which sees the African intellectual diaspora as a critical constituency in the development of African higher education—will have significant impact on the advancement of research and graduate education. However, as universities continue to be affected by brain drain, it is worth noting Hayward and Ncayiyana's (2014) warning: diaspora engagement will not be a meaningful endeavour without effectively curbing the continued unidirectional outflow of educated citizens.

REFERENCES

Adisa, Jinmi. 2017. 'The African Union Perspective on Diaspora'. In *Africa and Its Global Diaspora: The Policy and Politics of Emigration*, edited by Jack Mangala, 39–57. Cham: Palgrave Macmillan.

Akuffo, Hannah, Phyllis Freeman, Eva Johansson, Celestino Obua, Jasper Ogwal-Okeng, and Paul Waako. 2014. 'Doctoral Education and Institutional Research Capacity Strengthening: An Example at Makerere University in Uganda (2000–2013)'. *Higher Education Policy* 27 (2): 195–217.

Asongu, Simplice A., and Jacinta C. Nwachukwu. 2018. 'PhD by Publication as an Argument for Innovation and Technology Transfer: With Emphasis on Africa'. *Higher Education Quarterly* 72 (1): 15–28.

Ayiro, Laban P., and James K. Sang. 2011. 'The Award of the PhD Degree in Kenyan Universities: A Quality Assurance Perspective'. *Quality in Higher Education* 17 (2): 163–178.

Backhouse, Judy P. 2009. 'Doctoral Education in South Africa: Models, Pedagogies and Student Experiences'. PhD diss. University of the Witwatersrand, Johannesburg.

Bates, Imelda, Richard Phillips, Ruby Martin-Peprah, Gibson Kibiki, Oumar Gaye, Kamija Phiri, Harry Tagbor, and Sue Purnell. 2011. 'Assessing and Strengthening African Universities' Capacity for Doctoral Programs'. *PLoS Medicine* 8 (9): e1001068.

Bireda, Asamenew D. 2015. 'Challenges to the Doctoral Journey: A Case of Female Doctoral Students from Ethiopia'. *Open Praxis* 7 (4): 287–297.

British Academy, and the Association of Commonwealth Universities (ACU). 2011. *Foundations for the Future: Supporting the Early Careers of African Researchers.* London: The British Academy.

British Council, and German Academic Exchange Service (DAAD). 2018. *Building PhD Capacity in Sub-Saharan Africa.* London: British Council.

Bunting, Ian, Nico Cloete, and François van Schalkwyk. 2014. *An Empirical Overview of Eight Flagship Universities in Africa: 2001–2011. A Report of the Higher Education Research and Advocacy Network in Africa (HERANA).* Cape Town: Centre for Higher Education Transformation (CHET).

Colenbrander, Sarah, Jon Lovett, Mary Suzan Abbo, Consalva Msigwa, Bernard M'Passi-Mabiala, and Richard Opoku. 2015. 'Renewable Energy Doctoral Programmes in Sub-Saharan Africa: A Preliminary Assessment of Common

Capacity Deficits and Emerging Capacity-Building Strategies'. *Energy Research and Social Science* 5: 70–77.

Cross, Michael, and Judy Backhouse. 2014. 'Evaluating Doctoral Programmes in Africa: Context and Practices'. *Higher Education Policy* 27 (2): 155–174.

Desie, Yekoyealem, and Belay Tefera. 2017. 'Doctoral Students' Academic Engagements in Addis Ababa University, Ethiopia: Nature, Sources, and Challenges'. *International Journal of African Higher Education* 4 (1): 92–110.

Fallenius, Ann M. 1996. 'Research Capacity Building in Developing Countries: Some Comments Based on SAREC's Experience'. In *International Scientific Cooperation*, edited by Jacques Gaillard, 101–106. Paris: L'institut de Recherche Scientifique Pour le Développement.

Friesenhahn, Irene. 2014. 'Making Higher Education Work for Africa: Facts and Figures'. SciDevNet. https://www.scidev.net/global/education/feature/higher-education-africa-facts-figures.html (accessed 5 July 2018).

Gaillard, Jacques F. 1994. 'North–South Partnerships: Is Collaboration Possible between Unequal Partners?' *Knowledge and Policy* 7 (2): 31–63.

Garwe, Evelyn Chiyevo. 2015. 'The Status Quo of Doctoral Education in Universities in Zimbabwe'. *Journal of Studies in Education* 5 (3): 22–37.

Golde, Chris. M., and George E. Walker, eds. 2006. *Envisioning the Future of Doctoral Education: Preparing Stewards of the Discipline*. San Francisco, CA: Jossey-Bass.

Harle, Jonathan. 2010. *Scoping Study of Graduate Teaching Provision in the Social Sciences, Governance and Public Policy. Undertaken on Behalf of the Partnership for African Social and Governance Research*. Nairobi: Partnership for African Social and Governance Research (PASGR).

———. 2013a. *Doctoral Education in Africa*. London: Association of Commonwealth Universities.

———. 2013b. 'Strengthening Research in African Universities: Reflections on Policy, Partnerships and Politics'. *Policy & Practice: A Development Education Review* 16 (Spring): 80–100.

Hayward, Fred M. 2012. 'Graduate Education in Sub-Saharan Africa: Prospects and Challenges'. *International Higher Education* 66 (Winter): 21–22.

Hayward, Fred M., and Daniel J. Ncayiyana. 2014. 'Confronting the Challenges of Graduate Education in Sub-Saharan Africa and Prospects for the Future'. *International Journal of African Higher Education* 1 (1): 173–216.

IAU. 2011. *Changing Nature of Doctoral Studies in Sub-Saharan Africa: Challenges and Policy Development Opportunities at Six Universities in Sub-Saharan Africa*. Paris: International Association of Universities.

IAU, and ACUP. 2012. *IAU-ACUP International Seminar on Innovative Approaches to Doctoral Education and Research Training in Sub-Saharan Africa*. http://www.acup.cat/sites/default/files/final-report-iau-acup-seminar-innovative-approaches-doctoral-education_1.pdf (accessed 5 July 2018).

Jones, Nicola, Mark Bailey, and Minna Lyytikainen. 2007. *Research Capacity Strengthening in Africa: Trends, Gaps and Opportunities. A Scoping Study*

Commissioned by DFID on Behalf of IFORD. London: Overseas Development Institute (ODI).

Jørgensen, Thomas E. 2012. *CODOC—Cooperation on Doctoral Education between Africa, Asia, Latin America and Europe*. Brussels: European University Association.

Kassam, Faazil, Karim F. Damji, Dan Kiage, Chris Carruthers, and K. H. Martin Kollmann. 2009. 'The Sandwich Fellowship: A Subspecialty Training Model for the Developing World'. *Academic Medicine* 84 (8): 1152–1160.

Khodabocus, Fareeda. 2016. 'Challenges to Doctoral Education in Africa'. *International Higher Education* 85: 25–27.

Lulat, Y. G. M. 2005. *A History of African Higher Education from Antiquity to the Present: A Critical Synthesis*. Westport, CT: Praeger Publishers.

MacGregor, Karen. 2013a. 'Emerging Ideas for Building PhD Training Capacity. University World News.http://www.universityworldnews.com/article. php?story=20131215083542491 (accessed 5 July 2018).

———. 2013b. 'Where to from Here for the African PhD?' University World News. http://www.universityworldnews.com/article.php?story=20131102155412705 (accessed 5 July 2018).

———. 2015. 'African Research Universities Alliance Launched'. University World News. https://www.universityworldnews.com/post. php?story=20150310185922166 (accessed 5 July 2018).

Manabe, Yukari C., Elly Katabira, Richard L. Brough, Alex G. Coutinho, Nelson Sewankambo, and Concepta Merry. 2011. 'Developing Independent Investigators for Clinical Research Relevant for Africa'. *Health Research Policy and Systems* 9 (44). doi:10.1186/1478-4505-9-44.

Mkandawire, Thandika. 1995. 'Three Generations of African Academics: A Note'. *Transformation: Critical Perspectives on Southern Africa* 28: 75–83.

Molla, Tebeje, and Denise Cuthbert. 2016. 'In Pursuit of the African PhD: A Critical Survey of Emergent Policy Issues in Select Sub-Saharan African Nations, Ethiopia, Ghana and South Africa'. *Policy Futures in Education* 14 (6): 635–654.

Mouton, Johann. 2010. *African Experience with Collaborative Graduate Programs: Research Report*. Stellenbosch: University of Stellenbosch.

Muriisa, Roberts K. 2015. 'The State of Doctoral Education in Social Sciences in Uganda: Experiences and Challenges of Doctoral Training at Mbarara University of Science and Technology 2003–2010'. *Journal of Education and Practice* 6 (10): 204–213.

Mutula, Stephen M. 2009. 'Challenges of Postgraduate Research: Global Context, African Perspectives'. Presented at the 10th DLIS Annual Conference, September 9–10. University of Zululand, Richards Bay. http://www.lis.uzulu. ac.za/2009/Mutula-UZ2009DLISPaper.pdf (accessed 5 July 2018).

Obamba, Milton O. 2017. *Constructing 'Innovative' Doctorates: Scoping Evidence on Doctoral Structure and Practices from Six African Countries*. Nairobi: Partnership for African Social and Governance Research (PASGR).

Obanya, Pai. 1999. *The Dilemma of Education in Africa*. Dakar: UNESCO Regional Office, (BREDA).

Owusu-Manu, D., D. J. Edwards, S. K. Afrane, I. K. Dontwi, and P. Laycock. 2015. 'Professional Doctoral Scholarship in Ghana: A Case Study of the CDT–BEPS Framework'. *Industry and Higher Education* 29 (3): 197–207.

Quintana, Imma, and Adrià Calvet. 2012. *Current Situation and Future Challenges of PhD Studies in Sub-Saharan Africa*. Barcelona: Catalan Association of Public Universities (ACUP).

Robins, Lisa, and Peter Kanowski. 2008. 'PhD by Publication: A Student's Perspective'. *Journal of Research Practice* 4 (2): 1–20.

Sadlak, Jan., ed. 2004. *Doctoral Studies and Qualifications in Europe and the United States: Status and Prospects*. Bucharest: UNESCO.

Samuel, Michael A., and Hyleen Mariaye. 2014. 'De-colonising International Collaboration: The University of Kwazulu-Natal-Mauritius Institute of Education Cohort PhD Program'. *Compare: A Journal of Comparative and International Education* 44 (4): 501–521.

Stackhouse, Julie, and Jonathan Harle. 2014. 'The Experiences and Needs of African Doctoral Students: Current Conditions and Future Support'. *Higher Education Policy* 27 (2): 175–194.

Szanton, David L., and Sarah L. Manyika. 2002. *Programs in African Universities: Current Status and Future Prospects*. Berkeley, CA: The Institute of International Studies and Center for African Studies, University of California.

Teferra, Damtew. 2015. 'Manufacturing-and Exporting-Excellence and 'Mediocrity': Doctoral Education in South Africa'. *South African Journal of Higher Education* 29 (5): 8–19.

———. 2016. 'Beyond Peril and Promise—From Omission to Conviction'. *International Journal of African Higher Education* 3 (1): 7–18.

Tettey, Wisdom J. 2009. 'Deficits in Academic Staff Capacity in Africa and Challenges of Developing and Retaining the Next Generation of Academics: A Report Commissioned by Partnership for Higher Education in Africa'. http://www.foundation-partnership.org/pubs/pdf/tettey_deficits.pdf (accessed 10 December 2019).

———. 2010. *Challenges of Developing and Retaining the Next Generation of Academics: Deficits in Academic Staff Capacity at African Universities*. Partnership for Higher Education in Africa.

Timm, Lene. 2011. 'Promoting Excellence in PhD Research Programs in East Africa 2008–2011'. http://bsuge.org/fileadmin/user_upload/bsu-ge/Other_Reports/Prepare_phd_evaluation_10112011.pdf (accessed 5 July 2018).

Van de Laar, Mindel, Martin Rehm, and Shivani Achrekar. 2017. '"Community of Learning" for African PhD Students: Changing the Scene of Doctoral Education?' *Transformation in Higher Education* 2 (1): 1–9.

Williamson, Charmaine. 2016. 'Views from the Nano Edge: Women on Doctoral Preparation Programs in Selected African Contexts'. *Studies in Higher Education* 41 (5): 859–873.

Woldegiyorgis, Ayenachew. A. 2014. 'The Indelible Footmarks of the World Bank in the Higher Education of the Developing World: The Case of Ethiopia'. *International Journal of Research Studies in Education* 3 (3): 93–106.

World Bank. 2012. *Knowledge Economy Index 2012 Rankings.* Washington, DC: World Bank.

———. 2015. *Eastern and Southern Africa Higher Education Centers of Excellence Project (ACE II): Project Background, Description, and Results Framework.* Washington, DC: World Bank.

Chapter 10

Imperatives and Realities of Doctoral Education in South Africa

Damtew Teferra

This chapter discusses the history, profile and trends of doctoral education in South Africa. It starts with a presentation of the higher education system in general, including enrolment, qualification types and graduation figures, with a focus on doctoral education. This is followed by an analysis of trends in South African doctoral education since its inception, in terms of enrolment, completion rates and funding dynamics, among others. The chapter concludes by highlighting key points expected to contribute to the development of doctoral education in the country.

South African higher education institutions (HEIs) are the envy, and pride, of Africa. They are well endowed, more stable, more diverse and more comprehensive than their counterparts across the continent. As controversial as rankings may be, South African institutions dominate the top of any list of African HEIs, indicating that the country is a continental force in this area (Teferra 2015).

Nevertheless, the history of South African higher education is beset with racist and systematic discriminatory policies enforced by the apartheid system until it was dismantled in the 1990s. The impact of this infamous system, however, continues to be felt and manifested in the higher education system in a host of ways. According to Waghid (2015), the South African higher education system was profoundly shaped by racial discrimination and the inequalities of class, race and gender that spawned the systemic exclusion and marginalization of blacks, coloureds and Indians. The year 1994 marked the dawn of South Africa's transformation, terminating legal apartheid and ending university isolation (Council for Higher Education 2016; Jansen, McLellan, and Greene 2008). A new higher education policy kicked off in earnest with the establishment of a National Commission on Higher Education. Its mandate was to develop a policy framework to transform South African higher education, which at the time comprised of universities, technical and vocational schools called technikons and colleges of nursing, agriculture and teacher training. According to Scott (2009), the national education policy was 'radically engineered' with the goal of achieving equity, one of its main pillars.

After 1994, national policy identified the apartheid legacy and globalization as twin challenges to be addressed by higher education. Both the National Commission on Higher Education and the White Paper (Council for Higher Education 1997) set out the balancing act that South African higher education would have to perform in simultaneously serving the reconstruction and development needs of the country, confronting the challenges posed by globalization, and striving to address massive inequity issues (Council for Higher Education 2006; Jansen, McLellan, and Greene 2008; Sehoole 2005).

Currently, South Africa has, arguably, the best-developed higher education system in Africa. With a 20 per cent enrolment rate and more than one million students, it produces the largest share of academic research and publication on the continent. Yet the system also faces multiple systemic challenges, structural shortcomings and frequent strikes and crises—largely around issues of access, quality, funding, race and decolonization.

THE HIGHER EDUCATION SYSTEM IN SOUTH AFRICA: AN OVERVIEW

Doctoral education has taken centre stage as a vital avenue for the production of knowledge, which has become critical in fostering socio-economic development and making nations competitive globally. As a result, countries across the world are strengthening their offerings when it comes to graduate studies, especially PhD programmes (Teferra 2015). Accordingly, doctoral education has been identified as one of the key national development imperatives in South Africa (ASSAf 2010).

The South African public higher education system has three tiers: universities, comprehensive universities and universities of technology, though these are 'soft' and in some ways dubious categorizations (Jansen, McLellan, and Greene 2008). The higher education system also consists of increasingly expanding post-secondary institutions and colleges, both public and private. The largest producers of doctorates are the universities, or to be more specific, the historically white universities.

Currently, South Africa has 26 public universities, two of which opened just in the last couple of years. The University of Cape Town and Stellenbosch University are the oldest, and two of the most prestigious, in the country. In 2015, South African public HEIs enrolled 985,212 students, 58.3 per cent of them women, at the undergraduate and graduate levels (DHET 2018). That year, 53.6 per cent of the students in public institutions were enrolled in bachelor's degree programmes, while 16.6 per cent in postgraduate programmes, including doctorate programmes, and 27.6 per cent in undergraduate certificate and diploma programmes (DHET 2015). The National Development Plan (NDP) stipulates increasing university enrolment to about 1.62 million by 2030.

During the period 2009–2016, enrolments in doctoral degree programmes more than doubled, rising 104.3 per cent to 10,981. In that time period, the corresponding growth was 31.0 per cent or 13,567 for master's degrees; 30.9 per cent or 125,312 for undergraduate degrees and 23.3 per cent or 17,371 for postgraduate programmes below the master's level (DHET 2015). Other research has indicated that as many as 70 per cent of all doctoral students are studying part-time (Mouton 2016). There were 21,510 doctoral students in 2016 compared to 13,285 in 2011—a growth of more than 60 per cent (CHE–Vital Stats 2016).

South Africa is committed to scaling up the yearly production of doctorates to 5,000 by 2030, reaching 100 PhD graduates per million population (National Planning Commission 2011). In 2016, public HEIs produced 2,797 doctoral graduates, which was 10.6 per cent more than in 2015 (2,530 PhD graduates), and 102.7 per cent higher compared to 2009 (1,380 PhD graduates). (Please refer to Figures 10.1 and 10.2 for more detailed information by fields.) Despite a significant growth in the number of PhD graduates in existing public HEIs since 2009, hitting the Department of Higher Education and Training's (DHET) target of producing 12,000 PhD graduates by 2019 remains a challenge (DHET 2015). Higher Education South Africa (2014), now called Universities South Africa (USAf), a membership organization representing South Africa's public universities, noted that the target was 'too ambitious'.

THE DRIVE AND RAISON D'ÊTRE OF PhD PROGRAMMES

There is a broad consensus in South Africa that the quality of PhD graduates is insufficient to meet the developmental needs of the country. Expanding and consolidating doctoral education is thus driven by a heightened interest in advancing socio-economic development while staying globally competitive. In its 10-Year Innovation Plan, the department of science and technology (DST 2008) envisaged building 'a knowledge-based economy positioned between developed and developing countries' and South Africa needing 'to increase its PhD production rate by a factor of about five over the next 10–20 years' (DST 2008). With a compelling discourse and conceptual underpinning linking the economic wealth of nations with knowledge output, the department urged South Africa to increase its knowledge production substantially as a condition of joining the ranks of wealthier countries. According to a former minister of science and technology, in order to realize the national goal of building a knowledge-based economy, increased support for postgraduate study is imperative

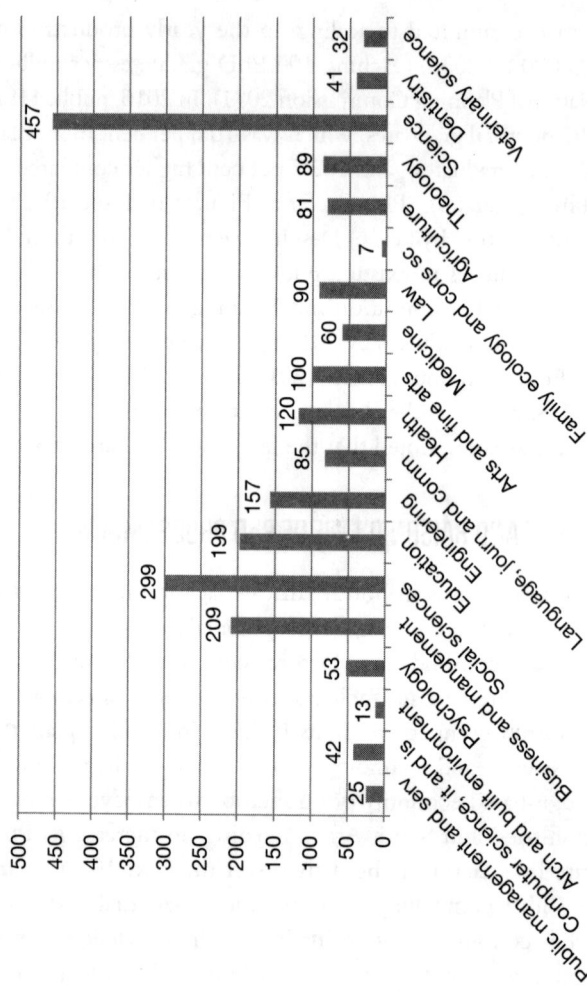

Figure 10.1 Headcount of the 2011 Cohort Graduating with Doctoral Degrees in Six Years (i.e., by 2016)

Source: CHE–Vital Stats (2016).

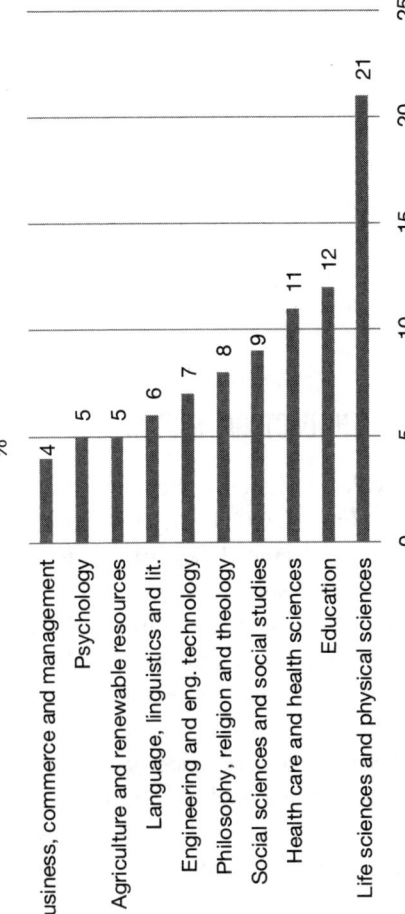

Figure 10.2 *Fields of Graduates*
Source: Herman (2017).

(Pandor 2011). The NDP envisages more doctorates in science, engineering, technology and mathematics for the country to become a leading innovator. The plan further expresses the ambition to double the number of graduate and postgraduate scientists and increase the number of black South African and women postgraduates, especially at the PhD level, in order to improve the research and innovation capacity and gender balance among university staff.

Accordingly, South Africa endeavours to increase the percentage of qualified PhD staff in the higher education sector from 34 percent (at the time of the promulgation of the NDP) to more than 75 percent by 2030. As mentioned above, it also plans to produce more than 100 doctoral graduates per million inhabitants per year by 2030. The South African government is thus determined to grow its knowledge production capacity through the expansion and consolidation of doctoral programmes.

THE DOCTORAL SECTOR

The first doctor of law degree (LLD) was conferred by the University of the Cape of Good Hope (UCGH) in 1899. Soon after, in 1907, the first doctor of science degree (DSc) was conferred by UCGH. By the 1920s, doctor of philosophy degrees (PhD and DPhil) were offered by both the University of Cape Town and the University of the Witwatersrand (Herman 2017). Herman (2017, 1441) indicates that in 2017, 21 per cent of all doctoral degrees were awarded in the life sciences and physical sciences, followed by education (12%), health care and health sciences (11%), and social sciences/studies (9%). (Figure 10.3 provides the number of doctoral graduates from 1899 to 2010.) The prominence of life sciences and physical sciences was particularly evident in the first decade of the 21st century due to policy emphasis on increasing output in these subjects.

A search on the South African Qualifications Authority database in March 2018 revealed 977 registered doctoral programmes in the country, along with information on the institutions where these programmes are granted. This is further accompanied by information on minimum credits and National Qualification Framework levels.

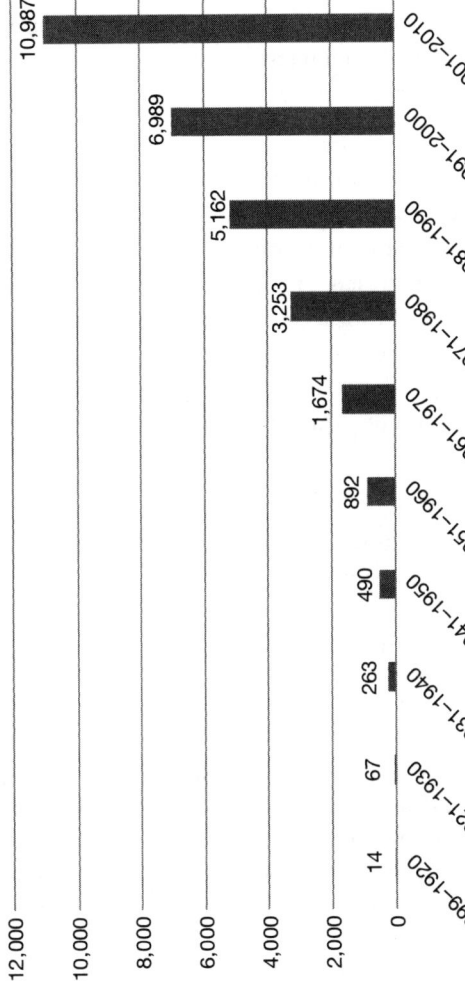

Figure 10.3 *Total Doctoral Graduates per Decade (Except for 1899–1920)*

Source: Herman (2017).

Most doctorates in the sciences have been produced in historically white institutions: the University of Cape Town has produced about 1,133 (17%) of all doctorates in life sciences and physical sciences, followed by the University of Witwatersrand with 987 (15%) and the University of Pretoria with 806 (12%). About 90 per cent of all doctoral degrees in South Africa have been awarded by eight historically white institutions. In particular, the University of Pretoria has consistently awarded the most doctorates per decade since the 1940s (Herman 2017, 1441–1442).

Historically advantaged universities still produce the majority of the PhDs in the hard/pure or hard/applied disciplines, while newly merged universities or previously black universities adhere to the national call to produce more PhD graduates by focusing mainly on soft/applied subjects, preserving the historical knowledge divide (ASSAf 2011). Given the heavy emphasis on science and technology, which happens to be stronger in the already advantaged institutions, it is conceivable that this divide will continue without any significant shift for some time to come.

Private HEIs also produce doctoral graduates, albeit in limited numbers. Of 39,686 students who graduated from these institutions in 2016, only 69 (0.2%) were doctoral candidates (DHET 2015). Of the 1,100 PhDs completed in 2006, only 7 per cent were produced at the five historically black institutions that were not merged with historically white institutions.

The NDP envisaged a 75 per cent graduation rate for all students entering doctoral programmes. This figure was later revised to 65 per cent, when empirical data showed that only around 50 per cent of national cohorts entering doctoral programmes would eventually graduate (Mouton 2016). Nearly halfway into the NDP, the growth pattern has only barely moved beyond the halfway mark. As mentioned above, USAf has challenged this goal as 'too ambitious'—presumably because South Africa's capacity to produce doctoral graduates only stood at 2,797 in 2016.

Over the past decade, the average doctoral completion rate in South Africa has remained below 50 per cent, with variations by institutional type, gender, race and age (Mouton et al. 2015). The average time-to-degree duration for doctoral students, 4.8 years in 2007, is consistent with international trends (MacGregor 2013; Mouton 2009, 2016). Seventy per cent of doctoral students study part-time, though quite a large number enrol full-time to benefit from the fee-free subsidy. DHET mandates subsidies for doctoral studies only up to three years, with, in a number of cases, an additional grace period of one year (Teferra 2015). Yet the three-year completion rate driven by funding imperatives tends to be an unrealistic expectation.

Thirty-four per cent of the doctoral cohort in 1996 were women. This rate has increased to 45 per cent in 2012, showing consistent growth from 38 per cent in 2000 to 41 per cent in 2004 and 43 per cent in 2008 (Mouton 2016). Typically, most women study in non-STEM (science, technology, engineering and mathematics) fields.

The average age of doctoral students at South African universities is high compared to international trends. According to ASSAf (2010), in 2007, only 12 per cent of doctoral graduates were under 30, with the average age at graduation being 40 years. While the proportion of graduates in the younger age group has remained relatively constant since 2000, the cohort of students over 30 has increased, with almost one in five being 50 at graduation.

The national average of production of PhD graduates in South African universities recorded remarkable growth, from 30 per cent in 2005 to 42 per cent in 2014—a 40 per cent increase. The highest growth trajectory was recorded by the universities of technology, with an increase from 9 per cent in 2005 to 17 per cent in 2014—nearly 90 per cent (Mouton 2016).

In 2015, DHET launched the Staffing South Africa's Universities Framework (SSAUF) with a focus on both research and teaching development, to ensure that academics acquire appropriate training and mentoring skills. The SSAUF consists of four core programmes linked to the academic development pathway, and a crosscutting support programme, particularly the New Generation of Academics Programme (nGAP), which will recruit new academics based on equity considerations and disciplinary needs. The nGAP scholars comprise master's and doctoral candidates, and postdoctoral emerging researchers, appointed to new academic positions still to be created.

Key components in the successful production of PhDs are the availability, and competence, of senior academics. Note that only two in five academics in the country's HEIs hold a PhD. Quite a sizeable number among them are in the early stages of their careers and may not be directly, and readily, deployed in the national PhD project. For that matter, the more senior academics in the system are not known to be productive, nor are they fully competent in terms of contributing to the training of PhD students. The incentive and the pressure for PhD supervision and completion are such that cases of 'enhanced' support for students have been reported in a handful of (especially) second-tier institutions, pushing ethical boundaries. It is somewhat intriguing that a study on the views of doctoral students on their supervisors by Blackhouse (2009) revealed a surprisingly favourable response, despite numerous gaps noted in the supervision process. Cloete, Mouton, and Sheppard (2015) concur with that observation, albeit with some reticence.

South Africa had 39 more professors and associate professors in 2013 (totalling 4,073) than in 2012 (4,034). Among these, 708 were black (17.4%) and 2,870 (70.5%) were white, while there was no information on race for 67 of them. Among the 2,175 full professors, 316 were black (14.5%), 101 coloured, 123 Indian and 1,593 white (73.2%), with no racial information for 42 professors. A quarter (552) of the professors were women—41 of them black (Africa Check 2014). According to a 2017 report by the minister of DHET, 66 per cent of all university professors in 2015 were white (Ramoupi 2017).

South Africa is concerned about aging faculty—a common phenomenon across Africa. In most universities, where the retirement age is 60, a crisis is looming: more than 1,430 professors and associate professors in 13 institutions will reach retirement age in the next 10 years (Govendar 2014). The workforce, including PhD supervisors, is expected to shrink as a result, although, according to Louw and Godsell (2015), there are variations among the departments that were interviewed. Succession strategies and efforts to expand the pool of supervisors by making use of emeritus or extraordinary professors are either in place or being considered.

For several reasons, there is an evident shortage of seasoned PhD supervisors and, hence, an overreliance on 'novices' in South African higher education. First, the funding regimes to support postgraduate supervision are attractive and generous. This highly incentivized system, funded by the government, prompts supervisors—novices and seasoned alike—to guide as many students as possible. In their study, Louw and Godsell (2011) pointed out that academics actually considered the 'heavy burden' of a large number of advisees to be an opportunity. Second, departmental and institutional leaders also have a vested interest in attracting a large body of students, thereby compounding the situation. For instance, graduating a PhD and a (research) master's student earns an HEI approximately ZAR340,000 (about US$28,200) and ZAR120,000 (about US$12,000), respectively, from the government (Teferra 2015).

Doctoral students and graduates are generously funded in the current framework. Doctoral research graduates are regarded as a research output unit with a weight of three, which means that a university 'earns' three times the subsidy of an accredited journal article with one doctoral graduate (approximately ZAR360,000 [US$36,000] in 2012; Cloete, Mouton, and Sheppard 2015). In times of financial constraints, this funding has the potential of softening the rigour of academic scrutiny (Teferra 2015).

ASSAf (2010) reports that approximately two doctoral students per supervisor appears to be the norm in the university sector, compared to a lower supervisory load of about 1.2 doctoral students per supervisor at universities of technology, where doctoral students are very few. Be that as it may, in a number of institutions the supervision role is much higher (Louw and Godsell 2015). For instance, at the University of KwaZulu-Natal, the senate mandates that senior academics supervise a minimum of six graduate students, but much higher figures are widespread. The number of advisees per academic is not mandated by the DHET, but by the guidelines of individual institutions.

The NDP, which acknowledges 'a shortage of academics' and looks to raise the current figure 70 per cent by 2030, identifies three new sources. First, local institutions with 'embedded research capacity' that should, in return for recognition of this niche, assist with supervision at other universities that only 'focus on teaching and learning'; second, partnerships with industry and commerce; and third, partnerships and exchanges with international universities (National Planning Commission 2012).

THE MODEL

Doctoral programmes in South Africa predominantly follow the traditional British apprenticeship model based on supervised research resulting in a thesis. Typically, this doctoral approach, which takes three to four years, lacks mandatory coursework; and if there are courses, they are non-credit bearing.

Another form of doctoral degree acquisition is the PhD by publication of a set number of articles on a particular focus area in refereed and accredited journals recognized by the DHET. The PhD by publication approach is practised by a small but growing number of university units. It is interesting to note, however, that while some university departments are increasing their numbers of doctoral students through PhD by publication (for instance, the social work department of North West University), others, such as the psychology department of the University of Johannesburg, reject that model. No department offers what is known as the American model, a PhD by coursework and dissertation (Louw and Godsell 2011).

Typically, doctoral students are admitted to a university upon review of their applications by a departmental committee in charge of recommending admission. Examinations or other forms of evaluation prior to admission are atypical. Generally, doctoral students seek out their own supervisor at the university where they intend to study. Departments can also assign supervisors following a successful application and review process. In general, students choose to have one supervisor, who often remains with the student even after the designated number of years for supervision has expired.

The assessment process does not include examinations or testing except at the time of proposal defence, yet even defence-related engagements tend to be rather lax. Exit (summative) public defences are not common either, though submission of work for publication in peer-reviewed journals prior to graduation is becoming more common and even mandatory in some institutions. It is important to note, however, that while some institutions advocate instituting the exit (summative) defence, others, such as the University of Pretoria's faculty of education, have moved away from it due to growing threats of fraud.

In a number of institutions, a much more organized and systematic way of advising doctoral students is practised in the form of a cohort model. This model of PhD training, which this author has followed at the school of education in the University of KwaZulu-Natal, supports groups of doctoral students in three phases, typically on a one-phase-per-year basis. If students fall behind their group and fail to complete their studies within the designated three-year period, they continue their supervision individually under their designated supervisors.

The growing pressure to produce more doctorates in South African universities has been well documented. In response, different approaches, practices and reforms are emerging at different levels in different institutions. It is important to note that doctoral studies are also offered as distance-education programmes and at private institutions, albeit in small numbers.

INTERNATIONAL DIMENSION

One of the attractive features of South African higher education for international students is its cost. Basically, PhD students do not pay tuition as long as they register as full-time students and complete their studies within three (extendable to four) years of subsidy. Government subsidies for postgraduate studies, by way of tuition fee remission, are the same regardless of nationality. International students, however, have to pay additional fees such as an international student levy.

Out of 72,959 foreign students enrolled in public HEIs in 2015, 7,725 (10.5%) were studying in doctoral programmes, both in regular

(84%) and distance mode (16%). The majority of foreign doctoral students came from English-speaking African countries, including Zimbabwe (24.8%) and Nigeria (16.1%; DHET 2015). A survey conducted among 1,700 international students at seven universities in South Africa in 2014 found that nearly 80 per cent came from Africa, 23 per cent of whom were studying for a master's degree, 19 per cent for a PhD and 1 per cent working as postdoctoral researchers (MacGregor 2014). International doctoral students constituted 19 per cent of all doctoral graduates in 2000, and this percentage went up to 34 in 2010. In other words, while the number of international students showed a growth of 365 per cent between 2000 and 2010, the number of South African graduates showed a growth of only 118 per cent (Herman 2017). It is important to note that the surge in the number of African students, especially in the physical sciences and agriculture, is linked to an increase in the number of international students from the Southern African Development Community countries and the rest of Africa.

In 2000, the number of black South African enrolments was almost twice (i.e., 990) that of students from the rest of Africa (526), but by 2012, there were 750 more enrolments from the rest of Africa (3,717) than from black South Africans (2,967). More surprisingly, the annual growth rate was almost twice as high for students from the rest of Africa (17.7% versus 9.6% for black South Africans).

The profile of graduates shows similar trends. While the number of black South African graduates increased by 78 per cent after 2000, the number of graduates from the rest of Africa increased by 644 per cent. By 2012, they outnumbered black South Africans by 496 to 325 (Mouton 2016). The South African higher education system is increasingly emerging as a major regional academic hub for African students, who now play a visible role in the country's 'knowledge project'. Some countries in Africa negotiate directly with the South African government and respective institutions to train their nationals in PhD programmes. The Ethiopian case is illustrative. In 2012, the Ethiopian ministry of education negotiated with the University of KwaZulu-Natal, one of the main South African universities, to enrol 50 doctoral students each year for five years in a host of PhD programmes, with particular emphasis on STEM fields. The reason for the particular interest of African nations in sending their students to South Africa is not simply its tuition-free postgraduate education, but rather the perception and expectation that these students will greatly benefit from this opportunity, which typically focuses on similar development challenges and issues as their own. Further, there is a firm intention to ensure that students return home once they complete their studies, thereby stemming the danger of brain drain.

These purported benefits, however, do not always become a reality. Quite a large number of doctoral graduates from abroad opt to remain in South Africa, which now has attractive visa policies for this highly trained group. In the case of Eritrea, for instance, a sizeable number of students who were sent to South Africa by the government in 2000 and 2001 (with the World Bank support) chose to stay, claiming that they would be subjected to political oppression should they return home. As a consequence, some 'threw their degree aside' and got involved in informal businesses (Connell 2015), while others joined the white-collar workforce.

One of the most common approaches to address the shortage of PhD graduates and build capacity in South Africa is what is typically known as 'growing one's own timber'. This motto is manifested in a number of ways, both good and bad. It spans from a fervent desire to train PhD candidates in the country and emphasizing self-reliance to a measure of occasional xenophobia towards international academics. South Africa's intention to reach self-sufficiency is commendable and needs to be supported. But it is important to stress that heightened competence and global competitiveness in higher education should be attained through the deployment and engagement of academics who have gained sufficient international exposure through the course of their studies and academic activities. The commendable endeavour of developing home-grown doctoral education capacity must beware of inbreeding, which is 'now rampant in many developing countries', including South Africa (Teferra 2015).

In any case, the South African PhD project is strengthened by a preferential immigration policy that encourages international doctoral students and postdocs to remain in the country after completion of their studies. According to the immigration policy document, most STEM graduates, university academic staff and others are granted preferential treatment and priority for a permanent residency permit. The possibility of permanently staying in the country after graduation is an additional incentive for international students in South Africa, especially for many Africans. As in other countries, such as the United States, this incentive has been instrumental in supporting graduate programmes in the country's universities.

FUNDING DYNAMICS

The issue of funding higher education in South Africa has had a treacherous history fraught with unrest, violence and nationwide crisis. The #FeesMustFall slogan, which advocated for free higher education, triggered an avalanche of social, economic and political upheavals that in the end contributed to the fall of President Jacob Zuma. In 2017, in a politically charged climate and under controversial circumstances, Zuma gave into the protestors' demands by declaring 'free higher education to all'. Just months later, Zuma was forced to resign from office, but the country's new president, Cyril Ramaphosa, has honoured Zuma's concession on educational fees.

In 2011, the government budget for higher education as a percentage of gross domestic product (GDP) stood at 0.75, which is substantially lower than the OECD's 1.21 and the world average of 0.84. Given the higher education transformation agenda and the NDP imperatives, a higher education budget to GDP ratio is considered of great importance (USAf). Currently, the South African government spends 0.77 per cent of its GDP on research and development (R&D), but seeks to increase this by 100 per cent to 1.5 per cent. The government stood as the largest funder of R&D at 43.9 per cent of the gross domestic expenditure on R&D, followed by the business sector at 40.8 per cent, foreign sources at 12.2 per cent and other local sources at 3.1 per cent. The most important trend is that the business sector has now replaced the higher education sector as the lead contributor to R&D spending (Pandor 2017). The National Research Foundation (NRF) makes funds available to support a small number of scholarships for full-time doctoral studies abroad, with the objective of increasing the number and quality of doctoral graduates in South Africa. The scholarships are exclusively reserved for South African citizens and permanent residents.

Support for doctoral programmes is granted on the assumption of their contribution to national imperatives (Blackhouse 2009). Accordingly, postgraduate education that is pursued on a full-time basis is tuition free. This is one of the most attractive aspects of South Africa's higher education system, not only for the beneficiaries but also from the perspective of the strategic interest of both universities and the government, which pursue the knowledge project with sustained commitment. The new funding framework was passed by the DHET in December 2003 and came into effect in 2004. Under this framework, the production of research master's and doctoral graduates is financially rewarded, so as to prompt universities to respond systematically and proactively. The reward system has, in fact, become the most significant incentive scheme to increase doctoral production (ASSAf 2010).

It could be argued that these funding modalities have been a factor in the considerable strengthening of PhD offerings since 2003–2004, when the funding model became operational (replacing the model from 1983, which provided no direct financial incentives for the enrolment and graduation of doctoral students). Since 2007–2008, universities have been recovering the fees accrued to doctoral students from the government, based on a provision set by the DHET. Two subsidy components are included in the doctoral funding framework: teaching-input grants and research-output grants. Teaching-input grants provide a subsidy for enrolments depending on level (such as undergraduate, honours, master's and doctoral) as well as weight per subject matter of the programmes. Education, law and psychology are at the lowest end; agriculture, health and sciences are at the highest. Research output grants are paid in a similar fashion (in total for the duration of registration) with variations among disciplines (Cloete, Mouton, and Sheppard 2015).

The South African government has invested in different strategies and projects to strengthen the research capacity of academics from marginalized groups and sectors. The Thuthuka programme of the

NRF, in particular, was established to improve the qualifications of researchers to the doctoral level in order to accelerate their progression into the mainstream of national and other research support opportunities. The programme also seeks to increase the number of NRF-rated researchers (Hay and Monnapula-Mapesela 2009).

EXCELLENCE AND MEDIOCRITY

In an article titled 'Excellence and Mediocrity', Teferra (2015) argued that South African higher education is not only a major hub of global excellence and eminence but also a citadel of mediocrity and ineptitude. Most of the leading universities in the country are renowned in Africa and beyond, and consistently appear at the top of regional rankings. South African academic pre-eminence was established globally on the occasion of the world's first human-to-human heart transplant in 1967. This excellence has been further consolidated by cutting-edge research and innovation in the treatment of HIV/AIDS and developments in space science. Such excellence and global visibility seem, however, to conceal inherent weaknesses in the system (Teferra 2015). These are manifested in the national PhD project, which so far has largely focused on numbers and transformation, not quality. As mentioned, the existing funding policy rewards numbers—the more graduates produced by supervisors and institutions the better, which generates extensive resources for individual academics as well as institutions. As mentioned above, the government pays universities the equivalent of ca. US$30,000 upon successful completion of a PhD programme, which is distributed to different institutional units and academics along government guidelines.

While incentives and rewards have been notable, so have the implications. In the interest of raising numbers, both institutions and academics have been known to push PhD production without ensuring quality. Academics may supervise two to three times more students than what is mandated. In a number of cases, this pressure has created loopholes in the system—like graduating doctoral students without (summative) exit defences, to mention but one—to expedite the process. These practices, which help conceal mediocrity, are particularly harmful to those nations that send many candidates to South Africa in an effort to build their own nascent systems (Teferra 2015). Alluding to this mediocrity, the NDP admits that the system 'can do better and is underperforming in a number of key areas. There are some institutions within the system that continue to show signs of instability and dysfunction'. Internal and external reasons for dysfunction and mediocrity abound, including widespread lacklustre doctoral supervision. Motivated by financial reward, spurred by shortages of supervisors and driven by the requirement to meet their academic contract with their institutions, doctoral supervisors, both seasoned and novice, are drawn into supervising even though their fields may only be distantly related to that of their students (Teferra 2015).

THE DOCTORAL MARKETPLACE

Only 0.07 per cent of the more than 1.4 million permanently employed individuals in corporate South Africa have PhDs. According to a study by Goneos-Malka (2015) on PhD graduates from 14 leading South African universities, 50 per cent experienced difficulties in finding a job or knew of other PhD graduates who had. Further, for 25 per cent it took up to a year to find employment, for 3 per cent up to two years, while 11 per cent said they were still unemployed. The study also found that 68 per cent were told they were overqualified for the employment they were seeking. The second part of the study looked at 350 top companies to determine how many of them employed PhD holders. It painted a dismal picture, with most major companies hiring on average no more than three PhD holders, in spite of employing tens of thousands staff.

As mentioned above, 70 per cent of PhD students are already studying on a part-time basis, presumably with full-time or part-time jobs. Thus, Goneos-Malka's study may largely concern students not previously employed during the course of their studies, or with prior employment not commensurate with their status, or working, but looking for more gainful employment. It is ironic that, at the same time South Africa is striving to build its doctoral production capacity, graduates have to grapple with finding gainful employment. It may be important, at this point, to undertake (tracer) studies in order to systematically identify areas of shortages and overproduction, so as to channel policy, resources and efforts appropriately.

PROMOTING DOCTORAL EDUCATION

South Africa is committed to increasing the number of doctorates produced annually in order to advance its economic growth and global competitiveness, and has considered a number of measures listed below.

Increasing Funding

According to Mouton (2016), the main hurdles to overcome when building doctoral education are finding sufficient funding for blacks (66%) and, for whites, finding sufficient time for studies (46%). It appears obvious that expanding funding opportunities for doctoral students, particularly for blacks, would go a long way in raising the number of doctorates in the country. But in the aftermath of the declaration of 'fee-free' higher education, finding additional funding may be a very difficult option.

Recruiting More Full-Time Students

A staggering 70 per cent of doctoral students in South Africa study on a part-time basis. This means that they take longer time to finish their studies and chances are that many drop out. Students should therefore be recruited as full-time students from the outset, and those already in the pipeline should be encouraged to study full-time. This, however, is not any easy task as the 'catchment area' for PhD studies is not growing and students' desire to give up full-time employment remains low.

Managing Throughput

Doctoral students spend, on average, about five years completing their degrees, and are on average between 33 years old (in the natural and agricultural sciences) and 41 years old (in the social sciences and humanities) when first enrolling in a doctoral degree (ASSAf 2010). Yet the doctoral subsidy offered by the DHET is only three years. 'Leaks' occur all along the pipeline, with increasingly smaller shares of students completing the subsequent level of education. The most severe blockages are located at the senior certificate level (85% of 2007 senior certificate candidates did not attain the minimum level of achievement to enrol for an undergraduate degree) and at the postgraduate level. When calculating the percentage of doctorates as a share of all under-graduate degrees conferred in 2007, only 2 per cent of undergraduates appear to have obtained a doctorate.

Diversity in Doctorate

There are now multiple ways of acquiring a doctorate, though they are not widely exercised in South Africa. The ASSAf report (2010) finds evidence that the traditional apprenticeship model, which is dominant in South Africa, may not be an efficient approach for the purpose of rapidly increasing the production of doctoral graduates. It identifies four main models for moving forward: the traditional apprenticeship model of individual mentoring, the coursework approach in addition to apprenticeship, the cohort-based model and the PhD by publication. Expansion, however, should not be pursued at the expense of quality.

Public Support

The PhD project in South Africa is largely the affair of the DHET, the DST and other relevant entities, including the universities. The project does not attract large or viable public support. In some institutions, the vigorous push by zealous vice chancellors to raise the number of faculty holding a doctorate through training opportunities has even been resisted. The NDP acknowledges that the government needs a greater understanding of the importance of science and technology, and higher education, in leading and shaping the future of modern nations. Government departments need to work together to develop a broad, enabling framework and policy that encourage world-class research and innovation.

In an endeavour to raise the quality of teaching and research, and to burnish their reputations, some institutions have been adopting strategic plans aimed at increasing the number of academics holding PhDs. In a few institutions, for instance the University of KwaZulu-Natal, the executive management has had to tussle with staff and the unions on the issue of implementing a mandatory policy on PhD acquisition, although this is funded by the universities.

In recognition of this trend, the ASSAf report (2010) recommended generating more public support for, and understanding about, the PhD. The idea here is to foster greater awareness and acceptance of the degree's significance for socio-economic development, beyond the personal gains of individual students. Developing a shared comprehension about the value of the doctorate is vital for garnering public support.

International Collaboration

International collaboration is one of the most common practices for capacity building in the academic and research arena. Through international cooperation for capacity building—the key rationale behind the internationalization of higher education in Africa (Teferra 2008)—doctoral programmes can be markedly enhanced, for instance, when it comes to doctoral advising, research mentoring, external examination and networking, among others.

CONCLUSION

South Africa has a commanding lead in the production of knowledge and research in Africa. It is estimated that half of Africa's knowledge is produced in South Africa. The key role of the PhD in sustaining this lead is evident. Unlike elsewhere on the continent, in South Africa, there are equally important centres of knowledge production outside of the universities; science and research councils, NGOs, the private sector, industry, government departments and state-owned enterprises are all involved in the production of knowledge. It is estimated that these entities produce 50 per cent of South Africa's knowledge.

The NDP has projected enormous increases in higher education enrolment within a relatively short span of time. To sustain the national system of innovation, many more doctoral students need to graduate. The economy requires a workforce with far higher skills to fulfil its development needs; research production needs to be stimulated and supported to respond to the demands of the knowledge economy and the next generation of academics has to be trained while transformation goals are being attended to—all in a climate of fiscal austerity. Managing the demands of different stakeholders while fostering the independence of a quality higher education sector and increasing knowledge production and relevance requires extensive skills in negotiation, prioritization and careful leadership, as well as a clear vision for the future of the system (Council for Higher Education 2016).

South Africa's plan to produce 5,000 doctorates annually may appear out of reach given the numerous challenges that the system faces, in particular, inadequate state funding, weak research infrastructure and deficiency in supervision capacities, among other obstacles. These numbers may be largely met by 2030, but not without further compromising the quality of PhD production in the country, which in turn has implications for the entire African continent.

REFERENCES

Africa Check. 2014. 'How Many Professors Are There in SA?' https://africacheck.org/reports/how-many-professors-are-there-in-sa/ (accessed 11 December 2019).

ASSAf (Academy of Science of South Africa). 2010. *The PhD Study: An Evidence-Based Study on How to Meet the Demands for High-Level Skills in an Emerging Economy*. Pretoria: ASSAf.

———. 2011. *Consensus Study on the State of the Humanities in South Africa: Status, Prospects and Strategies*. Pretoria: ASSAf.

Backhouse, J. P. 2009. 'Doctoral Education in South Africa: Models, Pedagogies and Student Experiences'. PhD thesis. Johannesburg: Faculty of Humanities, University of the Witwatersrand.

Cloete, N., J. Mouton, and C. Sheppard. 2015. *Doctoral Education in South Africa: Policy, Discourse and Data*. Cape Town: African Minds.

Connell, D. 2015. 'Eritreans Stranded in Hostile SA'. *Mail and Guardian*, 26 June. https://mg.co.za/article/2015–06–25-eritreans-stranded-in-hostile-sa (accessed 15 December 2018).

Council for Higher Education. 1997. *Education White Paper 3. A Programme for the Transformation of Higher Education*. Pretoria: Department of Education. https://www.che.ac.za/sites/default/files/publications/White_Paper3.pdf (accessed 11 December 2019).

———. 2006. 'Internationalization in the First Decade of Democracy. The Internationalization of Higher Education in South Africa', edited Roshen Kishun. Durban: International Education Association of South Africa. Pp: 65–80.

———. 2016. *South African Higher Education Reviewed - Two Decades of Democracy*. Pretoria: CHE. http://www.che.ac.za/sites/default/files/publications/CHE_South%20African%20higher%20education%20reviewed%20-%20%20electronic.pdf

———. 2018. *Vital Stats: Public Higher Education 2016*. Council on Higher Education, Pretoria, South Africa.

DHET. 2015. *Statistics on Post-School Education and Training in South Africa*. Pretoria: DHET.

———.2018. Statistics on Post-School Education and Training in South Africa: 2016—Released in March 2018. Pretoria: DHET.

DST. 2008. *Innovation towards a Knowledge-Based Economy. Ten-Year Innovation Plan 2008–2018*. Pretoria: DST.

Goneos-Malka, Amleya. 2015. 'PhD Students Battle to Get Jobs'. *Star Early Edition*, 29 June. https://www.pressreader.com/south-africa/the-star-early-edition/20150629/281711203301334 (accessed 24 November 2018).

Govender, P. 2014, April 6. 'Fear of Brain Drain as Profs Retire En Masse'. *Sunday Times*. http://academic.sun.ac.za/Health/Media_Review/2014/7Apr14/files/brain.pdf (accessed 11 December 2019).

Hay, D., and M. Monnapula-Mapesela. 2009. 'South African Higher Education before and after 1994: A Policy Analysis Perspective'. In *Higher Education in South Africa: A Scholarly Look behind the Scenes*, edited by E. Bitzer, 3–20. Stellenbosch: Sun MeDIA.

Herman, C. 2017. 'Looking Back at Doctoral Education in South Africa'. *Studies in Higher Education* 42 (8): 1437–1454.

Higher Education South Africa. 2014. South African higher education in the 20th year of democracy: Context, achievements and key challenges. Higher Education South Africa presentation to the Portfolio Committee on Higher Education and Training in Parliament, Cape Town, 5 March. http://www.hesa.org.za/hesa-presentation-portfolio-committeehigher-education-and-training.

Jansen, J., C. McLellan, and R. Greene. 2008. 'Internationalization and the Politics of Ambivalence in South African Higher Education'. In *Higher Education in Africa: The International Dimension*, edited by Jane Knight and Damtew Teferra,

387–420. Chestnut Hill, MA: Boston College; Ghana: Association of African Universities.

Louw, Johann, and Gillian Godsell. 2015. 'Multiple Paths to Success'. In *Doctoral Education in South Africa Policy, Discourse and Data*, edited by Nico Cloete, Johann Mouton, and Charles Sheppard, 125–172. African Minds: Cape Town.

MacGregor, K. 2013. Understanding demands and pressures of PhD production. *University World News*, 296. http://www.universityworldnews.com/article.php?story=20131115072244155 (accessed 15 November 2013).

———. 2014. 'Major Survey of International Students in South Africa'. *World University News*. http://www.universityworldnews.com/article.php?story=20140905134914811 (accessed 11 December 2019).

Mouton, J. 2009. *What We Know about the South African PhD and What This Means for Scaling-up Production*. Stellenbosch: Centre for Research on Science and Technology, University of Stellenbosch.

———. 2016, 25 February. 'The Doctorate in SA: Trends, Challenges and Constraints'. Bloemfontein: South Africa PhD Regional Conference.

Mouton, J., Van Lill, M., Botha, J., Boshoff, N., Valentine, A., Cloete, N. & Sheppard, C. 2015. A study on the retention, completion and progression rates of South African postgraduate students (Research report). Stellenbosch: Stellenbosch University.

National Planning Commission. 2011. National Development Plan: Vision for 2030. http://www.gov.za/sites/www.gov.za/files/devplan_2.pdf

———. 2012. *National Development Plan 2030: Our Future, Make It Work*. http://www.poa.gov.za/news/Documents/NPC%20National%20Development%20Plan%20Vision%202030%20-lo-res.pdf (accessed 11 December 2019).

Pandor, N. 2011. 'Science Funding Needs Improvement'. http://www.hsrc.ac.za/uploads/pageContent/1317/Science%20funding%20needs%20improvement.pdf (accessed 11 December 2019).

———. 2017. 'Minister Pandor's Statement on the R&D Survey 2014/2015'. http://www.dst.gov.za/index.php/media-room/media-room-speeches/minister/2163-minister-pandor-s-statement-on-the-r-d-survey–2014-2015 (accessed on 4 March 2018).

Ramoupi, N. L. 2017. 'Why Are There So Few Black Professors?' https://mg.co.za/article/2017-06-15-00-why-are-there-so-few-black-professors (accessed 2 July 2018).

Scott, I. 2009. 'Academic Development in South African Higher Education'. In *Higher Education in South Africa: A Scholarly Look behind the Scenes*, edited by E. Bitzer, 21–49. Stellenbosch: Sun MeDIA.

Sehoole, M. T. Chika. 2005. *Democratizing Higher Education Policy: Constraints of Reform in Post-apartheid South Africa*. New York, NY: Taylor & Francis.

South African Qualifications Authority. 2018. http://www.saqa.org.za/ (accessed 2 March 2020).

Teferra, D. 2008. 'The International Dimension of Higher Education in Africa: Status, Challenges and Prospects'. In *Higher Education in Africa: An International Dimension*, edited by Damtew Teferra and Jane Knight, 44–79. Chestnut Hill, MA: Boston College; Ghana: Association of African Universities.

———. 2015. 'Manufacturing—and Exporting—Excellence and "Mediocrity": Doctoral Education in South Africa'. *South African Journal of Higher Education* 29 (5): 8–19.

Waghid. 2015. 'Are Doctoral Studies in South African Higher Education Being Put at Risk?' *South African Journal of Higher Education* 29 (5): 1–7.

PART V

Asia

Chapter 11

Mainland China
Rapid Growth and New Strategies in Doctoral Education

Shuhua Chen

Mainland China (hereafter China) did not have doctoral education until 1978, although degree awarding documents may be traced back to 1935, before the People's Republic of China was founded (Wu, Lu, and Wang 2001). Yet, after four decades of development, China has become the largest doctorate producer in the world. Doctoral education plays an important role in providing talent for China's rising economy and strengthening the soft power of the country. At the same time, challenges and problems do exist. If not addressed appropriately, they will hinder the robustness of the system. In recent years, multiple reform projects have been carried out in doctoral education, and their implementation is raising questions about where China's doctoral education is going.

This chapter provides an overview of China's doctoral education, explores recent reforms and trends, and discusses problems and challenges both current and future. It starts with a brief historical review of the development of China's doctoral education, followed by an overview of its current state. After a brief introduction on the doctoral process, significant reforms and policies shaping the present system are summarized. Finally, the discussion and conclusion sections provide explanations for the trends in China's doctoral education and some thoughts on future developments.

BRIEF HISTORY

The Chinese word for doctorate is *bo-shi* (pronunciation similar to bə: ʃ). It literally means 'a person with broad knowledge'. In ancient times, *bo-shi* was a title for officials who worked directly for emperors and were in charge of keeping documents, writing books, consulting and teaching.

China's doctoral education began in 1978 (Zhu, Cai, and François 2017) when 18 doctoral students were admitted through national entrance examinations (Yang 2012). Mostly to address the shortage of faculty in higher education, China began expanding doctoral education soon after it was established. From 1982 to 1989, doctoral enrolments increased considerably, from 539 to 10,998 (Bao, Kehm, and Ma 2016). Between 2000 and 2003, graduate education (including doctoral education) experienced tremendous growth again, with an average annual increase rate of 26.6 per cent (Yang 2012). This was first due to the expansion of undergraduate education in the late 1990s. Also, the development of China's economy, science and technology was calling for more talent in all sectors, and many people felt the need to have an advanced degree for their work. Through years of development, Chinese universities, especially large research ones, had the capacity and resources to admit more students into graduate education (Zhang 2003). At the policy level, expanding graduate education was a response to China's strategic plan of building world-class universities (Zhou, Zhang, and Hua 2007). In November 1995, the Chinese government launched the '211 Project', whose goal was to build 100 key universities for the 21st century. In May 1998, China launched the '985 Project', a national initiative whose goal was to make Chinese universities more competitive worldwide. This project, named after the kick-off year (98) and month (5), aimed to improve the research performance of the 39 universities selected. After 2004, the growth

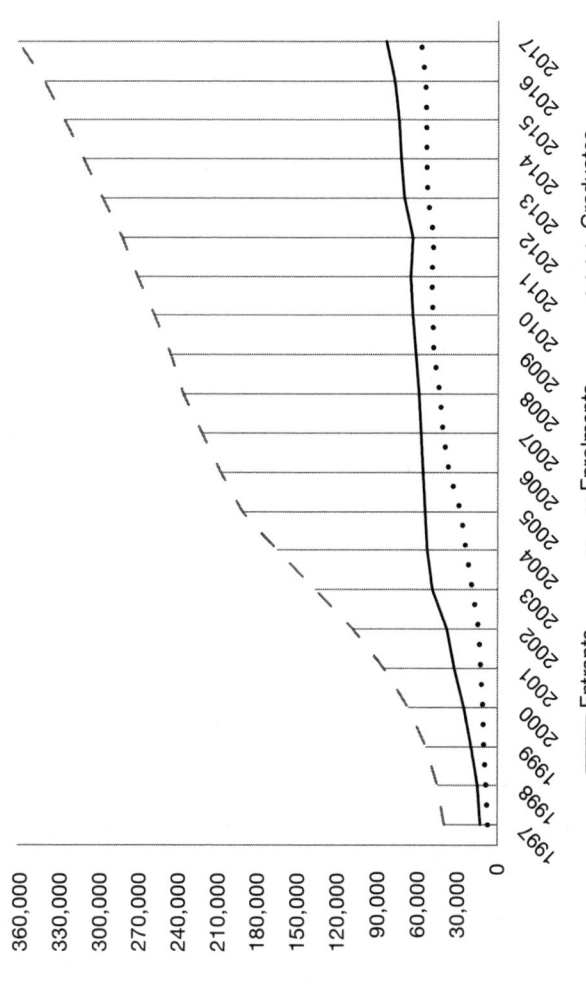

Figure 11.1 *Numbers of Entrants, Enrolments and Graduates (1997–2017)*

Source: Ministry of Education, http://en.moe.gov.cn/documents/statistics/2018/national/

rate of doctoral education has remained at 2–3 per cent each year. In 2016, China conferred 55,011 doctorates (Ministry of Education 2016) and for the first time exceeded the United States, which that same year conferred 54,904 (National Science Foundation 2018). During the past four decades, China has produced approximately 800,000 doctoral graduates in total (see Figure 11.1).

In developing graduate education, China borrowed heavily from the former Soviet Union, mostly due to historical reasons. The Soviet Union was the first nation to establish diplomatic relations with the new China. From 1949 to 1960, the Soviet government sent more than a thousand scholars and experts, including many in higher education, to help China recover from the wars. As a result, the Chinese higher education system maintains significant similarities with the Soviet system. In particular, the Chinese government invested much effort to develop the disciplines of natural sciences, engineering, agriculture and medicine; in contrast, social sciences and humanities received less attention and were not as fully developed (Yang 2012). This imbalance still exists today. As of 2016, the number of doctoral students in sciences, engineering, agriculture and medicine is nearly three times higher than the number of doctoral students in the social sciences and humanities (Ministry of Education 2016). Second, both universities and research institutes were allowed to award graduate degrees (Huang 2018). In the 1950s, there was also an increase in the number of specialized universities (as opposed to comprehensive universities), mostly offering degree programmes in engineering and agriculture (Huang 2018). Finally, the early doctoral students in China had little coursework, like in the Soviet Union (Maloshonok and Terentev 2018).

The Soviet influence began to diminish around the 1960s, following the Sino-Soviet split. With US President Richard Nixon's visit to China in 1972 and the establishment of Sino-US diplomatic relations in 1979, China started to look at the United States for higher education models. An additional driver was the Chinese government's launch of the open-door policy in 1978, which set Chinese higher education in a wider global context. Probably due to all these political and historical factors, China's earliest doctoral programmes adopted a less complicated model than the Soviet one—not requiring that students spend additional time completing the 'doctor of science' to become full faculty members after completing the 'candidate of science' (equivalent of the doctorate).

China's first doctoral programmes were offered mostly in Beijing and Shanghai, which set the tone for the distribution of doctoral education today. Doctoral programmes were established in geographic areas that were more industrialized, especially in large cities in the North, East and South (Yang 2012). Of the 575 doctorate granting universities, 50, which grant 60 per cent of China's doctorates, are located in large cities and 27 are in Beijing, Shanghai, Nanjing and Wuhan (Wang 2012). In contrast, Qinghai, Ningxia and Tibet—all western provinces—had no doctoral programmes at all as late as 2002 (Guo 2009). Until very recently, none of these provinces had more than 10 doctoral programmes.

Several government documents have shaped the development of China's doctoral education. From 1935 to 1940, before the new China was founded, the Nanjing government (Republic of China 1912–1949) issued a series of regulations regarding doctoral education. However, because of the wars, no doctoral students were recruited and no doctoral programmes were initiated. In 1980, the Academic Degrees Committee of the State Council (now the Department of Degree Management & Postgraduate Education under the Ministry of Education [MOE]) issued Regulations on Academic Degrees of the People's Republic of China. This document distinguishes three levels of academic degrees (bachelor's, master's and doctorate) by setting qualification standards for each of them. An accompanying document, Guidelines for Implementing the Regulations on Academic Degrees, was issued a year later, with details on coursework requirements and specifications on the procedure of doctoral examinations. These two documents are benchmarks for China's higher education. In 2010, the Outline of China's National Plan for Medium- and Long-Term Education Reform and Development (2010–2020) prioritized quality assurance in reforming doctoral education, and signalled a focus shift of China's doctoral education to quality control. Then, in 2013, a document issued by three departments (the MOE, the Ministry of Finance and the National Development and Reform Commission), the Memorandum on Further Reforming Graduate Education, proposed a new procedure for recruiting doctoral students—the 'application–examination' mechanism—which is expected to replace the former entrance examination mechanism.

CURRENT STATE

There are in total 2,914 higher education institutions (HEIs) in China, including 2,631 regular universities and 282 adult HEIs (excluding 800 private colleges; Ministry of Education 2017). Among the former, 575 confer doctorates. Besides HEIs, there are 215 independent research institutes that also grant doctorates (Ministry of Education 2016). Compared to universities, research institutes confer a much smaller number of doctoral degrees. For instance, in 2016, HEIs granted 53,641 doctorates, whereas research institutes conferred only 1,370 doctorates (Ministry of Education 2016). Doctorate granting institutions are publicly funded. None of the private HEIs confers doctorates, although a few (six as of 2016) offer master's programmes (Ministry of Education 2016). In October 2018, however, a private research-intensive university, Westlake University (WU), was established in Hangzhou, Zhejiang Province, and is expected to confer doctorates in the near future.

Types of Doctorates

The majority of the Chinese doctoral programmes confer only academic degrees, or doctor of philosophy. Professional doctorates first occurred in medicine in 1998. From 2009 to 2016, the ratio of academic doctorates to professional ones was nearly 20:1 (Ministry of Education 2016). Probably responding to a shrinking academic labour market, the 2013 Memorandum on Further Reforming Graduate Education clearly stated that China would develop professional doctorates. However, the progress has been slow and professional doctoral programmes remain very few. As of 2017, professional doctorates are offered within six fields (stomatology, medicine, veterinary medicine, education, engineering and Chinese medicine; Bao, Kehm, and Ma 2016). There is only a very small number of such programmes, for instance, 48 in clinical medicine, 25 in engineering and 15 in education (Yuan and Wang 2015).

Patterns of Enrolments

Between 1997 and 2016, doctoral enrolments in science and engineering programmes grew the fastest among all disciplinary areas. This pattern is certainly a legacy of the 1980s, when China was borrowing from the Soviet Union in building its own doctoral education. However, the rocketing growth in enrolments is probably also a result of the country's strategic plan for the development of higher education as well as a response to China's 13th Five-Year Plan on Innovation of Science and Technology (State Council 2016). The Memorandum on Further Reforming Graduate Education (Ministry of Education 2013) clearly stated, 'China will fully support ... fields in the frontiers of science and technology and areas that serve the country's significant demands'. The Five-Year Plan provided a list of priority areas, such as electronic engineering, manufacturing, pollution control and genetic engineering. In contrast, student enrolments in the social sciences and humanities were not growing as fast, and in a few disciplines (philosophy and history) enrolments remained the same throughout the decade.

Another pattern is women's increasing share in enrolments. In 1997, there were 7,394 women studying in doctoral programmes, whereas 20 years later, in 2016, this number increased 17 times to 132,132. In comparison, enrolments for men only increased 5.5 times (Ministry of Education 2016). There are no statistics regarding the fields in which female students are studying. However, the literature indicates that female students tend to pursue doctorates in the social sciences and humanities rather than in science and engineering. For instance, a study drawing on statistics on the employment status of engineering doctoral graduates of Tsinghua University between 2005 and 2014 (Jin et al. 2018) found that female students accounted for less than 20 per cent of the total graduates. Another study (Ma 2009) seems to show that, even in the social sciences, there are fewer female students.

Concerning their admission status, doctoral students are either 'state-planned' or contractual. State-planned students are funded by the government and usually full-time. In 2016, over 94 per cent of the entrants were state-planned (Ministry of Education 2016). Contractual students are often funded by companies and are expected to go back to work at those companies after graduation. These students may study either full-time or part-time. Before 2014, some students were 'self-financed'. These students were considered 'out of the plan' because they did not meet the admission standards. They were often full-time and paid a higher tuition fee compared to state-planned students. This category no longer exists now due to quality considerations.

Funding

Between 1978 and the mid-1980s, the government provided full financial support to all students in higher education. Both undergraduate and graduate students were exempt from paying tuition fees and received a monthly stipend to cover their living expenses (Zheng, Liu, and Lv 2016). After 1997, all HEIs began to charge undergraduate students for tuition and other fees (Shen and Xu 2002). Between the mid-1980s and 2013, a small proportion of doctoral students were required to pay, and three universities began to charge students enrolled in doctoral programmes (Zheng et al. 2016). Since 2014, all doctoral students pay for their study (Zhu et al. 2017) and tuition fees vary by fields and institutions.

At the same time, doctoral students receive financial aid from multiple sources. First, each full-time student receives an annual stipend from the government, often equal to the tuition fee. In 2017, this stipend was RMB13,000–15,000 per year (US$2,070–2,389; Ministry of Education 2018). Institutions usually have their own stipends that come in addition to these government subsidies. On top of the stipends, doctoral students receive performance-based fellowships during their study. They may also receive salaries, working as research, teaching and managerial assistants. There are also a variety of external fellowships (e.g., from industry) for which students can apply. Students with low family incomes may apply for governmental and institutional financial aid.

Supervision

As of 2016, China has 21,770 doctoral supervisors. The majority are men (85%) and nearly half (44%) are between 50 and 59 years old (Ministry of Education 2016). From 1981 to 1993, one had to be certified by the State Council (through the Academic Degrees Committee) in order to supervise doctoral students; since 1993, individual institutions approve their own doctoral supervisors (Chen 2013). Until 15 years ago, doctoral supervisor was a somewhat 'honorary' title awarded only to full professors; faculty members holding titles of assistant and associate professors were not permitted to be sole supervisors of doctoral students (Zhao and Shen 2011). In 2003, Peking University recognized the first associate professor as a doctoral supervisor (Zhao and Shen 2011); in 2010, Tsinghua University nullified the old mechanism and endorsed all associate professors as doctoral supervisors (Chen 2013). In 2016, Tsinghua allowed some assistant professors to supervise doctoral students (Tsinghua University 2016). To become doctoral supervisors, faculty members need to submit a formal application with supporting documents, including evidence of research productivity, capability to attract grants and supervising experience. In terms of supervision modes, each doctoral student may work with one supervisor, two supervisors or a supervisory team. With the rise of cross-disciplinary research, team-based supervision is becoming more common.

Career Prospects

Research indicates that more than 50 per cent of doctoral graduates from research universities still find employment at universities or research institutes, despite a shrinking academic labour market (Gao and Shen 2016). Yet, this number is decreasing and Chinese doctoral graduates work in a variety of sectors and positions (Gao and Shen 2016; Luo and Gu 2015). Generally speaking, graduates from the sciences and engineering are more likely to work in non-academic positions, and men are more likely than women to look for employment outside of universities (Gu and Luo 2013). A recent study (Gao and Shen 2016) drawing on the employment reports of 75 key Chinese universities found that, for the 2014 cohorts, and excluding graduates employed as postdocs in China and abroad, the employment rate was 51–97 per cent depending on institutions and disciplines. The same study also revealed that, in terms of employment sectors, only 20–40 per cent of graduates from top universities found faculty positions and around 20 per cent were employed in industry. A more recent study (Gu, Levin, and Luo 2018) based on surveys with 1,467 doctoral students from eight Chinese universities found that more than half of the students wanted to have non-academic positions after graduation, and that this pattern appeared to be even stronger among students at low prestige institutions. Although not yet a norm, postdoctoral positions are becoming more common than in the past, even in the social sciences and humanities; many doctoral graduates see postdoctoral experience as a stepping stone for a faculty position (Wang and Ren 2016).

Internationalization

The number of international students at the doctoral level has been increasing. In 2016, there were 18,051 international doctoral students studying in China, a nearly 10 time increase compared to 2004 (1,932; Wang 2017). However, doctoral students only account for 7 per cent of all international students, considerably fewer than students at other levels (18% at the master's level and 75% at the undergraduate level). Overall, the proportion of international students in doctoral pro-grammes is considerably lower than in high-income countries. For instance, in 2012, the proportion of international doctoral students in the United Kingdom, France, Australia, the United States and Japan were respectively 46.4 per cent, 40.0 per cent, 38.2 per cent, 31.0 per cent and 18.2 per cent, compared to only 1.9 per cent for China (Shen, Wang and Jin 2016). Few statistics are available on the distribution of international students by country of origin. However, Asian students account for the largest proportion at the graduate level. For example, the top five countries of origin for international doctoral students are Pakistan, South Korea, Vietnam, Thailand and Mongolia (Shen, Wang, and Jin 2016).

According to the Studying in China Plan (Ministry of Education 2010), China aims to become Asia's most popular destination for for-eign students by 2020. To reach this goal, the government is putting in place both policies and funding to attract international students. For example, the official website of the China Scholarship Council (CSC), campuschina.org, lists seven categories of state-level scholarship programmes supporting undergraduate, master's and doctoral studies, as well as multiple provincial, institutional, industrial and other scholarship programmes. International students are required to submit dissertations written in Chinese; yet many universities offer courses taught in English. International students pay much higher tuition fees than Chinese students; yet the special government fellowships available to them are also much higher.[1]

The Chinese government is sending students to top graduate schools in other countries with generous financial support. Between 2007 and 2011, the CSC funded 5,000 students each year to pursue doctorates abroad (Bao, Kehm, and Ma 2016). Since 2017, the government has increased this number to 9,000 (China Scholarship Council 2018). Sponsored students are required to return to China to work for two years after graduation (China Scholarship Council 2018). Further, joint doctoral training programmes are being established at the institutional and departmental levels, and students may apply for funding from universities and the CSC. The CSC and many research universities also have programmes to support doctoral students for stays abroad from 6 to 24 months (China Scholarship Council 2018). Through these programmes, students may take courses and participate in research projects abroad. As a result of a few joint initiatives, students may receive doctorates from partner institutions overseas.

Doctoral supervisors are becoming more international. In recent years, the central government has initiated multiple projects aiming to attract talent from abroad, the most prestigious being the 1,000 Talents Plan, launched in 2008, and the Chang Jiang Scholars Program launched in 2012. Provincial and local governments have launched similar initiatives. Through these programmes, numerous established Chinese scholars from overseas have been hired by China's universities and research institutes, many of them with doctoral supervising powers. Meanwhile, doctoral supervisors without overseas experience may apply for CSC financial support to become visiting scholars at top universities worldwide. All these initiatives contribute to making China's doctoral education more international.

---

[1] campuschina.org

THE DOCTORAL PROCESS

According to the Regulations on Academic Degrees of the People's Republic of China (State Council 2004), doctoral graduates are expected to 'have a solid and broad theoretical background and systematic and thorough knowledge in a field of specialization; be able to conduct scientific research independently; and make original contributions to science or specialized technologies'. This description, with its emphasis on original contributions of doctoral research and the independence of doctoral students, is in accordance with degree standards for doctoral recipients commonly accepted by universities and scholars worldwide (Lovitts 2017).

Chinese doctoral students usually graduate in three to five years, with the maximum completion time being eight years. The time to completion depends on admissions models, fields and institutions. Universities recruit students in three ways: fast-track doctorate, integrated doctorate and regular admission (Bao, Kehm, and Ma 2017). Students admitted through the fast-track model are master's students who show both the interest and potential to complete a doctorate. They are usually recommended to doctoral programmes by their supervisors or universities and have the option to complete a master's degree. The integrated doctorate is a recruitment mechanism for students who are completing their bachelor's degree. These students do not have the option to complete a master's degree but work directly on their doctorates. The fast-track doctorate and integrated doctorate are often referred to as the 'long programme' (Zheng and Liu 2017), as students recruited in this way are allowed to take a longer time to complete their doctorate than those recruited through regular admission. In practice, the operationalization of the long programme varies across institutions. Some universities recruit most of their students in this way, and others through regular admission. At some research universities, students in long programmes account for over 50 per cent of those newly admitted (Bao, Kehm, and Ma 2016). For regular admission, students traditionally take written entrance examinations organized by universities, followed by an interview. An emerging model is a combination of the American admissions model and the traditional model. That is, students submit an application package (a research proposal and supporting documents) and those selected take tests and attend an interview (Luo et al. 2016).

Students take courses in their first one to two years, and after completing coursework, they are required to take a comprehensive exam. Usually between the third and fourth semester (or later for students in the long programme), doctoral students submit a research proposal, which presents the research questions, methodology and a timeline for completing the dissertation. Passing the proposal defence is a milestone for students before officially beginning the dissertation work. However, it is common for many students to begin their projects (e.g., start collecting data) before that stage. During the dissertation research period, most universities require students to submit annual progress reports to supervisors and a mid-term report.

Before submitting the dissertation for external evaluation, most universities require students to attend a preparatory oral defence. This defence is usually arranged three months prior to the official submission of the dissertation, so students have time to do revisions. Once a student has passed the prep-defence and completed revising the dissertation, he/she submits the dissertation for external evaluation.

China seems to have a stricter evaluation system compared to many other countries in terms of using external examiners—experts/scholars from outside of a doctoral candidate's home university. Each dissertation is read by one to three external examiners, and at some universities even by four or five. External examiners are often nominated by supervisors; some universities randomly draw names from databases. In carrying out the evaluation, many universities are using a double-blind review mechanism, that is, a mechanism whereby the external examiners do not know the author of the dissertation under review and his/her supervisor(s), and vice versa. Normally, a doctoral candidate may proceed to the final oral defence only after all external examiners have approved the dissertation. A dissertation under review may be randomly selected for an internal review, usually organized by the graduate studies division of the doctoral candidate's home university. The evaluation committee for this round is composed of scholars who are different from those to whom the dissertation was originally sent to. In other words, a dissertation may be simultaneously evaluated by two groups of examiners. A veto from either group stops the candidate from proceeding to the final oral defence.

When the dissertation has been approved, the doctoral candidate defends it in front of a group of scholars in his/her field of specialization. Most oral defences are public and interested students and faculty members are allowed to attend. The result of the oral defence is based on a majority vote. Some universities post the names of the candidates who have recently passed the oral defence on their website for a certain period of time (e.g., three months) before awarding the degree. In China, doctorates are granted by HEIs and research institutes. However, the government sets qualification standards for doctoral programmes and decides whether individual programmes may continue recruiting students or not, according to periodical assessments.

Publishing in academic journals is a requirement for acquiring a doctorate, although it is not specified in any government documents, including the Regulations on Academic Degrees of the People's Republic of China. Depending on institutions, disciplinary areas and programmes, doctoral students need to publish one to four journal articles during their study, either in Chinese or in English, and they must be either the single author or the corresponding author. Some institutions and programmes have requirements concerning the quality of journals. For instance, at Shanghai Jiao Tong University, students in the sciences must publish at least one article in an SCI (Science Citation Index) journal. There is research indicating that not meeting the publication requirement is the major reason for Chinese doctoral students to postpone graduation (Li and Xie 2015). Fierce competition for publication spaces, due to the large number of doctoral candidates and the limited number of key Chinese journals, as well as difficulty in publishing in international journals, are further complicating the situation. Many students have to depend on publication in 'special issues' often 'specially added' to the regular issues of key journals, and on co-authoring with supervisors (He 2012).

Various statistics show that long-programme students are more likely to drop out—often before taking the comprehensive exam—often from lack of motivation; at some institutions, the attrition rate may reach 30 per cent (Wang, Zhang, and He 2016). Students who are regularly admitted, in contrast, have a very high completion rate. In recent years, there have indeed been calls to tighten doctoral examinations and eliminate less qualified students at earlier stages (Fu and Zhang 2015).

REFORMS AND TRENDS

China's doctoral education experienced tremendous growth in the 1980s and in the early years of this century. Nowadays, expansion is no longer a goal of development and the government and universities are shifting their attention to quality, accountability and international competitiveness. Accordingly, a more robust recruiting system and a stricter dissertation evaluation mechanism are being established, new initiatives are being put into practice and new types of universities are emerging.

The 'Application-Examination' Mechanism

Until 2007, when Fudan University began piloting a different admission procedure in its medical school, all students who wanted to pursue doctoral study had to pass entrance examinations (Zhou, Ma, and Ji 2015). The new model, known as the 'application–examination' mechanism, requires students to first submit an application for admission to the university where they want to study. An evaluation committee then reviews all submissions and selects those who are qualified. Once the review has been completed, selected applicants take written tests. Those who have passed the tests are interviewed and final decisions are made. Following Fudan University, Shanghai Jiao Tong University admitted 100 of all its doctoral students in this way in 2009 (Zhou, Ma, and Ji 2015). In 2013, the Memorandum on Further Reforming Graduate Education issued by the MOE clearly stated that the 'application–examination' system will gradually replace the old entrance examination. As of 2016, more than 100 universities are applying this new model in recruiting all or some of their doctoral students (Luo et al. 2016).

The application–examination mechanism gives more autonomy to universities and supervisors, focuses on the students' research potential and scholarly skills, and helps to select the best and most suitable students for doctoral study. It will thus ultimately enhance the overall quality of doctoral education (Shi 2017; Zheng and Liu 2017; Zhou, Ma, and Ji 2015). However, as a new mechanism, it is subject to misunderstandings and misconduct. Institutions differ in operationalizing the procedure, for instance, when it comes to assigning weight to the various components of the mechanism. Fairness in the admission process is therefore an issue (Luo et al. 2016). Other criticisms include the risk of corruption of faculty members and the overly formative nature of the admission interview (Zheng and Liu 2017).

Double-Blind Evaluation of Doctoral Dissertations

As the largest doctorate-granting country in the world, China puts emphasis on quality assurance more than ever before. At the top of its reform agenda are changes in the evaluation of doctoral dissertations. Currently, double-blind review is replacing other modes of dissertation evaluation (i.e., non-blind review and single-blind review).

While single-blind evaluation of doctoral dissertations has been used as early as 1995 at Tsinghua University (Sun et al. 2003), double-blind evaluation is a more recent phenomenon. For instance, Southeast University began sending dissertations for double-blind evaluation in 2002, with approval from the authors (Yao et al. 2011); Nanjing University of Agriculture required all doctoral dissertations to go through double-blind evaluation as of 2004 (Li, Luo, and Dong 2007) and Shandong University did the same as of 2005.

Double-blind evaluation is operationalized differently across institutions. Usually, universities and research institutes have databases from which they pull names of examiners for dissertation evaluation. These databases may be owned by academic departments, the graduate studies division or a third party. The number of external examiners differs depending on institutions, but most require two or three. Examiners are paid a courtesy fee, which varies across institutions.

The original purpose for using double-blind evaluation is to ensure fairness in the evaluating process and ultimately to enhance the quality of dissertations (Sun et al. 2003). Doctoral students tend to see blind reviewing as a better way of ensuring fairness than non-blind reviewing (Ma 2013). Case studies indicate that this mechanism is pushing students and supervisors to spend more time in revising dissertations before sending them out (Li, Luo, and Dong 2007). Overall, double-blind evaluation has considerably decreased the proportion of dissertations graded 'outstanding' (Li, Zhao, and Ma 2014).

Major problems with this procedure include a heavy workload for external examiners within a short turnaround time, difficulty in finding examiners (Yue 2011) and lack of scrutiny in selecting examiners (Zhao 2007). To partially address the workload problem, a few universities are using an exemption mechanism. That is, doctoral candidates with good publication records may be exempted from sending their dissertations for double-blind review. Additionally, institutions encourage students and supervisors to choose international examiners.

The Government's Quality Check on Dissertations

The Chinese MOE has conducted annual quality checks on doctoral dissertations since 2000. In 2014, the MOE launched a regulation that made the national quality check a systematic procedure. According to this regulation, the MOE randomly draws 10 per cent of the doctoral dissertations submitted in the previous year from the database of the National Library of China and sends them to three reviewers. A dissertation is considered 'problematic' if two of the reviewers grade it 'not satisfactory'. The MOE forwards the results of its quality check to individual universities and refers to its quality check records in assessing individual doctoral programmes. An accumulation of problematic dissertations for a doctoral programme may lead to its closure.

The regulation specifies that it is the MOE that organizes the annual quality check, yet many provincial departments of education also conduct dissertation quality checks. Considering the large number of doctoral graduates each year in China, state and provincial quality checks face many challenges, such as locating qualified reviewers, dealing with reviewer disagreement and the legitimacy of re-evaluating dissertations after submission (Cao, Xing, and Cai 2016).

The 'Double-World-Class' Project

The Double-World-Class (DWC) Project, launched in October 2015 by the State Council, is a strategic plan aiming to enhance the international competitiveness of Chinese universities. It largely replaced the previous 985 and 211 Projects, whose goals were also to improve the performance of research universities. 'Double' in the project name refers to world-class universities and world-class disciplines. The idea is to prioritize some universities and disciplines in accessing resources and thus expedite their development into the world-class league. The State Council's Overall Plan to Promote the Construction of World-Class Universities and World-Class Disciplines (2015) specifies a highly ambitious timeline for achieving this goal:

> By 2020, several universities and some disciplines will be ranked world class; several disciplines will approach the top end of world-class universities.
>
> By 2030, more universities and disciplines will become world class; several universities and some disciplines will lead the world-class rankings; the overall quality of China's higher education will be tremendously improved.
>
> By 2050, China will become one of the leading countries in terms of the quantity and quality of world-class universities and disciplines, and will on the whole have a strong higher education system.
>
> (English translation adapted from Huang 2017)

In September 2017, the MOE released a list of 42 universities, and 456 disciplines in 95 universities, as candidates for the DWC Project. All 42 universities are leading doctorate-granting institutions. There is no direct mention of doctoral education in the plan. However, prioritized access to financial and human resources will certainly make a difference to doctoral education in these institutions. They will be able to attract more highly qualified faculty and more talented doctoral students. In the long run, doctoral degree granting will become more concentrated in the universities on the list.

A common concern and criticism in academic communities is whether these lists will further marginalize smaller, more local and less renowned universities. Yan (2018) pointed out that the lists are not meant to pit Chinese universities against each other, but rather to encourage all of them to improve and work more closely with international counterparts. If this is truly the case, the DWC Project will further internationalize China's doctoral education through the exchange of information and resources with universities in other countries.

Emergence of New Research Universities

As previously mentioned, nearly 60 per cent of China's doctorates are granted by 50 large research universities. Now, their dominance might be challenged by the emergence of new universities. In 2012, the MOE approved the establishment of the University of the Chinese Academy of Sciences (UCAS), formerly known as the Graduate School of the Chinese Academy of Sciences (GSCAS). UCAS has an extremely high starting point in graduate education. As of December 2017, it has 153 CAS and Chinese Academy of Engineering (CAE) members and 6,000 doctoral supervisors. It has the largest doctoral enrolments (nearly 25,000) among Chinese HEIs, as well as the largest numbers of doctoral students in the sciences and international doctoral students.

Private research universities are emerging. In February 2018, WU, a privately funded institution located in Hangzhou, was formally approved by the MOE. The university website ambitiously says that the mission of the institution is 'to put China on the international map of science and technology research'. Accordingly, the university will recruit doctoral students, mostly in the sciences and engineering, before recruiting undergraduates. WU's leading faculty members are 1,000 Talents fellows and its first president is the former vice-president of Tsinghua University.

DISCUSSION

The development of China's doctoral education during the past 40 years shows a significant amount of borrowing and learning, reforms and changes, and achievements and problems. This section focuses on issues that seem most outstanding at present and provides thoughts on how they might continue to impact the system.

Top-Down versus Bottom-Up Reforms

The government plays a central role in reforming China's doctoral education. Almost all reforms are launched with government documents, such as the expansion of graduate education, adopting a new admissions model and applying the double-blind review mechanism. The top-down model has the advantage of effectively using resources to achieve goals. An example is the DWC Project, which clearly states that the Chinese HEIs and disciplines on the list will receive special financial and other corresponding support from the national and provincial governments. As the selected universities and disciplines are given priority in accessing financial and other resources, they stand a good chance of closing the gap with world-class universities.

Yet the risk with top-down reforms is that once mistakes are made, they spread considerably. China's recent reforms on doctoral education show that the government is using piloting to prevent such a risk. Most reforms are first practised at a few institutions (often prestigious research universities), and after a period of time, more institutions join in. For example, the application–examination mechanism in doctoral admissions began in a few programmes at a few universities before large-scale implementation. Another drawback is that the top-down model may make institutional identities invisible. It makes sense to distribute limited resources to HEIs based on their performance. Yet there are ways of grouping HEIs other than just making a list of candidate universities. Such lists encourage universities to only pursue goals similar to those of world-class universities and abandon other goals that are equally significant. For example, among the selected disciplines in the DWC universities, education is a listed discipline for Beijing

Normal University, a teacher-training institution established more than 100 years ago, but not for other 'normal' universities (teacher-training universities), some of which appear in the list only with disciplines unrelated to education.

The good news is that in recent years, universities have been given more autonomy and, as a result, reforms at the institutional level are becoming more common. One example is the approval of assistant professors becoming doctoral supervisors. In 2017, the MOE issued a document that grants universities further autonomy in carrying out reforms in doctoral education. Although implementation itself still reflects a top-down model (i.e., through a government document), the result is promising in that Chinese universities may initiate more reforms in the future.

Quality Control

In the past 15 years, China has shifted its attention in doctoral education from quantity (expansion) to quality. Quality control refers mostly to the evaluation of doctoral dissertations. In order to receive the degree, each doctoral student has to go through complicated and often intimidating procedures, including publishing in (often) specified journals, going through a rather formal preparatory oral defence and sending the dissertation to two or more external examiners for a double-blind review. Some students may be asked to submit a dissertation copy for a random quality check conducted by their own universities or the provincial or state educational authorities. This may take place before, during and after the formal evaluation of the dissertation. An unfavourable result at any stage of the evaluation will have serious consequences for students, supervisors and the corresponding academic units.

While China's dissertation evaluation procedure seems to be the most complicated in the world, whether it needs to be so remains a question. A comparative study between China and Canada on dissertation evaluation procedures (Chen 2018) points to several problems with China's current quality control mechanism. First, the Chinese system seems to depend too much on external examiners in ensuring quality in the evaluation process, yet in practice the eligibility for becoming one is often wrongly defined. Specifically, the Canadian system defines external examiners in terms of conflict of interests so as to ensure fairness in the evaluation, whereas the Chinese system defines external examiners mostly in terms of academic titles. Second, the fact that Chinese universities tend to use more than one external examiner seems to imply a lack of confidence in doctoral supervision. Finally, it is as important, if not more, to apply quality control to the process as to the product. For instance, universities should also focus on enhancing the learning experience of doctoral students, cultivating robust learning environments and training doctoral supervisors.

Global versus Local

As shown by the DWC Project, China wants to compete with other countries. Building world-class universities involves primarily building world-class faculty. By becoming more international as a result of national, provincial and institutional plans to attract talent from abroad, Chinese faculty has been greatly upgraded. When hiring assistant professors, HEIs, especially research universities, do show a preference for scholars with overseas experience. For instance, 60 per cent among new faculty members recruited by Peking University between 2009 and 2014 hold doctorates from foreign universities (Shen, Gao, and Wang 2016). Smaller and more local institutions can often offer better salaries and benefits in order to compete with larger institutions. The preference has put pressure on those holding doctorates from domestic universities. Indeed, many domestic doctoral graduates are going abroad for postdoctoral training immediately after graduation (Gao and Shen 2016).

As one of the world's largest exporter of international students, China has been challenged by brain drain. Statistics reveal that less than 10 per cent of Chinese doctorate holders in the United States returned to China between 2001 and 2005 (Shen, Wang, and Jin 2016). With China's economic development and a promising labour market for those holding foreign doctorates, the situation is changing. There are state, provincial and institutional programmes to attract junior scholars as well as preferential policies for those working outside of academia.

An emerging trend in the development of China's doctoral education is the localization of reforms. In its effort to develop doctoral education, China never stopped borrowing from other countries, while adding 'Chinese characteristics'. A good example is the application–examination recruitment mechanism. When adopting the recruiting procedure commonly used in other countries, few Chinese universities choose to completely abandon written tests, probably because the entrance examination model is viewed as more fair than the application-only model in the Chinese context. Another example concerns dissertation evaluation procedures. The overall structure resembles the North American one, yet implementation is different.

CONCLUSION

Literature, especially in English, addressing the trends in and challenges of doctoral education in China is scarce, and statistics are lacking. Therefore, this chapter may not give an entire overview. Yet, the author did consult abundant literature in Chinese in order to give a fair representation of current issues of concern. At the same time, when consulting Chinese scholars, one realizes how difficult it is to describe Chinese doctoral education in general terms, given the numerous variations existing across Chinese HEIs. The literature tends to focus on large research universities, marginalizing smaller universities and research institutes that also offer doctoral programmes. Literature on research institutes is almost non-existent in this regard.

In such a vibrant period of change for Chinese doctoral education, it is also difficult to cover all the reforms that are implemented. Multiple reforms take place—probably every day—at the provincial, institutional and departmental levels. Being a much younger system, China's doctoral education is far less stable than that in the United Kingdom or the United States, and is shaped by specific social, cultural and economic factors. Looking ahead, it is reasonable to predict that China will continue to develop a signature doctoral education, with borrowed international components and unique local features.

While existing HEIs continuously improve through multiple reforms, new research universities, including private ones, are emerging and questions are arising regarding what this means for the system as a whole, and who will follow whom in striving for excellence. With prestigious faculty members, including Nobel laureates, and state-of-the-art management, new universities are proving to be strong competitors to existing ones. Will China continue to launch new universities? Will smaller universities be further marginalized? How will Chinese HEIs be regrouped in the post-DWC Project period? Many questions remain open. What is certain for now is that China's doctoral education will continue its efforts to become one of the best in the world.

REFERENCES

Bao, Yanhua, Barbara M. Kehm, and Yonghong Ma. 2016. 'From Product to Process. The Reform of Doctoral Education in Europe and China'. *Studies in Higher Education* 43 (3): 1–18.

Cao, Lei, Rong Xing, and Dehao Cai. 2016. 'National Quality Check of Graduate Theses: Possible Problems and Recommended Solutions'. *Academic Degrees & Graduate Education* 33 (1): 52–55. (In Chinese).

Chen, Heng. 2013. 'History and Trends of China's Doctoral Supervision System'. *Education Research Monthly* 30 (7): 50–53. (In Chinese).

Chen, Shuhua. 2018. 'Dissertation Evaluation and Doctorate Granting Decision-Making: A Comparative Study of Top Universities in China and Canada'. Unpublished research report. Shanghai: Graduate Studies, Shanghai Jiao Tong University.

China Scholarship Council. 2018, January. 'Application Guide for CSC Fellowships 2018'. http://www.csc.edu.cn/article/1042 (accessed 26 August 2018).

Fu, Weidong, and Liqian Zhang. 2015. 'Reflections on the Application Mechanism in China's Doctoral Education'. *Journal of Higher Education Management* 9 (2): 107–113. (In Chinese).

Gao, Yao, and Wenqin Shen. 2016. 'Employment of Chinese Doctoral Graduates: An Analysis on the Employment Profiles of the 2014 Cohorts at 75 Institutions under MOE'. *Academic Degrees & Graduate Education* 33 (2): 49–56. (In Chinese).

Gu, Jianxiu, John S. Levin, and Yingzi Luo. 2018. 'Reproducing "Academic Successors" or Cultivating "Versatile Experts": Influences of Doctoral Training on Career Expectations of Chinese PhD Students'. *Higher Education* 76 (3): 427–447.

Gu, Jianxiu, and Yingzi Luo. 2013. '"Leakage from the Pipeline" or "Challenges of Doctoral Education": Rethinking China's Doctoral Education by Examining Chinese Doctoral Graduates' Career Paths'. *Journal of Higher Education* 34 (9): 46–53. (In Chinese).

Guo, Jianru. 2009. 'Expansion of Doctoral Education, Quality Distribution and Quality Assurance of Doctorates in Chinese Universities: A Perspective of the Institutionalism'. *Peking University Education Review* 7 (2): 21–46. (In Chinese).

He, Yuguo. 2012. 'The Academic Eco-system for Chinese Doctoral Students' Journal Publication: A Study on 15 Key Institution-Based Chinese Journals'. *China Postgraduates* 11 (1): 56–58. (In Chinese).

Huang, Futao. 2017. 'Double World-Class Project Has More Ambitious Aims'. University World News. http://www.universityworldnews.com/article. php?story=2017092913334471 (accessed 14 April 2018).

———. 2018. 'Changes and Challenges to Chinese Doctoral Education'. In *Doctoral Education for the Knowledge Society: Convergence or Divergence in National Approaches?* edited by Jung Cheol Shin, Barbara M. Kehm, and Glen A. Jones, 203–222. Cham: Springer.

Jin, Leili, Yiwei Wang, Chengtao Lin, and Dexin Hu. 2018. 'Career Choices of Women Doctorate Holders in Engineering'. *Journal of Graduate Education* 8 (3): 1–5. (In Chinese).

Li, Lan, and Yongsheng Xie. 2015. 'A Survey on the Publication Requirement in Doctoral Degree Awarding'. *Academic Degrees & Graduate Education* 32 (6): 60–64. (In Chinese).

Li, Yan, Shiqui Zhao, Luting Ma. 2014. 'An Empirical Study on Examiners' Comments on Doctoral Dissertations'. *Academic Degree & Graduate Education* 15 (10): 50–54. (In Chinese).

Li, Zhanhua, Yingzi Luo, and Weichun Dong. 2007. 'Reform and Practice of the Double-Blind Evaluation of Doctoral Dissertations'. *Higher Education Development and Evaluation* 23 (3): 51–56. (In Chinese).

Lovitts, Barbara E. 2007. *Making the Implicit Explicit: Creating Performance Expectations for the Dissertation.* Sterling: Stylus Publishing, LLC.

Luo, Yingzi, and Jianxiu Gu. 2015. 'Conflicts between China's Doctorates Production and the Labor Market and Solutions: A Study on Chinese Doctoral Students' Career Expectations'. *Academic Degrees & Graduate Education* 32 (10): 53–58. (In Chinese).

Luo, Yingzi, Zewen Liu, Jiale Zhang, and Xiaolin Wu. 2016. 'The Behavior Patterns of Stakeholders and Institutional Management of the Application–Examination Procedure'. *Research in Education Development* 37 (5): 58–64. (In Chinese).

Ma, Ling. 2013. 'The Effects of the Implementation of Double-Blind Evaluation of Doctoral Dissertations'. *Academic Degrees & Graduate Education* 30 (7): 11–15.

Ma, Ying. 2009. 'Gender Differences and Career Achievements of Doctoral Graduates'. *Journal of Chinese Women's Studies* 18 (6): 38–42. (In Chinese).

Maloshonok, N., and E. Terentev. 2018. 'National Barriers to the Completion of Doctoral Programs at Russian Universities'. *Higher Education* 22: 1–17.

Ministry of Education. 2010. 'Outline of China's National Plan for Medium and Long-term Education Reform and Development (2010–2020)'. http://old.moe.gov.cn/publicfiles/business/htmlfiles/moe/info_list/201407/xxgk_171904.html (accessed 16 February 2020) (in Chinese).

———. 2013. 'Memorandum on Further Reforming Graduate Education'. http://old.moe.gov.cn//publicfiles/business/htmlfiles/moe/A22_zcwj/201307/154118.html (accessed 16 February 2020) (in Chinese).

———.2016. 'Number of Postgraduate Students by Academic Field (Total)'. http://www.moe.gov.cn/s78/A03/moe_560/jytjsj_2016/2016_qg/201708/t20170822_311599.html (accessed 16 February 2020) (in Chinese).

———. 2018. 'Report on the Financial Support for Chinese Students 2017. http://www.moe.gov.cn/jyb_xwfb/xw_fbh/moe_2069/xwfbh_2018n/xwfb_20180301/sfcl/201803/t20180301_328216.html (accessed 26 August 2018) (in Chinese).

———. 2017. *Educational Statistics*. http://www.moe.gov.cn/s78/A03/moe_560/jytjsj_2017/ (accessed 15 December 2018). (In Chinese).

National Science Foundation. 2018. 'Doctorate Recipients from U.S. Colleges and Universities: 1957–2016'. https://www.nsf.gov/statistics/2018/nsf18304/data/tab01.pdf (accessed 15 December 2018).

Shen, Hong, and Donghua Xu. 2002. 'Exploring the Costs of China's Undergraduate Education in Relation to the Tuition Fee Charge'. *Educational Research* 24 (6): 72–76. (In Chinese).

Shen, Wenqin, Yao Gao, and Chuanyi Wang. 2016. 'An Analysis of Government Policies on Doctoral Education and Labor Market Demand in China: From the Dual-Demand Perspective'. *Education Research Monthly* 33 (12): 33–41. (In Chinese).

Shen, Wenqin, Chuanyi Wang, and Wei Jin. 2016. 'International Mobility of Ph.D. Students since the 1990s and Its Effect on China: A Cross-National Analysis'. *Journal of Higher Education Policy & Management* 38 (3): 333–353.

Shi, Guangjun. 2017. 'The Application–Examination Mechanism in Doctoral Admission: Purposes, Legitimacy and Improvement: From the Perspective the Supply-Side Reform'. *Journal of Graduate Education* 7 (5), 18–23. (In Chinese).

State Council. 2004. 'Regulations on Academic Degrees of the People's Republic of China'. http://www.gov.cn/flfg/2005-06/22/content_8526.htm (accessed 16 February 2020) (in Chinese).

———. 2016. 'Guidelines for the 13th Five-Year Plan for China's Economic and Social Development (Full Text)'. http://www.china.com.cn/lianghui/news/2016-03/17/content_38053101_15.htm (accessed 17 February, 2020) (in Chinese).

Sun, Xin, Hong Gao, Ying Liu, Wei Zhao, Haoming Chen. 2003. 'Thoughts on Reforms to Doctoral Dissertation Evaluation'. *Academic Degrees & Graduate Education* 20 (7): 23–26. (In Chinese).

Tsinghua University. 2016. 'Qiu Yong: The Quality of Doctoral Students Reflects the Level of Talent Cultivation and Academic Innovation of Top Universities'. http://www.tsinghua.edu.cn/publish/thunews/9649/2016/20161123152648619118000/20161123152648619118000_.html (accessed 10 December 2018).

Wang, Chuanyan, and Chao Ren. 2016. 'Postdoctoral Training in China: Challenges and Prospects'. *Science and Technology Management Research* 36 (16): 144–149. (In Chinese).

Wang, Xinhong, Junfeng Zhang, and Maogang He. 2016. 'An Empirical Study on the Attrition of Long-Program Doctoral Students'. *Journal of Higher Education* 37 (6): 50–58.

Wang, Zhanjun. 2012. *Academic Degrees and Graduate Education: Evaluation Theories and Methods*. Beijing: Higher Education Press. (In Chinese).

———. 2017. *Quality of China's Doctoral Education*. Beijing: Popular Science Press. (In Chinese).

Wu, Zhenrou, Shuyun Lu, and Taifu Wang. 2001. *A History of Graduate Education and the Academic Degree Systems of the People's Republic of China*. Beijing: Beijing Institute of Technology Press. (In Chinese).

Yan, Guangcai. 2018. 'The Radiation Effect of the Double World Class Initiative'. *Journal of Soochow University* 5 (1): 5–6. (In Chinese).

Yang, R. (2012). 'Up and Coming? Doctoral Education in China'. *Australian Universities' Review* 54 (1): 64–71.

Yao, Zhibiao, Keqin Lang, Bing Luo, Yangpei Kong, and Lu Zhang. 2011. 'Internal Control and External Monitoring of the Quality of Graduate Degree Theses: A Case Study of Southeast University'. *Journal of Graduate Education* 1 (5): 31–37. (In Chinese).

Yuan, Bentao, Chuanyi Wang. 2015. *Structure Adjustment of China's Graduate Education*. Beijing: Economic Science Press. (In Chinese).

Yue, Guofeng. 2011. 'Reflections on the Practice of the Double-Blind Evaluation of Doctoral Dissertations'. *Chinese Journal of Medical Education Research* 10 (2): 141–143. (In Chinese).

Zhang, Wei. 2003. 'A Comparison of the Scale and Structure of Graduate Education between China and the U. S'. *Academic Degrees & Graduate Education* 20 (7): 39–42. (In Chinese).

Zhao, Min. 2017. 'The Prospect of the Double-Blind Evaluation of Doctoral Dissertations'. *China Higher Education* 22 (12): 36–37. (In Chinese).

Zhao, Shikui, and Wenqin Shen. 2011. 'A Comparison of Doctoral Supervision Systems between China and Western Countries'. *Academic Degrees & Graduate Education* 28 (5): 71–77. (In Chinese).

Zheng, Feizhong, Jie Liu, and Jianxin Lv. 2016. 'The Characteristics of Paid Graduate Education and Optimization of the Tuition Fee System: A Historical Perspective'. *Academic Degrees & Graduate Education* 33 (2): 57–61. (In Chinese).

Zheng, Ruoling, and Mengqing Liu. 2017. 'The Practice of the Application–Examination Mechanism in Doctoral Admission: The Case of X University'. *Fudan Education Forum* 15 (2): 94–100. (In Chinese).

Zhou, Jianmin, Xiaofeng Zhang, Huihui Hua. 2007. 'Exploring the Legitimacy of the Expansion of China's Graduate Education'. *Academic Degrees & Graduate Education* 24 (10): 61–65. (In Chinese).

Zhou, Shanbao, Guangfu Ma, and Jingtao Ji. 2015. 'Rethinking the Application–Examination Mechanism in Doctoral Admission Practice'. *Journal of Graduate Education* 5 (1): 44–47 (In Chinese).

Zhu, Chang, Yuzhuo Cai, Wen-qin Shen, and Karen François. 2017. 'Perceptions of European and Chinese Stakeholders on Doctoral Education in China and Europe'. *European Journal of Higher Education* 7 (3): 227–242.

Chapter 12

The Role of Doctoral Education in Developing Research Capacities in India

N. V. Varghese

A doctoral degree is considered the most prestigious and most international of all academic degrees (Nerad and Evans 2014). It prepares students to be future academic leaders and trains researchers in knowledge generation. Knowledge economies recognize the value of research and knowledge production. 'Research universities stand at the center of the twenty-first century global knowledge economy' (Altbach 2011, 65). The high priority given to research and to the large-scale employment of graduates in knowledge economies has fuelled a worldwide expansion in higher education.

Higher education institutions contribute to knowledge production through their engagement in research and development (R&D) activities in two distinct, but related ways. The research carried out by universities and specialized research institutions is a regular source of knowledge production. Similarly, universities have been at the forefront in training the knowledge producers of the future—doctoral students. Even when knowledge production has partially moved away from universities to specialized institutions, research training has remained an almost exclusive domain of the university sector. Doctoral programmes remain a major component of all research-intensive universities.

Public investment and public institutions have traditionally been the sources of research and knowledge production. However, this trend has been changing in recent decades. Public investment in R&D activities is declining in high-income countries and continues to be very low in less developed countries. This decade has seen stagnation, or even a decline, in public expenditures on R&D activities in OECD countries. Between 2009 and 2016, the government share of total R&D funding in OECD countries decreased by four percentage points, dropping from 31 to 27 (OECD 2018). While the public sector continues to play a dominant role in R&D activities in less developed countries, these nations still lack both the financial and human resources to promote research and knowledge production (Sanyal and Varghese 2007). Private sector investments in R&D activities have increased and corporate sector engagement with knowledge production is on the rise globally, especially in high-income countries.

Doctoral studies are an important initial step in research training and creating capacities for knowledge production in the future. Without a doubt, the increasing economic value of knowledge production and the massification of the higher education sector have been influencing factors in promoting doctoral studies in many countries (Shin, Postiglione, and Ho 2018). The importance attached to research and publications in the global ranking of universities is a factor favouring the extension of the boundaries of research and knowledge generation in institutions of higher education. A pool of talented doctoral students and postdoctoral researchers has become a necessary condition to sustain the world-class university status attained by many higher education institutions. It is also true that doctoral degree holders experience higher employment rates and enjoy higher salaries (OECD 2017).

This chapter will analyse the trends in research programmes in India by focusing on doctoral-level degree studies offered by institutions of higher education. The next section provides an introduction to higher education provision in India, followed by a section on the evolution of doctoral programmes at Indian universities. Next will be a discussion of enrolment trends in, and expansion of, research study programmes in India. Trends in research and in the awarding of doctoral degrees in India will be analysed, and the final section attempts to draw some conclusions.

HIGHER EDUCATION IN INDIA: INSTITUTIONAL DIVERSITY IN PROVISION

India has a highly diversified institutional arrangement for providing higher education. One can seek higher education in India through both universities and non-university institutions. India has an affiliating system whereby students can pursue their studies for a university degree in colleges that are not authorized to award the degrees. Some of the most prestigious institutions in India such as the Indian Institutes of Technology (IITs) and the Indian Institutes of Management (IIMs) are not part of the university structure, although they are authorized to award degrees.

The university system in India consists of central universities, state universities, private universities and 'deemed-to-be' universities. Central universities, created by acts of the national parliament, are fully funded by the central government through the University Grants Commission (UGC, the highest regulatory body in Indian higher education), and have mostly unitary structures with no colleges affiliated with them. Among the 45 central universities in India in 2017–2018, some like Banaras Hindu University and University of Delhi do have affiliated colleges. In fact, University of Delhi has the largest number of affiliated colleges among all central universities.

State universities are established by acts passed by state legislatures. Although they receive partial financial support from the central government, they are funded and managed mostly by their respective state governments. State universities have an affiliating system and a large number of colleges are affiliated with each of the state universities. One of the state universities (Agra University) has more than 1,000 colleges affiliated with it. The public university sector in India, including both central and state universities, mostly enrols students at the master's and doctorate degree levels. In 2017–2018, there were 370 state universities in India.

Beginning at the turn of this century, India permitted private universities to open and operate. These too are established by state legislatures and are regulated under UGC rules passed in 2003. Within a short span of one and a half decades, the number of private universities in India has increased to 263. Private universities are not affiliating universities and they offer programmes mostly at the undergraduate level.

In the non-university sector, affiliated colleges are the most widespread providers of courses leading to degrees, mostly at the undergraduate level. These colleges may be owned and managed by the government, or be aided by the government or operate without any governmental support at all. Government colleges account for 22 per cent of the total, while aided private colleges account for 13.3 per cent and unaided private colleges for 64.7 per cent. These unaided private colleges began to proliferate in the 1980s, mostly offering technical and professional degrees, and were referred to as capitation fee colleges. They do not rely on the government for funds. However, they also have no authority to develop their own study programmes or award degrees.

Another category of institutions, called 'autonomous colleges', began to emerge in India in 1978. These colleges are free to develop courses, evaluate students and conduct examinations. However, those with the authority to award degrees are few in number. At present, there are 621 autonomous colleges in India. The country also has open universities and distance education programmes offered by dual-mode universities. There is one national open university, 14 state open universities and more than 200 dual-mode universities offering distance education courses. Distance education programmes account for nearly 20 per cent of the enrolment in higher education.

With more than 900 universities, 41,000 colleges and 36 million students as of 2017–2018 (MHRD 2018), India has the second largest higher education system in the world. The gross enrolment ratio (GER) in India is still low at 25.8 per cent. Nearly 80 per cent of the students are enrolled in undergraduate level programmes, 8 per cent in diploma programmes, 11 per cent in master's-level programmes and less than 1 per cent in research programmes.

DOCTORAL STUDIES IN INDIAN UNIVERSITIES

University education in India started during the colonial period with the establishment of the first set of universities in the Calcutta, Bombay and Madras Presidencies in 1857. These first universities were modelled after the University of London, and their role was mostly to conduct examinations and award degrees. The actual teaching took place in colleges, and research was an underdeveloped domain.

Most of the colleges and universities in India remained teaching institutions until the early 20th century. In his 1907 convocation address at Calcutta University, Sir Asutosh Mukherjee, the then vice chancellor, questioned whether universities should be confined to issuing degree certificates and argued that they needed to emerge as centres of learning (Bose 1964). Mukherjee invited eminent scientists to join the university and develop their respective departments into centres of learning and excellence. These initiatives led to introduction of doctoral studies at Calcutta University. Other universities in India followed this example, and thus doctoral programmes became part of Indian universities in the early decades of the 20th century.

India had a small but active group of outstanding academics, trained mostly at foreign universities, who carried out world-class research and published in the world's leading academic journals. These scholars were instrumental in establishing many of the reputed research departments and centres at existing Indian universities. Between 1904 and 1920, 13 doctorates were produced in India, 12 of them by the University of Calcutta (Sen 2015). In fact, India became a leader in doctoral education and academic research compared with other Asian countries (except Japan), even before its independence in 1947 (Chatterjea and Moulik 2006).

India gave higher education and research high priority during the post-Independence period. In 1948, the first commission on education appointed by the government of newly independent India was one focused on higher education. The Radhakrishnan Commission's recommendations emphasized improving the quality of research and teaching in higher education institutions. Subsequent committees and commissions also preferred to maintain high quality research and instruction, and to expand access to higher education only slowly. Public policies on higher education were highly influenced by the recommendations of these committees and commissions. It seems that the committees feared a dilution in the quality of research and instruction if the sector was allowed to expand too quickly. It is not surprising then that the higher education sector in India remained a slow growing sector for decades after Independence. In 2001, more than 50 years after Independence, the GER in Indian higher education remained at 8.1 per cent. Doctoral studies were a slow moving segment of the entire higher education sector. According to research from the IndCat INFLIBNET Centre, India had produced nearly 128,000 doctoral theses by 2000; this number almost doubled to 237,400 theses by 2010 and increased to 274,200 by 2018.

The commissions and committees specified a division of labour among institutions of higher education in India. University departments and research centres were assigned to carry out graduate studies and research programmes, while affiliated colleges were expected to focus more on undergraduate teaching. Thus, research and doctoral studies became mostly a part of the university system, while colleges became teaching institutions. The establishment of technological institutions and centrally funded universities in the post-Independence period further reinforced this division of labour by promoting research in the university sector and teaching in the affiliated undergraduate colleges. The expansion of higher education took place more through the admission of students to undergraduate courses in the affiliated colleges rather than through admissions to graduate courses offered in the universities.

ENROLMENT IN RESEARCH AND DOCTORAL PROGRAMMES IN INDIA

A doctoral programme in India, like in other countries, requires several years of intense study and research in a specified area, the generation of evidence-based knowledge and the preparation of a thesis that is reviewed by a group of examiners. According to UGC regulations, candidates for admission to an MPhil/PhD programme shall have a master's degree, or its equivalent, with at least 55 per cent marks in aggregate, or its equivalent grade 'B' on the UGC seven-point scale, or an equivalent grade in whatever grading system is followed. Scores are relaxed by 5 per cent for students belonging to disadvantaged groups.

Indian education follows a pattern of 10+2+3+2+1, or 2+3. That is 12 years of school, followed by three years for the undergraduate degree, two years for the master's, then either one or two years of coursework for the MPhil, and finally three years for the doctoral degree. According to UGC regulations, the MPhil programme shall be of a minimum duration of two consecutive semesters (one year) and a maximum of four consecutive semesters (two years). The PhD requires a minimum duration of three years, including coursework, and a maximum of six years. The UGC does not approve PhDs acquired through distance learning. In all, a doctoral degree in India assumes around 22 years of continuous study.

Historically, there have been two approaches to doctoral studies in India. The first is the direct PhD, in which students start research work immediately after admission to a doctoral programme. In the second approach, students go through coursework after admission. The former is more aligned with the European approach, while the latter is closely related to the US approach (Ghosh 2008). Now, there is a new approach common in most universities in India—an integrated MPhil and PhD programme. Under this framework, a student has to complete the MPhil and maintain a university-mandated minimum score, or cumulative grade point average, in order to progress to a PhD programme. The MPhil comes after the master's, and is for a period of one year without a thesis, or two years with coursework and a thesis. The UGC discourages part-time doctoral studies. In many universities, however, part-time doctoral studies, although not preferred, are permitted after completing the MPhil. In any case, coursework has become an integral part of doctoral study programmes in India. According to a more recent UGC regulation in 2016, all doctoral students must not only take courses, but also defend their doctoral study proposals.

Fellowships are given to full-time doctoral students if they qualify in competitive examinations conducted at the national or institutional level. All universities admit MPhil/PhD students through an entrance test conducted at the institutional level, following UGC guidelines for minimum eligibility criteria. The UGC conducts a National Eligibility Test (NET) to select suitable candidates for teaching positions in universities and colleges. As part of the NET, junior research fellowships are awarded to qualifying students. Organizations such as the Council for Scientific and Industrial Research and the Indian Council for Social Science Research, and other agencies also provide fellowships and financial support to doctoral students. Most of the full-time doctoral students in India receive some form of financial support that may partially, or fully, cover the direct cost of their studies.

In this century, Indian higher education has moved away from slow growth and low GER and into an accelerated growth and fast expansion mode, leading to the massification of the sector (Varghese 2015). As noted earlier, in 2018, India had nearly 42,000 institutions and 36.5 million students, accounting for a GER of 25.8 per cent (MHRD 2018). How did the expansion and massification of the sector affect enrolments in research and doctoral studies? An analysis of enrolment in higher education indicates that in 2000–2001, nearly 88 per cent of the enrolment in Indian higher education was at the undergraduate level, while nearly 11 per cent was at the graduate level, 0.6 per cent in research studies and 1 per cent in diploma programmes. The massification of the sector in this decade has led to a redistribution. In 2016–2017, the share of students enrolled in undergraduate study programmes declined to 78 per cent, and in research programmes to 0.41 per cent. However, the enrolment in diploma programmes, which are considered postsecondary education but not equivalent to a university degree, increased to 8 per cent.

This change in the share of student enrolment at different levels of higher education is primarily due to two reasons: the emergence of private universities and the expansion of enrolment in open universities. Private universities came into existence in India at the turn of this century and offer programmes, mostly at the undergraduate level, in technical and professional domains such as engineering, medicine, management, law and other vocational courses. The proliferation of private providers in these selected domains of study has resulted in 'disciplinary distortions' in higher education (Anandakrishnan 2010). These institutions are producing too many poor quality graduates in technical and professional subject areas, which has led to high unemployment rates. This fast expansion of undergraduate-level education in private institutions has also led to a decline in the relative share of students enrolled in research programs. Private universities have yet to establish their presence in the area of doctoral programmes. While private institutions (both aided and unaided) account for more than 77 per cent of all higher education institutions and a major share of overall student enrolment, they account for only 13 per cent of the enrolment in doctoral programmes (MHRD 2018).

The share of enrolments in open universities and distance education programmes has increased to around 20 per cent of the total. Open and distance learning modes do not encourage research study programmes, and doctoral studies account for only 0.01 per cent of the total open university enrolment (Varghese 2018b). Thus, these two factors—the expansion of enrolment in the private universities, mostly at the undergraduate level, and the surge in enrolment in open universities—have contributed to a relative decline in the share of students enrolled in research and doctoral programmes in India, dropping from 0.6 per cent in 2000 to around 0.44 per cent in 2011–2012.

However, this decline in the share does not imply a decrease in the total number of students pursuing doctoral programmes in India. In fact, overall enrolment numbers in doctoral programmes have increased during this decade. In 2010, the UGC stipulated that a doctoral degree was necessary (if one has not passed the NET) in order to be recruited for faculty positions in higher education institutions. This led to increased demand for admissions to research study programmes in India. The enrolment in doctoral programmes increased from 81,000 in 2011–2012 to 161,000 in 2017–2018 (Table 12.1), which accounts for 0.44 per cent of the total higher education enrolment. The enrolment in MPhil programmes more or less stagnated at around 34,000 during the same period, its share declining to 0.09 per cent of the total. Thus, the share of students in doctoral programmes in relation

Table 12.1 *PhD and MPhil Enrolment by Major Discipline and Gender (2017, in %)*

Discipline	PhD			MPhil		
	Male	Female	Total	Male	Female	Total
Agriculture	3.57	3.35	3.48	0.23	0.11	0.16
Commerce	2.26	3.48	2.78	7.41	8.68	8.22
Education	4.06	5.15	4.52	4.43	4.32	4.36
Engineering and technology	28.93	17.34	23.98	0.08	0.20	0.16
Fine arts	0.37	0.53	0.44	1.45	1.09	1.22
Foreign language	1.95	3.02	2.41	7.39	10.11	9.13
Indian language	4.55	5.28	4.86	13.31	11.72	12.29
IT and computer	1.30	1.91	1.56	3.06	5.81	4.82
Journalism and mass communication	0.46	0.42	0.44	0.79	0.39	0.53
Law	1.07	1.42	1.22	0.24	0.13	0.17
Management	5.46	6.43	5.87	1.82	1.53	1.63
Medical science	4.34	4.46	4.39	0.81	1.07	0.97
Science	24.59	27.72	25.92	18.81	27.26	24.22
Social science	10.61	12.41	11.38	23.52	16.65	19.13
Veterinary and animal sciences	0.72	0.59	0.66	0.00	0.00	0.00
Others	5.76	6.50	6.07	16.67	10.92	12.99
Grand total	100	100	100	100	100	100
Grand total in numbers	92,570	68,842	161,412	12,287	21,822	34,109

Source: MHRD (2018).

to total enrolment in higher education increased to 0.53 per cent in 2017–2018.

While this increase in enrolment at the doctoral level was shared equally by men and women, the increase in enrolment at the MPhil level was accounted for by women only. In fact, the enrolment of men in MPhil courses declined during this period by around 3,600. This is a trend one can also see at the master's level; the enrolment of men stagnated, while the enrolment of women increased by around 584,000. In 2017–2018, the women's share in enrolment was 56 per cent at the master's level, 64 per cent at the MPhil level and 42.6 per cent at the doctoral level.

A deeper analysis of doctoral and MPhil degree level enrolment by gender (Table 12.2) shows a similar pattern over the years. In 2017, more than 60 per cent of men and 55 per cent of women were accounted for by the social sciences, sciences and engineering, and technology subject areas. In fact, of the total enrolment at the doctoral level, women have become a majority in the subject areas of commerce, fine arts, foreign languages and information technology and computers. The overall gender parity index favours women at the master's and MPhil levels, and women are improving their relative position in enrolment at the doctoral level.

In addition to increased enrolment in doctoral studies domestically, a number of Indian doctoral students are studying abroad. In 2017, the UNESCO Institute for Statistics reported that there were around 305,000 Indian students pursuing higher education abroad. A breakdown of those figures in terms of stages of higher education is not readily available. However, it is known that a significant number of Indian students pursue doctoral studies abroad. A large share are enrolled in doctoral programmes in the United States, the United Kingdom and Australia. In 2016, there were 1,093 Indian students enrolled in doctoral programmes in Australia, accounting for nearly 2.6 per cent of all Indian students in Australian universities. The National Science Foundation's 'Survey of Earned Doctorates' reports that, in 2015, US universities awarded 2,230 doctorates to Indian students, which accounted for 13.9 per cent of all doctorates awarded that year to

Table 12.2 MPhil and Doctorate Degrees Awarded by Faculty

Faculty	2000–2001 (%)	2010–2011 (%)	2014–2015 (%)
Science and technology disciplines (A)			
Science	3,727 (32.3)	9,720 (34.0)	15,560 (31.0)
Engineering/ Technology	778 (6.7)	1,728 (6.1)	4,385 (8.7)
Medicine	221 (1.9)	648 (2.3)	1,515 (3.0)
Agriculture	889 (7.7)	661 (2.3)	1,821 (3.6)
Veterinary science	110 (1.0)	186 (0.7)	238 (0.5)
Total (A)	5,725 (49.59)	12,943 (45.31)	23,519 (46.83)
Arts disciplines (B)			
Arts and humanities	4,398 (38.1)	9,737 (34.1)	15,849 (31.6)
Commerce	621 (5.4	2,808 (9.8)	5,295 (10.5)
Education	399 (3.5)	1,128 (4.0	1,633 (3.3)
Law	105 (0.9)	240 (0.8)	289 (0.6)
Others	296 (2.6)	1,711 (6.0)	3,641 (7.3)
Total (B)	5,819 (50.4)	15,624 (54.7)	26,707 (53.2)
Total (A + B)	11,544 (100)	28,567 (100)	50,226 (100)

Source: University Grants Commission. Various years, Annual Reports.

international students in the United States. In 2015–2016, more than 17,000 Indian students were enrolled in doctoral programmes in US universities (Group of Eight 2017). A large number of Indian doctoral students pursue their studies in science and technology subject areas, and a majority of these students do not return to India after their doctoral studies. In this sense, students pursuing doctoral studies abroad contribute to a brain drain for India and a brain gain for host countries.

TRENDS IN DOCTORAL DEGREES AWARDED IN INDIA

Higher education research in India is broadly divided into two areas: science and technology, and the arts. The data presented in this section on doctoral degrees awarded follows this pattern, although a more detailed disciplinary categorization is given in the tables. The number of research degrees (MPhil and PhD) awarded in India increased from 11,544 in 2000–2001 to 50,226 in 2014–2015 (Table 12.2). It is impressive—a growth rate of more than four times within a period of just one and a half decades. Although the sciences and the arts grew comparably, the increase in the number of degrees awarded seems to favour arts subjects, which increased at a rate of around 4.7, while science and technology disciplines grew at a rate of about 4.1 during those years. The change in numbers has also affected the relative share for the subject areas. For example, in 2000–2001, science and technology subjects accounted for 49.6 per cent of the total research degrees awarded by universities in India. That share had declined to 46.8 per cent in 2014–2015. Meanwhile, the share of doctoral degrees awarded in arts subjects showed a corresponding increase, from 50.4 per cent to 53.2 per cent, during the same period.

An analysis of research degrees awarded by discipline reveals that more than 70 per cent of the doctoral degrees were in science and in the arts and humanities in 2000–2001. However, their combined share declined to around 62 per cent in 2014–2015 (Table 12.3). This was primarily due to an increase in the number of doctoral programmes offered in other subject areas. For example, among the science and technology disciplines, the share of research degrees in agriculture was halved during the period between 2000–2001 and 2014–2015, while other subject areas within science and technology increased their share (Table 12.3). Although there has been a decline in the overall share of science degrees, from 32.3 per cent to 31.0 per cent, the number remained high at around two-thirds of all doctoral degrees awarded in all science and technology disciplines in 2000–2001 and in 2014–2015.

The trend also shows a decline in the share of doctoral degrees awarded in arts and humanities subjects, from 38.1 per cent in 2000–2001 to 31.6 per cent in 2014–2015 (Table 12.3). Within that, however, the number of research degrees in commerce doubled, while those in the 'others' category almost trebled. The largest increase in the number of research degrees was in commerce, which increased its share from 5.4 per cent to 10.5 percent (from 621 degrees in 2000–2001 to

Table 12.3 *Doctoral Degrees Awarded by Faculty*

Faculty	2010–2011	2014–2015
Science and technology disciplines (A)		
Science	5,271 (32.8)	7,617 (27.9)
Engineering/Technology	1,682 (10.5)	4,340 (15.9)
Medicine	601 (3.7)	1,395 (5.1)
Agriculture	586 (3.6)	1,690 (6.2)
Veterinary science	162 (1.0)	204 (0.8)
Total (A)	8,302 (51.6)	15,246 (55.8)
Arts disciplines (B)		
Arts	4,998 (31.1)	6,890 (25.2)
Commerce	1,259 (7.8)	2,305 (8.4)
Education	645 (4.0)	763 (2.8)
Law	223 (1.4)	254 (0.9)
Others	666 (4.1)	1,869 (6.8)
Total (B)	7,791 (48.4)	12,081 (44.2)
Total (A+B)	16,093 (100)	27,327 (100)

Source: University Grants Commission. http://nstmis-dst.org/PDF2017/Table13.pdf (accessed 12 December 2019).

Note: Figures in the bracket are percentages to the total.

5,295 in 2014–2015). The 'others' category increased its share from 2.6 per cent to 7.3 per cent during the same period.

The decline in the number of degrees awarded in traditional subject areas at a time when the overall number of students pursuing doctoral degrees is increasing shows that doctoral studies have been slowly but steadily spreading to non-traditional disciplines and responding to market demand in India. For example, the increase in the number of doctorates in commerce indicates the changing demand for degrees in an economy with a financial sector that is growing quickly. Many graduates in commerce are not entering teaching professions, but work instead in the private and corporate sectors, where employment opportunities are brighter and salary levels are higher.

Doctoral degrees maintain a high share of the total number of research degrees (MPhil and PhD) awarded in India. Doctorates accounted for 59.3 per cent of the total in 2010–2011 and 54.4 per cent in 2014–2015. The share of doctoral degrees awarded in the arts declined from nearly 50 per cent in 2010 to around 45 per cent in 2014–2015. Science and technology disciplines showed a corresponding increase (Table 12.3). Table 12.3 also shows a relative increase in MPhil degrees as a share of the total for arts subjects, while the MPhil share remained more or less unchanged in science and technology.

The All India Survey on Higher Education data (MHRD 2018) shows that the country awarded 34,400 doctoral degrees in 2017–2018. Nearly 60 per cent of those went to men. According to this survey, the number of doctoral degrees awarded in science increased from 5,393 to 8,880 during the period from 2011–2012 to 2017–2018. The increase was impressive in both engineering and technology. In fact, science and engineering subjects accounted for more than two-thirds of the doctoral degrees awarded in science and technology disciplines. This again reflects the demand for doctoral graduates in the knowledge economy sectors of India.

In the social sciences, education is the discipline with the largest number of doctoral degrees awarded during the period between 2010 and 2014. This was followed by economics and commerce. More than 50 per cent of the doctoral dissertations in the social sciences were in education, commerce, economics and management (Pandita and Singh 2017), and more than 80 per cent of doctoral theses were in those subjects plus political science, sociology, psychology and law. In other words, eight subject areas accounted for more than four-fifths of all social science doctoral theses from 2010 to 2014.

It is also interesting to look at the geographic breakdown of doctoral degree awards. Eight of India's states accounted for nearly two-thirds of the doctoral degrees awarded between 2010 and 2014. In fact, three states alone—Gujarat, Maharashtra and Andhra Pradesh—accounted for more than one-third of the doctoral degrees awarded during this period. Surprisingly, the states that produce the largest number of doctoral degree graduates are not those with the highest density of higher education institutions or those with the top-ranking universities in the country.

In 2017, more than 60 per cent of the doctoral degrees in social sciences were awarded by 20 universities in India, while the remaining 40 per cent were shared by 151 others (Pandita and Singh 2017). In terms of the average number of social science doctoral theses produced, Jawaharlal Nehru University (JNU) in New Delhi ranked first, followed by Maharshi Dayanand University (MDU), Haryana, and Dr. Babasaheb Ambedkar Marathwada University in Maharashtra. JNU produced the largest number of doctoral theses in political science, sociology and economics, while MDU produced the largest number of doctoral theses in education.

As mentioned, a large number of doctoral degrees were awarded in the field of education between 2010 and 2014. MDU awarded the largest number of doctoral degrees in education, followed by Dr. Babasaheb Ambedkar Marathwada University in Maharashtra, and then H. N. Gujarat University and Saurashtra University, which are both in Gujarat (Koul and Pandita 2017). In fact, there has been a proliferation of higher education institutions offering courses and programmes in education in recent decades. A major share of the research in education departments at universities has focused on pedagogical dimensions at the school level (Varghese 1992), and this trend continues today. Research on higher education has been relatively absent. Interestingly, more research on broader issues related to higher education and development has been carried out in social science departments rather than education departments (Varghese 2018a).

Overall, the trends indicate that the nature of doctoral studies is changing in India. Universities and programmes are increasingly responding to the needs and requirements of the knowledge-based production sectors of the economy. This will also have effects on the nature of doctoral programmes, as they move away from training graduates for teaching and research positions, and instead try to transform them into knowledge workers. While regulating bodies are encouraging research skills as an essential entry qualification for positions in universities, employment opportunities and higher salaries are increasingly found in the knowledge-based production sectors of the economy. The relatively slow recruitment of faculty members in higher education institutions reduces employment opportunities for doctoral graduates in India, compelling them to take up jobs in other sectors. The increasing share of doctoral degrees in commerce and technology, and a decline in the share of doctoral degrees awarded in education, are reflections of increasing employment opportunities in the knowledge sectors of the economy. This will have an effect on the shaping of Indian doctoral programmes in the future.

CONCLUDING OBSERVATIONS

Doctoral programmes are expanding in the context of massification of higher education in India. The UGC regulation of 2010, which made the doctoral degree a necessary qualification to become an academic faculty member in an Indian university, has contributed to the expanding enrolment in research degree programmes in India. An analysis of the subject areas in which that expansion is taking place indicates that Indian doctoral programmes are responding to the demands of employment sectors other than universities, and of professions other than teaching. The increase in the share of doctoral degrees awarded in subject areas such as commerce, engineering and technology indicates that research studies are reacting to the quickly expanding sectors of the knowledge economy.

The expansion of doctoral programmes and the increase in student enrolment at the doctoral level are challenges in India. Faculty members qualified to supervise doctoral students are limited in number, and hiring rates are not keeping pace with the rate of expansion. A recent stipulation by the UGC to strictly adhere to the required student–teacher ratio has resulted in the cancellation of admissions offers to doctoral students at many prestigious universities. Such trends further reduce the scope and quality of doctoral study programmes, since they affect the relatively better placed universities rather than the poorly placed ones.

Teacher shortages are a reality in Indian higher education. These shortages are felt more in public institutions, many of which are strong pillars of research and doctoral programmes in the country. Strict enforcement of student–teacher ratios at a time when teacher vacancies are not filled limits the expansion of the country's research base. Therefore, the main challenge and immediate concern is how to expand the base of research programmes in India, while at the same time ensuring their quality. The teacher shortages are not due to a lack of qualified candidates, but rather the absence of recruitment at some of the universities for several years. An immediate solution lies in filling these faculty vacancies quickly, and with highly qualified individuals. The lack of teacher recruitment not only contributes to shortages of teachers but also to the growing unemployment of doctoral graduates. These factors—teacher shortages and unemployment of doctoral graduates—are two sides of the same coin, because a major source of employment for Indian doctoral graduates continues to be universities and research institutions.

Admissions to research programmes are regulated through entrance tests at the university level and at the national level through examinations such as NET. This helps ensure the quality of the students entering doctoral programmes. However, it needs to be emphasized that it is not always the best students who are attracted to doctoral programmes. Many of the best students from good institutions are not willing to invest four to five more years of study after completing their master's. Moreover, demand for these graduates in the employment market is high, and hence the opportunity costs of pursuing doctoral studies are becoming relatively high.

One of the main concerns in doctoral education in India is the quality of doctoral theses. There are universities endowed with highly qualified faculty with plenty of research experience, but this is confined to a limited number. The majority of institutions are poorly placed to provide academic guidance, and so their students produce doctoral theses of low quality. At many of these institutions, the infrastructure needed to carry out doctoral studies, especially in science subjects, is also far from satisfactory. Taken together, these two factors adversely affect the quality of doctoral theses produced by Indian universities. The slow pace of teacher recruitment adds to these concerns, as does the lack of funding and support for doctoral students. The UGC has increased the fellowship amount for doctoral students, but the majority of students pursuing doctoral degrees do not get UGC fellowships. They get either state government fellowships or fellowships provided by their own universities, which are worth far less than a UGC fellowship. Therefore, there is a need to increase both the overall number of fellowships and the amount of money given through existing fellowships, especially non-UGC ones.

There are also concerns about how doctoral degrees are awarded. The thesis is evaluated by two external examiners, who must be carefully selected. The dissertation defence sessions (viva voce) need to test the candidate's in-depth knowledge of his or her subject area, while also evaluating the empirical evidence generated by the candidate and his or her analytical competencies as reflected in the thesis. It is also now mandatory that the doctoral student has two published articles before he or she submits the thesis. While this is a welcome step, the publications produced by many candidates are of questionable quality.

Another important concern for Indian doctoral graduates is acute unemployment. Recent advertisements for clerical-level positions in states such as Uttar Pradesh and Telangana have attracted applications from a large number of doctorate degree holders. This trend shows that unemployment is slowly but steadily spreading among doctoral graduates. One of the reasons for this is the absence of recruiting by Indian universities to fill teaching positions. Students who graduate from less prestigious universities feel the incidence of unemployment most acutely. It seems that the low quality of doctoral studies and the high incidence of unemployment among doctoral graduates from poorer quality institutions are closely related.

In conclusion, the major challenge facing doctoral studies in India is one of quality. There is a need to attract good students and to strengthen academic guidance, support and funding for research students in India. Equally important, though, is the need for supporting teachers so that they can improve their research supervision skills and competencies.

REFERENCES

Altbach, P. G. 2011. 'The Past, Present, and Future of the Research University'. *Economic & Political Weekly* 56 (6): 65–73.

Anandakrishnan, A. 2010. 'Accountability and Transparency in University Governance'. *University News* 48 (45): 18–23.

Bose, Satyendra Nath. 1964. 'The Problem of Education in Bengal and Asutosh'. In *S. N. Bose: The Man and His Work, Part II: Life and Lectures and Addresses, Miscellaneous Pieces*, edited by S. Chatterjee et al. Calcutta: S. N. Bose National Centre for Basic Sciences.

Chatterjea, A., and S. P. Moulik. 2006. 'Doctoral Education and Academic Research in India'. CHERI Working Paper No. 87. Ithaca, NY: Cornell University.

Ghosh, N. 2008. 'Research in Engaged Social Sciences: A Few Concerns'. *Economic & Political Weekly* 43 (4): 77–79.

Group of Eight. 2017. *Report of the Go8-India PhD Advisory Taskforce on Two-way Mobility of PhD Students between India and Australia*. Canberra: Group of Eight Universities.

Koul, M., and R. Pandita. 2017. 'Doctoral Dissertations Awarded in Education in India: A Study'. *International Journal of Information Dissemination and Technology* 17 (4): 233–237.

MHRD. 2018. *All India Survey of Higher Education 2017–2018*. New Delhi: Department of Higher Education, MHRD.

Nerad, M., and B. Evans. 2014. *Globalization and Its Impacts on the Quality of PhD Education: Forces and Forms in Doctoral Education Worldwide*. Rotterdam: Sense Publishers.

OECD. 2017. *Education at Glance*. Paris: OECD.

———. 2018. *Science, Technology and Innovation Outlook 2018*. Paris: OECD.

Pandita, R. K., and S. Singh. 2017. 'Doctoral Research Output in Social Sciences in India during 2010–2014: A Study'. *DESIDOC Journal of Library and Information Technology* 37 (5): 328–336.

Sanyal, B. C., and N. V. Varghese. 2007. *Knowledge for the Future: Developing Research Capacities in the Developing Countries*. Paris: IIEP/UNESCO.

Sen, B. K. 2015. 'Doctorate Degrees from India: 1877 (First Award) to 1920'. *Indian Journal of History of Science* 50 (3): 533–534.

Shin, J. C., G. A. Postiglione, and K. C. Ho. 2018. 'Challenges for Doctoral Education in East Asia: A Global and Comparative Perspective'. *Asia Pacific Education Review* 19 (2): 141–155.

University Grants Commission (UGC). 2016. *Minimum Qualifications for Appointment of Teachers and Other Academic Staff in Universities and Colleges and Measures for the Maintenance of Standards in Higher Education*. New Delhi: University Grants Commission.

————. Various years. *Annual Reports*. New Delhi: University Grants Commission.
Varghese, N. V. 1992. 'Interdisciplinarity and Educational Research in India'. *Perspectives in Education* 8 (2): 65–78.
————. 2015. 'Challenges of Massification of Higher Education in India'. CPRHE Research Paper Series no.1. New Delhi: CPRHE/NIEPA.
————. 2018a. 'Education Research and Emergence of Higher Education as a Field of Study in India'. In *Higher Education Research as a Field of Study in Asia*, edited by Jisun Jung, Hugo Horta, and Akiyoshi Yonezawa, 299–313. Singapore: Springer.
————. 2018b. 'Digital Technology and the Changing Nature of Distance Learning'. Convocation address. Hyderabad: Dr. B. R. Ambedkar Open University.

Chapter 13

From Quantitative Expansion to Qualitative Improvement
Changes in Doctoral Education in Japan

Futao Huang

Doctoral education in Japan has undergone several major changes since the late 19th century, developing distinctive characteristics during the process. On the one hand, Japan's doctoral education still maintains some historic traditions. On the other hand, the country has launched several national-level reforms since the late 1980s, aiming to modernize the system. Japan's doctoral education is significantly different from that of many Western countries, including Germany, the United Kingdom and the United States, and neighbouring Asian countries such as China and Korea. From a historical perspective, Japan established its modern higher education system in the late 19th century, modelled on Western ideas, especially on the practices of German research universities. Soon after the Second World War, Japan reformed its national higher education system by learning from US models, including the introduction of an American form of doctoral education, but the system did not achieve any comprehensive expansion and development in terms of organization and curriculum until the early 1990s. Recent reforms to Japan's doctoral education have resulted in its rapid expansion and qualitative improvement. However, it is confronted with numerous issues. For example, in contrast to the United States and even China, the percentage of doctoral students is still low compared to total undergraduate enrolment. Thus, it faces the challenges of attracting talented students—deterred by insufficient financial support—to doctoral programmes, growing criticism from industry and business, limited employment opportunities for doctoral graduates, especially in the academic market, and low numbers of international students, particularly from non-Asian countries.

This chapter provides an overview of doctoral education in Japan, highlighting and analysing current thinking and developments. Through both a literature review and an original analysis of national statistics and several national surveys, it focuses on the particular characteristics of Japan's doctoral education (starting with a brief history) and presents the reforms that have been launched and the changes that have occurred, with a particular focus on reforms since the 1990s. The study concludes by arguing that, since the 1980s, Japanese doctoral education has moved from a phase of quantitative expansion until the end of the 1990s to a focus on qualitative improvement starting in the 2000s. This change is characterized by a progression from unsystematic teaching and training activities to the establishment of more formal and comprehensive doctoral training. The significant impact of the central government and of Japanese industry and business in doctoral education is emphasized.

CONTEXT AND STRUCTURE

When the Meiji government established the modern Japanese higher education system in the late 19th century with influence from various Western countries, there was no clear national policy on doctoral education, nor was there any systematic doctoral education and training at the institutional level. According to the 1886 Imperial University Order, an 'Imperial University has as its goal the teaching of, and the fundamental research into, arts and sciences necessary for the state'. In terms of its educational and research organization, the Tokyo Imperial University, founded in 1887, consisted of colleges and graduate schools. The former recruited graduates from senior high schools and provided them with professional training. Most research activities took place in the latter, which offered postgraduate courses to college graduates. Because of this structure—similar to that of US universities—the establishment of colleges and graduate schools in Japan's first modern university is thought to have been largely influenced by the US model. Postgraduate programmes were comparable to those at US universities, but there is no clear evidence that any of these programmes were developed to match those at US research universities. As for accreditation, graduates of the University of Tokyo were awarded bachelor's degrees soon after its establishment. However, according to the 1886 Imperial University Order (MEXT 1980), bachelor's degrees functioned as a title for graduates of the university, rather than as an academic diploma. According to the 1887 Academic Degree Order, only two types of degrees, doctoral degrees (*hakushi*) and great doctoral degrees (*daihakushi*), were awarded at the University of Tokyo and other imperial universities. They initially covered five disciplines—law, medicine, engineering, literature and science—but later expanded to nine. Doctoral degrees were basically awarded to two categories of candidates. The first category included students who had completed their studies at a graduate school and passed a relevant examination. The issuance of degrees for this category was determined directly by the minister of education. The other category included scholars deemed to have a similar level of achievement and who were recommended by the Imperial University Council. In practice, however, few doctoral degrees were ever conferred, partly because of extremely high requirements and heavy bureaucratic procedures. It was not until the promulgation of the 1920 Academic Degree Order that the authority of conferring doctoral degrees was transferred from the ministry of education to individual imperial universities.

It is still unclear which overseas ideas or models influenced the early forms of Japanese doctoral education and training. Further, little is known of the extent to which doctoral students were trained in Japanese universities before the Second World War. Because the fundamental mission of almost all national universities in the Meiji period was to foster government officials and professionals in law, engineering, medicine and other fields at the undergraduate level, more focus was placed on undergraduate education in almost every institution (Ito 1995).

After the Second World War, influenced by US ideas under the ongoing occupation of Japan, the government's 1947 Education Act introduced a system of graduate education, including doctoral education. According to Japan's Ministry of Education, Culture, Sports, Science and Technology (hereafter MEXT; 2018), in contrast to the pre-war period, graduate schools were established as independent institutions also providing postgraduate education. Regulations governing graduate school programmes were initially set by the Japanese University Accreditation Association under the 'Standards for Graduate Schools' in April 1949. In 1953, 'Academic Degree Regulations' were issued by the ministry of education. The first four graduate schools were established in March 1950 in private universities, followed by graduate schools in both national and local public universities in 1953. Back then, both master's-level programmes and doctoral programmes were initially used as training programmes for students and teaching staff who would become academics or researchers, in other words to build the academic profession in Japan. Master's-level programmes generally consisted of a two-year course, and doctoral programmes required an additional three years. The length of study at both master's and doctoral levels did not considerably differ from current practice.

Three factors seem to have contributed to the start of doctoral education after the war. First, because of the strong demand from US occupying authorities for the widespread reform of Japan's national education system following the US model, both the ministry of education and the Japanese University Accreditation Association made huge efforts to introduce the general structure of the US university system to Japan. This included graduate education consisting of master's degree programmes and doctoral degree programmes. Second, with the implementation of two key national policies—also a requirement of the US occupying authorities, aimed at democratizing and increasing access to higher education in Japan—a large number of so-called 'newly established universities' were founded at the national and local levels. Some of these were actually new, while others were created through mergers between existing colleges and other educational institutions.

The quick expansion of these new universities required training a large number of faculty at the doctoral level. Finally, there was also a high demand for high-level researchers and scientists to contribute to rebuilding post-war Japan, and to stimulate the development of science and technology. In contrast to many European countries (in which independent research institutes outside of the university system also play an important role in fostering young scientists, researchers and academics), Japanese universities, and especially national universities, play a decisive role in undertaking scientific research and cultivating talented young academics.

No significant changes occurred in the basic structure of Japanese doctoral education from the early 1950s to the 1960s. Despite steady growth, government data shows that there was no huge expansion of doctoral education in terms of student enrolments (Figure 13.1). For example, the number of doctoral students only increased from 7,429 in 1960 to 11,683 in 1965, 13,243 in 1970, and 14,904 in 1975. It was only during the 1970s, when the 'Standards of Establishment of Graduate Schools' were promulgated, that the expansion of doctoral education began in earnest. In 1974, the central government stressed the necessity of strengthening the existing structure of faculty members involved in graduate education and improving facilities and conditions for graduate education, but still no fundamental changes happened to doctoral education. According to Kobayashi (1995), the quantitative expansion and qualitative changes in Japanese graduate education, including doctoral education, did not really occur until the 1980s. However, from that point through the 1990s, there was rapid and widespread growth as more national-level reforms on graduate education were adopted. Figure 13.1 clearly indicates that the number of doctoral students expanded rapidly between 1985 and 2005.

BASIC STRUCTURE AND SCALE

Currently, there are two basic pathways for doctoral candidates to obtain their degrees in Japan. One is to earn their doctoral degree by completing all required courses, submitting a dissertation and passing an oral examination within a standard period of time (normally three

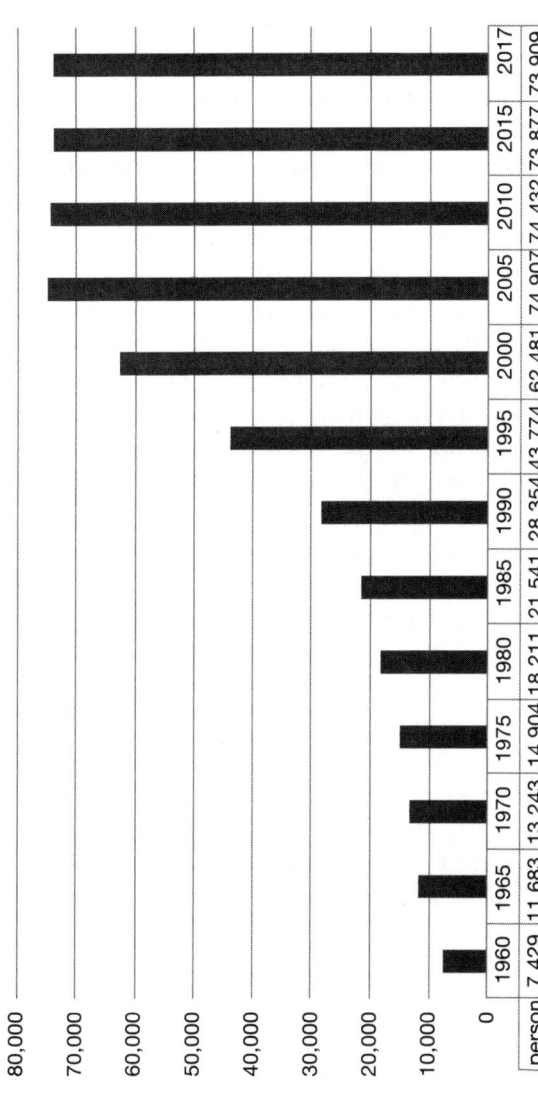

person	1960	1965	1970	1975	1980	1985	1990	1995	2000	2005	2010	2015	2017
	7,429	11,683	13,243	14,904	18,211	21,541	28,354	43,774	62,481	74,907	74,432	73,877	73,909

Figure 13.1 *Changes in the Numbers of Students in Doctoral Courses*
Source: MEXT (2018).

years, but it varies considerably by discipline and university). These students are known as *Katei* doctors. Normally, they are awarded degrees as long as they meet all requirements. The other pathway is to receive a doctoral degree by submitting a doctoral dissertation to a graduate school or publishing a number of research papers. Candidates in that category are called *Ronbun* doctors. In most cases, they are conferred doctoral degrees rather a long time after graduation, and while working in universities or other academic fields. One of the most important reasons behind this system is that, as mentioned earlier, there already existed two pathways to receive doctoral degrees. One could be regarded as a model strongly impacted by the European influence, particularly that of the German research-intensive university. The other seems to have been more influenced by the US model. Prior to the late 1980s, when national-level doctoral education reforms were launched and the US model of training doctoral students through the provision of coursework was taken into full consideration, a large number of professors or researchers, especially those from the humanities and social sciences, were *Ronbun* doctors. Normally, they received their doctoral degrees after completing required doctoral courses and submitting a dissertation to an examination committee or publishing a book or several research papers, often while working in universities or research institutes as faculty or researchers. Despite differences by discipline, university and applicant, many *Ronbun* doctors received their degrees while in their mid-30s or 40s, and some were more than 60 years old (Ushiogi 1999, 308–310). Recently, with the increase in the number of international students and the further internationalization of Japan's doctoral education, more students are becoming *Katei* doctors. However, the traditional way of becoming a *Ronbun* doctor through academic publications still exists in the contemporary Japanese doctoral education system.

Quantitative Trends in Doctoral Education

The implementation of national policies placing priority on the development and expansion of graduate schools has led to rapid growth in the number of both graduate schools and doctoral students. Still, compared to the enrolment ratio of 50.6 per cent of students at the undergraduate level (excluding mature students), the percentage at the doctoral level is only 0.7 (MEXT 2017a). To illustrate this, as of 2016 there are 121 doctoral degree holders per 1,000,000 persons in Japan, compared to 344 in Germany, 286 in the United Kingdom, 274 in Korea, 266 in the United States and 179 in France. This clearly indicates that the scale of Japanese doctoral education is still limited compared to these countries (NISTEP 2017).

Table 13.1 shows the number of doctoral students and universities offering doctoral programmes, among others. Compared to North America and countries in continental Europe, there are relatively more private universities in Japan, followed by local public and national universities. The proportion of private universities is 77.5 per cent of the total number of universities. Among these, 58.3 per cent (455) are qualified to provide doctoral programmes. By sector, 69.7 per cent of private universities, 16.9 per cent of national universities and 13.4 per cent of local public universities provide doctoral programmes. A large proportion of private universities are involved in the provision of doctoral programmes, but in contrast to undergraduate education

Table 13.1 Number of Students and Universities Offering Doctoral Degrees as of 1 May 2017

	Total	National	Local Public	Private
Number of universities	780	86	90	604
Universities providing:				
Master's courses	599	86	78	435
Doctoral courses	455	77	61	317
Professional degree courses	131	60	7	64
Number of students at graduate school	250,891	151,711	16,091	83,089

Source: MEXT (2017). Gakkou kihon chousa (Basic Investigation of Schools).

Note: Number of students at graduate school includes those studying in master's courses, doctoral courses and professional degree courses.

(in which 70% of students study in private universities and colleges), 66.9 per cent of graduate students, including master's-level students in professional schools, study at national and local public universities. Further, among graduate students, 63.9 per cent are master's-level students, 29.5 per cent are doctoral students and 6.6 per cent are enrolled in professional programmes such as business and law. Students from professional schools and programmes are all counted as master's-level students.

There are remarkable variations among private universities in terms of quality of doctoral education. The large private institutions that were established in the late 19th century in big cities such as Tokyo, Kyoto and Osaka seem to enjoy a higher academic and social reputation than more recent ones established in smaller cities. Except for a few leading private institutions such as Waseda University and Keio University, the quality of doctoral education in the vast majority of private universities is not considered as good as that of national universities.

As for numbers of doctoral students per discipline, the largest numbers are enrolled in medical science and health (39.3%), followed by engineering (17.2%). The main reason for the dominance of medical sciences and health is that most medical graduates continue to study for a doctorate, which makes them more trustworthy and attractive to future clients when opening their own practice (Ushiogi 1999). In contrast, in public hospitals, earning a doctoral degree is not a precondition for medicine, dentistry or pharmacy graduates. However, nowadays, it is difficult for graduates in these disciplines to be hired as academics or researchers in university hospitals, to say nothing of becoming professors, if they do not hold a doctorate.

Organization of Doctoral Study

Unlike in China, for instance, or in other countries in Asia, a master's degree in Japan is not considered an independent academic degree, but is instead viewed as a preparatory programme for students who want to pursue a doctoral degree. In most cases, a master's degree education has two functions. On the one hand, it provides students with an opportunity to learn fundamental or comprehensive knowledge in a specific discipline or specialization, including research methodology, and stimulates their interest in doing research at the doctoral level. On the other hand, it also provides students and their advisors with opportunities to discuss and determine whether the students may be accepted into doctoral programmes based on their academic achievements and their career plans. Therefore, master's programmes in Japan are normally considered the first stage of graduate education, while doctoral courses are seen as its completion. This is the main reason why the general term 'graduate education' is used in many national policies and government reports for both programmes, with very few addressing the topic of doctoral education per se.

In terms of the standard length of graduate education, traditional students need to study for two years in a master's course. Individual graduate schools have the authority to extend the length of the students' programmes, and mature students can study for as many as eight years. Forms of examinations and entry requirements vary considerably by universities and disciplines, but normally, there is a written entry examination and an oral interview for master's-level applicants. The normal way for students to receive a master's degree is to obtain about 34–36 credits within two years, and then pass an examination or successfully defend a dissertation. There are considerable variations in this regard among universities and disciplines.

The standard length of study for doctoral education is three years; it takes four years for students in medicine, dentistry, pharmacy and health science. Like many other countries, the basic requirement for new entrants is a master's degree, a degree from a professional school or a functional equivalent. In most cases, applicants only have to submit to an interview for admission to a doctoral programme. Based on the results of the interviews, faculty members or members of the examination committee in individual doctoral programmes determine whether applicants may be accepted as doctoral students. Regarding supervision, since the 1990s, a coursework system based on US practice has been developed and is being implemented more and more broadly—again with huge differences among universities and disciplines. Meanwhile, traditional patterns of doctoral training, like individuals' training without any systematic coursework, have been declining. Team supervision is the normal way of training doctoral students. In most cases, a team is required to include a principal advisor who should be a full professor and qualified to supervise and award doctoral degrees, two professors acting as co-advisors and one or two junior faculty, if required. As far as coursework, doctoral students earn credits from basic courses in their first year, followed by courses on research methodology, specific topics and other subjects provided by faculty at the programme-level or at the level of the graduate school. From the start, students are supervised by their principal advisors based on their research proposal. Generally speaking, doctoral students have to successfully defend their research proposal before the supervision team pass an oral mid-term examination, take a final examination in the form of presenting their original research outcomes and finally submit their doctoral dissertation. The minimum requirements for doctoral students to be conferred their degrees include: (a) studying at graduate schools for at least five years, including two years of master's courses and obtaining more than 30 credits; and (b) receiving required supervision, submitting a doctoral dissertation, having it successfully reviewed and examined and passing the final graduation examination. Not all universities or disciplines require students to publish peer-reviewed research papers, but increasingly, doctoral students are being asked to publish two such papers as part of their doctoral dissertation, especially in leading universities and within STEM (science, technology, engineering and mathematics) disciplines.

RECENT POLICIES AND REFORMS

The report *Adjusting and Strengthening Graduate Education* was released in 1991 by the University Council, a consultative committee of the ministry of education that is comprised of university leaders, prestigious researchers and professors, and influential or knowledgeable persons from various fields of society (MEXT 1991). Because of the required reforms it laid out, this report had a profound impact on the quantitative growth and qualitative changes in Japanese doctoral education. Individual universities were asked to establish graduate schools distinct from existing undergraduate programmes. Graduate education was to be strengthened in terms of faculty positions, facilities and equipment.

Next, universities were required to improve the condition of graduate students by increasing the number of scholarships and loans available to them, expanding both the number and the duration of postdoctoral contracts and introducing a system of teaching and research assistantships. Finally, to help foster human resources for fields other than higher education and research, it was suggested that the overall scale of graduate education be expanded by a factor of two by the year 2000. Meanwhile, it was also necessary to enhance the quality of teaching and research within graduate education and to strengthen relevant systems.

Due to national policies designed to give priority on graduate school education, remarkable changes have occurred in Japanese universities. First, they have restructured to emphasize the development of graduate education. Faculty members in most research-intensive universities have become affiliated with newly created graduate schools. Within these graduate schools, doctoral education and training have become more systematic and institutionalized. Yet, as they did in the past, faculty still teach programmes for undergraduate students. In most cases, aside from being more engaged in accepting graduate students, faculty responsibilities have not changed much. Further, as mentioned above, there was constant and rapid growth in the number of both graduate schools and graduate students in the 1990s. As shown in Figure 13.1, the number of students in doctoral courses increased from 28,354 in 1990 to 62,481 in 2000. Finally, the mobility of graduate students between universities accelerated. For example, among all doctoral students enrolled, the proportion of those who had graduated from a different university prior to entry into their current doctoral programmes increased from 22.8 per cent to 31.7 per cent over the same period (Kobayashi 2004).

Amendments to the School Law in 2004 also had a profound impact on changes in graduate education. For example, the amendments communicated more explicitly that the aim of graduate education should be to foster highly skilled professionals, and so professional schools within business and law began to be established. The significance of several reports issued by the MEXT since 2005 cannot be overstated, because all have significantly shaped and affected the basic policies and systems of graduate education. In contrast to prior policies, the 2005 report paid much greater attention to improving essential parts of graduate education and stressed the importance of general and systematic reforms. According to the report (MEXT 2005), more coursework was to be introduced in graduate schools. Based on the missions and goals at individual universities, graduate schools and programmes were encouraged to strengthen their education in a more systematic and comprehensive way. Further efforts were also made to substantiate graduate education. As a result, for example, most universities have created and implemented diploma policies (used in a broad sense and referring to the provision of detailed regulations and requirements that students must meet to be awarded academic degrees or just certificates/diplomas prior to graduation), curriculum policies and admissions policies. In addition, more universities have also broadened their coursework in a systematic way (MEXT 2017b).

In January 2011, the Central Council for Education (a consultative council for the MEXT) reemphasized the importance of improving the quality of Japan's doctoral education, and implemented a series of national policies designed to foster doctoral graduates who could be active at a global level. This strategy hinged around the following points (MEXT 2011). First, it sought to develop closer, more direct partnerships and collaborations between government, universities and industry. Second, the government tried to ensure consistent doctoral education (normally five years), by combining master's-level programmes and doctoral programmes with the same educational goal. This new, more cohesive model of doctoral education is expected to produce graduates better equipped to undertake innovative and independent activities. Third, the government implemented 'Leading Doctoral Programs' in 2011, with the intention of establishing several 'bases' to function as centres of excellence for doctoral education. By selecting and allocating additional financial resources to several leading Japanese universities and important disciplines, the Japanese government expects these institutions to take the lead in improving Japan's doctoral education. Finally, the government, individual universities and industry have tried to stimulate the internationalization of Japan's doctoral education by encouraging academic exchanges and collaborations between domestic and international doctoral students, hiring more international faculty and researchers and providing more financial support for doctoral students to go abroad and undertake international research.

Previous research identifies three main characteristics in the changes in Japanese graduate education since the early 1990s (Ehara 2010). First, in order to improve the international competitiveness of the Japanese economy, facilitate research and the development of advanced technology, and train researchers and professionals, the existing system was restructured and the scale of postgraduate education expanded at a systemic level. At the same time, individual universities were encouraged to bring graduate education in line with their own missions and establish new types of graduate education in collaboration with other universities. Second, reforms were launched to make the system of graduate education more flexible and easier for new applicants to be accepted and obtain degrees. For example, master's and doctoral programmes were set up for mature students, with correspondence courses, night classes and programmes taught via television and other media. Still, there was no significant expansion in the number of doctoral students enrolled in distance-only doctoral programmes. For example, 54 students were enrolled in the Open University in 2018; only four of them were graduates from doctoral programmes. More importantly, the majority were between 50 and 60 years old (The Open University of Japan 2018). Compared to those who received their doctoral degrees from universities, these course programmes are less prestigious. Third, more and more universities have founded independent graduate schools and moved faculty from undergraduate to graduate schools. This is especially true in the case of the former 'Imperial Universities' and other national universities, where more emphasis is placed on research than teaching. Similarly, a few private universities also began to devote more efforts to the provision of graduate education programmes.

To sum up, since the early 1990s, when Japan increased its efforts to expand and reform graduate education, it seems that two different policies have been implemented. Throughout the 1990s, more stress was placed on quantitative growth in terms of both graduate schools and students. Since the early 2000s, substantial reforms on qualitative aspects of graduate education, including fundamental elements such as curriculum, degrees and admissions, have been carried out.

One of the outcomes of these reforms is that the traditional model of doctoral education focusing on the composition of doctoral dissertations has been greatly changed, and a new way of producing doctorates by combining coursework and a doctoral dissertation has been widely adopted. According to MEXT statistics (2014), in 1985, only 38 per cent of all doctorate holders earned their degrees through the completion of coursework and passing exams associated with their dissertations (*Katei* doctors). That same year, as many as 62 per cent were awarded doctoral degrees by submitting a book-length dissertation after graduation (*Ronbun* doctors). However, as of March 2014, as many as 86 per cent of graduates were *Katei* doctors, while only 14 per cent were *Ronbun* doctors.

DOCTORAL EDUCATION AND SOCIETY

The Labour Market and Doctoral Graduates

By the early 1990s, according to Ushiogi (1993, 310), doctoral degree holders were employed only in the academic profession, mostly in universities and research institutes. Neither government departments nor private enterprises were interested in hiring doctoral degree holders. The job market for doctoral graduates was extremely limited and they did not have many options after graduation. In recent years, employment opportunities have become more diverse. For example, relevant data from a national survey of doctoral degree holders suggests that as of 2012, 60 per cent became academics (52.6% were employed in universities and 7.4% in public research institutes). Among those who found work outside academia, 26.1 per cent worked in private enterprises, 7.7 per cent in non-profit organizations, 3.5 per cent were self-employed and 2.8 per cent were independent and unaffiliated to any workplace (NISTEP 2016, 11). However, there were notable differences in employment destinations among the various disciplines.

In terms of employment situation (MEXT 2017c), as of 2014, 38.7 per cent of doctoral graduates obtained a permanent position, 23.6 per cent were hired on a fixed-term basis and 11.8 per cent were mature students who continued to work in their original workplace after graduation. In general, the largest number of doctoral graduates belonged to 'others' (20.6%, mainly including medical doctors), followed by individuals who continued to study and worked part-time (16.6%), university faculty (16.2%), employees of private enterprises (13.2%) and postdoctoral students (12.2%). By discipline, a high proportion of doctoral graduates from the humanities and arts belonged to 'others' (including those who continued to study and work part-time); along with 'unknown', they accounted for over half of the total. Within the so-called 'soft sciences', the majority of doctoral degree holders from the humanities (36.1%) and arts (40%) chose to continue to study and work part-time, whereas the majority of graduates from the social sciences (23.9%), home economics (31.4%) and education (44%) became university faculty. In contrast, the largest number of graduates from the natural sciences (32.3%) became postdoctoral students, those from engineering (36.5%) were hired in private enterprises and those from agriculture (16%) and health (43.8%) worked in 'others', as well as medical doctors.

Despite the fact that since the 1990s, the employment destinations of doctoral graduates have gradually diversified, from the perspective of industry and business there is still a mismatch between doctoral education and the needs of the labour market. According to the report by Keidanren (Japan Business Federation; 2007), industries, businesses and universities all believe that the reason private employers are reluctant to hire doctoral graduates is because they think top talent does not often pursue a doctorate and the capacity and added value of doctoral graduates is unclear. Further, because Japanese doctoral programmes focus on training researchers for academic professions, they are rarely relevant to other career paths. Specific issues concerning doctoral programmes include overemphasizing research at the expense of equipping graduates with other capacities; a narrow focus on certain academic fields or research topics and a lack of interdisciplinary research; doctoral candidates devoting too much effort to their dissertations without learning other things; lack of familiarity with technology among students; and a preponderance of research topics and doctoral dissertations that are irrelevant and unimportant to industry and business. As a result, most enterprises prefer to employ graduates from master's programmes.

These findings are confirmed by recent research. Of all the countries where one can graduate with a PhD, Japan is arguably among the worst when it comes to employment opportunities. The country's steady population decline means fewer 18-year-olds headed off to universities, which in turn means fewer teaching and other academic opportunities for PhD holders. Moreover, Japanese industries and businesses remain uninterested in employing doctoral graduates, still preferring to hire graduates from lower levels of higher education who can be trained on the job (Cyranoski et al. 2011).

Economic Issues Faced by Doctoral Students

Doctoral students in Japan seem to bear a heavier economic burden than their counterparts in North America and continental Europe. With the exception of law school, tuition and fees at all national universities in Japan total approximately $7,500 per year for doctoral education, while private universities charge even more. Unlike in Australia and the United States, international students pay the same rate as domestic students. Then there are living expenses, which can run, at a minimum, about $1,300 per month, although big cities such as Tokyo and Osaka are more expensive. In short, very few doctoral students receive sufficient public funding to cover their living expenses, study and research. For example, according to Table 13.2 (MEXT 2017d), as of 2015, when excluding those receiving loan-type scholarships, only 10.4 per cent of doctoral students were supported with more than US$16,200 per year (the minimum living wage in Japan). Further, 52.2 per cent of doctoral students received no financial support, no exemptions for tuition or fees and no other loans. This is also one of the main reasons why very few excellent university graduates are willing to enrol in doctoral programmes.

CHANGES IN DOMESTIC AND INTERNATIONAL DOCTORAL STUDENTS

Domestic Doctoral Students

As noted earlier, policies placing a priority on graduate education have led to the rapid expansion of graduate schools and the number of graduate students since the early 1990s. However, these changes occurred

Table 13.2 *Amount of Allowance for Living Expenses per Doctoral Student (per Year)*

Amount of Allowance	Ratio (%)
No allowance	52.2
Less than 5,400 US dollars	24.9
5,400–10,800 US dollars	7.5
10,800–16,200 US dollars	4.4
16,200–22,000 US dollars	2.8
More than 22,000 US dollars	7.6

Source: MEXT (2017). *Cyuo kyoiku shingikai daigaku bunkakai daigakuin bukai* (81). [Session of Graduate Education of Branch of University, Central Council for Education]. http://www.mext.go.jp/component/b_menu/shingi/giji/__icsFiles/afieldfile/2017/07/24/1386653_05.pdf (accessed 3 April 2018) (in Japanese).
Note: The amount includes tuition reduction but excludes loan-type scholarships.

predominantly in master's programmes. As Table 13.3 shows, although changes in the number of doctoral students were not constant, their total number decreased slightly from 74,811 in 2007 to 73,909 in 2017. Interestingly, there was no substantial change in the overall distribution of doctoral students by discipline from 2007 to 2017. The top three disciplines of doctoral students in 2007 were medical science and health (31.9%), followed by engineering (18.6%) and others (11.6%). In 2017, this distribution was similar: the top was medical science and health (39.4%), followed by engineering (17.2%) and others (12.1%). Further, in the period from 2007 to 2017, there was a decline in the number of doctoral students in the humanities (from 10.3% to 7.7%), social sciences (from 10% to 8.1%), natural science (from 7.7% to 6.6%), engineering (from 18.6% to 17.2%), agriculture (from 5.7% to 4.8%), home economics (from 0.5% to 0.3%) and arts (from 1.0% to 0.9%), whereas the number of doctoral students in medical science and health, education and 'others' increased from 31.9 per cent to 39.4 per cent, from 2.6 per cent to 3.1 per cent and from 11.6 per cent to 12.1 per cent, respectively.

Table 13.4 reveals that the number of doctoral graduates/awarded doctoral degrees also saw a minor decrease from 15,973 in 2006 to

Table 13.3 *Changes in the Numbers of Doctoral Students in Total and by Discipline*

	2007	2012	2017
Number of students	74,811	74,316	73,909
Students' ratio by disciplines (%)			
Humanities	10.3	8.7	7.7
Social science	10.0	9.0	8.1
Natural science	7.7	7.0	6.6
Engineering	18.6	18.5	17.2
Agriculture	5.7	5.1	4.8
Medical science and health	31.9	35.1	39.4
Home economics	0.5	0.4	0.3
Education	2.6	3.1	3.1
Arts	1.0	0.9	0.9
Others	11.6	12.3	12.1

Source: Compiled by the author based on MEXT's statistics in Gakkou kihon chousa (Basic Investigation of Schools) from 2007 to 2017.

15,773 in 2016. This is largely because the number of admissions at the doctoral level was almost the same as the number of doctoral graduates in that same period. However, when including the number of those who earned their doctoral degrees by submitting dissertations or book-length research papers (*Ronbun* doctors), the number of awarded doctoral degrees exceeded those of doctoral graduates in 2006, 2007, 2008, 2010 and 2011.

As for time spent obtaining a doctoral degree by discipline, according to the MEXT survey (MEXT 2017e), the proportion of doctoral students in the humanities, social sciences and education who spent more than three years was higher than in science, engineering, agriculture, health, home economics, arts and 'others'. For example, about 23 per cent of doctoral students in the humanities, 14 per cent in education and about 11 per cent in the social sciences spent four years getting their degrees. In contrast, it took only 1 per cent of doctoral

Table 13.4 Changes in the Numbers of Doctoral Graduates and Awarded Doctoral Degrees

	2006	2007	2008	2009	2010	2011	2012	2013	2014	2015	2016
Number of graduates	15,973	16,801	16,281	16,463	15,842	15,892	16,260	16,445	16,003	15,684	15,773
Number of degrees awarded	17,860	17,291	16,735	15,872	16,760	15,911	15,902	15,390	15,045	–	–

Source: Compiled by the author based on MEXT's statistics in Gakkou kihon chousa (Basic Investigation of Schools) from 2006 to 2016.

Note: Number of doctoral degrees also include Ronbun doctors (obtaining doctoral degrees only by submitting dissertations after graduation).

students in engineering and 0.8 per cent in science that long to earn their doctoral degrees.

International Students

The implementation of the policy of accepting 300,000 international students to Japanese campuses, launched in 2008, has led to a steady growth in the number of international graduate students. According to MEXT statistics (2017f), as of 2017, there were 16,292 international doctoral students in Japanese universities. This accounts for 22 per cent of the total (73,909), much higher than the proportion of international students at the undergraduate level, which only makes up for 3.4 per cent of the total. By discipline, the largest number of international doctoral students are in engineering (30.2%), followed by medical science and health (12.1%), social science (10.5%), humanities (10.1%), agriculture (8.7%) and science (7.5%). Further, a 2018 report by the National Institute of Science and Technology Policy (NISTEP) reveals that the largest number of international doctoral students in Japan comes from China (44.1%), followed by other Asian countries (29%), North America, Europe and Latin America (9.8%), Korea (7.7%), 'other' (6.2%) and Taiwan (3.2%; NISTEP 2018, 80).

No national data has been published by the Japanese government on the destinations of international doctoral students upon graduation. The NISTEP survey suggests that 50.3 per cent stayed in Japan, while 49.7 per cent had moved to other countries (NISTEP 2018, 20). Many international doctoral students coming to Japan for their studies are required to return to their home countries if they are funded by national governments or other sponsoring institutions. Still, it seems that in recent years, there are three reasons why international doctoral graduates are determined to stay and work in Japan. First, more and more of these students are privately funded, and therefore under no obligation to return to their home countries. Second, due to a rapid decline in the number of Japanese entering university, the government has become more open to accepting and hiring international doctoral graduates to address this demographic gap. Finally, universities, industries and businesses have all identified hiring high-level international doctoral graduates as an effective way of enhancing their international competitiveness. Recent research suggests that up to 40 per cent of full-time international faculty at Japanese universities studied in Japanese universities and received their highest degrees from Japanese universities (Huang 2018). Although no clear data is available, as pointed out, it is much easier for graduates in the hard sciences to find employment in industry and business than those in the soft sciences. Thanks to policies aimed at further internationalizing Japan's universities and society by attracting more high-level international students from English-speaking countries, and by hiring more international faculty in Japanese universities, we can anticipate that more international students who have obtained their doctoral degree in Japan will stay in the country.

CONCLUDING REMARKS

This study presents an overview of doctoral education in Japan and its most striking characteristics, based on the analysis of national statistics and several national surveys. It also analyses the main factors that have affected changes in Japanese doctoral education.

In order to improve the quality and, especially, the international competitiveness of doctoral education, it is clear that both the government and individual institutions should continue to make efforts to attract 'the best and the brightest' students to go into doctoral programmes; to better adapt doctoral programmes to the expectations of society, industry and business; and to provide more financial support for doctoral students.

REFERENCES

Cyranoski, David, Natasha Gilbert, Heidi Ledford, Anjali Nayar, and Mohammed Yahia. 2011. 'The World Is Producing More PhDs than Ever Before. Is It Time to Stop?' *Nature* 472: 276–279.

Ehara, Takekazu. 2010. *Tenkanki nihon no daigaku kaikaku: Amerika tono hikaku* [Japanese Higher Education Reforms at a Turning Point: From Comparative Perspectives between Japan and the United States], 154–159. Tokyo: Toshindo. (In Japanese).

Huang, Futao. 2018. 'Foreign Faculty at Japanese Universities: Profiles and Motivations'. *Higher Education Quarterly* 72 (3): 237–249.

Ito, Akihiro. 1995. 'Nihon no daigakuin no rekishi' [History of Japanese Graduate School]. In *Gendai no daigakuin kyouiku* [Modern Graduate Education], edited by Shogo Ichikawa and Kazuyuki Kitamura, 19–25. Tokyo: Tamagawa University Press. (In Japanese).

Keidanren (Japan Business Federation). 2007. *Daigakuin hakase katei no genjyou to kadai* [Current Situation and Issues of Doctoral Education], 7–8. https://www.keidanren.or.jp/japanese/policy/2007/020/chukan-hokoku.pdf (accessed 12 June 2018; in Japanese).

Kobayashi, Shinichi. 1995. 'Daigakuin he no shingaku to daigakuinsei no syusyoku' [Going to Graduate School and Students' Career]. In *Gendai no daigakuin kyouiku* [Modern Graduate Education], edited by Shogo Ichikawa and Kazuyuki Kitamura, 52–53. Tokyo: Tamagawa University Press. (In Japanese).

———. 2004. 'Daigakuin jyutenka seisaku no kouzai' [The Merits and Demerits of Placing Priority on Developing Graduate Schools]. In *Daigakuin no kaikaku* [Reform of Graduate Education in Japan], edited by Takekazu Eraha and Toru Umakoshi, 64–68. Tokyo: Toshindo. (In Japanese).

MEXT. 1980. 'Japan's Modern Educational System'. http://www.mext.go.jp/b_menu/hakusho/html/others/detail/1317336.htm (accessed 13 December 2019).

———. 1991. *Daigakuin no seibi jyujitsu nitsuite* [Adjusting and Strengthening Postgraduate Education]. http://www.mext.go.jp/b_menu/shingi/chukyo/chukyo4/gijiroku/03052801/003/001.htm (accessed 7 June 2018; in Japanese).

———. 2005. *Shinjidai no daigakuin kyouiku* [Graduate Education in a New Era]. http://www.mext.go.jp/b_menu/shingi/chukyo/chukyo0/toushin/05090501/all.pdf (accessed 7 June 2018; in Japanese).

———. 2011. *Hakse katei kyouiku kaikaku ni kansuru sankoushiryou* [References for Reforms on Doctoral Education Programs]. http://www.mext.go.jp/b_menu/shingi/chukyo/chukyo4/004/gijiroku/__icsFiles/afield-file/2012/02/15/1315482_05.pdf (accessed 28 November 2018; in Japanese).

———. 2014. *Gakui jyuyo jyoukyou* [Situation of Awarding Academic Degrees]. http://www.mext.go.jp/component/a_menu/education/detail/__icsFiles/afieldfile/2017/01/26/1299723_10.pdf (accessed 7 June 2018; in Japanese).

———. 2017a. 'Distributed Materials for the Committee of Graduate School No. 81 on May 30'. http://www.mext.go.jp/component/b_menu/shingi/giji/__icsFiles/afieldfile/2017/07/24/1386653_05.pdf (accessed 20 May 2018; in Japanese).

———. 2017b, October 31. 'Summary of Discussion of Committee of Graduate School'. No. 82. http://www.mext.go.jp/b_menu/shingi/chukyo/chukyo4/houkoku/1366897.htm (accessed 20 May 2018; in Japanese).

MEXT. 2017c. *Daigakuin katsudou jyoukyou chousa* [Survey of Graduate School Activities 2014]: 24. http://www.mext.go.jp/b_menu/shingi/chukyo/chukyo4/004/gijiroku/__icsFiles/afieldfile/2016/09/06/1376885_12.pdf (accessed 12 May 2018; in Japanese).

———. 2017d, May 30. 'Distributed Materials for the Committee of Graduate School. No. 81. http://www.mext.go.jp/component/b_menu/shingi/giji/__icsFiles/afieldfile/2017/07/24/1386653_05.pdf (accessed 20 May 2018; in Japanese).

———. 2017e. *Daigakuin katsudou jyoukyou chousa* [Survey of Graduate Education Activities 2014]: 29. http://www.mext.go.jp/b_menu/shingi/chukyo/chukyo4/004/gijiroku/__icsFiles/afieldfile/2016/09/06/1376885_12.pdf (accessed 12 May 2018; in Japanese).

———. 2017f. *Gakkou kihon chosua 2017* [Basic Investigation of Schools 2017]. (In Japanese).

———. 2018. 'Japan's Modern Educational System'. http://www.mext.go.jp/b_menu/hakusho/html/others/detail/1317447.htm (accessed 18 May 2018).

NISTEP. 2016. *Gaiyou: Hakase jinzai tsuiseki chousa 2ji houkokusho* [Outline: 2nd Report of Japan Doctoral Human Resource Profiling]. http://www.nistep.go.jp/wp/wp-content/uploads/NISTEP-NR174-SummaryJ.pdf (accessed 15 May 2018; in Japanese).

———. 2017. *Kagaku gijutsu shishou 2017* [Indicators of Science Technology 2017]: 170. http://www.nistep.go.jp/wp/wp-content/uploads/NISTEP-RM261-statistics_J.pdf (accessed 15 May 2018; in Japanese).

———. 2018. Hakase jinzai tsuiseki cyosa dai ni ji houkokusyo 2nd [Report on "Japan Doctoral Human Resource Profiling (JD-Pro)"]. 80. http://hdl.handle.net/11035/3190 (accessed 20 July 2018) (in Japanese).

The Open University of Japan. 2018. *Facts and Figures*. https://www.ouj.ac.jp/eng/pdf/FactsandFigures2016.pdf (accessed 23 December 2018).

Ushiogi, Morikazu. 1993. 'Graduate Education and Research Organization in Japan'. In *The Research Foundations of Graduate Education: Germany, Britain, France, United States, Japan*, edited by Burton R. Clark. Berkeley, CA: University of California Press.

———. 1999. 'Nihon ni okeru daigakuin kyouiku to kenkyu soshiki' [Graduate Education and Research Organization in Japan]. In *Daigakuin no kenkyu* [Research into Graduate Education], edited by Burton R. Clark, 420. Tokyo: Toishindo. (In Japanese).

Chapter 14

Development and Transformation of Doctoral Education in Kazakhstan

Aliya Kuzhabekova

The process of modernization of doctoral education in Kazakhstan has been ongoing since the country gained independence from the Soviet Union in 1991. However, a quarter century since the launch of the reforms, one can observe varying degrees of change in funding mechanisms, admission parameters, the supervision process, graduation requirements, assessment procedures and criteria, as well as institutional arrangements supporting doctoral education.

Much of the thinking about the structure and nature of doctoral training was influenced by the Bologna Process, of which Kazakhstan became an official cosignatory in 2010. This came after the country signed the Lisbon Convention in 1997. The reforms were aimed at readjusting the isolated post-Communist system of higher education inherited from Soviet times to a more open and globally integrated configuration appropriate for the needs of a capitalist knowledge economy and an increasingly globalized world (Kuraev 2014). The main approach to this readjustment was restructuring the system in accordance with 'European standards' (Tampayeva 2015) to make the country 'open to the free flow of people, ideas, capital, and labor, so that it could ride the crest of globalization' (Dixon and Soltys 2013, 66).

This chapter provides an overview of the transformations that have occurred in Kazakhstani doctoral education over more than two decades of the country's independence. It summarizes the initial configuration of the system, created during Soviet times. It then provides an explanation of the rationale for the changes and describes the current system, the result of the implementation of Bologna-driven reforms. This is followed by a descriptive analysis of available statistical data on the dynamics and the present state of doctoral education, and, finally, by a summary of the main issues faced by the Kazakhstani system of doctoral education.

THE SOVIET ORIGINS OF DOCTORAL EDUCATION IN KAZAKHSTAN

The oldest doctoral degree granting university in the country, the Kazakh Pedagogical University, was established by the Soviets in 1928 (Asylbayev 2006). Kazakhstan had enormous reserves of mineral resources, vast amounts of land with a massive agricultural potential and a sparse population. In the course of time, these lands came to be viewed by the central Soviet government as appropriate sites for aerospace and military testing. The exploitation of the republic's industrial, agricultural and military potential necessitated access to a trained workforce, including scientists. Hence, the Soviets created a system of universities, government-owned industrial enterprise research labs, as well as the republic's own branch of the Academy of Sciences, with a network of research labs and institutes. This network of government-funded and centrally controlled institutions conducted research and trained the scientific workforce through doctoral programmes.

Unfortunately, accurate data on doctoral education in Soviet Kazakhstan is not easily available. In 1986, five years prior to independence, there were 55 postgraduate degree-conferring universities and 30 research institutions, which were a part of the Academy of Sciences system (Education and Science in Kazakh S. S. R. 1990). In 1973, there were 253 doctoral and 3,325 candidate of science degree holders in the republic, compared to 29,806 doctoral and 288,261 candidate of science degree holders for the whole of the Soviet Union (Central Statistical Agency of the USSR 1974). Given that Kazakhstan had the second largest territory among the Soviet republics and made a significant contribution to the economy in terms of agricultural and industrial production, the scale and the output of doctoral education in the republic was unimpressive. The number of doctorates produced was insufficient to satisfy the needs of the education and economic sectors, and therefore the republic relied on a supply of doctoral graduates trained in Russia and other Soviet republics. As of 1980, only 2 per cent of university faculty had a doctor of science degree and only a half had a candidate of science degree (Ermekbay, Zh. A., 2016).

Doctoral training was implemented in two stages. The first stage, *aspirantura*, corresponded to Western PhD programmes and involved predominantly independent work on writing a scholarly dissertation. Upon successful defence, this led to the conferral of the degree of candidate of science (*kandidat nauk*). The second stage was similar to the German *Habilitation*; it consisted of completely independent work on a scholarly dissertation and accompanying publications or industrial prototypes, culminating in a defence followed by the conferral of the degree of doctor of science (*doktor nauk*).

Having a postgraduate degree was relatively prestigious in the Soviet Union. Studies in postgraduate programmes were attractive to young people because doctoral education was free and supported by a stipend that was more than an average salary (PhD в России 2018). To be admitted to an *aspirantura*, individuals needed to complete two years of postgraduation employment, submit a letter of nomination from their undergraduate institution, pass an exam and have an acceptable average grade.

The duration of the programme was three years for full-time students and four years for part-time students. To obtain a degree, students needed to pass the 'Candidate Minimum' exam, which covered the 'Foundations of Dialectic and Historic Materialism'. They had to show proficiency in both a foreign language and their area of specialization, and defend their dissertations.

The degree of *doktor nauk* was expected to be completed without formal supervision, but it implied affiliation with a research institute, where the individual would pursue research on their topic under the supervision of a professor (Tokarev 2016). The conferral of the degree required a candidate of science degree, successfully defending a doctoral dissertation and the publication of a set number of scholarly papers. Dissertations were more important in the Soviet Union than publications, which were required as a formality (Mironin 2018). Highly bureaucratized candidate dissertation defences were conducted publicly by a national dissertation committee of 11–25 individuals nominated by a governmental body called the Higher Attestation Committee. This national dissertation committee considered dissertations in a particular area of specialization for a set of institutions (Soviet of the Ministers of the USSR 1975). Upon successful defence before the Higher Attestation Committee, dissertations were then further considered by a committee of experts, also nominated by the government.

Several issues with the system of conferral of academic degrees emerged in the later days of the Soviet Union (Mironin 2018). First, because degrees were necessary for promotion through academic ranks and in terms of prestige, salaries and social benefits, the bureaucratic process of dissertation defences became corrupt. Having proper connections in the decision-making bodies and being able to return the favour of a positive decision became more important than the quality of the dissertation. Second, obtaining a postgraduate degree became an end in itself, with dissertations not leading to practical applications or a significant advancement of scientific knowledge. This was due to the relative unimportance of publications, or practical outcome, in the decision of dissertation committees. In combination, these two factors led to a lesser-qualified research body and to a decline in the prestige of a career in research.

DOCTORAL EDUCATION REFORM IN POST-SOVIET KAZAKHSTAN

The dissolution of the Soviet Union and a resulting decline in economic production had a significant impact on academia in the newly independent Kazakhstan. During the early days of independence, many researchers, the majority of whom not ethnic Kazakhs, left the country in order to escape the economic decline and an uncertain future in the country (Mukhtarova 2010). According to Anderson, Pomfret, and Usseinova (2004), higher education in Kazakhstan was severely hit by the economic crisis of the transition period. The financial crisis impacted research and the research training capacity of universities. As the Soviet system collapsed, some of the local research institutions died out, while others barely made ends meet. Research links between Kazakhstan and other countries of the former Soviet Union weakened. Chronic underfunding led to aging infrastructure and shrinking salaries. These developments, in turn, undermined the prestige of scientific and academic professions and pushed many of the remaining scientists and scholars into other employment.

Given the deficit in public resources, the focus of early reforms was on radical privatization. Subsequently, this initial 'reactive' approach to reform, appropriate given the economic crisis, changed to a more strategy-driven one. This new approach was made possible, and necessitated by, new economic and political realities—the discovery of huge oil reserves in Kazakhstan, and the ascendance of the republic as an important geopolitical player in the region.

The old systems of higher and postgraduate education were considered incapable of preparing citizens to operate in the new market economy. In search of possible solutions for the educational reform conundrum, the government turned to the Bologna Process (Tampayeva 2015). As a result, Kazakhstan introduced the credit-based system of accounting for academic hours, as well as academic transcripts, in an effort to support the Bologna Process's principles of life-long learning and academic mobility. Kazakhstan also adopted the three-level degree structure (bachelor's, master's, PhD) to ensure compliance with Western standards, along with credit transferability and international degree recognition. Additionally, the country created an academic accreditation system to ensure quality control, established a National Qualification Framework for professionals, and began an admissions regime based on nationwide testing.

In 2004, in accordance with the Bologna Process's three-level degree structure, Kazakhstan introduced the PhD with the intent to replace the old sequence of candidate plus doctor of science degrees. The decision to change from a lengthier two-degree sequence to a shorter single degree was largely due to the urgent need to increase the number of doctoral degree holders among university faculty in order to meet international accreditation requirements. To increase the low number of PhD holders inherited from the Soviet Union, it was essential to shorten the duration of doctoral training and remove the bureaucratic barriers to obtaining research degrees. Hence, the decision was made to simplify the process by adopting the Bologna alternative.

As an experiment, several universities in Kazakhstan introduced PhD programmes in 2004. The expectation was that the last cohort would be able to graduate by 2010, by which time the nationwide switch to PhD programmes was expected to be complete. The process of transition, however, was somewhat slow, and some universities struggled. They were unable to ensure the required level of doctoral degree holders among the faculty to support the new PhD format, and so continued to deliver Soviet era degrees (Kassevitch et al. 2005).

Kazakhstan's final move to the contemporary PhD system happened in 2010, and was influenced by three circumstances: the negative side effects created by the introduction of privately funded postgraduate education, the rise of a policy emphasis on economic growth driven by innovation and the official recognition of Kazakhstan as the 47th member of the European Higher Education Area.

Unexpectedly, a new supply of fee-based postgraduate programmes, which emerged as a result of privatization, met a high level of demand among individuals who did not intend to be scholars in the future. There were incentives for enrolment in these programmes in the public service, where having a research degree increased one's chances for promotion. Because only a limited duration of residence was required for obtaining some form of research degrees in the old system, and because the dissertation defence process was so corrupt, many public servants preferred to pay their way through by offering bribes to pass courses and, eventually, by purchasing a dissertation from somebody else in order to graduate (Anonymous 2014). The proliferation of holders of purchased degrees completely discredited the old system of researcher training and increased the level of corruption in the already imperfect process of defence.

In the meantime, to increase research productivity and therefore facilitate innovation-driven economic growth, the government adopted a system of output-based incentives. These were based on research contributions linked to internationally recognized publications and patents. This new system made the old approach to research training, which had focused on dissertations rather than publications, largely irrelevant.

Finally, in 2010, Kazakhstan was recognized as an official member of the Bologna Process. Prior to that year, the government tolerated variability in the tempo of transition. But in an attempt to demonstrate a marked achievement in education policy, the official announcement was made in 2010 that adhesion to the Bologna Process had been successfully completed, and that Kazakhstani universities had to either immediately move to offer PhD programmes or stop offering doctoral degrees altogether. As the next section will demonstrate, while this transition has indeed led to shorter periods of study, many aspects of the previous system were inherited by the new system, and high levels of both centralization and bureaucratization persist.

THE CURRENT FORM OF DOCTORAL EDUCATION IN KAZAKHSTAN

Since 2010, the only form of doctoral education offered in Kazakhstani universities has been a formal training programme leading to a PhD. It is now available at all national and regional public universities, as well as some private institutions. To be admitted to a PhD programme, an individual needs to have a master's degree and three years of employment experience. Other requirements include passing a foreign language test and an oral exam on the appropriate subject (Government of the Republic of Kazakhstan 2012).

Most of the students pursuing a PhD degree currently receive a grant from the government, which covers tuition fees and provides a monthly stipend. To avoid the previously described problem of 'purchased dissertations', only international students and local students sponsored by their employers can choose to pay for themselves. However, few students choose to pursue a PhD at their own expense. According to the Erasmus+ Report (2017), in 2014–2015, the annual tuition fee for doctoral education in Kazakhstani universities was EUR6,500 (KZT1,307,000). Few students could afford being enrolled on a fee-paying basis, given that the average annual salary that year was KZT 1,490,724.

According to the newly formulated State Standards on Doctoral Education (Ministry of Education and Science of the Republic of Kazakhstan 2011), the duration of the PhD programme should be at least three years and the programme should be full-time. Any additional years are to be paid for by the student. While the Bologna requirements do not set an expectation with respect to the number of credit hours for doctoral programmes, PhDs in Kazakhstan are based on a credit hour accounting for at least 75 credits. Of those, at least 15 should be in theoretical courses, 5 each in teaching and a research practicum, and at least 50 credits in dissertation research. Upon completing the coursework, a student is also expected to pass a comprehensive exam.

The coursework and dissertation can be completed in Russian or Kazakh, the main languages in the country. In several private universities hiring international faculty and offering Western-style programmes, the coursework and dissertation can be done in English. However, all students, regardless of the language of instruction, have to take classes and pass exams in Kazakh, the official language, and in English, which is considered the language of international research communication.

With respect to graduation, the most notable change was the introduction of more rigorous requirements for the number and quality of publications. Students are now expected to publish seven scholarly papers based on their dissertations prior to defence. Out of those seven papers, at least one should be published in an international peer-reviewed journal, and at least three should be published in the proceedings of international conferences.

This publication requirement is hard to fulfil, especially if the student's advisor is not actively publishing in international journals, or if English is a barrier. While prior research (Kuzhabekova and Mukhamejanova 2017) revealed that students who pursue their degrees within established research schools, and who effectively utilize their international mobility funding, manage to produce the required publications, many others struggle. Some fulfil the requirement by preparing a manuscript in English, and then paying for a professional translation. Others pay to get their papers published, with prices ranging from $1,000 to $1,500. The proliferation of publications by Kazakhstani researchers in predatory journals, and of presentations at predatory conferences, indicate how this strict requirement is being fulfilled in practice by many students. According to a Ministry of Education and Science official, 10 per cent of the degrees in Kazakhstan in 2014 were not conferred by dissertation committees because candidates published in predatory journals or plagiarized their articles (*Forbes Kazakhstan* 2015).

The process of dissertation writing and advising remains similar to what it was in the days of the Soviet Union, with some minor changes in the composition of the advisory committee. As in the past, coursework is minimal, and the student is expected to learn and to write the dissertation with limited assistance from an advisor. Comprehensive methodological training is not available, especially in the social sciences. This is partly due to the lack of broad methodological knowledge among the supervising faculty. Meanwhile, independent learning is further complicated by poor access to modern textbooks and the most current research literature. As a result, the quality of doctoral education remains low. Faculty trained in the Soviet Union or in the early days of independence remain largely isolated from the global research community. In turn, they end up producing doctoral graduates who also have trouble integrating into that community.

As a countermeasure, the Regulations on Conferral of Scientific Degrees (Ministry of Education and Science of the Republic of Kazakhstan 2011) now require a PhD advisory committee to include one member from a university outside of Kazakhstan. This innovation was introduced to ensure quality control by exposing doctoral students to foreign faculty, who can provide training in modern methods and theories. According to Kuzhabekova and Mukhamejanova (2017), the benefits of this arrangement are realized if the student's local advisor intentionally chooses someone outside of Kazakhstan who is a collaborator and expert in the same field. In this case, the student then receives good support from not only one, but two individuals. However, if a student is supervised by a local faculty member who takes a hands-off approach, then the student alone is responsible for finding the right external advisor.

As was the case during the Soviet era, the process of dissertation defence and degree conferral remains unnecessarily complicated, multi-layered and centrally controlled, with much of the process being external to the university. Most universities still do not confer doctoral degrees and have little control over the final decision, which continues to rest with the Ministry of Education. The process remains largely non-transparent and subjective. In fact, for most doctoral students, the process of the defence, and therefore the outcome of their studies, stays obscure right until the end. Predictability is there only for those whose advisors are well connected with the members of the corresponding government committees. In Kazakhstan, as in the Soviet Union, it is still more important to know who's who, and to be able to return favours, than to produce quality scientific and academic work.

A NEW MODEL OF DOCTORAL EDUCATION AT NAZARBAYEV UNIVERSITY

In 2010, the Kazakhstani government's dissatisfaction with the overall pace of reforms in higher education, as well as its increased commitment to developing national research and innovation capacity to ensure the country's economic competitiveness, led to the establishment of the country's first world-class aspiring university, Nazarbayev University (NU). Today, NU operates in partnership with several leading universities from around the world, including the University of Cambridge, the University of Pennsylvania, the Lee Kuan Yew School of Public Policy at the National University of Singapore, the University of Wisconsin–Madison and Duke University. In addition to delivering world-class research and education, NU is expected to be a flagship institution that sets an example for other universities. Its creation was meant to speed up the process of changes in higher education by showcasing mechanisms for adoption, testing and dissemination of best international practices (Kuzhabekova et al. 2017). To fulfil its mission, NU has not only received ample funding, which has allowed it to hire 80 per cent of its faculty from abroad, but has also been granted a special autonomous status.

Doctoral programmes at NU have only recently been launched, and their organization generally follows North American or British conventions. These programmes are administered independently by the government. The curriculum, the admission requirements, the length of the programmes, as well as the procedures for supervision, comprehensive exams and the defence of dissertations are all determined by individual departments rather than by external authorities at the Ministry of Education. The dissertation defence is conducted within the department conferring the degree; external graders and committee members are invited to participate by the degree conferring units. Importantly, within these new programmes, the main requirement for graduation is the dissertation. Publications are not required from doctoral students.

At present, however, the graduation requirements at NU are viewed by outsiders as being too lax. This makes the future of NU doctorates somewhat ambiguous right now when it comes to employability. However, given the governance reforms expanding university autonomy that are being currently implemented across Kazakhstan, there is hope that the NU model will gradually be adopted at other universities, and that the decentralized version of doctoral education will produce researchers who are more globally competitive.

THE STATE OF DOCTORAL EDUCATION IN NUMBERS

More than a hundred universities currently offer PhD programmes in Kazakhstan. Seventy of those are public and 39 are private (Committee on Statistics of the Republic of Kazakhstan 2017). The number of PhD students in Kazakhstan has been steadily increasing, from 400 at the beginning of 2003, to 3,603 at the beginning of the 2017–2018 academic year (Committee on Statistics of the Republic of Kazakhstan 2017). Much of this growth has occurred at universities in the major cities, Astana and Almaty.

Complete and reliable statistics on degree progression are not forthcoming, but the available data shows that the dropout rate is low. According to the Committee on Statistics of the Republic of Kazakhstan (2017), only 3 per cent of students withdrew from doctoral programmes prior to graduation, and only 1 per cent did not graduate on time in 2017. As was mentioned above, in 2014, 10 per cent of dissertations were failed due to plagiarism and publication in predatory journals. While official statistics on failed defences are not available for 2017, given the figures noted above on degree progression during the same year, it can be assumed that most dissertations were successfully defended on time. This can be explained by the unaffordability of tuition if a student fails to graduate within the standard time frame, as well as by the presence of several layers in the defence process. Unacceptable dissertations, for example, can be sent back for improvement at earlier stages before they are seen by the decision-making body. There is also persistent corruption in the process; money can assure that a failure of a defence can be avoided.

With respect to demographics, according to the Committee on Statistics of the Republic of Kazakhstan (2017), most of the students pursuing PhD degrees are in their 30s. Interestingly, age does not seem to be a barrier for entrance into a PhD programme. In fact, four current PhD students in Kazakhstan are older than 60. Doctoral education seems to be most attractive, or most accessible, for the Kazakh majority, which represents 99 per cent of students. Women (59%) outnumber men (41%), with the difference increasing in the new cohort, where women comprise 62 per cent of the class. The most likely explanations for the gender imbalance are the lack of jobs for women, along with wage discrimination. Many women prefer to invest further in their education in the absence of attractive employment opportunities. This is particularly true for women in their 20s and 30s, who may be discriminated against in hiring and promotion by employers, and who may prefer to spend time in PhD programmes during their maternity leaves.

In terms of country of origin, only 1 per cent of PhD students in local universities come from outside Kazakhstan. In an effort to send more Kazakhstani doctoral students abroad, the government began offering special Bolashak scholarships in 2006. While the number of

PhD students educated abroad is increasing, with many students being funded by these Bolashak scholarships, the number of such students is insignificant. Between 2005 and 2013, only 213 students were Bolashak recipients (Perna, Orosz, and Jumakulov 2015). Most of those students were educated in the United Kingdom, the United States and Russia.

Table 14.1 shows student enrolment by field of specialization in 2017 (Committee on Statistics of the Republic of Kazakhstan 2017). Almost a quarter of the students enrolled in doctoral programmes in Kazakhstan specialize in engineering, followed by social sciences and education. Seventy-five per cent of education students are women. In fact, women outnumber men in many disciplines, including medicine and veterinary science, as well as in the social sciences, arts and humanities. Men dominate only in two specializations—law and engineering.

Unfortunately, data on employment and wage premiums associated with doctoral degrees is not reported in Kazakhstan. However, given the low level of research activity within the Kazakhstani private sector and government, and the pressures on universities to increase the ratio of PhD holders among the faculty to meet international accreditation requirements, it is fair to say that most PhD programme graduates find employment at universities or public research institutes.

Transition from a PhD programme to a job in academia or the public research system is somewhat complicated. First, a degree obtained outside Kazakhstan has to undergo a lengthy degree recognition procedure. Second, there remains much ambiguity about the correspondence between the new PhD degrees and the old Soviet degrees. Third, the rank at which PhD degree holders should be hired is often unclear. Technically, PhD degrees should be considered equal to doctor of science degrees, but there is still a perception that the doctor of science degree is worth more. This is reflected by the fact that doctor of science holders are paid twice as much as PhD degree holders. In addition, many recent doctoral graduates, including graduates from universities abroad, are employed as junior researchers on part-time contracts, which do not offer acceptable salaries or job security.

While obtaining a doctoral degree does increase the salary of a scholar, the average wage of a PhD degree holder remains lower than

Table 14.1 Enrolled PhD Students by Area of Specialization as of 2017–2018

Specializations	Enrolled					Admitted					Graduating				
	Total	Men	%	Women	%	Total	Men	%	Women	%	Total	Men	%	Women	%
Education	421	107	25	314	75	211	58	27	153	73	71	17	24	54	76
Humanities	406	148	36	258	64	210	77	37	133	63	72	27	38	45	63
Law	269	139	52	130	48	130	78	60	52	40	30	18	60	12	40
Arts	55	23	42	32	58	22	6	27	16	73	11	2	18	9	82
Social Sciences	633	246	39	387	61	307	120	39	187	61	87	21	24	66	76
Natural sciences	329	123	37	206	63	171	61	36	110	64	66	22	33	44	67
Engineering	855	456	53	399	47	381	159	42	222	58	198	95	48	103	52
Services	52	22	42	30	58	23	8	35	15	65	12	4	33	8	67
Military	8	4	50	4	50	5	1	20	4	80	1	0	0	1	100
Medicine	295	95	32	200	68	110	34	31	76	69	85	25	29	60	71
Veterinary	52	17	33	35	67	25	9	36	16	64	13	5	38	8	62
Total	**3,603**	**1,467**	**41**	**2,136**	**59**	**1,671**	**640**	**38**	**1,031**	**62**	**721**	**259**	**36**	**462**	**64**

Source: Committee on Statistics of the Republic of Kazakhstan (2017).

the salaries in occupations that do not require doctoral training. In 2017, the average salary of university faculty, for example, was KZT113,000, which is 5 per cent below the average salary in the country that same year (Zakon.kz 2018). Wages for women in academia are lower than wages for men, and this tendency persists even for PhD degree holders.

The premium from a PhD degree obtained from abroad, especially from Western institutions, is higher. Most of the holders of Western PhD degrees are now employed by NU. They receive salaries that are not only higher than salaries at other universities, but also higher than the salaries of their NU colleagues without such degrees. However, few of the internationally educated Kazakhstani PhD holders are hired at the level of faculty at NU, due to the pervasive perception that they are not as well prepared as their international counterparts.

Until recently, many international PhD degree holders faced the same lack of long-term job security as graduates of domestic universities. There is much demand for PhD degree holders in academia and public research institutions, and recent graduates often view a career in academia or research as highly desirable. However, there is some evidence from our other study (Kuzhabekova, Sparks, and Temerbayeva 2019) that some PhD degree holders leave academic professions and careers in research after several years of being employed on part-time contracts, and that many face problems when applying for full-time faculty positions.

DISCUSSION AND CONCLUSIONS

This section discusses some of the key positive developments and issues that have emerged over the period of reform in Kazakhstan. As should be clear from the findings summarized above, the country has succeeded in realigning the structures of doctoral education to achieve greater consistency with the European Higher Education Area. Moreover, the credit hour academic accounting system allows universities to plan their curricula in accordance with the approaches utilized in the West, as well as to facilitate academic mobility and degree recognition. In addition to making structural changes, financial mechanisms for supporting PhD education have been created, and the government has retained its important role in providing the necessary funding. Compared with the original state of the system, when the Soviet scholarly community existed in almost complete isolation from the global research community, modern doctoral programmes incorporate both an international advisor and a provision for academic mobility of graduate students. In short, the positive developments are hard to ignore.

Some issues, however, have yet to be addressed. One of the key problems, which may also be typical for other countries with lower levels of research capacity, is the lack of well-qualified local PhD supervisors who are active researchers at the international level. In the absence of such advisors, who have good knowledge of recent theoretical and methodological developments, the socialization of doctoral students into research professions is problematic. The situation could be improved with a better integration of recent graduates from doctoral programmes abroad, who are motivated to engage in international-level research and who have up-to-date knowledge of theories and methods. However, these graduates have trouble integrating into the Kazakhstani higher education system.

Another issue typical for other countries with lower levels of research capacity is the poor quality of both the curriculum and the teaching at the PhD level. While there are various effective models for doctoral education in the world, those models, which are based on limited coursework, may not be the most effective for countries like Kazakhstan. In the absence of quality supervision, it is very difficult for students to orient themselves among the numerous theories and methodological approaches via independent study. Formal coursework could provide some introduction to the field for students. While initially it may be difficult to find professors able to teach foundational and novel theories and methods to students, faculty could focus on mastering material for a course and improve their own skills over time. As a result, the overall quality of preparation of students could change for the better in the longer term.

While doctoral students in the West increasingly feel pressured to produce publications prior to graduation, and in some fields, to complete the dissertation as a sequence of published papers, requiring students to produce both a dissertation and publications is not realistic in some countries. As the example of Kazakhstan demonstrates, students can end up with a low quality of both. Unable to figure out the publication process by themselves, some students do not spend enough time on their dissertation, while others turn to publishing in questionable journals, thus undermining the global reputation of Kazakhstani scholarly community. In general, instead of focusing on the output requirements, reformers should focus on the inputs—the quality of facilities, the curriculum and instructors, as well as on continuing to improve the overall process of doctoral education.

When it is properly organized, international mobility seems to have a huge potential for improving the quality of doctoral education in countries with lower levels of research capacity. In Kazakhstan, students benefit from trips overseas if they are supervised by a domestic faculty member with both an active research agenda and connections abroad, as well as by a foreign advisor who tries to accommodate the needs of the student. Most students, however, do not receive this level of help and feel disoriented because their Kazakhstani advisors do not engage with them, and they have little clarity about the amount, duration and the conditions of their funding.

As the experience of Kazakhstan demonstrates, countries with lower levels of research capacity are not attractive for international students at the doctoral level. Much of the quality of doctoral training in countries of the global North is connected to the diversity of the student body, as well as a higher quality of students selected not from a constrained geographic area, but from around the world. In Kazakhstan, the quality of international cohorts could increase if the pool of competitors became larger. Domestic students could learn various world views and generate creative ideas in discussions with international students. They could also build networks with future scholars from other parts of the world. This potential, however, is underutilized because Kazakhstan is not a desired destination for talented future scholars from other parts of the world.

Another issue common for countries with lower national income levels is the insufficient financial support provided to PhD students during their studies. The stipend paid to students in Kazakhstan is below market salary averages, and the decision to enter a PhD programme ultimately comes down to the choice between a call of the heart and the hunger pangs one can expect to experience during years of frugal existence as a student. This situation leads to another common problem. Because men have to perform the role of breadwinners in the family and face better employment opportunities outside academia, they are less attracted to PhD programmes than women. The under-representation of men in certain majors could be problematic in the future, as certain scholarly fields will not sufficiently incorporate their perspectives as gender and will not benefit from the creative potential of gender diversity.

Many of the issues discussed above are related to efficiency. In Kazakhstan, doctoral scholarships are distributed among a large number of universities, most of which do not have the material or human resource capacity to support doctoral students. Efficiency and effectiveness could be increased if the number of institutions offering doctoral programmes was reduced, and scholarships were allocated to a small number of research-intensive universities, which would then receive a greater level of funding to be able to improve their laboratories and libraries, and to attract better faculty via higher salaries. This would create optimal conditions for intellectual exchange and research, as well as lead to the development of scholars and the emergence of a new generation of faculty for all universities.

Two key challenges in Kazakhstan, plagiarism and corruption, are also common in other post-Soviet countries. While the problems have been inherited from the Soviet period, their scale has increased since independence. Plagiarism has become pervasive, due to a combination of unrealistic graduation expectations and poor quality of training in disciplinary theories and methods. When students have committed several years of their life to a poorly paid 'occupation', expecting to get a return from a degree, they will go to great lengths to satisfy their graduation requirements, including purchasing a dissertation and stealing the work of others. If left unchecked, these unethical practices will perpetuate the current situation; scholars will not be able to produce international-level research or to teach the next generation of scholars.

Corruption in doctoral education is manifested in several ways in Kazakhstan. First, universities may give preferential treatment when it comes to applicants from their own ranks. This contributes to academic inbreeding, and prevents well-qualified applicants from other universities from entering high-quality programmes. Second, some degree of corruption is reported at the stage of the dissertation defence, where the likelihood of success is higher for those whose advisor is well connected and more influential in old Soviet scholarly circles. Finally, there is a lack of transparency and fairness in the hiring process for academic and research positions, as it is more important for a PhD graduate to be well connected than to have a high level of expertise. This affects in particular the graduates of universities abroad, who do not have the necessary connections (Kuzhabekova, Sparks, and Temerbayeva). Overall, whatever form corruption takes, it has negative effects on the quality of doctoral education, as well as on the prospects for a young generation of scholars in the academic job market.

Another issue common to post-Soviet countries is the over centralization of doctoral programme administration. Governments in these countries should give universities greater autonomy in administering doctoral programmes and should strengthen market incentives for universities to pursue quality. Presently, in Kazakhstan, training institutions are somewhat isolated from the evaluation of the training that they provide. The function of choosing external reviewers, and all final decision-making, is performed by the Higher Attestation Commission, which may not have the proper expertise in narrow fields of specialization to identify appropriate assessors. In addition, it is hard to guarantee that the Higher Attestation Commission acts in the interest of the public when ensuring high quality versus collecting self-serving favours.

Universities would be interested in more quality control if it creates institutional, or individual, faculty benefits in the form of enhanced reputation, increased demand for the programme (and consequently profits from fees), increased research funding, higher salaries, etc. Mechanisms for creating such incentives are abundant in international practice. They range from reputational measures, such as comprehensive programme and university rankings based on feedback from experts from other universities, alumni and employers, to differentiated allocation of research money and variable salary scales reflecting the reputation and research productivity of a particular programme or university. There are also existing solutions for quality control of dissertations defended at the university level. In other countries, dissertation committees may include an external evaluator who does not personally advise the student, thereby remaining more objective in evaluating quality.

Despite the issues indicated above, there are clear signs that positive developments are on their way in Kazakhstan. Previous efforts of the government are expected to pay off over time. There is hope that the Bolashak stipends, provided to talented Kazakhstani students for PhD study abroad, as well as the substantial investments in the creation of the world-class aspiring NU, will eventually bear fruit. As Bolashak returnees and NU graduates penetrate the Kazakhstani higher educational system and scholarly community, the quality of PhD student supervision and research in general can be expected to increase. NU is also creating a model of a highly effective and productive research system, which is expected to be emulated by other universities, and thus produce massive spillovers into other research universities in Kazakhstan. Many faculty and researchers at NU employ postdoctoral students from other universities, serve as external members of dissertation committees throughout Kazakhstan and support visiting doctoral students and faculty. By doing this, they contribute to a better understanding of alternative approaches to doctoral education and enhance the research capacity of scholars in other institutions.

NU has only recently launched its doctoral programmes and still needs time to calibrate the process of doctoral training and assessment. However, it is already actively sharing its experience with other universities by conducting an annual Higher Education Leaders Forum, as well as through conferences and workshops on current issues, theoretical developments, research methods, publication processes and university management for faculty, students and administrators from other universities. It is also influencing policymakers by offering consultations and conducting evaluations, and by implementing policy-relevant research.

It has huge potential to change educational policy in Kazakhstan, particularly with regard to doctoral education.

REFERENCES

Anderson, Kathryn H., Richard Pomfret, and Natalia Usseinova. 2004. 'Education in Central Asia during the Transition to a Market Economy'. In *The Challenges of Education in Central Asia*, edited by Stephen P. Heyneman and Alan DeYoung, 131–152. Greenwich, CT: Information Age Publishing.

Anonymous. 2014. 'Problems in Attestation of the Research Cadre and in Promotion to Academic Ranks'. Zakon.kz, 6 March. https://www.zakon.kz/4622234-problemy-attestacii-nauchnykh-kadrov-i.html (accessed 18 August 2018).

Asylbayev, D. S. 2006. 'The Development of Higher Education and the Stages in the Evolution of Governance of Universities in Kazakhstan'. *Vestnik of the Kazakh–American Free University* 4: 17–22.

Central Statistical Agency of the USSR. 1974. *Statistical Materials Published for the 250th Anniversary of the Academy of Science of the U.S.S.R.* Moscow: Statistika.

[Центральное Статистическое Агенство, СССР. 1974. *Статистические материалы опубликованные к 250-летнему юбилею Академии Наук СССР*. Москва: Статистика.]

Committee on Statistics of the Republic of Kazakhstan. 2017. 'On Postgraduate Education in the Republic of Kazakhstan. The State at the Beginning of 2017–2018 Academic Year'. http://stat.gov.kz/faces/wcnav_externalId/homeNumbersEducation?_afrLoop=4233825399904633#%40%3F_afrLoop%3D4233825399904633%26_adf.ctrl-state%3D16itpef57v_51 (accessed 18 August 2018).

[Комитет по Статистике Республики Казахстан. 2017. *О послевузовском образовании в Республике Казахстан на начало 2017–2018 учебного года.*

Dixon, J., and Dennis Soltys. 2013. *Implementing Bologna in Kazakhstan: A Guide for Universities.* Almaty and Astana: Academpress.

Education and Science in Kazakh SSR. 1990. *Statistical Compendium.* Almaty: R.I.I.Ts.

[Образование и наука в Казахсклй ССР. 1990. Статистический сборник. Алматы: РИИТ.]

Erasmus+. 2017. 'Overview of the Higher Education System in Kazakhstan'. http://www.erasmusplus.kz/attachments/article/196/countryfiche_kazakhstan_2017.pdf (accessed 18 August 2018).

Ermekbay, Zh.A. (2016). The formation and development of science in Soviet Kazakhstan. *Vestnik of Tomsk State University*, (413), 103–110.

Forbes Kazakhstan. 2015. 'Are Kazakhstani Scholars Paying for Publication Abroad?' 15 June. https://forbes.kz/process/science/platyat_li_kazahstanskie_uchenyie_za_svoi_publikatsii/ (accessed 18 August 2018).

[*Forbes Kazakhstan*. 2015. Платят ли казахстанские ученые за свои публикации.]

Government of the Republic of Kazakhstan. 2012. 'Decree about the Order of Admission to Educational Organizations, Which Deliver Spot Graduate Professional Education Programs'. 19 January, no. 109. http://adilet.zan.kz/rus/docs/P1200000109 (accessed 18 August 2018).

[Правительство Республики Казахстан. 2012. Об утверждении Типовых правил приема на обучение в организации образования, реализующие профессиональные учебные программы послевузовского образования.19 января, 2012, № 109].

Kassevitch, V., N. Rozina, G. Lukichev, E. Gevorkyan, A. Minayev, A. Talonov, and V. Chistokhvalov. 'Russian National Report on the Bologna Process, 2004–2005'. http://www.Bologna-bergen2005.no/EN/national_impl/00_Nat-rep–05/National_Reports-Russia_050117.pdf (accessed 18 August 2018).

Kuraev, Alexey. 2014. 'Internationalization of Higher Education in Russia: Collapse or Perpetuation of the Soviet System? A Historical and Conceptual Study'. PhD diss., Lynch School of Education, Boston College. http://hdl.handle.net/2345/3799 (accessed 18 August 2018).

Kuzhabekova, Aliya, and Dinara Mukhamejanova. 2017. 'Productive Researchers in Countries with Limited Research Capacity: Researchers as Agents in Post-Soviet Kazakhstan'. *Journal of Studies in Graduate and Postdoctoral Education* 8 (1): 30–47.

Kuzhabekova, Aliya, Soltanbekova, Arailym, Almukhambetova, Ainur, and Mukhametzhanova, Assel. 2017. 'Educational Flagships as Brokers in International Policy Transfer: Learning from the Experience of Kazakhstan'. *European Education* 50 (4): 353–370.

Kuzhabekova, A., Sparks, J., & Temerbayeva, A. (2019). 'Returning from Study Abroad and Transitioning as a Scholar: Stories of Foreign PhD Holders from Kazakhstan'. *Research in Comparative and International Education* 14(3), 412–430.

Ministry of Education and Science of the Republic of Kazakhstan. 2011. 'State Standard on Doctoral Education'. 17 June, no. 261.

[Министерство Образования и Науки Республики Казахстан. 2011. Государственный Общеобразовательный Стандарт Образования Республики Казахстан. Послевузовское Образование. Докторантура. 17 июня, № 261.]

Mironin, S. 2018. 'Two Approaches to the Development of Science and the History of Dissertation Issue'. *Biometrics*. http://www.biometrica.tomsk.ru/naukoved/mironin (accessed 18 August 2018).

Mukhtarova, N. 2010. 'Brain Drain in Kazakhstan in 1999–2008'. Master's thesis. Prague: Charles University in Prague. https://dspace.cuni.cz/handle/20.500.11956/32208 (accessed August 2018).

Perna, L. W., Kata Orosz, and Zakir Jumakulov. 2015. 'Understanding the Human Capital Benefits of a Government Funded International Scholarship Program: An Exploration of Kazakhstan's *Bolashak* Program'. *International Journal of Educational Development* 40 (2015): 85–97.

PhD in Russia. 2018. '*Aspirantura* in the USSR'. http://phdru.com/study/ussr/ (accessed August 2018).

[PhD в России. 2018. Аспирантура в СССР.]

Soviet of the Ministers of the USSR. 1975. 'Resolution on the Regulations on the Conferral of Scientific Degrees and Academic Ranks'. file:///C:/Users/Aliya/Dropbox/My%20documents%2012.08.15/Research/Articles%20and%20Chapters%20in%20progress/Book%20on%20Doctoral%20Education%20with%20Yudkevich/Зашита%20в%20CCCP.html (accessed August 2018).

[Совет Министров СССР. 1975. Резолюция по правилам присуждения научных степеней и академических званий.]

Tampayeva, G. Y. 2015. 'Importing Education: Europeanisation and the Bologna Process in Europe's Backyard—The Case of Kazakhstan'. *European Educational Research Journal* 14 (1): 74–85.

Tokarev, N. V. 2016. *The Academy of Sciences of the Byelorussian Soviet Socialist Republic: The Years of Conception and Development (1945–1991)*. Minsk: Byelorusskaya Nauka.

Vestnik of the Academy of Sciences of Kazakh SSR. 1980. 8: 9–10.

Zakon.kz. 'Experts Counted the Salaries of University Faculty in Kazakhstan'. 21 February. https://www.zakon.kz/4904976-kakaya-zarplata-v-sfere-obrazo-vaniya.html (accessed August 2018).

[Zakon.kz. Эксперты посчитали зарплаты преподавателей в Казахстане]

Chapter 15

Rapid Development and Current Rethinking in Doctoral Education in South Korea

HeeJin Lim, Seung Jung Kim and
Jung Cheol Shin

Doctoral education in South Korea (hereafter Korea) began to attract policy attention in the late 1990s as a response to the rise of a knowledge society. The Korean government introduced various programmes, for example, the Brain Korea 21 (BK21) project and the World-Class University project, to improve the research competence of local universities and researchers. As a result, the productivity of Korean researchers improved rapidly and the number of doctoral students and PhD graduates increased significantly. However, due to this rapid expansion, doctoral education in Korea is now facing various challenges, including a mismatch between the number of PhD graduates and available jobs, especially in academia. Other issues involve the country's hierarchical academic culture, student exploitation and limited financial support for doctoral students. This chapter addresses the historical formation of the doctoral education system in Korea, as well as its general characteristics. We will also discuss major items on Korea's policy agenda on doctoral education and related challenges.

DOCTORAL EDUCATION DEVELOPMENT IN KOREA

Korean doctoral education has experienced rapid growth in response to the development of the country's increasingly knowledge-based economy. The number of doctoral students in 1970 was only 470, but grew to 75,342 in 2017. Korean universities are producing approximately 14,000 new doctorates each year, which makes the country a world leader in the number of research and development (R&D) workers per capita. Korean doctoral degree programmes were relatively underdeveloped until the 1990s. They suffered from poor research infrastructure, which led to a dependency on foreign degree holders, mainly from the United States. However, both the Korean government and universities were ambitious in their efforts to establish 'world-class universities', which resulted in improvements in the quality of doctoral education. These efforts included increases in research funding and more stipends for doctoral students.

In the 1960s, following the Korean War, undergraduate enrolment began to grow and the size of graduate schools expanded accordingly. This sudden expansion revealed the poor quality of the nation's graduate schools. Critical educational problems included the lack of differentiation between undergraduate and postgraduate programmes, as well as an insufficient number of faculty members who could advise graduate students effectively (Lee et al. 2013). Also, graduate students' level of academic commitment was very low, because their main interest was simply to obtain a degree, rather than pursue scientific enquiry (Seoul National University 2006).

After the revision of the Education Law in 1975, Korean universities started to adopt an American-style, coursework-based model of doctoral education. This transformation largely took place under the guidance of faculty members who were trained in US universities (Umakoshi 1995). Another major shift during the 1970s was the increased recognition of a university's research function. This was due to Korea's rapid economic development. During this period, the Korean government aimed to transform its economy from 'labour-intensive' to 'heavy-technical' industry. As a result, the government established various government-funded research institutes, including the Korea Advanced Institute of Science and Technology (KAIST), to support rapid industrial development (Shin and Lee 2015).

In the expansion period, and especially from the late 1990s, the number of graduate students (including doctoral students) started to increase even more dramatically, along with undergraduate enrolment. This was because of the Korean government's active effort to improve the research competence of its universities through the introduction of various large-scale government-driven graduate education support projects, such as the BK21 project and the World-Class University project, as responses to the rise of the knowledge-based economy (Shin 2009).

For a long time, the Korean government's major policy concern was improving the quality of undergraduate education. However, because of an increase in the perceived importance of universities' roles in knowledge production, government policies rapidly expanded to include the graduate education sector, especially doctoral education. The fast growth of graduate education in such a short period of time has resulted in various problems. When it comes to doctoral graduates, supply and demand remain mismatched in Korea. As noted above, there are also concerns about Korean education's hierarchical nature and about the exploitation of students. Later in this chapter, we will discuss how and why these problems push many Korean students into pursuing doctoral study abroad.

ORGANIZATION OF KOREAN DOCTORAL EDUCATION
Types of Graduate Schools

The graduate education system in Korea includes both master's and doctoral levels, and there are three main systems: general graduate school, professional graduate school and graduate school for continuing education. These systems differ from one another in terms of roles and functions. General graduate schools aim to cultivate future scholars and focus on providing in-depth academic research training. Almost 90 per cent of all doctoral degrees are awarded by general graduate schools. Professional graduate schools strive to cultivate highly specialized professionals in more than 100 majors, including medicine, law, business management, interpretation and translation, theology, social welfare, international studies and public administration. Although professional graduate schools offer professional degrees, some institutions also grant academic doctoral degrees, depending on the university's rules and the academic discipline. In 2017, approximately 10 per cent of doctoral degrees were awarded by professional graduate schools. Finally, graduate schools for continuing education target working professionals and the general adult population, but only award master's degrees. Continuing graduate schools are also called 'specific' graduate schools, because they offer master's degrees in specific industrial fields. Each university may establish all three types of graduate schools if they meet government requirements, but some professional school subjects such as medicine and law are restricted to a few universities due to enrolment quota regulations (Ministry of Education 2014). For example, at Seoul National University, there are 72 departments that offer doctoral programmes in general graduate school, and 11 professional graduate schools in fields such as medicine, dentistry and international studies. This shows that a single institution can establish various types of graduate schools according to needs.

A recent trend in Korean higher education is an increase in the number of doctoral students enrolled in professional graduate schools. However, general graduate schools are still the dominant providers of doctoral education, accounting for 90.1 per cent of doctoral student enrolment in 2017, compared to 9.9 per cent in professional graduate schools. This chapter's focus will largely be on the characteristics and issues related to general graduate school.

Doctoral Student Enrolment Trends

In 2017, there were 74,342 doctoral students studying in Korea. Interestingly, the number of graduate students has been consistently increasing, while the enrolment rate of undergraduate students at two- and four-year colleges has been declining. The rate of increase for doctoral students is also higher than that of master's students. For example, from 2000 to 2013, the annual rate of doctoral student growth was 5.3 per cent, whereas for master's students, it was only 0.8 per cent (Ministry of Education 2014).

Table 15.1 *Changes in Numbers of Doctoral Students by Discipline*

	1999	2001	2005	2009	2013	2017
Humanities	3,157	3,922	5,467	7,000	7,925	9,122
Social science	4,287	5,198	8,430	10,448	12,890	14,185
Education	1,310	1,555	2,987	3,760	4,783	5,289
Engineering	8,660	9,413	9,312	10,476	16,215	19,648
Natural science	5,754	6,113	6,693	7,698	10,787	12,262
Medicine	5,156	6,039	7,761	7,308	8,962	9,549
Arts and physical science	600	1,165	2,822	3,696	4,326	4,287
Total	28,924	33,405	43,472	50,386	65,888	74,342

Source: Korea Education Statistics Service.

Table 15.1 details the changes in the number of doctoral students from 1999 to 2017. The number of doctoral students increased approximately 2.5 times during that time. Among the student population, the proportion of those studying science and engineering accounted for 49.8 per cent in 1999 (engineering 29.9%, natural sciences 19.9%), but declined to 42.9 per cent in 2017 (engineering 26.4%, natural sciences 16.5%). On the other hand, the rate of increase in some academic fields exceeded the average. Education numbers grew fourfold, social sciences threefold and arts and physical sciences a little more than sevenfold. Moreover, there is clear evidence of a rapid increase in the number of female doctoral students in Korea. Following increases in female enrolment at the bachelor's and master's levels, the proportion of female doctoral graduates rose from 1,264 (20.5%) in 2000, to 5,385 (37.6%) in 2017.

Another recent trend is the growth in the number of international doctoral students studying at Korean universities. In 2016, international students made up approximately 9.3 per cent of the doctoral student population; only a little more than one-quarter of those students received scholarships from the Korean government, their home governments or from a university. That means a majority of international students were 'self-paying'. As for fields of study, the share of international students is highest in the social sciences (36.5%), followed by engineering (19.6%), the humanities (17.9%) and science (10.2%).

Most international doctoral students in Korea are from other Asian countries (87.7%), with China (36.3%) sending the largest number of students. The ratio of students from ASEAN (Association of Southeast Asian Nations) countries is also gradually increasing. However, the share of international students in Korean doctoral programmes is still very low compared to other countries such as the United States, the United Kingdom and Australia.

The language issue is one of the critical factors that limits the successful academic adjustment and socialization of international students. Despite the importance of local language skills, the Korean government has recently lowered the standard for Korean proficiency for admission in order to attract more international students. Although the Korean government and universities have expanded the number of classes taught in English, most instruction is in Korean, which makes international students' learning experiences more difficult. In addition, most international students are from non-English speaking countries, which makes classes taught in English ineffective. In many cases, international students are allowed to complete their dissertations in Korean or English.

THE DOCTORAL EDUCATION MODEL AND DEGREE PROCESS
Doctoral Education Model

As mentioned earlier, doctoral programmes in Korea began to adapt the coursework-based US model in the mid-1970s. Students are required to complete up to two years of structured coursework. After completion of the coursework, students then must pass a comprehensive or qualifying exam before beginning work on the dissertation. However, one of the major differences between Korean and US doctoral programmes is the limited range of courses offered for doctoral students, due to the relatively small faculty size in each department. The size of university departments is usually much larger in US universities, which allows for more diverse course options for doctoral students. But in Korea, the range of courses is limited and students have fewer choices (Lim et al. 2016). Also, compared to US doctoral programmes, qualifying or comprehensive exams in Korea are generally less strict, so 'weeding out' weak candidates through the examination process is relatively rare (although it differs by department and institution).

Admissions Requirements

Students who wish to enrol in Korean doctoral programmes should hold a master's degree or the equivalent as recognized by law. For integrated master's–PhD programmes, students can apply directly after finishing their undergraduate degrees. Integrated degree programmes are more common in science and engineering fields. In general, doctoral students are selected based on a department's or specific programme's criteria. For example, some programmes may require a research proposal and an interview. But in some hard disciplines, especially in master's–PhD integrated programmes, applicants are required to pass an assessment of their basic academic ability. However, unlike the Graduate Record Exam or Graduate Management Admission Test in the United States, there are no standardized exams needed to apply for a Korean doctoral programme. The majority of graduate schools do require a certain level of English proficiency as part of their admissions and graduation criteria, because most learning materials and publication activities are in English.

When it comes to tuition, most doctoral students in Korea pay their own way, although some institutions and programmes (mostly in science and engineering) support the cost of tuition and offer a stipend. As of 2018, the average tuition for doctoral programmes in Korean universities was approximately US$4,800 per year for public and national universities and $8,293 for private universities.

Graduation Requirements

Doctoral student dissertations are usually evaluated by a review committee of five members, including one external reviewer. The specific requirements for graduation and the format of doctoral dissertations differ by institution and discipline. For example, science and engineering students in research-focused institutions are required to publish a certain number of papers in peer-reviewed journals first (mainly in globally recognized Science Citation Index journals with high impact factors), and then elaborate on those papers for their dissertations (PhD by publication). Therefore, a student's publication output is considered very important, especially in STEM (science, technology, engineering and mathematics) departments in research-focused institutions. On the other hand, students in the social sciences and humanities can submit a dissertation without having to publish first, although doctoral students in non-STEM fields are also required to have a certain publication output in order to fulfil their graduation requirements. The pressure for non-STEM students to publish in international journals is relatively low compared to the hard sciences, because in many cases non-STEM students can publish their articles in domestic journals.

According to the Doctoral Recipients Survey published by the Korea Research Institute for Vocational Education and Training in 2015, new doctoral degree holders published 2.33 articles in domestic peer-reviewed journals, and 2.78 articles in international peer-reviewed journals on average during the course of their doctoral programmes (Song et al. 2015). When looking at difference by disciplinary field, those in the natural sciences had the highest rate of publication in international peer-reviewed journals (4.54 articles), which reflects the importance of global publication in that discipline. It also shows that doctoral students in Korea are actively engaged in international publication activities, due to the strong emphasis on research productivity at both the governmental and institutional levels. The same survey also investigated average time to degree for doctoral students, which varies across disciplines. The average for all subjects was 5.1 years; the arts and humanities had the longest time to degree (6.4 years) and medicine the shortest (4.1 years).

Although it varies by discipline and institution, most doctoral students in Korea are not required to teach during the course of their doctoral programmes. Instead, some students participate in their supervisor's undergraduate class as teaching assistants. They may be assigned tasks such as checking attendance and grading. In general, doctoral students have limited pedagogical training and experience during their doctoral programmes, partly because the government has encouraged universities to provide undergraduate courses taught by full-time faculty members in order to ensure quality (the full-time faculty to student ratio is a university evaluation indicator). This limits opportunities for doctoral students to engage in teaching activities before they obtain their degrees.

Characteristics of Doctoral Degree Granting Institutions

Table 15.2 shows the number of doctoral degrees awarded by universities, classified based on their research functions and productivity. According to data collected in 2017, Seoul National University, which belongs to Research Group 1, awarded 9.5 per cent of all

Table 15.2 Doctoral Degree Holders by Categorized Universities (2017)

	Name of Institution	Doctoral Degree Holders	Rate of Total Doctoral Degree Holders (%)
Research Group 1	Seoul National University	1,248	9.5
Research Group 2	Yonsei University	715	17.2
	Korea University	588	
	Sungkyunkwan University	444	
	Hanyang University	510	
Research Group 3	KAIST	638	6.6
	POSTECH	242	
Research Active	13 other institutions	3,323	25.2
Others	Others	5,498	41.6
Total		13,206	100

Source: University Information by Korean Council for University Education.

doctoral degrees (1,248). That is the highest number of doctoral degrees from a single institution in Korea. Research Group 2 consists of major private universities located in the Seoul area, such as Yonsei, Korea, Sungkyunkwan and Hanyang. These institutions awarded 17.2 per cent of all doctoral degrees. Research Group 3 is composed of two major institutions specializing in science and engineering (KAIST and POSTECH), and together they accounted for 6.6 per cent of doctoral degree awards. The Research Active group consists of other major public institutions such as Kyungpook National University and Pusan National University, and 25.2 per cent of doctoral degrees were granted from this group. Finally, a substantial proportion (41.6%) of doctoral degrees were awarded by the 'other' category. These are institutions with fewer resources and less orientation towards research. It is likely that most doctoral students enrolled in these institutions are part-time, and that their motivations for studying are for professional development.

POLICY EFFORTS TO IMPROVE DOCTORAL EDUCATION IN KOREA

Efforts to Establish World-Class Research Universities and Graduate Education

The Korean government actively joined the global competition to establish world-class universities in the late 1990s (Shin 2009). The BK21 project was introduced in 1999 with the aim of improving the graduate education system and ultimately establishing world-class research universities. The project's two decade agenda has evolved over three phases: BK21 first phase (1999–2005), BK21 second phase (2006–2012) and BK21 Plus (2013–2020). The ultimate goals of this project are to improve the rankings of Korean universities by strengthening both the quantity and quality of research produced by selected universities and departments, and to provide financial support for graduate (both master's and doctoral) students. Seventy per cent of the budget is allocated to support graduate students and junior academics in order to create more stable and effective research environments.

Selected participants in the BK21 project are required to be full-time students who can dedicate at least 40 hours a week to research and coursework. Financial aid is offered in the form of 'research scholarships', and doctoral students are entitled to receive US$1,000 per month. Moreover, BK21 students enjoy other benefits, including coverage of their travel costs to participate in international conferences, and assistance with article evaluation and submission fees. In 2017, 33,000 graduate students in master's and doctoral programmes (29,000 students in science and engineering and 4,000 in arts and humanities) received financial support from the project (Ministry of Education 2017).

The BK21 project has been praised for its achievements, but also criticized for some side effects. The research productivity of participating BK21 teams (faculty and graduate students) has increased significantly, because project selection and evaluation are heavily focused on quantitative measurements (Baik and Park 2007; Kim, Yi, and Jang 2014). For example, many of the teams mandate that students publish articles in international journals (the Science Citation Index, the Social Sciences Citation Index and the Arts and Humanities Citation Index) and present at international conferences. Thus, the BK21 project has contributed to enhancing the global competency of graduate students in domestic institutions by encouraging more active participation in the global research arena. However, the size of financial support provided to graduate students is still not sufficient to reduce the financial burden, or attractive enough to induce more top students to enrol in domestic programmes. Also, the high level of government oversight on university research has meant 'evaluation fatigue' for many faculty, staff and students.

The current BK21 Plus project is expected to run through August 2020. The Korean government is preparing to introduce what it is tentatively calling BK21 FOUR when the Plus programme comes to an end. Although it is still in the planning stages, the government aims to address the various limitations of the existing BK21 projects. The government wants to reduce the number of participating departments from 542 to 350 in order to increase the size of financial support that each team receives. Also, the amount of financial support that doctoral students receive will increase from US$1,000 to US$1,500 per month. However, there are concerns that this will result in increased pressure on universities and departments to compete, as well as generate inequity issues because fewer doctoral students will be able to receive financial support.

Another major policy initiative targeted at improving the research environment and attracting talented students to domestic doctoral programmes is the 'Global PhD Fellowship',' or GPF, which was introduced in 2011. The major difference between the BK21 project and the GPF programme is how doctoral students are selected for funding. Doctoral students who wish to apply to the GPF programme submit a research proposal directly to the National Research Foundation (NRF). If successful, they can receive $30,000 per year for three to five years, depending on the programme type. The GPF programme resembles the National Science Foundation's Graduate Research Fellowship Program in the United States, and Japan's Special Researcher Program (Jang 2013). Approximately 200 students are selected each year for the GPF, and although the programme is available in all disciplines, approximately 80 per cent of the recipients are in science and engineering and are mostly enrolled in research-focused universities.

EFFORTS FOR QUALITY ASSURANCE IN KOREAN DOCTORAL EDUCATION

For a long time, the Korean government's education policy focused largely on undergraduate programmes and there was no direct, government-driven evaluation specifically for graduate education. Instead, universities were required to self-evaluate their graduate programmes and publish the reports on their university websites. However, rapid growth in the number of postgraduate students and social demand for accountability in graduate education have resulted in the government seeking more direct intervention. In 2014, the Ministry of Education announced a plan to expand the scope of evaluation to include graduate education starting in 2016.

Then, in July 2016, the government withdrew its plan for graduate education evaluation due to strong opposition from Korean universities. Nevertheless, the government exercises indirect control by linking each institution's undergraduate programme evaluation result to its graduate programme. Since 2015, the Korean government has been undertaking strict assessments to achieve university reform. It wants to improve the quality of college education, as well as respond to the country's rapid school-age population decline. Institutions with high evaluation scores may increase their doctoral student enrolment quota by reducing undergraduate and master's student quotas, which can directly affect the research performance of the university. On the other hand, institutions with low scores must increase the proportion of undergraduate student enrolment and reduce their existing graduate student quotas.

As a result, there are no direct quality control measures for the graduate education sector in Korea. Instead, the government indirectly controls it through university self-evaluation, relying on the institutions themselves to improve the quality of education internally and voluntarily. Also, the government uses specific evaluation criteria in order to spur institutions to compete for large financial subsidy programmes like BK21 Plus. Consequently, universities who wish to obtain funding are actively trying to fulfil the evaluation criteria. However, current quality control mechanisms may not be as effective in improving the accountability of less prestigious institutions that have a low chance of receiving government subsidies, yet still produce a substantial number of doctoral degree holders. The end result may be a kind of 'Matthew effect' or 'winner-take-all' phenomenon, in which support and resources are concentrated on already high-achieving universities.

ISSUES AND CHALLENGES IN KOREAN DOCTORAL EDUCATION
Supply and Demand Issues

When it comes to Korean doctoral graduates' employment prospects, there is currently a mismatch between supply and demand. The market for jobs in academia is shrinking. At the same time, Korea produces one of the highest number of graduate students per capita in the world. For example, in 2003, there were 5.3 graduate students per 1,000 people, which is much higher than other high-income countries such as the

United States (3.8), France (2.5) and Japan (1.6) (Ban 2003). Because of this, some institutions like Seoul National University attempted to reduce quotas for doctoral student enrolment in the early 2000s in an effort to improve job prospects and the quality of education. In the late 2000s, however, doctoral student quotas started to rapidly increase again because of the role universities were asked to play in the development of the national R&D system.

Each year, approximately 13,000 new doctoral degree holders are entering the Korean job market, but one in four of them fails to secure any form of employment (Yoo et al. 2017). This unemployment rate is increasing, and the figures are particularly bad in disciplines with more limited career options, such as the arts, humanities and natural sciences. Ironically, the employment rate of doctoral students in lower-tier universities tends to be higher, because most of these students are part-time and go back to largely non-academic jobs (public servants, school teachers, etc.) when they finish. Doctoral graduates who do succeed in finding a job in academia often face a low level of job security. Most new academic jobs in Korea are short-term, contract-based and have low salaries.

Problems with Doctoral Student Exploitation

The cultural nature of Korean academe is often defined as 'hierarchical and authoritative' (Shin 2012). It is derived from a traditional Confucian culture that places great importance on respecting elders and on the authority of the teacher (especially university faculty). In this cultural context, the academic advisor's level of authority is particularly strong in Korean universities. In fact, advisors have great influence on a student's graduation, future career and even daily life. With such an unbalanced power relationship between doctoral student and faculty member, numerous cases have been reported of students suffering abusive treatment by their academic advisors. Some experience verbal and physical abuse, as well as various forms of exploitation, including embezzlement of the student's scholarship money and sexual misconduct. It also leads to ethical dilemmas, such as when an academic advisor takes authorial credit for work done entirely by a student. Under these circumstances, it is usually very difficult for doctoral students to raise any dissenting opinion because they fear it will threaten their learning experience and future. In fact, some studies have pointed out that it is exactly this 'cultural' issue that drives so many Korean students to study abroad (Kim 2008; Lim 2018).

The recognition of the human rights of graduate students is growing. However, such initiatives are not being driven by institutions, but rather through the 'voice' of the students themselves. For a long time, the human rights issues of graduate students were situated in a 'blind spot' because of their sensitive nature. Then, in 2014, the first Graduate Students Bill of Rights was announced by the graduate student association at KAIST. It emphasized the 'freedom' and 'rights' of graduate students, and focused specifically on preventing student exploitation. In the years that followed, students at other major institutions such as Seoul National University and Korea University formed their own graduate student councils. Efforts to secure student rights have also been introduced by the government, which tries to consistently monitor and prevent any student mistreatment, especially regarding the embezzlement of student scholarships by academic advisors. Controversially, Kim (2007) pointed out that the loyal and close relationships between advisors and graduate students are exactly what have enabled Korean universities to increase their research productivity in such a short period of time. True world-class universities, however, should be able to have both high research competence and a democratic academic culture that can effectively mix creativity and autonomy (Shin et al. 2018).

Brain Drain Issues

Despite the continuous efforts of the Korean government and universities to improve domestic doctoral education programmes, there are still many students who choose to study abroad. As of 2016, 223,908 Korean students were studying overseas at all educational levels. This included language exchange programmes. Among those outbound students, the ratio of postgraduate students enrolled in both master's and doctoral programmes was approximately 15 per cent (33,167 students). The data shows that Korean students' most popular destination for postgraduate study is the United States (53%), followed by China (11.4%), Germany (7.6%), Japan (7.2%) and the United Kingdom (5.3%). Doctoral students' destinations differ by discipline; for example, countries such as Germany and France are preferred by students who wish to specialize in the humanities, whereas those studying economics and engineering tend to prefer the United States. In 2015, 1,323 Koreans reported that they obtained a PhD degree overseas, the biggest share of those in the United States.

Two major forces drive students to study outside Korea. First, as mentioned earlier, some students choose to study abroad due to the cultural problems that exist in Korean universities. Second, there is a clear tendency for universities, especially the more prestigious ones, to prefer foreign degree holders when recruiting faculty. As of 2016, approximately 33 per cent of all faculty members in Korean universities obtained their degrees from foreign universities. However, the ratio of foreign degree holders increases significantly when one looks at more prestigious universities. For example, more than 80 per cent of the faculty members in soft disciplines at the major research universities (Seoul National, Yonsei and Korea) are foreign degree holders, mostly from US universities. A study by Lee (2013) pointed out that domestic doctoral degree holders are more likely to be hired by lower-tier universities. For this reason, prospective doctoral students, especially those who obtained undergraduate degrees from higher-tier institutions, fear that it is vital to obtain a doctoral degree from abroad in order to become faculty at one of the major Korean universities. For a long time, there was also a strong perception that foreign degree holders had more research competence and advanced knowledge. However, some recent studies have pointed out that there is no difference between the research productivity of domestic and foreign degree holders, especially when it comes to publications. In fact, domestic degree holders perform even better in some cases (Shin et al. 2014; Sung 2017). In the longer term, these trends may help change the perception of domestic doctoral programmes as underrated.

One of the main remaining challenges regarding outbound doctoral students is brain drain. Substantial numbers of overseas PhD graduates do not return to Korea after completing their degrees. This is particularly true of STEM graduates. At the same time, there is also an increase in number of domestically trained STEM doctoral graduates choosing to seek employment opportunities in other countries. For example, out of 97,000 doctoral researchers in Korea, 36.4 per cent indicated their intention to leave due to pressure on short-term research output, job insecurity, lack of research funding and the suppressive research environment in Korea (Kim 2010).

Limited Financial Support for Doctoral Students and Graduates

Although the Korean government has introduced various initiatives to increase financial support for doctoral students, this area needs further improvement. Among recent PhD graduates, only 35.7 per cent indicated they received any form of scholarship (including the BK21 project) to cover their tuition fees and provide a stipend during their doctoral programmes. Although the BK21 project is a significant milestone that improved financial support for graduate students, the amount students receive is still not sufficient to relieve their financial burdens. For example, doctoral students who participate in the BK21 project receive approximately US$12,000 annually, which makes it difficult to cover living costs in the Seoul area. Moreover, if the student is taking coursework and the affiliated programme or lab does not cover it, there are additional tuition fees ranging from US$4,800 to $8,293 depending on the university or programme. The situation is very different compared to other advanced countries like the United States or the Nordic countries, where a doctoral student often receives competitive financial assistance in the form of a scholarship, fellowship or salary.

One of the reasons for limited financial assistance at Korean universities may be due to a mismatch between available resources and number of students. Also, universities in Korea rely heavily on the government to support graduate students and put very little effort into increasing their own contributions. This is because most of their financial subsidies are focused on supporting undergraduate students. On the other hand, there are limited public and university financial support programmes (postdoctoral fellowships) offered to doctoral graduates in Korea. In

2017, NRF offered 2,506 fellowships (1,650 in the humanities and social sciences and 847 in science and engineering) that were targeted at new doctoral graduates. However, the size of this public programme is very limited compared to the number of doctoral graduates produced each year (ca. 13,000 as noted above). The scarce public funding for postdoctoral research fellowships in science and engineering puts serious constraints on new doctoral graduates who wish to pursue an academic career, because postdoctoral research experience is considered almost mandatory for those who wish to find a placement in academia.

Limited financial support for domestic postdoc programmes leads to brain drain as locally trained PhD graduates find placements in overseas institutions (Oh 2017). Although postdoctoral positions are known for their lack of job stability in many countries, they are particularly unstable in Korea because of short-term contracts and poor salaries. As a result, Korean doctoral students often want to acquire postdoctoral experience in other advanced countries, not only to become better researchers, but also to improve their job prospects. In order to overcome these issues, NRF has increased the salaries offered to postdoctoral researchers, from $29,000 in 2010 to $45,000 in 2018 (for science and engineering). The organization has also encouraged more students to pursue postdoc positions in domestic institutions. In fact, the foundation gives selection preference to those who wish to work in Korea, and provides higher salaries for those who apply to domestic programmes (US$45,000 for one or two years) than for those who apply for overseas programmes (US$40,000 for one year only).

Issues with External, Project-based STEM Doctoral Education

The Korean government has continuously increased R&D investment in order to make the nation more competitive and innovative in the global economy. In 2016, 4.24 per cent of total GDP was spent on R&D. Until the mid-1990s, Korean universities did not contribute much to the national research system because they were focused on teaching activities. However, in the late 1990s, the role of universities in the national R&D system started to expand rapidly, which meant that academics began to actively engage in research projects funded by government and industry. Close research collaborations between universities, industries and the government, offer various advantages, especially in STEM fields. For example, they allow doctoral students to be able to link theory with actual practice and access cutting-edge technologies. Also, collaboration may help students find job placements after graduation (Behrens and Grey 2001; Mendoza 2007). Despite these advantages, academic participation in externally funded projects may also cause problems for doctoral students. For example, students can have limited research autonomy in such projects. The quality of supervision may be low because advisors spend too much time securing funding, or are engaged in other project management roles (Deuchar 2008; Wichmann-Hansen and Hermann 2017).

Although this 'project-driven' trend in STEM doctoral education is seen in many countries, it seems to be more problematic in Korea. Lim (2018) points out that when university academics are highly involved in externally funded projects, the learning experience of doctoral students is affected. For example, doctoral students have difficulty setting long-term research agendas in their interest areas because they are assigned too many activities unrelated to their own research. This leads to a clear mismatch between the work they are asked to undertake and the actual research they wish to pursue. For example, a recent study found that only 15.5 per cent of Korean doctoral students indicated they had freely chosen their research topic (Um et al. 2013). Most importantly, the quality of supervision was often found to be very poor because many advisors would not let students pursue their own lines of research. Instead, advisors broadened or changed their students' research areas in order to try to secure what little government funding is available on a limited range of topics. Also, when comparing domestic and foreign degree holders, it was found that those who were trained in domestic institutions spent significantly longer hours in administrative tasks related to external projects and much less time on their own research, compared to those who were trained overseas (Hong et al. 2015).

In summary, doctoral students are on the front lines in a nationally supported research system, but their contributions and sacrifices are often neglected by the university and government. This leads doctoral students to question their identities (student versus employee), and many wonder if they are nothing but cheap labour for their universities and departments. This is why, in many cases, doctoral students argue that they should be regarded as employees and receive salaries and benefits commensurate with their actual contributions.

CONCLUSION

From the 1960s onwards, doctoral education has experienced rapid expansion in Korea, fuelled by a demand for doctoral graduates in the job market as the knowledge economy emerged. The Korean government and universities have pushed to improve research productivity, which naturally led to an increase in the number of doctoral students, who are the main contributors to research activities. With these educational and societal changes, the number of R&D personnel in Korean companies increased from 6.5 per 1,000 employees in 2000, to 13.3 per 1,000 in 2016. This puts Korea on par with Sweden according to OECD data. In addition, the Korean government has been expanding financial investment in doctoral students through large projects like BK21. The competitiveness of doctoral degree holders produced by Korean universities is increasing, as a recent comparative study demonstrates (Shin et al. 2014).

However, as we have pointed out, there are numerous challenges in Korean doctoral education that need attention: student exploitation, the hierarchical academic culture, problems associated with limited financial support and the mismatch between supply and demand when it comes to doctoral graduates. Little attention has been paid to the students' employment perspective and little effort made to resolve imbalances in the job market. There are substantial numbers of doctoral graduates experiencing difficulty in securing stable jobs, especially in fields with limited employment potential like the humanities and natural sciences. In this context, it is critical for the government and individual academic advisors, as well as doctoral students themselves, to be aware of the changing job market. In many research-focused universities, academic advisors are still too focused on training scholars suitable for careers in academia. But, in reality, the academic job market is very limited, and it is expected to shrink even further due to Korea's population decline. As a result, many PhD graduates who aspire to work in academia will be forced onto different career paths. Some will not be fully prepared, and some will end up unemployed. Responses to this changing environment must include more training in transferrable skills and a better understanding of career alternatives. Korea is also struggling with the loss of talented doctoral students to Western countries, especially the United States. This is related to the 'signal effect' of the overseas educational experience, and the fact that domestic doctoral degree holders are often underestimated in the job market (Shin et al. 2014). What is more, domestic doctoral degree holders in the natural sciences and engineering prefer to do their postdoctoral research abroad in an effort to make themselves more competitive.

These challenges require transformative changes in Korea's academic culture, as well as in educational structure, funding, research policy, faculty hiring practices, etc. The reality, however, is that universities do not pay much attention to doctoral education because their main internal policy interests are still largely focused on undergraduate education. Also, the Korean government is not actively involved in resolving the issues surrounding doctoral education. Undergraduate admission policy is still at the core of the national political agenda, and therefore gets more attention and interest from the general public. Until now, the Korean government has not implemented direct quality control mechanisms in doctoral education. Instead, it has increased quantitative support (funding) for doctoral education as a surface-level way to enhance the quality of research environment, leaving other issues to be resolved internally at the institutional and individual academic levels. This can be even more problematic because more than 40 per cent of doctorates are granted in non-research-intensive universities. Doctoral students in these universities may lack experience in effective academic socialization, which can harm their overall research competence and career readiness.

Finally, Korean doctoral programmes should pay more attention to strengthening the teaching competence of students, especially those seeking to pursue careers as university teachers. Lim's study (2019) finds that junior academics at Korean universities enter their faculty roles without the interest or teaching skills needed. This inevitably has a negative impact on the overall quality of college teaching.

Behind all of these challenges and issues, we should also point out the lack of scholarly interest paid to doctoral education in Korea. Many academics believe that doctoral education is based on individualized, 'apprenticeship' mechanisms that occur between academic supervisors and their doctoral students, with a high level of discretion. However, a few studies have revealed that the quality of such supervision is questionable (Lim 2018; Kim 2017). Individual supervisors have a great deal of autonomy in training their doctoral students. In order for the doctorate to be effectively institutionalized as part of an entire educational system, there should be more in-depth academic research focusing on doctoral students' experiences and on the system as a whole. Rigorous academic research might attract attention from policymakers and institutional leaders and trigger transformative changes in Korean doctoral education.

REFERENCES

Baik, Il Woo, and Kyung Ho Park. 2007. 'The Influence of 1st Stage BK21 Project on Universities Research Performance'. *The Journal of Educational Administration* 25 (4): 435–453. (In Korean).

Ban, Sang Jin. 2003. 'A Study on Graduate Education Quality Improvement in Knowledge Based Society'. Policy report. Sejong: Ministry of Education and Human Resources. (In Korean).

Behrens, Teresa R., and Denis O. Gray. 2001. 'Unintended Consequences of Cooperative Research: Impact of Industry Sponsorship on Climate for Academic Freedom and Other Graduate Student Outcome'. *Research Policy* 30 (22): 179–199.

Deuchar, Ross. 2008. 'Facilitator, Director or Critical Friend? Contradiction and Congruence in Doctoral Supervision Styles'. *Teaching in Higher Education* 13 (4): 489–500.

Hong, Sungmin, G. Cho, S. Kim, M. Kim, and K. Son. 2015. 'Research on Ways to Link Education and R&D Policy Together for Human Resources in Science and Technology Sector'. Policy report. Sejong: STEPI. (In Korean).

Jang, Dukho. 2013. 'An Analysis of the Differences in Research-Related Constructs: Serial Comparison of the Graduate Students in Global PhD Fellowship and Brain Korea 21 Projects'. *Engineering Education Research* 16 (3): 20–27. (In Korean).

Kim, Bongeok. 2010. 'A Study on STEM Doctoral Researchers Brain Drain Characteristics and Factors'. Policy report. Seoul: Korea Institute of S&T Evaluation and Planning.

Kim, Jongyeong. 2008. 'In Pursuit of Global Cultural Capital: Analysis of Qualitative Interviews Revealing Korean Students' Motivations for Studying in the United States'. *Korean Journal of Sociology* 42 (6): 68–105.

Kim, Kiseok. 2007. 'Great Leap Forward to Excellence in Research at Seoul National University'. *Asia Pacific Education Review* 8 (1): 1–11.

Kim, Seong Jin, Pil Nam Yi, and Deok Ho Jang. 2014. 'An Analysis on the Research Outcomes of World-Class University Project comparing with BK21 Project in Korea'. *The Journal of Economics and Finance of Education* 23 (3): 61–88.

Kim, Seung Jung. 2017. 'A Study on Development of Academic Identity of Doctoral Students in the Field of Humanities and Social Science'. *The Journal of Educational Administration* 35 (4): 317–345.

Lee, E. 2013. *Analysis of Structural Relation Between Faculty's Doctoral Origin and Academic Affiliation*. Master's Thesis, Seoul National University.

Lee, Jungmi, E. Y. Kim, Kim E. Y., S. H. Im, G. J. Lee, D. H. Jang, K. H. Han, and S. H. Shin. 2013. 'Study on Actual Condition and Development Plan of Graduate School Education'. Seoul: Korean Educational Development Institution. (In Korean).

Lim, Heejin. 2018. 'STEM Doctoral Students' Research Stress: Causes and Coping Strategies'. PhD diss. Seoul: Seoul National University.

———. 2019. 'A Study on Junior Faculty's Adaptation Process on Teaching Activities: A case of College of Education. *The Journal of Korean Teacher Education*, 36(1), 359–384.

Lim, Heejin, Haeyeon Park, Sohyun Kim, and Kyungho Kim. 2016. 'A Study on Master Students' Graduate School Experience in Korean Research University'. *Asia Journal of Education* 17 (3): 379–408. (In Korean).

Mendoza, Pilar. 2007. 'Academic Capitalism and Doctoral Student Socialization: A Case Study'. *The Journal of Higher Education* 78 (1): 71–96.

Ministry of Education. 2014. 'A Plan for 2015 Graduate School Enrollment Adjustment'. Press release. Sejong: Ministry of Education. (In Korean).

———. 2017. 'Management Plan for 2017 BK21 Plus Project'. Press release. Sejong: Ministry of Education. (In Korean).

Oh, Hyungchul. 2017. 'The Issues of Postdoctoral Fellowship Program in Korea'. *CNU Journal of Educational Studies* 38 (1): 317–336. (In Korean).

Seoul National University. 2006. 'Seoul National University: 60 Years History'. 60 Years History Compilation Committee. Seoul: Seoul National University. (In Korean).

Shin, Jung Cheol. 2009a. 'Building World-Class Research University: The Brain Korea 21 Project'. *Higher Education* 58 (5): 669–688.

———. 2009b. 'Classifying Higher Education Institutions in Korea: A Performance-based Approach'. *Higher Education* 57 (2): 247–266.

————. 2012. 'Higher Education Development in Korea: Western University Ideas, Confucian Tradition, and Economic Development'. *Higher Education* 64 (1): 59–72.

Shin, Jung Cheol, and Soo Jeong Lee. 2015. 'Evolution of Research Universities as a National Research System in Korea: Accomplishments and Challenges'. *Higher Education* 70 (2): 187–202.

Shin, Jung Cheol, Jisun Jung, Gerard A. Postiglione, and N. Azman. 2014. 'Research Productivity of Returnees from Study Abroad in Korea, Hong Kong, and Malaysia'. *Minerva* 52 (4): 467–487.

Shin, Jung Cheol, Seung Jung Kim, Eunyoung Kim, and Heejin Lim. 2018. 'Doctoral Students' Satisfaction in a Research-Focused Korean University: Socio-environmental and Motivational Factors'. *Asia Pacific Education Review* 19 (22): 1–10.

Song, Changyong, Kim, Yumi and Kim, Haejung. 2015. National Survey on Newly Graduated PhD Degree Holders. KRIVET report (in Korean).

Sung, Siyoon. 2017. 'Domestic Doctoral Degree Holders Outperform Foreign Degree Holders in Research Productivity'. *Joongang Daily News*. https://news.joins.com/article/22043795 (accessed 5 December 2018).

Um, M., K. Park, H. Kim, Y. Lee, and D. Park. 2013. 'A Study on How to Support the Graduate Schools in Science and Engineering'. Policy Report. Sejong: STEPI. (In Korean).

Umakoshi, T. 1995. *The Establishment and Development of Modern University in Korea*. Translated by Yongjin Han. Seoul: Kyoyook Book. (In Korean).

Wichmann-Hansen, Gitte, and Kim Jesper Herrmann. 2017. 'Does External Funding Push Doctoral Supervisors to Be More Directive? A Large-Scale Danish Study'. *Higher Education* 74 (2): 357–376.

Yoo, H. G., S. W. Min, H. J. Kim, H. J. Son, and E. H. Lee. 2017. 'Doctoral Degree Holder Survey 2017'. Seoul: Korea Research Institute for Vocational Education Training. (In Korean).

PART VI

Latin America

Chapter 16

Building Research Capacity and Training
Brazilian Dilemmas in Doctoral Education

Ana Maria Fonseca de Almeida, Maurício Ernica and Marcelo Knobel

Doctoral education has grown rapidly in Brazil since its organization as part of a national graduate system in the 1960s. Its rise was a direct result of investments made by the Brazilian state in technological capacity-building, and in training high-level specialists needed for the economic development plans developed in that period. When this structure was defined, in the middle of the 1960s, only 11 doctoral programmes were fully functioning in the country (Balbachevsky 2005). Thirty years later, in 1998, those programmes numbered 773, with an enrolment of 26,697 students. By 2017, there were 2,219 programmes with an enrolment of 112,004 students. In that same year, 21,591 doctorate degrees where awarded (Geocapes 2018). This constitutes a rather significant growth. Between 1998 and 2016, the number of students enrolled in doctoral programmes increased by a factor of four while, in that same period, the general population increased by a factor of 1.2 (Simões 2016). This chapter describes the current configuration of doctoral studies in Brazil. We identify the dynamics that have contributed to the expansion of doctoral programmes while also examining the challenges they have faced and some of the reforms currently under consideration.

BUILDING A NATIONAL GRADUATE SYSTEM

The first Brazilian doctoral degrees were awarded in the 19th century, mostly delivered by professional schools of medicine or engineering long before the establishment of any university in the country. The few doctoral degrees awarded in that period had no significant value in the job market (Schwartzman 1991). A doctoral education or title was not required to get a position in any of the few professional schools or public research units that existed at the time. A larger number of such positions became available in the 1930s, when the federal government began to organize the first universities in the country. This was also when, as part of fierce competition with the central government, São Paulo, the wealthiest state, created the first university with a strong research component, the University of São Paulo, in 1934.

Higher education was widely reformed in the 1960s. A national system of federal universities was created through the establishment of new institutions and, more frequently, by federalizing existing public and private professional schools. A US model of university organization was also implemented in close collaboration with experts funded by the United States Agency for International Development. As a result, the department became the most important unit in a university's organizational structure, and the adoption of the US academic credit system helped to reorganize undergraduate curricula. At the same time, a university professor career path was implemented. This provided tenure, progression based on merit and special retirement benefits for those who passed public exams.

As part of these extensive reforms, a national system of graduate education was also created. Graduate studies were, and still are, organized along two tracks: *lato* and *strictu sensu*. The first refers to all specializations offered after undergraduate studies, including MBA-like degrees; the second pertains to master's and doctoral studies. The US model was also the reference point for the *strictu sensu*. Its main goal was to train students for careers in higher education teaching and in research.

More recently, a professional track has been developed, encompassing the master's and doctoral levels. These kinds of programmes are intended for professionals who seek to advance their competence in specific techniques, processes and themes demanded in the job market. The US model is still in place today and is not being challenged. The programmes are closely regulated by the Brazilian federal government, and are very similar throughout the country, across all fields of knowledge and all types of higher education institutions.

In Brazil, a two-year academic master's programme normally precedes doctoral studies. The master's degree allows the student to apply for doctoral education, with admission contingent on passing competitive examinations. After acceptance, the doctoral programme lasts three to five years. In order to be awarded a master's or a doctoral degree, a student has to follow predefined coursework with a minimum number of credit hours in mandatory and/or optional courses. If enrolled in a master's programme, the student then prepares a dissertation, or a thesis if enrolled in a doctoral programme. Despite the common ground that unifies the system at large, there is wide variation among fields and programmes regarding the emphasis put on coursework and/or research. Some programmes require students to develop proficiency in a larger set of discipline fundamentals—theory and methods, for example. Programmes of this type emphasize coursework, allowing less time for research. Most programmes, however, require a strong commitment to research. Students are required to conduct original research leading to novel and significant contributions to their fields. Finally, some programmes will have a more flexible set of requirements, allowing the student to choose either to emphasize coursework (and thus general formation) or research (and thus specialization). These variations lead to differences in terms of professional profiles, ranging from less to more specialized ones, with the clear predominance of the latter.

In all cases, master's and doctoral studies are pursued under the supervision of a faculty member affiliated with the specific graduate programme in which the student is enrolled. The supervisor should be a specialist in the chosen field of study, and should closely follow the students' work, participating in coursework choices as well as in theoretical or methodological research decisions. After some intermediary evaluations, the student has to defend his or her dissertation or thesis in a public oral examination before a committee of specialists assembled by the supervisor specifically for this occasion. The students are expected to publish their results in highly regarded journals in Brazil and abroad. In fact, student publication rates and patterns are taken into consideration when doctoral programmes are evaluated by the federal government. The push to increase student and faculty publication rates is quite strong, leading some programmes to require students to publish at least some of their results before being awarded degrees. Still, it is worth mentioning that since there is no explicit demand of this sort from government regulatory agencies, this practice is far from the norm.

FINANCING DOCTORAL EDUCATION

With the rise of graduate education during the 1960s, a number of Brazilian federal agencies that were created a decade earlier in order to support the advancement of science and technology were put in charge of channelling resources to newly created or regulated doctoral programmes. Most of these resources were, and still are, directed to research centres and groups where doctoral students develop their research. Since the flow of resources depends exclusively on the quality of the work proposed by scientists, academic fields have begun to develop more autonomy.

One of these agencies, the National Campaign for the Advancement of High Ranking Civil Servants (known by its Brazilian acronym CAPES), was created in 1951 with the main goal of training enough civil servants to meet the development needs of the country. This agency, subordinated to the Ministry of Education, became responsible for university programme accreditation and evaluation in the 1980s. This formed the basis upon which a university's share of the resources would be defined in a very centralized way. Since then, a rather complex evaluation framework has been developed by university professors and scientists who were chosen on the basis of their scientific reputation. CAPES operates with a great degree of autonomy. The National Council for Scientific and Technological

Development (Brazilian acronym CNPq), part of the ministry of science and technology, was another federal agency created in that same period. Today, it plays an important role in research funding. It sponsors a broad programme of graduate scholarships, and distributes substantial grants for larger research projects that are often connected to doctoral work.

Until recently, similar agencies have not existed at the state level. The notable exception is the São Paulo Research Foundation (FAPESP), which was founded in 1960 in order to support research developed in the universities and research institutes located in São Paulo state. This support was available to all institutions, regardless of their status as public or private, federal or state controlled. Nowadays, FAPESP is one of the most important research funding bodies in the country in terms of budget, and its graduate scholarship programme accounts for an important part of the doctoral student funding in the state of São Paulo.

In the case of federal universities, the ministry of education became responsible for providing the resources needed for professorial and staff salaries, buildings and facilities construction, equipment acquisition and maintenance. State universities, for their part, depend totally on state governments for these expenses. This latter group of institutions is quite heterogeneous in terms of numbers of students, investment in research, undergraduate or graduate profile and budget. A few of them in richer states are research intensive, and run well-regarded doctoral programmes. This is the case in the states of Rio de Janeiro, Paraná and, most notably, São Paulo, where the three state universities—the University of São Paulo, the University of Campinas and the State University of São Paulo—receive a fixed proportion of the state sales tax (9.57% for the three universities). This financial arrangement, which is unique in the country, has protected these institutions from the fiscal whims of government officers.

It is worth noting that, since the 1960s, the flow of resources to doctoral programmes has been rather stable. Until now, it has not really been interrupted, even when the country faced drastic government changes or economic and political crises that have significantly diminished its investment capacity in different periods. This reveals a determination that is rare in other policy areas in Brazil.

THE EXPANSION OF BRAZILIAN DOCTORATE STUDIES

Besides the need to create research capacity, the impulse to expand doctoral studies also grew out of demands to expand higher education generally. The processes of rapid industrialization and urbanization during the first half of the 20th century resulted in a more complex class structure, giving rise to new segments of urban upper and middle classes. In the 1960s, these groups became quite vocal and demanded access to higher education, which was seen as a key resource in gaining access to new jobs that became available in that period. A large university reform ensued, establishing, among other changes, a university professor career path that required a doctoral degree for advancement and for reaching higher leadership positions. This new path offered the same benefits as those awarded in the higher civil service sector. As a result of these developments, a great number of job positions for doctorate holders were created in higher education, mostly in public universities. This proved decisive in securing the value of the doctoral degree, in terms of both employment benefits and prestige.

These reforms changed the higher education landscape in Brazil. On the one hand, they made possible the creation of research-intensive universities, in which doctorate holders could get jobs and career progression was based on qualifications. This model was adopted widely in the public sector, as well as by a few non-profit private institutions. A dynamic, for-profit higher education sector also surged in this period, fed by tax breaks. It offered more precarious academic jobs with lower salaries and fewer pension benefits. Access to research facilities or doctoral programmes was practically non-existent, since these for-profit institutions were predominantly dedicated to teaching. As a result, they rarely hired doctorate holders, despite the fact that the number of such degree holders among faculty members was, and still is, one of the factors taken into account by the ministry of education in its periodic evaluations of higher education institutions.

This differentiation led to a marked segmentation in the higher education system. The public and non-profit private research-intensive universities rapidly became regarded as top tier, while for-profit institutions, dedicated mostly to undergraduate education, were relegated to less prestigious positions. The former became responsible for educating, at the undergraduate level, top-ranked public service officials and professionals, as well as, at the graduate level, the scientists needed to expand research in the country. The latter, meanwhile, educated lower-level public servants and private managers, as well as K-12 teachers. For a long time, the public and non-profit private sectors remained reserved for the children of the upper classes, as well as some middle and lower-middle class students who would go, for the most part, to study teacher training or some other less prestigious, more work-oriented major. Meanwhile, the for-profit institutions received the larger part of the demand from middle and lower-middle class students.

Finally, it should be noted that although Brazilian universities were granted academic autonomy, the oversight of doctoral programmes—be they run by public or private bodies at the federal, state or community level—is centralized in the ministry of education, which was, and still is, in charge of their accreditation and evaluation.

DOCTORAL EDUCATION IN BRAZIL TODAY

As mentioned above, doctoral studies are usually offered by public universities, which, by Brazilian law, are forbidden to charge tuition fees, even to foreign students. Therefore, the cost of pursuing a doctoral education is relatively low. Many students can support themselves with temporary jobs while pursuing their studies. In addition to that, a steady supply of scholarships allows more than one third of the graduate student population—locals and foreigners alike—to fully dedicate themselves to their studies (Geocapes 2018). The monthly stipend is quite generous by Brazilian standards, and the students who receive one are not required to work in any capacity. Some of these scholarships allow, or even require, a period of time spent studying abroad, during which students are supposed to develop part of their research alongside renowned research groups.[1] This international component makes doctoral studies even more appealing for many students.

Since the 1950s, providing Brazilian doctoral students with funds for study abroad has been seen by policymakers as a strategic way to increase the country's exposure to the global research environment. For many years, Brazilian students were encouraged to pursue doctorate studies in prestigious institutions in Europe, North America and Asia. Returning researchers were instrumental in establishing Brazilian doctoral education. As national programmes expanded and consolidated, the government scaled back this investment, reorienting more resources towards funding short-term internships in well-regarded research institutions abroad.

In 2012, a larger and more ambitious international mobility programme, called Science Without Borders, was launched, with a focus on undergraduate students. The results have been quite impressive. By 2016, the number of scholarships awarded was 92,880. Around 78.9 per cent of those (73,353) went to undergraduate students to spend a year studying abroad, while around 10.4 per cent (9,685) went to doctoral students to undertake research internships abroad for periods of 3–12 months. Close to 3.6 per cent (3,353) were given to students to pursue a four-year doctoral education abroad (Ciência sem Fronteiras 2018). Since the programme is quite recent, it is rather difficult to evaluate its outcomes. For doctoral education in particular, it seems that the awards did not change the pattern that was already in place.

With regard to student mobility, it is worth noting that Brazilian doctoral programmes attract a small share of students from other countries. In 2016, 2 per cent of doctoral students in Brazil were foreigners. This is not a large proportion when compared to other Latin American countries, such as Chile (8%) or Mexico (3%) but is nonetheless significant in absolute terms (OECD 2018).

This flow of students is probably explained by a variety of factors. First, Brazilian doctoral education is nowadays part of research system that is more institutionalized and more dynamic than in other countries

---

[1] See http://fapesp.br/en/bepe

in the region. Second, the financial cost of pursuing doctoral education in Brazil is lower, with both the free tuition and the ample number of scholarships mentioned above. Economic and political events also seem to have an impact on the way Latin American student flows have been shaped in recent times, implying that domestic circumstances also play a role in student mobility in the region.

CONSOLIDATION AND EXPANSION OF BRAZILIAN DOCTORAL PROGRAMMES (1998–2016)

In this section, we will examine more closely the fast expansion of doctoral studies in Brazil, which reached a rate of 7.6 doctorate degrees awarded per 1,000 inhabitants in 2013. Even though this is a considerable number in the Latin American context (e.g., the corresponding rates are 4.2 for Mexico and 3.4 for Chile), it is lower than the 20.6 rate of the United States or the 40.1 rate of the United Kingdom in that same year (Revista Fapesp. 2016).

In the period that followed higher education reforms and the regulation of graduate education, Brazilian universities and research centres were stimulated to create doctoral programmes in all fields, which resulted in accentuated growth. Today, most doctoral programmes are offered by universities, with only a handful offered by autonomous research centres. As can be seen in Figure 16.1, most doctoral programmes are offered by public institutions, either federal or state-run. Since the 2000s, the growth in the number of programmes has been progressively concentrated at federal institutions.

The growing number of federal programmes corresponds to an increase in the number of degrees awarded by federal institutions (universities and research institutes), as shown in Figure 16.2.

A steady stream of students has been attracted to these new programmes, resulting in a significant increase in the number of doctorate holders in the country, as shown in Figure 16.3.

Doctoral education in Brazil is not evenly distributed, and has not grown at the same pace among various fields of study. Degrees awarded in health and STEM (science, technology, engineering

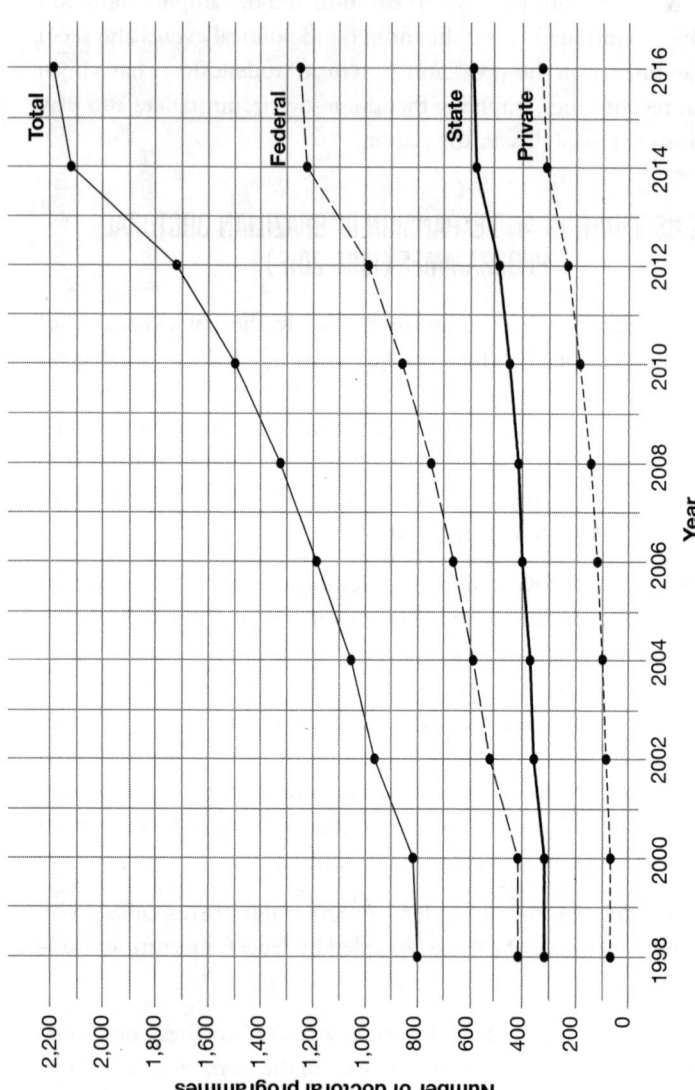

Figure 16.1 *Number of Doctoral Programmes in Brazil by Type of Higher Education Institution from 1998 to 2016*
Source: By authors, data from Geocapes 2018.

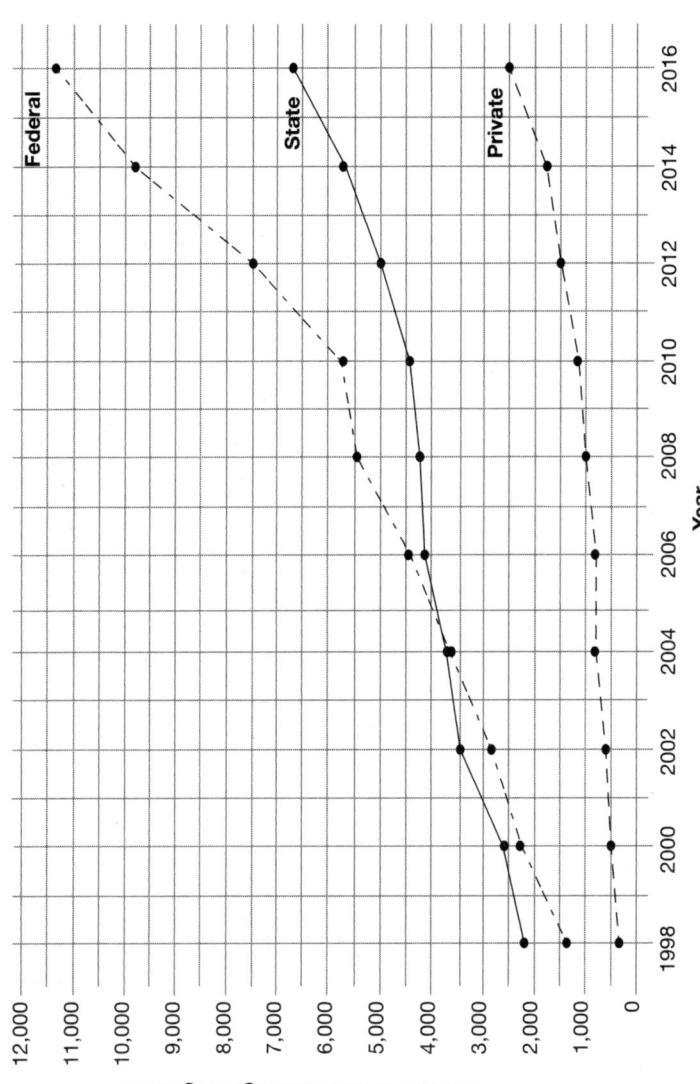

Figure 16.2 *Number of Doctoral Degrees Awarded in Brazil by Type of Higher Education Institution from 1998 to 2016*

Source: Geocapes 2018, by authors.

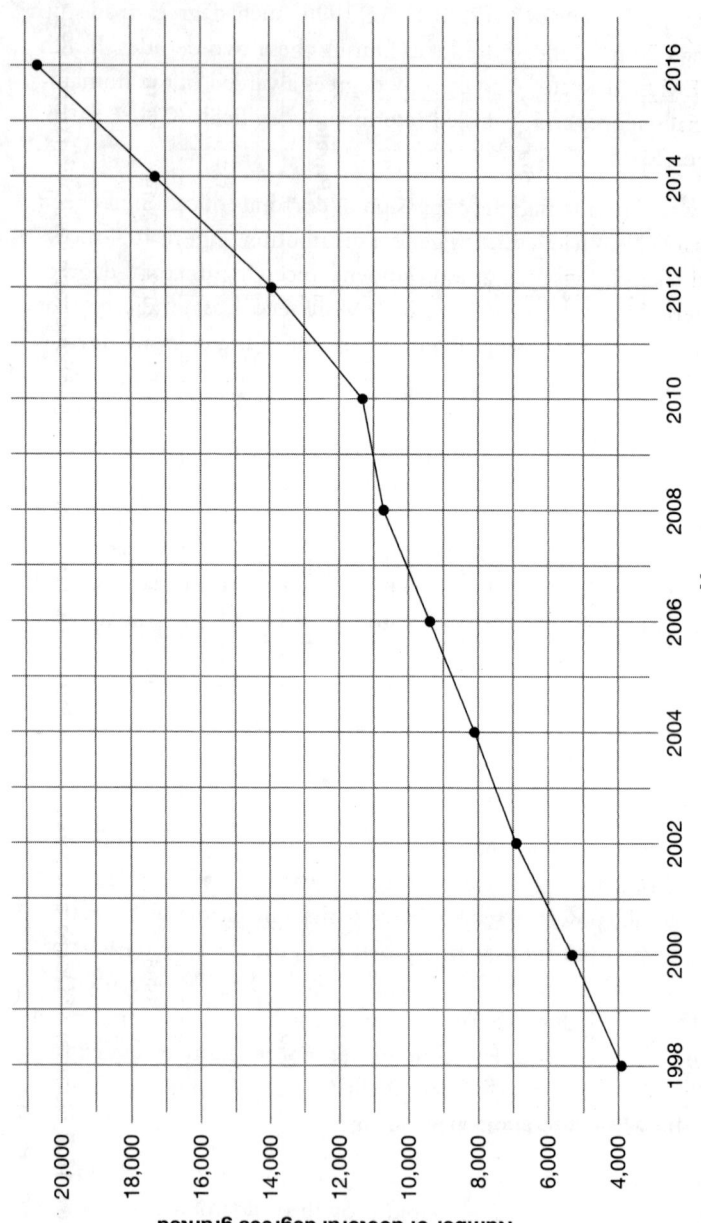

Figure 16.3 *Total Number of Doctoral Degrees Awarded in Brazil per Year from 1998 to 2016*

Source: Geocapes 2018, by authors.

and mathematics) areas accounted for a little less than 60 per cent of all degrees awarded in 2017. Back in 1996, such degrees made up more than 70 per cent of the total. During these two decades, health and STEM fields were overtaken by degrees awarded in the humanities, social sciences and so-called interdisciplinary fields (CGEE 2016; Geocapes 2018).

It is worth noting that the expansion of doctoral education has been accompanied by changes in the gender distribution. Figure 16.4 shows the lead taken by women among students receiving doctoral degrees in the period between 1996 and 2008. More recent data indicates that women receive a little more than 50 per cent of the doctoral degrees awarded annually (Almeida and Zanlorenssi 2018). These advances have been seen as the result of other changes in Brazilian society. In the middle of the 1980s, women surpassed men in terms of number of years spent in school. Their proportion in the working population has more than doubled since the 1960s, and the birth rate has declined sharply since then. Careers in public service have been quite attractive to women, and since doctoral degrees tend to lead to teaching and research positions in the public sector, they have been attractive to women as well. Changes in the offer of doctoral education have also significantly helped bridge the gender gap. As mentioned above, the proportion of degrees awarded in fields traditionally more sought after by women in Brazil, such as the humanities and social sciences, grew substantially during this period.

Strong regional concentration of doctoral programmes is another feature of Brazilian graduate education, favouring the wealthier and more politically powerful states where the first universities were created. Although new institutions were established in the 1960s, and each state gained its own federal university at that point, this was not sufficient to modify the original imbalance. Neither the gradual development of research centres in more peripheral regions, nor the more recent expansion of public universities beyond traditional centres, has significantly altered this general picture.

The overall expansion of higher education enrolment has also played a role in the relatively rapid growth of doctoral education in Brazil. Increased undergraduate enrolments led to a sharp increase

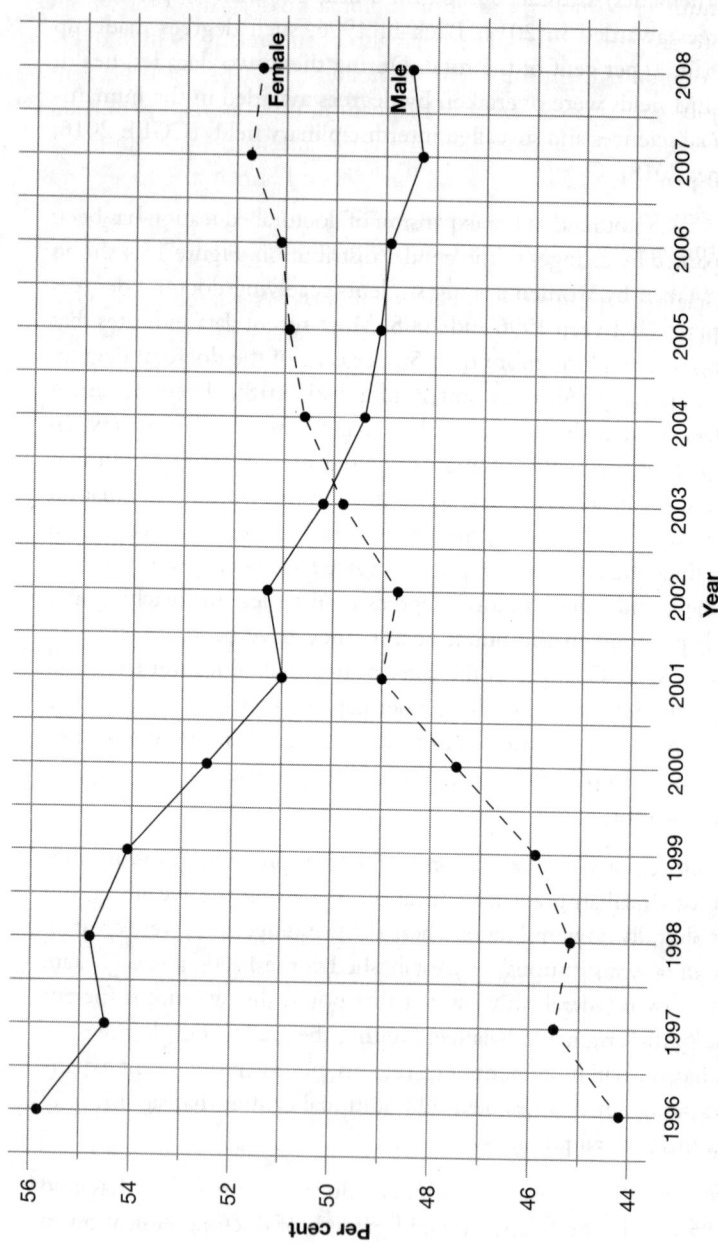

Figure 16.4 *Relative Percentage of Doctoral Degrees Awarded in Brazil, by Gender, from 1996 to 2008*

Source: Viotti et al. (2010).

in the number of higher education diploma holders, many of whom sought to progress further. There has also been a relatively high overall rate of employment for doctorate holders; in 2014, 79.1 per cent found jobs within five years after graduation, up from 63.9 per cent a decade earlier. This employment rate varies among fields, from more than 80 per cent in STEM, social sciences and humanities to around 70 per cent in the biological sciences. For health and agricultural sciences, the employment rate is about 75 per cent (CGEE 2016).

In Brazil, the job market for doctorate holders is largely restricted to higher education, because that is where most research-oriented positions are. The main result of the public investment in doctoral education has therefore been in research and education capacity building. The increase in the number of higher education faculty holding a doctorate is a good indicator: in 2007, of 317,041 faculty, 37.4 per cent held a doctorate degree. By 2017, that number had risen to 380,673 or 41.33 per cent (Brasil-INEP 2017). Only a small proportion of doctorate holders have research careers at non-educational institutions. These accounted for only 4.8 per cent of all graduate degree holders employed in 2009, decreasing to 3.4 per cent in 2014 (CGEE 2016). Doctorate degree holders also work in high public service positions. Between 2009 and 2014, they accounted for 12 per cent of the total number of graduate degree holders employed during this period (CGEE 2016). Beyond that, those with doctorates work in numerous functions not related to research.

The job market for doctorate holders is shaped by four interconnected dynamics. First, the financial returns for doctorate holders are rather impressive, considering that most of them work in higher education. In 2014, doctoral graduates employed in either academic or non-academic jobs 'earned ... around 5.7 times more than the average Brazilian worker' (CGEE 2016). Estimates based on the 2010 census indicate that a doctorate holder earns 35 per cent more than a master's degree holder. Master's and doctorate holders together receive 83.6 per cent more than undergraduate degree holders. Undergraduate degrees holders, in turn, earn 170 per cent more than those who only finish high school (CGEE 2016). Furthermore, even though the expansion of higher education in the last decades has been mostly due to the growth of the for-profit private sector, which offers few positions for doctorate holders, the expansion of the public sector has also been quite significant since the 1970s. This has led to the creation of an important number of research-intensive universities that are dependent on doctorate holders to staff their faculties.

In addition, faculty positions in public universities come with good benefits. After passing a competitive public hiring process, doctorate holders become civil servants. As such, they are entitled to tenure after three years on the job, and earn good salaries by Brazilian standards. Until about a decade ago, faculty who were hired by public institutions were also entitled to retirement with full salaries and benefits.

Finally, the Brazilian job market has become virtually closed to foreign doctorate holders. Although the work of foreign scholars was seen as crucial in building research capacity in the country in the 19th and early 20th centuries (Figueirôa 1998; Massi 1989; Schwartzman 1991), this trend reversed after the 1930s. That is when nationalization laws first prevented foreigners from holding teaching positions in Brazil, and forbade teaching in languages other than Portuguese (Seyferth 1997). Until the end of the 1980s, Brazilian public universities needed a special waiver in order to hire foreign citizens. Even after this requirement was abandoned, the hiring process remained biased against foreigners. The majority of undergraduate classes are taught in Portuguese, and, in most cases, the public selection of professors is conducted in Portuguese— despite the fact that universities and research centres are allowed to use other languages for teaching and hiring purposes. As a result, despite the relatively high numbers of exchanges and collaborations between Brazilian scientists and their counterparts in Latin America, Europe and North America, language remains a real obstacle to getting a job in a Brazilian public university. This has left foreigners who graduated in Brazil and mastered the Portuguese language with some reservations about applying for a position (Almeida, Ernica, Digiampietri and Knobel, 2017). Moreover, the Brazilian state is quite bureaucratic. Foreigners are required to provide a lot of documentation if they want to obtain a regular position in the country. This troublesome process has been singled out as a major drawback for foreign scholars. These job market dynamics could have led to a shortage in the supply of doctorate holders for Brazilian universities. But this scenario has not happened, thanks to a regular supply of Brazilian-trained doctorate holders, made possible by the steady interest of Brazilian students in doctoral education and its relatively low cost.

It is worth stressing that the expansion of doctoral programmes in Brazil has been based on continuous public investment, and has been geared towards training professionals for the expanding public higher education system. To a lesser extent, these programmes also prepare students for careers in public administration, and, to an even lesser extent, in research institutions. Research and development (R&D) is still quite limited, except for a few companies with local R&D teams.

Policymakers in charge of regulating doctoral programmes in the 1960s saw them as a fundamental tool for economic development. At that time, investment in science and technology was intended to reduce Brazil's dependence on technology imported from industrialized countries. The results of these investments are currently under discussion. With regard to technological development, there is no doubt that some sectors advanced considerably due to highly skilled labour at the doctoral level. This is the case in agriculture, health, energy (petrol and ethanol) and, more recently, in software. However, the country still predominantly imports technology in other sectors with rather weak R&D intensity, a fact that some analysts attribute to the lack of a critical mass of human capital. Others put the blame on the way the productive sector itself is organized. With regard to Brazilian scientific development, even though output has been growing, it has had a relatively low impact on the global scientific space.

In just 50 years, Brazil has been able to create a solid graduate system that has supported the expansion of higher education. Since doctoral education put such an emphasis on research, it has become a very important source of technological and scientific production, with significant impacts on scientific innovation and discovery. With all this in mind, it is important to ponder why this system is still engaged in capacity building and tends towards academic isolation and inbreeding. It is also worth noting here that the expansion of higher education in the 2000s was not sufficient to offset some imbalances in, for example, the regional distribution of programmes or the overconcentration of programmes in some fields. In order to adequately address these issues, the system requires resources that have become scarce in the current context of deep economic crisis and political instability.

RECENT DEVELOPMENTS, DEBATES AND POLICY CHANGES

Brazilian doctoral studies have been strongly affected by two more or less recent developments: the central government's increasing control over graduate programmes beginning in the 1990s and the economic crisis that started in 2014. The Ministry of Education manages the assessment of all graduate education through the agency mentioned above, CAPES. In 1998, this system went through a major overhaul, resulting in the adoption of criteria that put a lot of emphasis on faculty publishing output (Fonseca 2001). The assessment committees constructed, and still periodically revise, a ranking of national and international journals in their respective fields. In some subject areas, the committees also produce similar rankings for books published inside and outside the country. For assessment purposes, emphasis has been placed on the international exposure of Brazilian science, and thus articles published in journals indexed in the Web of Science and Scopus databases are more highly valued. As part of the increasing quantification, other activities in which faculty members are involved (teaching load, number of completed supervisions, etc.) were counted and evaluated as well. This gave rise to the time-consuming task of recording all activities of faculty involved in doctoral programmes, as well as tracking the flow of doctoral students.

The quantitative dimension of publishing and the logic of ranking have spread rapidly throughout the system. All graduate programmes now receive a grade from 1 to 7, which guides the accreditation process and also the distribution of resources. Programmes graded below 3 in two evaluation cycles can be closed down, while programmes rated 6 or 7 will receive a larger share of the resources. This system has also been widely employed by other research support agencies in their decisions about grant allocations and fellowships for researchers.

The rise of the new evaluation system has changed academic practices in Brazil in a number of ways and with mixed results. The focus on quantitative research outputs has led to a sharp increase in the number of articles published in national and international journals. But some analysts argue that this might be impairing research endeavours in the country. They might be right. Some studies have shown that the increase in the number of published articles authored by researchers based in Brazil was not followed by a corresponding increase in the number of citations of those articles (Pena 2010).

As discussed above, Brazilian doctoral education has had a significant impact on the country. It has trained the faculty needed for the expansion of research-intensive universities, and has helped to consolidate a national scientific community, giving support for important technological and scientific advancements that have greatly benefited the economy and the population. From this point of view, it has been mostly successful. However, policymakers believe that the impact of Brazilian science should be stronger, and some believe that in order to achieve this, doctoral education should be reformed. So far, this conversation has focused mainly on ways to improve the evaluation system (Almeida and Guimarães 2013; Sobral 2016; Sobral and Santos 2018).

Steady government support has been instrumental in securing reliable and continuous funding for university research endeavours and, as a consequence, in supporting research training at the doctoral level. However, this arrangement is now at risk, mostly because the increasing need for funding for the expansion of undergraduate education. Also, the economic crisis that began in 2014 has significantly restricted state investment and funding in general. For these reasons, funding conflicts within the higher education system have intensified, leading to a decrease in the number of job offers in the academy and falling salaries. As the crisis also touches other sectors of the economy, a decline in job offers in the corporate world is expected as well, curbing the fragile growth in the number of doctorate holders employed in this sector.

CURRENT CHALLENGES

Three recent developments have triggered significant effects on Brazilian doctoral studies: the economic crisis faced by Brazil since 2014; the recent approval of a constitutional amendment establishing a strict maximum value for public expenses, which may impose a long period of limited resources for public universities and, finally, the likely approval of broad pension reforms aimed at ending coveted benefits enjoyed by faculty at public universities.

Taken together, the economic crisis and the public expenditure restriction have already imposed limits on the expansion of the higher education system and doctoral studies. To fully understand how, one has to go back to the 1990s and early 2000s, when a previous economic crisis and hyperinflation restricted Brazilian government expenditure and, consequently, faculty hires and changes. After this period of hardship ended in the second half of the 2000s, public universities intensively hired new professors. But the long period without new hires created a generational gap, with harsh consequences for those entering academic careers in the first half of the 2000s and for the functioning of doctoral programmes.

This problem had recently started to recede, but now, with the current economic crisis that began in 2014, a new generation gap is imminent. New hires are becoming rarer, salaries are not being adjusted, career progression is getting more difficult, facilities are not being built or even maintained and resources for research are limited. Also, when universities do hire, many experienced professors with consolidated careers and reputations, not to mention accumulated scientific savoir faire, have already retired or are about to do so. Further, the possibility of a pension reform is inciting these older professors to retire earlier, in order to keep the benefits to which they are entitled under the current law. This wave of early retirements is leading to a lack of leadership and mentorship in doctoral programmes. The significant decrease in the number of professors in departments also affects the working conditions of younger faculty, who are expected to engage in administrative duties more intensely than would be the case under normal circumstances. Thus, one of the main challenges faced by doctoral programmes is guaranteeing that their dynamism, made possible by the renovation of existing programmes and the creation of new ones, does not cool down.

Depending on their peculiarities, doctoral programmes will be affected differently. It is possible to identify three distinct cases. The first regards consolidated programmes located in established, well-regarded universities. Usually, these are the programmes with the best scientific reputation. Above all, they will face challenges in guaranteeing that the professional development of newly hired faculty does not stall due to the administrative demands placed upon them. While retired faculty are authorized by law to continue to work as researchers and even to receive grants from funding agencies, they are forbidden to hold administrative positions. As public university governance in Brazil is strongly based on peer management, the removal of senior professors from these functions can impose a significant overload on younger faculty, potentially turning them away from research activities. Also, as noted above, the distribution of resources to doctoral programmes is currently linked to evaluations that emphasize published output. If younger professors are overloaded by administrative tasks, this will have a negative impact on their academic production and, consequently, on the evaluation of their programmes. This can in turn lead to problems securing funding.

The second case refers to new doctoral programmes in established, well-regarded universities. As for the more established programmes, the new ones will also suffer from the administrative overload of younger faculty. These newer programmes receive less funding because they are new: any decline in public expenditure tends to penalize them more, even though, paradoxically, their success is dependent on more intensive investments. Simply put, the strong reliance on a rough quantification of published output to guide the distribution of resources, without taking into account its impact in terms of innovation, is an impediment to the development of newer doctoral programmes, because the effects of the economic crisis and pension reforms are amplified.

The last case concerns programmes created in new universities, or at new campuses of older universities, during the expansion that happened between 2000 and 2010. These programmes were supported by a wave of new hires, and were for the most part created in reputable research centres. But stagnant salaries, diminished prospects for career progression and a lack of investment in facilities may hinder the consolidation of research in these institutions. Furthermore, in the case of programmes located outside of established research centres, budget restrictions will impose limits on mobility and exchange, with higher costs to programme development and quality.

These recent developments will also have an impact on the internationalization of doctoral programmes. As mentioned above, the growing and uninterrupted investment that took place in the last 20 years increased the number of foreign students in Brazilian doctoral programmes and sustained a significant international circulation of Brazilian students and researchers. This investment is already showing some results in the growth of collaborative research as well as in the number of articles published in English language journals and the number of citations these articles have received. Obviously, the recent economic downturn threatens this internationalization, but it is unclear how different fields will be affected. In STEM areas, exchanges with foreign research groups happen more frequently than in the social sciences and humanities, which are more domestically oriented. It is likely that new restrictions will hit STEM fields harder.

Besides the economic crisis and the institutional changes affecting the working conditions of doctorate holders employed in higher education and research centres, analysts have raised two other sets of issues regarding Brazilian doctoral programmes. Some question whether their growth can be sustained, arguing that programmes will not be able to induce and support the production of new knowledge if scholars are working in less than ideal research environments. Others question the lack of synergy between academia and industry. In fact, these two sets of issues are closely related. The concentration of work positions for doctorate holders in universities and research institutions is considered by some analysts to be excessive, and is seen as an indicator, and sometimes even as the cause, of a certain malfunction in Brazilian doctoral education. Their argument goes like this: in the current and future research landscape, where just a few universities will likely have the structure needed to support innovative research, it seems misguided to invest in the intensive training of doctorate holders who will be absorbed by ill-equipped universities. Also, too much investment in new universities or new campuses is considered by some to actually be a hindrance to the production of new knowledge, since newer institutions will take longer to establish a research infrastructure, or will not be able to do so at all in the long run.

Faced by what they see as a contradiction—the expansion of universities lacking basic research infrastructure and, simultaneously, the expansion of doctoral programmes in those same universities—some argue that the focus should instead be on training scientists motivated by the drive of discovery. Otherwise, doctoral programmes might just be training researchers to reproduce knowledge. Some structural characteristics of the Brazilian academic landscape are seen as contributing to this pattern. The first is the weight of programme evaluations that give little consideration to the scientific nature of the programmes, or the original contributions they offer to a specific knowledge area. As these evaluations have an impact on a programme's certification, and thus on the distribution of resources, they can strongly influence the way research is organized. Also to be considered is the relative isolation of Brazilian researchers, which serves to reinforce domestic research agendas at the expense of contributing to the international scientific debate. Finally, there is an urgent need to prepare faculty for the ever-expanding higher education system, which has led to a decrease in the average time doctorate holders take to get a job after graduating. In addition to a shortened period of training, it is common for these newly minted PhDs to begin their academic careers right after obtaining their degrees. These positions are usually offered by newly created universities, in which the research structure itself has yet to be established and new hires cannot find adequate mentorship.

The lack of synergy between universities and the corporate world is seen as one of the most important challenges facing doctoral education in Brazil. Analysts note the following obstacles in bridging this gap: the progressive deindustrialization of the country; the widespread tendency in some sectors to import technology instead of establishing local R&D initiatives and, finally, the recent economic crisis, which has put the structure of Brazilian research and doctoral programmes at risk. In this context, it is worth remembering that the research-intensive sector of the higher education system, which encompasses doctoral programmes, has relied heavily on public resources. The sector's stability, therefore, depends upon the governing elite's decision to continue to prioritize it. Since the 1950s, these elites have shared a tacit assumption that the social benefits of this arrangement largely outweigh the costs, and so the influx of resources has never been under real threat. However, the recent economic and political instability has led to the election of a new governing group whose views about such matters are not yet clear. If a radical, short-term, pro-market view of investment in research and higher education gains traction, the traditional arrangement could be under threat. It is not difficult to envision the deleterious ways in which cuts in investment in this area could lead to the fast dismantlement of Brazil's research and training capacity, which has been built at great cost over the course of the last 60 years.

REFERENCES

Almeida, Ana M. F., Mauricio Ernica, Luciano Digiampietri, and Marcelo Knobel. 2017. 'International Faculty in a Brazilian University'. In *International Faculty in Higher Education: Comparative Perspectives on Recruitment, Integration, and Impact*, edited by Maria Yudkevich, Philip G. Altbach, and Laura Rumbley. New York, NY: Routledge.

Almeida, Elenara C. A., and Jorge A. Guimarães. 2013. *A Pós-Graduação e a Evolução da Política Científica Brasileira*. [Graduate Studies and the Evolution of Science Policy in Brazil]. São Paulo: Senac.

Almeida, Rodolfo, and Gabriel Zanlorenssi. 2018. 'What Is the Gender and Age of Masters and Doctors in Brazil'. Nexo. https://www.nexojornal.com. br/grafico/2018/05/23/Qual-o-g%C3%AAnero-e-a-idade-de-mestres-e-doutores-no-Brasil (accessed 20 November 2018).

Balbachevsky, Elisabeth. 2005. 'A pós-graduação no Brasil: novos desafios para uma política bem sucedida' [Graduate Studies in Brazil and the Challenges of a Successful Policy]. In *Os desafios da educação no Brasil* [Education Challenges in Brazil], edited by Colin Brock and Simon Schwartzman, 285–314. Rio de Janeiro: Nova Fronteira.

Brasil–INEP–Instituto de Estudos Pedagógicos. 2017. 'Censo da Educação Superior: Notas Estatísticas 2017' [Higher Education Census 2017]. http://download. inep.gov.br/educacao_superior/censo_superior/documentos/2018/censo_ da_educacao_ superior_2017-notas_estatisticas2.pdf (accessed February 2019).

CGEE (Centro de Gestão e Estudos Estratégicos). 2016. *Mestres e doutores 2015— Estudos da demografia da base técnico-científica brasileira* [Masters and PhDs. 2015 – Studies of the Techno-Scientific Workforce in Brazil]. Brasília: CGEE.

Ciência sem Fronteiras. 2018. http://cienciasemfronteiras.gov.br/web/csf/o-programa

Figueirôa, Silvia F. 1998. 'Mundialização da ciência e respostas locais: sobre a institucionalização das ciências naturais no Brasil (de fins do século XVIII à transição ao século XX)' [Mondialisation of Science and Local Responses: On the Institutionalization of Natural Sciences in Brazil—from the end of the 18th century to the 20th century]. *Asclepio* 50 2: 107–123.

Fonseca, Claudia. 2001. 'Avaliação dos programas de pós-graduação do ponto de vista de um nativo' [Evaluation of Graduate Programs from the Viewpoint of a Native}. *Horizontes Antropológicos* 7 16: 261–275.

Geocapes Dados Estatísticos. 2018. https://geocapes.capes.gov.br/geocapes/ (accessed 15 August 2018).

OECD. 2018. *Education at a Glance 2018: OECD Indicators*. Paris: OECD Publishing.

Massi, Fernanda Peixoto. (1989). 'Franceses e Norte-Americanos nas Ciências Sociais Brasileiras (1930–1960)' [French and North Americans in Social Sciences in Brazil], in S. Miceli (org.), História das Ciências Sociais no Brasil [History of the Social Sciences in Brazil] (vol. 1). São Paulo, IDESP/Vértice/ Finep, pp. 410–460.

Pena, Sergio D. J. 2010. 'O estado da ciência no Brasil. Como dar um salto de qualidade?' [The State of Science in Brazil. How is it Possible to Achieve a Leap in Quality?] *Parcerias Estratégicas* 15 31: 115–128.

Revista Fapesp. 2016. 'Doutorados per capita no mundo' [Doctorates Per Capita in the World] No. 246. http://revista- pesquisa.fapesp.br/2016/08/19/ doutorados-per-capita-no-mundo/ (accessed 15 April 2018).

Schwartzman, Simon. 1991. *A Space for Science*. University Park, PA: Pennsylvania State University Press.

Seyferth, Giralda. 1997. 'A assimilação dos imigrantes como questão nacional' [The Assimilation of Immigrants as a National Question]. *Mana* 3 1: 95–131.

Simões, Celso Cardoso Silva (2016), Breve histórico do processo demográfico [Brief History of the Demographic Process], in Figueiredo, Adma Hamam de (editor), Brasil: uma visão geográfica e ambiental no início do século XXI [Brazil: a Geographical and Environmental Vision in the Beginning of the XXIst Century], Instituto Brasileiro de Geografia e Estatística-IBGE, pp. 39–73. Available in https://biblioteca.ibge.gov.br/visualizacao/livros/ liv97884_cap2.pdf (Accessed in 02/17/2020).

Sobral, Fernanda. 2016. 'A dimensão econômica e social da política brasileira de ciência, tecnologia e inovação' [The Economic and Social Dimensions of the Policy on Science, Technology, and Innovation in Brazil]. In *Sociedade, Conhecimentos e Colonialidades*, edited by Maíra Baumgarten. Porto Alegre: Editora da UFRGS.

Sobral, Fernanda, and Gilberto L. Santos. 2018. 'Avaliação de Políticas Públicas de Ciência, Tecnologia e Inovação: abordagens a partir de casos concretos' [The Evaluation of Public Policies on Science, Technology and Innovation: Approaches Based on Concrete Cases]. *Tecnologias, Sociedade e Conhecimento* 5 1: 8–26.

Viotti, Eduardo Baumgratz, Oliveira Jr., C., Viotti, R., Pinho, R., Daher, S., Vermulm, R. (2010). 'Doutorados e doutores titulados no Brasil: 1996–2008' [Doctoral Programmes and Doctors in Brazil: 1996–2008]. In Centro de Gestão e Estudos Estratégicos-CGEE, 2010, Doutores 2010: estudos da demografia da base técnico-científica brasileira [Doctors 2010: Studies on the Techno-Scientific Workforce in Brazil] - Brasília, DF: Centro de Gestão e Estudos Estratégicos.

Chapter 17

Reassessing the Progress of Doctoral Education in Chile

Ana Luisa Muñoz-García and
Andrés Bernasconi

There is a general consensus that doctoral education is relevant for training new generations of scientists and scholars and for scientific development and innovation, which are connected to the idea of the economic competitiveness of a nation (Devos and Somerville 2012). The knowledge society—the advancement of research and technology, participating in the global economy and interconnection among nations—requires people with advanced leadership capacities (David and Foray 2002; Popescu, Sabie, and Comanescu 2016). Doctoral graduates are expected to generate new knowledge from positions in academia, government and the business and third sectors, which in turn is supposed to contribute to the next generation of innovations (Meissner, Gokhberg, and Shmato 2016). Globally, governments are investing in the expansion of doctoral education (Nerad 2004), as policymakers understand the increasing importance of knowledge in sustaining economic growth and prosperity (Pedersen 2014).

Over the past decade, the Chilean government has followed this trend, paying substantial attention to the higher education system and the construction of an advanced human capital capacity for the country.

Several reports issued during the past decade on the strengths and weaknesses of higher education in Chile have identified at least five major challenges (Consejo Asesor Presidencial 2008; Muñoz and Sobrero 2006; OECD 2007; Rojas and Bernasconi 2009; Sanchez 2011). First, the system needs to continue to expand in order to accommodate up to 80 per cent of the 18–25 age cohort. Second, higher education as a whole has to promote quality through a transparent and rigorous system of accreditation. Third, the system has to increase and diversify public funding for institutions. Fourth, higher education needs to increase scientific and technological research. Finally, internationalization has to become a relevant policy focus in higher education.

Following these studies—and in line with the global discourse on human capital accumulation as an indicator of capacities for innovation and productivity—advanced human capital has been recognized by the Chilean government as an important driver of economic and social development (CONICYT 2013a, 2008, 2012). There is now a widely held vision among policymakers that highly skilled professionals are crucial for scientific and economic advancement in Chile (Consejo Asesor Presidencial 2008). Thus, numerous initiatives have been developed to increase the numbers of doctorate holders and to promote scholarships for Chileans pursuing PhDs at home or abroad.

Furthermore, since 2015, the higher education system has been moving forward with a reform process that was pushed by the government of President Michelle Bachelet (2014–2018) and her coalition in Congress. That process is articulated around five core objectives: (a) consolidate the higher education system, (b) guarantee quality of education and uphold public trust, (c) advance equity and inclusion, (d) strengthen public higher education and (e) improve technical and vocational education (MINEDUC 2015). The most salient aspect of this reform is free tuition for students from families in the six lower deciles of income (Delisle and Bernasconi 2018). While the reform does not involve the postgraduate level directly, it does impact doctoral degree programmes through changes in funding for institutions, and through the promulgation of policies related to knowledge, diversity and the equity of the system.

Two main features characterize the current state of doctoral education in Chile. There has been a rapid increase in enrolments in doctoral programmes and in the number of scholars with doctoral degrees. Yet rising enrolments have not been matched by increases in research funding or in number of academic jobs available. As a result, doctoral holders find themselves trapped by the lack of demand for their skills in the system. This chapter presents the main trends in doctoral education in Chile in the larger context of Chilean higher education. Next, we describe the scope and features of doctoral education in numbers. We then turn to recent policies aimed at promoting doctoral education, both in Chile and for Chileans studying abroad. In the final section, we elaborate on the challenges and opportunities ahead for strengthening advanced human capital formation.

THE CONTEXT AND EVOLUTION OF DOCTORAL EDUCATION IN CHILE

In 2017, Chilean higher education was composed of 152 public and private institutions (SIES 2017b). The Council of University Rectors (CRUCH) is comprised of 27 universities, including 18 public ones and 9 private, not-for-profit institutions that are referred to as the G9 group. The universities that are part of CRUCH are Chile's oldest, created before the expansion of the educational system began in 1980. All of Chile's 43 professional institutes (*Institutos Profesionales*, IP) and 48 technical training centres (*Centros de Formación Técnica*, CFT) are private (see Figure 17.1). As part of its higher education reform, the government is in the process of establishing 15 state-owned CFTs by 2022 (OECD 2017). Unlike private universities, private IPs and CFTs are allowed to operate for profit.

About 40 per cent of the funding for higher education comes from the government. The rest comes from private sources, mostly in the form of tuition payments by students and their families. Both private and public institutions charge tuition, although in the past, students coming from the lower deciles of family income have been eligible for scholarships. Since 2016, however, lower-income students have qualified for free tuition at both state and private institutions. In 2018,

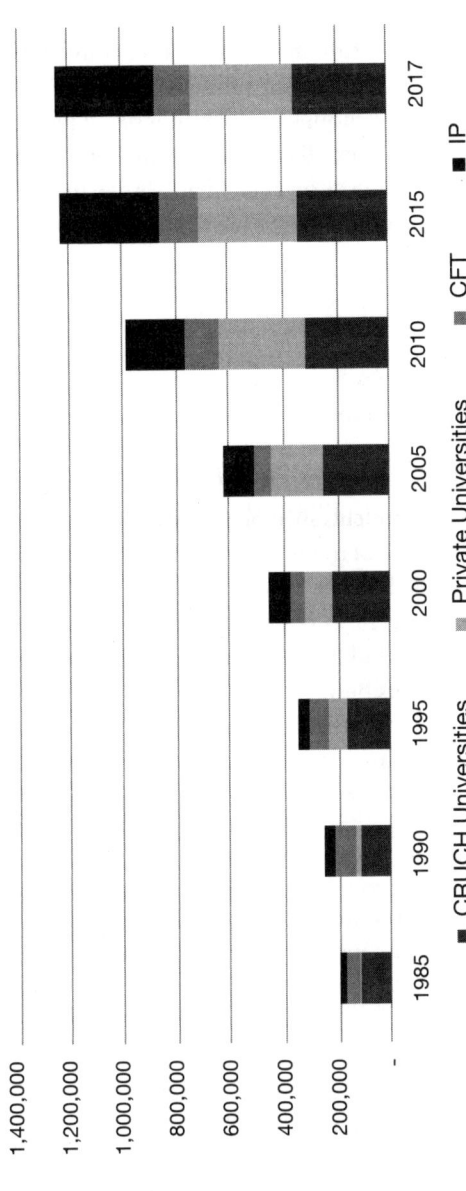

Figure 17.1 *Enrolments in Higher Education in Chile (1985–2017), by Type of Institution*

Source: SIES (2017a).

some 30 per cent of undergraduate students were enrolled in the free tuition programme (Delisle and Bernasconi 2018).

Private higher education has a long tradition in Chile, with the founding of the first private university dating back to 1888. Interestingly, private institutions have outnumbered public ones since the 1920s and currently enrol 85 per cent of the total student population. That does not mean, however, that private institutions are of higher quality. Good and mediocre institutions exist in both sectors.

During the past 20 years, Chilean higher education has experienced a boom in enrolments. In 2016, 7 out of 10 students were the first from their families to access higher education. From 1990 to 2017, the gross higher education enrolment ratio increased by more than 400 per cent. In terms of raw numbers, total enrolments have increased from about 249,482 students in 1990 to almost 452,325 in 2000. By 2017, the number stood at 1,176,727 (SIES 2017c). Data for 2017 indicates that 84.7 per cent of students in Chile are enrolled in private institutions, making Chile one of the world's leaders in private enrolment in higher education. The breakdown of enrolments by type of institution is as follows: 15.2 per cent in public universities and 41.3 per cent in private universities (including both the early members of CRUCH and new private universities), 31.8 per cent in IPs and 11.7 per cent in CFTs. Table 17.1 provides data about the evolution of enrolments by type of institution since 1985. It shows how both CRUCH universities at the top of the prestige ladder and technical training centres at the bottom have lost enrolment share to private universities and professional institutes.

The past 50 years have seen an accelerating expansion of doctoral programmes and enrolments in Chile. There were just 16 doctoral programmes enrolling 97 students in total in the mid-1980s. By 2017, there were 284 programmes with more than 5,500 students, 60 per cent of them men. From 16 doctoral graduates in 1985, the figure went up to 685 in 2015. The number of doctoral graduates has multiplied by 42 in the past 30 years (Baeza 2017, 180).

Baeza (2017) distinguishes three stages in the development of doctoral education in Chile. The initial one, from 1968 to 1982, saw

Table 17.1 *Share of Enrolments in Higher Education by Type of Institution (1985–2017)*

Type of Institution	1985	1990	1995	2000	2005	2010	2015	2017
CRUCH universities	59	45	47	48	40	32	27	28
Private universities	3	8	20	23	31	33	30	31
CFT	26	31	21	12	10	13	12	11
IP	13	16	12	18	19	23	31	30
Total	**100**	**100**	**100**	**100**	**100**	**100**	**100**	**100**

Source: SIES (2017b).

the creation of the first doctoral programmes in the sciences (biology, chemistry, physics and mathematics) and the humanities (philosophy and history). These were fields with larger concentrations of research faculty in the universities, many of whom had earned their doctorates abroad. The structure of doctoral programmes has remained consistent from the beginning: two years of coursework followed by two years of research and thesis work. There are no empirical studies evaluating the relevance of this US model vis-à-vis other possible ones, but there is a dearth of experimentation with other models, at least among accredited programmes, due to the accreditation criteria. Further, there is no research on the prevalence of the US model in Chilean doctoral education, but past collaborations between Chilean universities and organizations such as the Ford Foundation and the Fulbright Scholarship Program can perhaps account for such a strong US influence. Also, the current institutional accreditation model, based on US experience and advice, may help explain why Chilean doctoral programmes have followed the US pattern. Across all disciplines, the expected product of a Chilean doctoral programme is a monograph-style dissertation. The publication of research papers is often added as a programme requirement or encouraged as a form of résumé building. Only recently has graduation by published and/or accepted papers emerged as an alternative to the dissertation in some fields, such as the sciences and social sciences.

The second historical stage (1983–1998) was characterized by public funding instruments that promoted growth in doctoral education. In 1982, Chile's National Fund for Scientific and Technological Development (known by its Spanish acronym FONDECYT) began allocating grants to researchers based on a competition among individual research projects. These grants included funding for doctoral theses. By 2000, FONDECYT had financed 588 dissertations. Another funding instrument was the Advanced Human Capital Formation Program. From 1988 to 1998, it granted 548 doctoral scholarships, mostly in the natural sciences. In that same decade, 42 doctoral programmes opened, all of them at CRUCH institutions. Eighty per cent of these programmes were in the OECD areas of natural sciences, engineering and technology, and humanities (Baeza 2017, 189–190).

According to Baeza, the third stage began in 1999, the first year of operation of the Program for Improving Quality and Equity in Higher Education (MECESUP). This was a World Bank sponsored initiative that lasted for 15 years and went through three rounds of funding. Throughout the programme's lifetime, one of its goals was the expansion and improvement of doctoral education. More than 200 programmes were created in those years, and for the first time, private universities joined the effort by creating 43 doctoral programmes. Indeed, from 2007 to 2016, doctoral programmes in the 16 state universities grew by a factor of 1.9; they multiplied by 1.7 in the 9 private universities that are members of CRUCH. In private universities outside of CRUCH, the number of programmes expanded by a factor of 5.6 and the total number of students in those programmes grew from 10 to more than 600, for an annual average growth rate of 100 per cent (Baeza 2017, 190).

CURRENT PROFILE OF DOCTORAL EDUCATION

Distribution of Enrolment

Overall, one trend is clear in Chilean higher education—expansion. Like other emerging economies (OECD 2013), Chile has expanded its postgraduate programmes (Munita and Reyes 2012). In 2018, some

74,000 students were enrolled at the master's, PhD and postgraduate specialization levels, almost twice as many as in 2008. While roughly 5,500 students at the doctoral level seems a modest number in a higher education system of 1.2 million students, the shape of the curve in Figure 17.2 speaks to the intensity of the expansion in recent years. In 1990, there were 241 students enrolled in doctoral programmes in Chile, and in 1996, just 408. By 2000, the number had reached 1,053—a 300 per cent rise from 1990. The number continued to increase from 2000 to 2017. In 2010, enrolments reached more than 2,000, and in 2017, there were 5,540 doctoral students in programmes in Chile (see Figure 17.2).

Funding

Doctoral students in Chile apply for grants once they have been admitted to a programme. Although a student's advisor will typically support the application, the final decision on the allocation of grants among applicants rests with the funding agency. In the late 1990s and in the 2000s, there was some experimentation with state-funded scholarships that were both administered and allocated by doctoral programmes themselves, but this approach was not successful and has since been phased out.

Doctoral Studies Abroad

To gauge the magnitude of the doctoral education endeavour in Chile, one must also include Chilean students pursuing PhDs outside of the country. Counting scholarships that have been awarded gives a good indication of the number of doctoral students abroad, because most of them fund their studies through Becas Chile, a scholarship programme for Chileans studying outside the country that started in 2008 as a complement to the domestic scholarships initiated in the 1980s. The aim of the Becas Chile programme is to significantly stimulate the development of human capital in terms of quantity and quality, through an out-of-country investment in technical, professional and graduate education. The programme seeks to double the number

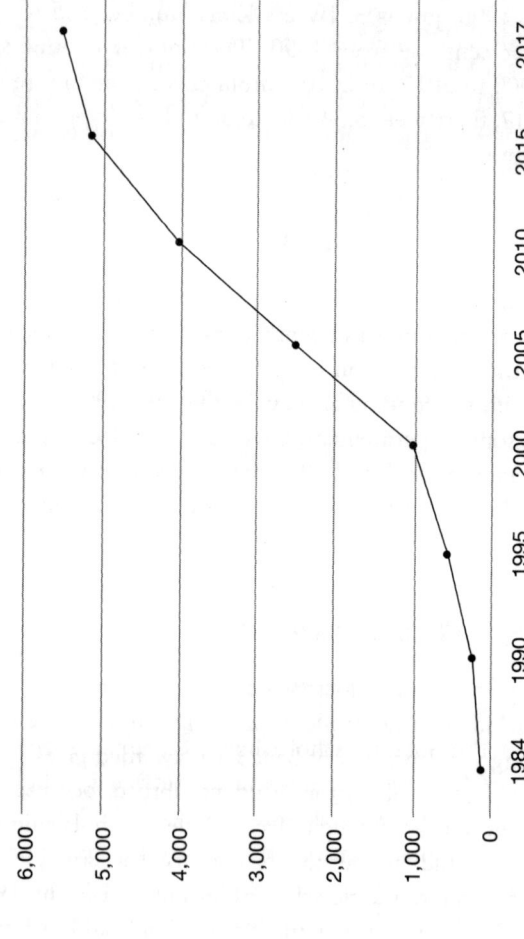

Figure 17.2 *Enrolments of Doctoral Students in Chile (1984–2017)*

Source: SIES (2017c).

PhD enrolments as a step towards strengthening the tertiary education workforce and the research capacity of the Chilean economy (OECD and World Bank 2010, 13). From 2008 to 2017, Becas Chile awarded more than 3,770 fellowships to pursue doctoral programmes abroad. The programme has maintained an average of 377 scholarships per year, which represents around 40 per cent of the total number of scholarships for national doctoral programmes awarded annually.

A study on the distribution of Chilean doctoral students who went abroad between 2008 and 2016 (CONICYT 2017) found that Europe was their preferred destination, with 68 per cent of women and 62 per cent of men choosing to go there. Far behind, the second most popular destination was North America, with 20 per cent of women and 26 per cent of men. Finally, Oceania was chosen as a destination by 9 per cent of women and 8 per cent of men.

When disaggregating Becas Chile doctorate scholarships by country, one finds that the United Kingdom was the most popular destination, with 26 per cent of both men and women choosing to go there. The United States was the second most popular for men (22%) and the third for women (17%). In terms of the OECD disciplines, the highest proportion of Chilean scholars in the United Kingdom studied subjects in the humanities and social sciences, while the most prevalent destination for study in the agricultural sciences, engineering and technology was the United States (31%).

Results

Currently, some 1,100 doctoral scholarships are granted every year. The graduation rate for beneficiaries oscillates between 75 per cent and 90 per cent, depending on the cohort (Dirección de Presupuestos 2017, 21, 25). Another official source puts the average graduation rate at 77 per cent over the past 10 years across all scholarship programmes and cohorts (CONICYT 2018, 1). Time to degree was calculated at six years for those studying in Chile and seven years for Chileans abroad (Dirección de Presupuestos 2017, 25). By one estimate, these figures translate into 1,000 Chilean doctoral graduates per year, both at home and abroad (CONICYT 2018, 3).

While this gives a sense of the flow, a question remains: what is the total number of PhD graduates receiving support from all scholarship programmes since 1988? Santelices and Bouchon (2018) put the figure at 9,500, including those still in process. The gender breakdown for the national scholarship programme is 55 per cent men and 45 per cent women. In the case of the Becas Chile programme for doctoral study abroad, the percentages are the same (CONICYT 2018). These new graduates will join an older generation of scholars (around 7,600 in 2009, Dirección de Presupuestos 2017, 14). Some overlap with the previous figure may exist for those who studied in the late 1980s and early 1990s, but their numbers are small compared to the most recent cohorts.

Employment Prospects

What are the employment prospects for the doctoral graduates mentioned above? According to Chile's ministry of economy, 75–80 per cent of doctoral graduates are employed in universities (MINECON 2016). More fine-grained data on graduates of national programmes suggests that, as of 2015, 70 per cent of those who graduated between 2007 and 2014 were employed in Chilean universities. The majority of the rest were working as postdoctoral researchers through government-funded programmes, while some 10 per cent were employed either in business or in government. Unemployment was estimated at 6 per cent (CONICYT 2018, 5). The lack of employment opportunities in the private sector is a result of various possible factors: an industrial sector that rarely relies on science-based innovation, opting instead to import technology and the training that goes with it (Comisión 2015); an economy that relies mostly on commodities with low added value and a lack of openness in universities to the demands of the business sector (CONICYT 2018, 8).

Chilean universities are the main employers of PhD graduates across all disciplines, including engineering and technology. This situation differs from that in other OECD countries. While education dominates as the main sector of employment for individuals with doctoral degrees, the variation across the OECD is high. For example, only about one-third of PhD holders in Belgium, Denmark and the Netherlands work in academia. In Poland and Portugal, however, the figure is close to four-fifths, which is more in line with Chile. The second most important sector is usually business or government. For example, the business sector employs at least one-third of doctorate holders in Belgium, Denmark and the United States.

While the Chilean private sector has not been a significant employer of doctoral graduates so far, universities do have the demographic potential to employ all PhD graduates, including those abroad. Only 27 per cent of university faculty in Chile have a PhD. In terms of full-time equivalent positions, faculty without PhDs account for 23,400 jobs. If universities were able to replace faculty without PhDs with new doctoral graduates, the situation would be very different. However, this is beyond the financial and political capabilities of almost all universities in Chile.

Brain drain is not considered a problem in the Chilean context. Scholarship grantees are required to return to Chile after finishing their studies, and they must remain in the country for twice the duration of their scholarship. To promote decentralization, the Chilean government allows grantees who decide to live outside of the capital, Santiago, to do so for only the same amount of time as the duration of their scholarships. However, the requirement to return does not seem to sufficiently explain the tendency of Chileans to come back to their country. Unfortunately, this phenomenon has not been studied in detail.

Enrolments

As mentioned above, according to data by the National System of Information in Higher Education (SIES), there were 5,540 doctoral students in the country in 2017 (41.6% women and 58.4% men; SIES 2017a). In spite of the scholarship programmes established by the government since 2008, the number of research and development (R&D) personnel per 1,000 people in Chile stands at less than 1, which is much lower than the OECD average of 7.6 (Comisión 2015, 32). This figure underscores the gap that needs to be bridged and the limits of a strategy that outsources doctoral training to universities abroad (Pedraja-Rojas, Rodriguez, and Araneda 2016).

While growth in enrolments was a healthy 52.7 per cent between 2008 and 2017 (SIES 2017a), these gains have not been spread across all universities in the system. Table 17.2 shows how the distribution of enrolments is highly concentrated in programmes at universities that are members of CRUCH. Those account for 88.4 per cent of enrolments, while new private universities account for only 11.6 per cent. This illustrates the uneven level of development at Chilean universities.

Similar to international trends, the development of doctoral programmes by discipline is not homogeneous in Chile. Science programmes account for 33 per cent of the total, followed by the social sciences, economics and law with a combined 18 per cent. Engineering, construction and industry account for 17 per cent. On the other hand, the disciplines with the fewest programmes are services (0.3%), agriculture (6.3%) and education (6.9%). Programmes in engineering, construction and industry almost doubled their enrolments between 2010 and 2017.

While women's participation in doctoral programmes grew between 2007 and 2017, gender gap persists. The main gap can be found in engineering, construction and industry, where women accounted for just 26 per cent of enrolments in 2007 and 31 per cent in 2017. Women are also poorly represented in the sciences, the subject area with the largest share of enrolments and a gender gap that is actually growing.

Table 17.2 *Enrolment in Doctoral Programmes by University Type (2017)*

Type of University	Doctoral Enrolment
CRUCH public universities	2,343 (42.3%)
CRUCH private universities	2,554 (46.1%)
Private universities	643 (11.6%)
Total	5,540

Source: SIES (2017a).

In 2007, women represented 43 per cent of students in science doctoral programmes. In 2017, this figure had dropped to 40 per cent.

Enrolments are unevenly distributed across fields and are generally in line with the availability of programmes. In 2017, the percentage of students enrolled in basic sciences was 38.5, followed by technology with 15 per cent of enrolments. In disciplines such as the arts and architecture, the percentage of enrolments that year reached 1.7. In business, it was 1.4 per cent. Together with enrolments, the number of doctoral programmes in the country has also increased, with the greatest number of programmes found in the universities that are part of CRUCH. Meanwhile, there has been a substantial increase in the number of programmes offered in some private universities as well. As we can observe in Table 17.3, doctoral programmes offered by CRUCH universities are 81 per cent of the total (SIES 2017b). This can be explained by the strong ties these institutions have with scientific development and by their ability to foster conditions that support research.

Moreover, the national distribution of doctoral programmes shows a clear tendency towards centralization in the three most populous regions of the country: Metropolitana, which includes the capital, Santiago (53%), Valparaíso (12%) and Bío Bío (13%). Furthermore, the fact that private universities do not develop doctoral programmes in the regional areas contributes to the overall centralization of programmes in the Metropolitan region. In 2017, there were only four doctoral programmes in private universities outside of Metropolitana.

Table 17.3 *Doctoral Programmes Offered by Institutions (2017)*

Type of Institution	Number
CRUCH state universities	116
CRUCH private universities	114
Private universities	54
Total	284

Source: SIES (2017).

The number of doctoral graduations increased 60 per cent between 2007 and 2016, as was expected from the increase in enrolments. However, the 1,570 PhDs awarded nationally during this period seems a low figure when compared to the 284 doctoral programmes operating in 2017. Similar to enrolments, degrees awarded are concentrated in CRUCH universities, with 91 per cent of the total.

A survey-based study undertaken by the higher education division of the Chilean ministry of education looked at a set of 93 Chilean doctoral programmes (MINEDUC 2014). The study found that 84 per cent of the 2,110 students who responded to the survey (with close to a 70% response rate) said they felt supported in their professional goals by their academic advisor. Only 4 per cent stated they were not supported. Also, 82 per cent of the respondents said they received appropriate counselling at the time of enrolment, and 57 per cent reported that they received information about expectations regarding their academic progress while in the programme. In terms of skills developed through the programme, the two most important were identified as 'giving presentations to academic audiences' and 'drafting articles for publication'. According to the students surveyed, one important aspect of the academic profession that was largely absent from their training was the opportunity to teach undergraduates and graduates. Preparation for work interviews and managing research projects was also reported as missing from their training.

Accreditation

The quality assurance framework for higher education provides for voluntary accreditation for doctoral programmes and is entrusted to the National Commission for Accreditation. Accreditation can be granted for anywhere from 2 to 10 years, depending on the judgement of the commission. The criteria for accreditation (Comisión Nacional de Acreditación 2013) set the regulatory framework for programme structure and duration, as well as faculty and graduation requirements. Herein lies the requirement of a thesis as the product of the programme and of passing a qualification or candidacy examination before beginning the thesis. If the candidacy exam is not based on the dissertation proposal (for instance, if it consists only of an evaluation of coursework), then a separate evaluation of the proposal must be undertaken. The minimum period of residence for a doctoral student is 2.5 years if full-time or the equivalent if part-time. Standards set by the commission have helped buttress the quality of doctoral programmes by defining, for instance, the requirements that faculty must meet to be entitled to supervise doctoral dissertations in terms of minimum numbers of publications and research projects (Celis and Véliz 2017). The guidelines also lay out the requirements for any university wishing to start a new doctoral programme. The host university must exhibit well-established research lines, and no fewer than seven full-time faculty members who are actively researching the subject matter of the doctoral programme must be core faculty members of that programme. There are joint programmes linking two or more national or international universities (although the degree must be issued by at least one Chilean university to be considered part of the national system). Through scholarships, the National Commission for Scientific and Technological Research (CONICYT) supports doctoral internships abroad for a minimum of 3 months and a maximum of 10 months.

The rules of the National Accreditation Commission do offer some flexibility when it comes to curriculum. For example, the study plan in the first two years can consist of coursework, seminars, research units or even some other structure without any teaching components at all. Also, the thesis or dissertation can be replaced by original published work by the candidate.

To date, based on data from the ministry of education's Higher Education System Information (SIES 2017c), we can see that only 26 per cent of doctoral programmes in private universities have accreditation. CRUCH public and private universities have, respectively, 64 per cent and 78 per cent of their programmes accredited. Until now, non-accredited doctoral programmes have been allowed to continue to operate. But a comprehensive Higher Education Reform Act passed in May of 2018 requires that, starting in 2020, all doctoral programmes must be accredited in order to remain licenced. Lack of accreditation will lead to the closing of the programme. This will likely hit the private sector hardest because most unaccredited programmes are run by private universities.

Even though there are differences in the number of years for which programmes are accredited and in the perceptions of students about their doctoral experiences (Tornero, Epstein, and Vicuña 2016), the evaluation of quality is relevant because the decision of the accrediting agency has a direct impact on financial aid. Only students in accredited programmes are eligible for scholarships awarded by CONICYT. These scholarships cover tuition fees and provide a living allowance (worth US$1,000), along with some additional funding for research stays abroad. For students, the value of attending an unaccredited doctoral programme is unclear. There may be some value for senior faculty who never obtained a PhD in their youth, or for those who cannot afford full-time study or are otherwise restricted in their options. As mentioned above, holding a doctorate remains rather exceptional among Chilean faculty; only 27 per cent of university full-time or equivalent staff had a doctorate in 2017. Thus, uncredentialed faculty may seek to obtain a qualification—any qualification—as a formality for promotion or for mere legitimacy. Yet under the new regulations, the option to undertake an unaccredited programme will soon cease to be available in Chile.

POLICIES TO PROMOTE DOCTORAL PROGRAMMES IN CHILE

Over the past decade, a number of government strategies have been designed to directly or indirectly promote and strengthen doctoral education and doctoral programmes in Chile. This is appropriate, given the shortage of research personnel in the country generally and at universities in particular. If all FTE faculty without a doctorate in Chilean universities were to be replaced by PhD holders, close to 24,000 FTE positions would need to be filled. Other indicators also underscore Chile's deficits in this regard. In 2017, Chile had 587 PhDs per one million inhabitants. In 2009, this figure was 1,800 for Spain; 2,300 for the United States; 4,400 for Germany and 18,500 for Switzerland (Dirección de Presupuestos 2017, 14). Across the whole population of Chile, only 0.2 per cent have earned a PhD, while the OECD average is 1.5 per cent (Dirección de Presupuestos 2017, 18).

Another way of assessing this shortage of research staff is through the estimates generated by the Presidential Commission on Science for the Development of Chile, which issued its report in 2015. Nowadays, approximately 700 personnel with PhDs are added to Chile's R&D activities each year. If nothing is done to increase this figure, in 16 years the net addition of people with doctorates will only increase to 850 per year (Comisión 2015, 33). If, on the other hand, Chile wants to triple its share of R&D personnel per 1,000 individuals in the workforce, raising it from the current 0.9 to a level of 2.7 (still about one-third of the OECD average of 7.6), the number of R&D staff with PhDs would need to increase from the current 4,943 to 27,782 by year 2030 (Comisión 2015, 31). To attain this goal, the public budget for R&D would need to expand by 9 per cent per year over the next 15 years, and the share of private investment as part of total investment (public and private) would need to increase to 50 per cent from the current level of 35 per cent. Measured in US dollars, the public budget for R&D would need to grow from the current level of $750 million per year to $2.8 billion by 2030 (Comisión 2015, 31–32). Note that these figures do not include the cost of training staff, but only their salaries and installation and operational costs.

What is the likelihood of this happening? Not very high, we surmise. The free tuition policy is already costing US$1.5 billion per year, and that is not considering the additional resources that would be necessary for its proposed expansion to students above the current cut-off point of family income in the six lowest deciles. In fact, free tuition for all undergraduates would bring the cost to US$3.1 billion (Delisle and Bernasconi, 2018). Most likely, investment in developing research personnel will continue to increase piecemeal, if at all, and only slowly register in the indicators mentioned above.

At any rate, three things are worth noting about Chile's policies for advanced human capital. First, with ebbs and flows, they have put an emphasis on increasing the number of people in the workforce qualified at the doctoral level. Second, they have attempted to strengthen policymaking through a new ministry of science of technology. Third, they have become increasingly aware of the problem of ensuring employability for advanced human capital in Chile.

Increasing Chile's Doctoral Workforce

The government has increased the availability of scholarships to promote the education of advanced human capital within the country. Since 2008, the Scholarship Program for National Doctorates has awarded about 500 scholarships per year (CONICYT 2013b). This has increased in recent years; since 2015, the number has been more than 700, compared to 64 in 2000 and 500 in 2010. In 2017, national doctoral fellowships were awarded to 735 students (CONICYT 2017). In order to attract more scholars to pursue PhD programmes in Chile, fellowship benefits have been expanded. For instance, students now have the option of doing an internship abroad, which allows them to participate in an international environment that can offer opportunities for academic and scientific collaboration on a more global scale. In addition, students now have the option of requesting extra funding to cover the costs of completing the doctoral thesis, or asking for an extra semester to finish writing it.

As stated above, the Becas Chile programme has awarded 40 per cent of the scholarships allocated to students admitted to doctoral programmes abroad. These cover tuition fees and living expenses. The cost per student of the international programme is much higher than the national programme, though, and Becas Chile has always faced pressure from scientists and scholars in Chile who would prefer that funding to go to domestic programmes. Yet there is an excess capacity in domestic programmes estimated at 51 per cent of enrolments, due to insufficient applications by qualified candidates (SIES 2017c). This suggests that Chilean doctoral programmes face a demand problem as well—not just issues of supply or availability of financial aid.

Scholarship programmes have never prioritized specific fields of study. Candidates can apply for admission to whatever field they choose and applications are funded solely on the merit of the applicant and the quality of the programme and university. In general, scholarships have always been centralized in the national scholarships programme, which selects candidates among all applicants in accredited programmes. As a rule, scholarships are not allocated by doctoral programmes.

In spite of the enormous need for more people trained at the doctoral level in Chile, between 2013 and 2017, the public budget for scholarships decreased by 15 per cent in the national programme, and by 19 per cent in the Becas Chile programme (CONICYT 2018, 18).

Creation of a Ministry of Science and Technology

In June of 2018, a bill to create a ministry of science and technology was passed by the National Congress of Chile, after having been on the congressional docket during the previous two administrations. The creation of the new ministry stems from the realization that there is a dearth of national, full-scale planning and coordination of science and technology policy, which is currently fragmented across several ministries and government agencies, the most important being CONICYT.

The creation of a single ministry alone is unlikely to have an impact on either the scale or quality of doctoral education in Chile. Currently, 20 per cent of CONICYT's funding supports graduate scholarships (CONICYT 2015), and the question of whether to increase that share and decrease the share of funding allocated to research by established scholars is a political one. In other words, given the fiscal restrictions outlined above, the overall budget for R&D is unlikely to increase, with or without a ministry. More funding for doctoral education would have to come at the expense of research projects and other CONICYT programmes or programmes from the new ministry. This would pit potential scholars against established ones, and the latter would undoubtedly prevail.

Employment Opportunities for New Doctoral Graduates

As indicated above, jobs for new PhD graduates in Chile are scarce outside of the academic sector. Gonzalez and Jiménez (2014) point out that between 2013 and 2018, the number of researchers with PhDs in Chile should have doubled. But the national system for research and innovation lacks the capacity to absorb them. There are few policies that specifically tackle this absorption problem, and universities remain dependent on state funds to finance research. Since 2010, that funding has been stagnant, with investment in R&D stuck at 0.35–0.38 per cent of GDP, compared to the OECD average of 2.4 per cent.

For the past 20 years, funding for new academic positions in universities has been made possible through enrolment growth. Unfortunately, the past two years have seen enrolments plateau, due to the shrinking college age population and the levelling off of student aid. As a result of these trends, universities are not expanding their faculty numbers, which limits opportunities for new PhDs to insert themselves into tenure track positions.

In fact, the expansion of available scholarships, both for programmes in Chile and abroad, is often criticized for not considering the demands that a greater number of PhD graduates would place on the higher education system. In its last policy report on human capital formation, CONICYT (2018, 5) acknowledges this conundrum. The report mentions all the potential avenues for ensuring jobs for new doctorates: making accreditation requirements for graduate programmes more demanding in terms of numbers of faculty with PhD; expediting the replacement of senior academics in universities with younger scholars; increasing the number of postdoctoral positions and creating adjunct research positions in government-funded research centres. Which of these will it be? The report does not say. Rather, it defines two key guiding policy questions (CONICYT 2018, 8). What postgraduate programmes does Chile need, and among those, which ones should be pursued overseas? And what obligation does Chile have to secure positions for these postgraduates once they return?

The criterion for funding a domestic postgraduate programme is that it be 'of equal or greater academic quality compared to equivalent programmes abroad (CONICYT 2018, 11). That is an extremely tall order. If one is to take it at face value, there is no chance that a doctoral programme in Chile would ever be declared eligible, unless 'equivalent' here is meant to refer to programmes in other middle-income countries. The report then sets out to delineate the extent of the state's responsibility for providing jobs to graduates. It proposes to identify priority areas, defined politically by cabinet ministers, within which the government will guarantee 'to facilitate job opportunities' to graduates (CONICYT 2018, 12). Those who decide to study in a field other than the selected ones will do so at their own peril. Another CONICYT policy in this respect is the proposed authorization for graduates to remain overseas as long as they serve Chile in some form: 'Retribution must be substantial in activities to foster the development of the country ... to be carried out in Chile, or abroad, or both'. (CONICYT 2018, 12).

Beyond these policy proposals, the responses to this stalemate have been twofold: require government funded centres and large projects to hire adjunct, non-tenure track researchers, and provide state-funded retirement incentives for senior faculty in public universities. Whether this two-pronged approach will suffice to secure jobs for some 1,000 new PhDs graduating each year remains to be seen, considering that the private sector and the government have not been major employers of doctorate holders.

CHALLENGES AND OPPORTUNITIES

The nature of the doctoral degree, the structure of its curriculum and the overall quality of the programmes (at least the accredited ones) are not contentious in Chile at this time. Rather, the problem is understood to be bigger—the participation of Chile in the knowledge economy. The shortcomings of Chile in this regard are numerous. According to the World Economic Forum's World Competitiveness Index, Chile ranks 108th out of 140 countries in terms of quality of primary education, 107th in mathematics and science education, 86th in terms of the overall quality of its education system and 92nd in terms of private spending on R&D. Chile is not prepared for the development of a knowledge-driven economy. Business executives identify the country's 'inadequately educated workforce' and 'insufficient capacity to innovate' as the second and fourth most problematic factors for doing business in Chile (OECD 2017, 38).

Moreover, with only 0.39 per cent of GDP spent on R&D in 2017, Chile ranks last among all OECD nations, which average out at 2.36 per cent (OECD 2014a, 2015c). In fact, Chile ranked among the bottom five OECD member countries on 11 out of 19 different indicators used by the OECD to measure the comparative performance of national science and innovation systems (OECD 2014a). As stated previously, Chile also has the lowest number of researchers per thousand workers (0.9 compared to the OECD average of 7.6). These numbers reveal specific challenges, not only in terms of increasing investment in research, development and innovation, but also in terms of fashioning a long-term policy to promote the training of advanced human capital that is connected to a national policy for research.

Most R&D activity is unequally distributed in Chile, not because of an unequal distribution of innovation needs across the country, but because of the concentration of advanced human capital in three regions in the country: Santiago, Bío-Bío and Valparaíso (OECD 2016a). For example, in 2010, half of R&D expenditure and personnel were located in the Santiago Metropolitan region (OECD and World Bank 2010), which also accounts for more than half of all doctoral programmes. The challenge here is to create new and more prominent incentives to build research centres outside of these three regions—places where research can be done to stimulate the development of other areas of the country. Here, again, universities can be key actors at the regional level. They have the best scientific capacities, as well as the infrastructure and equipment for doing research.

Chile needs to greatly expand its R&D personnel in order to bridge its capacity gap with OECD benchmarks. At the same time, it has to find a way to open slots for tenure track positions at universities at a time when these institutions are not expanding. The country must also support overall increases in R&D funding to take advantage of increased human capital capacities. The above-mentioned difficulties in providing academic jobs to graduates are pushing Chilean universities to rethink the purpose and curriculum of their doctoral programmes. Albeit incipient, there are discussions about preparing students for job markets beyond academia, along the lines of the so-called third mission (Santelices and Bouchon 2018). Such preparation would include developing oral and written communication skills and teaching abilities, project acquisition and management capabilities, learning about intellectual property and technology transfer, acquiring tools for business development and entrepreneurship, and improving one's fluency in English. These discussions are taking place in a broader context of insufficient policy development, and an overall lack of any comprehensive national strategy for research, development and innovation involving government, industry and universities. According to Balbontin, Roeschmann, and Zahler (2018), one of the weaknesses of doctoral training in Chile at the policy level is the lack of coordination between universities, agencies linked to science and the training of human capital, and entities that have as their central focus the productivity of the economy. If basic research and capacity building are part of the same value chain as innovation and technology transfer, these two processes ought to be better connected than they are now. At this time it is still unclear whether the new ministry of science, technology and innovation will be able to better articulate the links between the formation of human capital and the agencies pushing for productivity. The current mismatch is a consequence of this lack of vision and planning. Hopefully, the new ministry will be able to strengthen the institutional side of the equation and give prominence and better coordination to R&D policies, for Chile to fully participate in the global information and knowledge society.

REFERENCES

Baeza, P. 2017. 'Diversidad y diferenciación en la oferta de programas de doctorado en Chile'. *Calidad en la Educación* [*Quality in Education*] 47: 179–214.

Balbontín, Rodrigo, Juan Andrés Roeschmann, and Andrés Zahler. 2018. *Ciencia, Tecnología e Innovación en Chile: Un Análisis Presupuestario* [*Science, Technology and Innovation in Chile: An economic analysis*]. Santiago: Ministerio de Hacienda.

Celis, Sergio, and Daniela Véliz. 2017. 'La acreditación como agente de mejora continua en los programas de postgrado en ciencia y tecnología' [*Accreditation as a factor on improvement of postgraduate programs in science and technology*]. In *Series Cuaderno de Investigación en Aseguramiento de la Calidad*. Santiago: Comisión Nacional de Acreditación.

Comisión Nacional de Acreditación. 2013. Criterios para la acreditación de programas de postgrado [Critera for accreditation of postgraduate programs]. https://www.cnachile.cl/Documentos%20de%20Paginas/Criterios%20vigentes%20para%20la%20Acreditaci%C3%B3n%20de%20programas%20de%20postgrado%20a%20partir%20del%2004%20de%20noviembre%20del%202013.pdf (accessed September 4, 2018).

438 | Ana Luisa Muñoz-García and Andrés Bernasconi

Comisión Presidencial Ciencia para el Desarrollo de Chile. 2015. *Un sueño compartido para el futuro de Chile. Informe a la Presidenta de la República, Michelle Bachelet.* [Presidential Commission of Science for the Development of Chile. 2015. A shared dream for the future of Chile. Report to the President of the Republic, Michelle Bachelet].

CONICYT. 2008. *Capital Humano Avanzado: Hacia una política integral de becas de postgrado* [*Advance Human Capital: Towards a integral policy of postgraduate scholarships*]. Santiago: Comisión Nacional de Investigación Científica y Tecnológica.

———. 2012. *Hacia una Institucionalidad Pública para el Desarrollo de la Ciencias en Chile* [Towards a Public Institutionalisation for the Development of Science in Chile]. Santiago: Comisión Nacional de Investigación Científica y Tecnológica.

———. 2013a. *25 años de Becas de Doctorado* [25 years of Doctoral Scholarships]. Santiago: Comisión Nacional de Investigación Científica y Tecnológica.

———. 2013b. *Compendio Estadístico: Concursos de CONICYT, 2008–2010* [Statistical Compendium: CONICYT Funding, 2008–2010], edited by CONICYT. Santiago: Comisión Nacional de Investigación Científica y Tecnológica.

———. 2015. *Principales Indicadores Cienciométricos de la Actividad Científica Chilena* [Main Scientometric Indicators of Scientific Activity in Chile], edited by Scimago. Santiago-Madrid-Viña del Mar: MINEDUC.

———. 2017. *Resultados de Selección: Concurso Doctorado Nacional Año Académico 2017* [Results of Selection: National Doctorate Scholarships for the Academic Year 2017], edited by Programa de Capital Humano Avanzado. Santiago: Comisión Nacional de Investigación Científica y Tecnológica.

———. 2018. Becarios Programa Formación de Capital Humano Avanzado. [Doctorates of the Advance Human Capital Program]. https://www.conicyt.cl/becasconicyt/estadisticas/informacion-general/ (accessed 4 March 2020).

Consejo Asesor Presidencial. 2008. *Los desafíos de la educación superior chilena: Informe del Consejo Asesor Presidencial para la Educación Superior* [Challenges of Higher Education in Chile: Report of the Presidential Council for Higher Education]. Santiago, Chile: Ministerio de Educación.

David, Paul A. and Dominique Foray. 2002. An introduction to the economy of the knowledge society. *International Social Science Journal* 54(171): 9–23.

Delisle, Jason, and Andrés Bernasconi. 2018. "Lessons from Chile's Transition to Free College." *Evidence Speaks Reports* 2 (43):1–14.

Devos, Anita, and Margaret Somerville. 2012. 'What Constitutes Doctoral Knowledge? Exploring Issues of Power and Subjectivity in Doctoral Examination'. *Australian Universities Review* 54 (1): 47–54.

Dirección de Presupuestos. 2017. Informe final de evaluación programas gubernamentales (EPG) Programas: Becas nacionales de posgrado y Becas Chile [Final report of the evaluation of government programs (EPG), National Graduate Scholarships and Chile Scholarships]. Santiago, CONICYT.

Gonzalez, Horacio and Alejandro Jiménez. 2014. Inserción Laboral de Nuevos Investigadores con Grado de Doctor en Chile. [Access to Employment of New Researchers with a Doctorate Degree in Chile]. *Journal of Technology, Management and Innovation* 9(4): 132–148.

Meissner, Dirk, Leonid Gokhberg, and Natalia Shmato. 2016. "The Meaning of Doctorate Holders fo Human Capital Development of Nations." In *The Science and Technology Labor Force: The Value of Doctorate Holders and Development of Professional Careers*, edited by Leonid Gokhberg, Natalia Shmatko and Laudeline Auriol, 343–350. Switzerland: Springer.

MINECON. 2016. *Resultados Desagregados CDH* [Disaggregated Results CDH], edited by Ministerio de Economía. Santiago, Chile. http://www.economia. gob.cl/estudios-y-encuestas/encuestas/encuestas-de-innovacion-e-id/segunda-encuesta-trayectoria-de-profesionales-con-grado-de-doctor-cdh-ano-de-referencia-2014 (accessed on 2 November 2018).

MINEDUC. 2014. Estudio evaluativo de un conjunto de programas doctorales chilenos 2013–2015. Santiago de Chile: Ministerio de Educación. [Evaluation study of a set of Chilean doctoral programs 2013–2015]. http://dfi.mineduc. cl/usuarios/MECESUP/File/2014/eventos/NASNRC/04122014/EvalDrs-Chile-Informe%20Preliminar%20041214.pdf

———. 2015. *Bases para una Reforma al Sistema de Educación Superior*. Santiago: Ministerio de Educación.

Munita, Maria I., and Javiera Reyes. 2012. *El Sistema de Postgrado en Chile: Evolución y Proyecciones para las Universidades del Consejo de Rectores* [The Postgraduate System in Chile: Projections for the Universities of the Council of Rectors]. Santiago: Consejo de Rectores de las Universidades Chilenas (CRUCH).

Muñoz, Ana Luisa, and Viviana Sobrero. 2006. 'Proyecto Tuning en Chile: Análisis del proceso de internacionalización de la educación superior' [Tuning Project in Chile: Analysis of the Internationalisation Process in Higher Education]. *Revista Calidad en la Educación* 24 (1st semester): 249–271.

Nerad, M. 2004. 'The PhD in the US: Criticisms, Facts, and Remedies'. *Higher Education Policy* 17: 183–199.

OECD. 2007. *Country Background Report—Chile*, edited by OECD. Paris: OECD.

———. 2013. *Reviews of National Policies for Education: Quality Assurance in Higher Education in Chile 2013*, edited by OECD Publishing. Paris: OECD.

———. 2014. OECD Science, Technology and Industry Outlook 2014. Paris.

———. 2015. Chile: Policy Priorities for Stronger and more Equitable Growth. Paris: OECD

———. 2016. Gross domestic spending on R&D (indicator).

———. 2017. *Education at a Glance 2017: OECD Indicators*. Paris: OECD.

OECD, and World Bank. 2010. *Reviews of National Policies for Education: Becas Chile scholarship program*. Paris: OECD.

Pedersen, Heidi Skovgaard. 2014. 'New doctoral graduates in the knowledge economy: trends and key issues'. *Journal of Higher Education Policy and Management* 36 6: 632–645.

Pedraja-Rojas, Liliana, Emilio Rodriguez, and Carmen Araneda. 2016. 'Doctoral Education and Government Funding in Higher Education Institutions: An Approach from Chile'. *Contemporary Issues in Education Research* 9 2: 67–75.

Popescu Gheorghe H., Oana Sabie and Mihaela Comanescu. 2016. The Role of Human Capital in the Knowledge-Networked Economy. *Psychosociological Issues in Human Resource Management* 4(1): 168–174

Rojas, Alvaro, and Andres Bernasconi. 2009. 'El gobierno de las universidades en tiempo de cambio' [University Governance in Changing Times]. In *Desafíos y Perspectivas de la Dirección Estratégica de las Instituciones Universitarias*, edited by Nicolas Fleet. Santiago: Gráfica, LOM.

Sánchez, Ignacio. 2011. *Los desafíos de la educación superior en Chile* [The Challenges of Higher Education in Chile], edited by Centro de Políticas Publicas UC. Santiago: Pontificia Universidad Católica de Chile.

Santelices, Bernabé, and Pedro Bouchon. 2017. Desarrollo de la ciencia, la tecnología y la innovación. [Development of Science, Technology and Innovation]. In *Ideas en Educación II. Definiciones en tiempos de cambio*, ed. Ignacio Sánchez, 645–681, Santiago: Ediciones de la Pontificia Universidad Católica de Chile.

SIES. 2017a. *Informe de Matrícula 2017 en Educación Superior* [Report of Enrolments in 2017 in Higher Education]. Santiago: Ministerio de Educación.

———. 2017b. *Listado de Instituciones Educación Superior* [List of Higher Education Institutions]. Santiago: MINEDUC.

———. 2017c. *Matrícula 2017 (Pregrado y Postgrado)* [Undergraduate and Postgraduate Enrolments in 2017], edited by MINEDUC. Servicio de Información de Educación Superior. Santiago: MINEDUC.

Tornero, B., L. Epstein, and M. I. Vicuña. 2016. *Consistencia entre percepciones de estudiantes sobre la calidad de sus doctorados y la evaluación de CNA* [Consistency between student perceptions of the quality of their doctorates and the evaluation of CNA], No. 3, Vol. 3 of *Cuadernos de Investigación*. Santiago: Comisión Nacional de Acreditación (CNA-Chile).

PART VII

Middle East

Chapter 18

United Arab Emirates
A Doctoral Education Start-Up

Tatiana Karabchuk

This chapter is devoted to the description and discussion of the relatively recent establishment of doctoral education in the United Arab Emirates (UAE). The UAE has a very young, oil-rich, postcolonial economy. Its population is slightly more than nine million people, of whom 85 per cent are expatriates from 200 different countries (FCSA 2016; Gonzalez et al. 2008). This large number of expatriates affects the country's provision of higher and doctoral education. The UAE's young universities face many challenges in attracting and retaining the best faculty from across the globe, and in recruiting the most talented students. Further, they are tasked with developing the research infrastructure necessary to be competitive in the global education market and placing highly in international rankings.

Despite its emerging economy, the UAE prioritizes research development by making enormous investments in higher and doctoral education. Thanks to high oil revenues, the UAE has made a historically unprecedented leap, moving from a very traditional society to a highly modernized one over the last 20 years (Samier 2014). Moreover, the country is becoming the regional leader in higher education and research by increasing the number of universities, improving the quality of its doctoral programmes and raising its number of publications. Gross enrolment ratios in tertiary education jumped from 15.55 per cent in 2008 to 36.85 per cent in 2016. Even higher numbers were observed in terms of enrolment of women, with an increase from 27.7 per cent in 2008 to 53.2 per cent in 2016 (UNESCO 2016). All of these factors make the development of doctoral education in the UAE an interesting and relevant case study.

Before discussing the historical peculiarities of higher education in the UAE, it is important to understand the country's position in the context of recent global developments in doctoral education. The world is experiencing a general shift from national public research institutions towards universities (OECD 2016a). In OECD countries, universities are seen as the main performers of public research. This is due to their ability to closely link teaching and research and involve students in research activities (OECD 2016b). The UAE is following this logic as well, and is strengthening research capacity in its universities. The total UAE expenditure on education is already around 1 per cent of GDP (FCSA 2018). According to the Ministry of Education, expenditure on research and development will reach 1.5 per cent of GDP in 2021.

Postgraduate education and academic research have become global endeavours for many nations and for supranational organizations such as the OECD, UNESCO and the World Bank. Via policy recommendations, these entities are enhancing doctoral education's contributions to national and regional economic growth (Nerad 2010). Countries' hopes for social development and economic growth are often dependent on an increase in the number of highly educated elites. However, the growing discrepancy between the expanding number of doctoral graduates and the number of jobs available in labour markets is an important drawback. As discussed in an article in *Nature*, science PhD graduates may never get a chance to take full advantage of their qualifications, as their supply considerably exceeds demand (Cyranoski et al. 2011). Doctoral graduates outnumber available positions in the Unites States and Japan, accounting for the considerable unemployment rate among PhD holders (Cyranoski et al. 2011). There is a similar trend in Europe; however, the 2.2 per cent unemployment rate among PhD holders in 2009 was much lower than the overall unemployment rate (Eurostat 2009). This raises important questions regarding the status of doctoral education in the UAE. Does the UAE have too many PhD graduates? Is there, perhaps, a mismatch between the qualifications of doctoral degree holders and labour demand? The short answer is 'no'. The UAE is currently becoming a research-oriented country focused on enhancing educational policies and introducing PhD programmes at some universities. Some of the numerous challenges in establishing and developing doctoral education in a highly traditional, religious society (albeit one with a flourishing, oil-rich economy) are discussed below.

HISTORICAL DEVELOPMENT OF HIGHER AND DOCTORAL EDUCATION IN THE UAE

The country's first university, United Arab Emirates University (UAEU), was established in 1977 with an enrolment of 400 bachelor of arts students. Now, UAEU aspires to become a comprehensive, research-intensive university. It currently enrols approximately 14,000 students at the undergraduate and postgraduate levels combined. Most of its students are Emirati, but there is also a small proportion of international students. UAEU is the oldest of the three public universities affiliated with the Ministry of Higher Education and Scientific Research; the other two are the Higher Colleges of Technology and Zayed University. Public universities offer tuition-free education to UAE nationals and a limited number of expatriates. In 2016–2017, only 7.5 per cent of individuals studying in the UAE's public universities were expatriates. In contrast, up to 59 per cent of students at private universities were expatriates (FCSA 2018). Initially, federal universities promised all graduates jobs in new governmental institutions (Burden-Leahy 2009; Gonzalez et al. 2008).

Since 1997, the UAE has witnessed a tremendous expansion of both public and private higher education institutions, reaching 87 by 2017 (FCSA 2017). That places the UAE among the top Gulf Cooperation Council (GCC) countries. Higher education has always been of high importance in the UAE's developmental policies (Jose and Chacko 2017). The government is constantly investing significant resources to develop the country's education and research capacities, with up to 22.5 per cent of the 2010 budget going towards these goals (Ibrahim 2011, 149).

The UAE has always emulated the best practices from the West, modernizing itself in the same fashion as high-income states (Al Farra 2011; Donn and Al Manthri 2010; Jose and Chacko 2017). Yet it has retained and preserved its own traditions (Burden-Leahy 2009). Early partnerships on issues of higher education began with Egypt, then turned towards high-income, English-speaking countries. Unlike other postcolonial countries, the UAE did not receive any funding from international organizations like the World Bank (although its advice was taken into account) for the advancement of higher education as a nation-building tool (Burden-Leahy 2009). It is worth underscoring the state's key role in the development and power structure of higher education (Burden-Leahy 2009; Wilkins 2010). The UAE government can afford to fund mass state higher education for the foreseeable future. Unlike other Arab World countries, women and rural citizens do not face a lack of educational opportunities (Burden-Leahy 2009), and higher education is seen as a crucial element in developing national identity and solidarity, as well as providing expertise to manage the economy (Burden-Leahy 2009).

The rising number of (mainly private) higher education institutions in the UAE has been driven by multiple factors during the last 15 years. Among them are the country's economic growth and private sector investments in the Gulf region's institutions of higher education (Jose and Chacko 2017; Lefrere 2007). The expansion and diversity of private higher education institutions in the UAE reflect the global trend of turning education into a commercial product (Altbach 2015; Bennell and Pearce 2003; Lefrere 2007; Wilkins 2011). The predominance of private higher education institutions in the Emirates can easily be seen in Table 18.1. It is important to note that while private universities might also receive government investments because royal family members 'own' them, these institutions are not governed or administered as if they were public (Samier 2014).

Table 18.2 provides the latest statistics on the total number of students enrolled in higher education institutions (including postgraduate

Table 18.1 *Total Number of Public and Private Higher Education Institutions[a] in 2017 (by Emirate)*

Sector	Public		Private	
Emirates:	Total Number of Higher Education Institutions	Including Number of Universities	Total Number of Higher Education Institutions[a]	Including Number of Universities
Abu Dhabi	3	2	29	7
Dubai	2	1	34	13
Sharjah	1	0	7	4
Ajman	0	0	4	2
Umm Al Quwain	0	0	1	0
Ras Al Khaimah	1	0	2	2
Fujairah	1	0	2	1
Grand total	8	3	79	29

Source: FCSA statistics online (from Ministry of Education).

Note: [a]'Higher education institution' means here an institution providing undergraduate (higher) education in the country. These include colleges, institutes, academies and universities. https://data.bayanat.ae/en_GB/dataset/total-of-higher-education-institutions-by-emirate-and-sector (accessed 4 March 2020).

Table 18.2 *Total Number of Students Enrolled in Higher Education Institutions in the UAE (2013–2017)*

	2013–2014	2014–2015	2015–2016	2016–2017
Women	72,946	79,857	81,200	81,183
Men	55,333	59,548	58,359	56,072
Total	128,279	139,405	139,559	137,255

Source: FCSA statistics online (from Ministry of Education). https://data.bayanat.ae/en_GB/dataset/number-of-students-in-higher-education-institutions-by-emirate-sector

programmes) in the UAE for the last five years. It is evident that there has been huge growth in the number of higher education students, increasing from 400 in 1977 to 137,255 in 2017. Unexpectedly, since the end of the 1990s, the number of Emirati women enrolled in higher education has begun to exceed the number of men. However, this dominance did recently decrease from 70 per cent in 2008 (Fox 2008) to 60 per cent in 2017.

Postgraduate education has been one of the main challenges faced by the UAE in establishing a knowledge-based economy (Hijazi et al. 2008), and the country is still addressing it. By the end of 2017, despite the impressive increase in the number of master's programmes (to 179), only eight universities offered doctoral degrees. All 20 of the available PhD programmes are taught in English.

The first doctoral degree programmes in the country emerged very recently, in 2009–2010. As a public university, UAEU has been a leader in the process of establishing and developing doctoral education in the country. Only much later did private universities also open doctoral degree programmes. Among them are New York University Abu Dhabi, Khalifa University (with Masdar Institute of Science and Technology), American University of Sharjah and Abu Dhabi University. Despite its private status, Khalifa University recently proclaimed that it wanted to become a world-class graduate school with a strong focus on research. That status helps to attract young talent at both the national and international levels, and provides students with high quality mentorship and teaching.

The typical Emirati PhD programme is very similar to the European or UK model, with four years of paid fellowship and a thesis submission and defence at the end of one's studies. Only master's degree holders are eligible to enrol in PhD programmes. The US variant of combined master's/PhD programmes is not that popular in the country. For example, foreign students can only apply for PhDs if they already have their master's degrees. At the same time, UAEU very recently opened a combined master's/PhD track, which provides tuition support. This programme is available only to talented Emirati students (with GPAs higher than 3.5), and covers their master's studies as well as their doctoral education.

A worthwhile question to ask is why students from other countries would come to do doctoral work in the UAE. The country hardly ever provides citizenship to people of other nationalities, migration policies are very strict and doctoral programmes do not yet have the reputation necessary to attract young, ambitious PhD candidates. Hence, how can the UAE attract talented students from abroad? First, the country's universities are the Gulf region's leading institutions, and they do provide high quality education. Some higher education institutions providing PhD degrees are regional branches of well-known Australian, French, UK and US universities. Second, students usually receive substantial stipends and do not need to pay tuition fees. Third, the UAE's high standard of living and safe environment make it an extremely appealing country to live. Fourth, the UAE is known to be quite an attractive work destination in the Arab world, and so students may plan to stay in the country after graduation. Finally, a warm climate and excellent living conditions might also contribute to their decisions.

Unfortunately, no official statistics are publicly available on either the number of students currently enrolled in Emirati PhD programmes or the number of doctoral graduates in the UAE. The only data available from the Ministry of Education are the number of national PhD graduates who completed their education outside the UAE and the number of PhD scholarships given by the ministry to nationals studying abroad. Both are indicators of the government's support for those wanting to get a degree outside the country. In fact, the government provides excellent opportunities for nationals who want to receive a doctoral degree abroad and then return to work in the UAE. Through the three federal public universities' scholarship programmes, Emirati citizens can apply to study abroad for their PhDs and be fully funded for tuition fees, air tickets, accommodation and even salaries. One of the country's missions is to develop a large, highly qualified reserve of human resources. This will allow the UAE to meet society's demands for various specializations, thereby contributing to the country's economic and social development. An 'Emiratization' programme provides Emirati nationals who receive a PhD abroad with comprehensive benefits for coming back and working at their home universities. The return rate is very high. The UAE takes great care of its citizens, and thus PhD graduates abroad have a significant motivation to come back and continue their academic careers at home. Emiratis do not tend to stay abroad longer than the time allotted for their studies.

Until now, the UAE government has concentrated more on sending students abroad (to the United Kingdom, the United States, Australia and Canada) to receive high-quality PhDs, rather than on developing the country's own doctoral education system. For the last three years, the total number of students receiving doctoral degrees abroad has not exceeded 100 per year (about 60% of them women). Considering that the population of Emiratis in the country is just over one million people, we can estimate that roughly 0.009 per cent of UAE nationals per year either receive a doctoral degree or become PhD students abroad. As a comparison, about 0.006 per cent of Saudi Arabia's population held doctoral degrees in 2015, while the proportion of doctoral graduates ranges from 0.021 per cent in the United States to 0.04 per cent in the United Kingdom (calculations based on data from OECD 2016a), countries considered to be PhD 'factories'.

Why, despite the highly attractive benefits, is the number of Emirati youth going abroad for PhDs still so low? The general lack of high-quality education at public schools and the lack of research-oriented tracks at public universities do not allow Emirati nationals to be competitive in doctoral programmes at US or UK universities. Additionally, the availability of good jobs in the government sector for university graduates does not motivate Emiratis to aim for a PhD abroad. Another restricting factor is the highly traditional values that limit women's mobility abroad (Simadi and Kamali 2004).

As previously discussed, Emirati women outnumber men in pursuing undergraduate and graduate degrees in the UAE. Thus, unlike other countries, scientific fields in the UAE may soon include a majority of women. This is in line with the country's general policies for gender equality, and especially for gender equity in all areas of the economy. However, in today's faculty gender structure, the Western pattern of dominance by men is evidenced. This is particularly true in the ranks of associate and full professors (Table 18.3). The gender gap in public universities is less pronounced than in private ones (32% women versus 41% women, respectively). Yet it may still take a decade before a science and faculty distribution in Emirati universities becomes gender balanced.

The total number of professors and lecturers in higher education institutions in the UAE is fewer than 7,000. At first glance, one could think number is rather low compared to Western countries. In the United States, Russia or the United Kingdom, this might equal the number of faculty from just a couple of universities. However, given the UAE's population of nine million, the relative proportion of researchers and academicians is not as small as it may seem. Still, the low number of associate and full professors (potential supervisors of PhD students) could also explain the low numbers of both PhD programmes and doctoral students within the country.

Despite the lack of professional faculty in the region, the UAE (like other Gulf countries) is trying to develop and considerably improve doctoral education. Within the last five years, the UAE has opened 17 new PhD programmes at various universities. Usually, the length of a full-time doctoral programme is three to four years, but it is also possible to complete a part-time PhD degree within six years. All doctoral programmes are accredited by the UAE Commission for Academic Accreditation. Higher education institutions are encouraged to provide more variety for PhD degree seekers. There is a demand for this from both employers and from a younger generation of Gulf youth

Table 18.3 *Number of Faculty Members (by Gender and Status) in Public and Private Higher Education Institutions in the UAE (2014–2017)*

Public Higher Education Institutions	2014–2015			2016–2017		
	Men	Women	Total	Men	Women	Total
Professor	162	26	188	150	23	173
Associate professor	261	77	338	256	84	340
Assistant professor	275	181	456	295	218	513
Lecturer/Faculty	807	636	1,443	1,046	892	1,938
Total	1,505	920	2,425	1,747	1,217	2,964

Private Higher Education Institutions	2014–2015			2016–2017		
	Men	Women	Total	Men	Women	Total
Professor	419	46	465	347	56	403
Associate professor	623	127	750	586	127	713
Assistant professor	1,349	556	1,905	1,007	437	1,444
Lecturer/Faculty	615	547	1,162	782	675	1,457
Total	3,006	1,276	4,282	2,722	1,295	4,017

Source: FCSA statistics online (from Ministry of Education). https://data.bayanat.ae/en_GB/dataset/number-of-faculty-members-at-federal-higher-education-institutions

who are much more motivated than their counterparts were five to seven years ago.

Structured and online doctoral degrees, as well as part-time and full-time PhD programmes, are available in the country. All online doctoral programmes are paid for and provided by private higher education institutions. Thus, any eligible candidate can apply for either a scholarship or a paid doctoral programme. Online doctoral degrees may be obtained via interactive, smart learning platforms. This allows PhD students to take courses from anywhere in the world without disrupting their schedules. The study process is based on a blended learning model, accredited and supported by the UAE Ministry of Education's Commission for Academic Accreditation. For example, among the online doctoral degree offerings, one may find the doctor of philosophy in health care management, the doctor of philosophy in total quality management and the doctor of philosophy in educational leadership.

Doctoral education is free of charge for Emirati nationals. International students can apply for postgraduate research scholarships or pay for their studies. It is usually emphasized that the PhD programmes prepare individuals for a wide array of careers, including academia, scientific research, consultancies in higher education and working in schools in the UAE (or in higher education institutions in the Gulf, Middle East and worldwide). Doctoral graduates can also pursue careers in research, international organizations and business and industry.

As in all other countries, PhD applicants must meet certain criteria. For example, UAEU requires applicants to have the following: (a) a minimum cumulative GPA of 3.3 on a 4.0 scale (or equivalent) from their master's degree (b) a score of 6.5 or higher on the IELTS academic exam, or equivalent proof of English proficiency. Additionally, applicants are asked to take the Graduate Record Examination (GRE) and submit their official scores. PhD seekers must also provide CVs, letters of recommendation and proof of their previous research experience, preferably in the form of publications.

International applicants are encouraged to apply, and receive a full support package, including a full tuition waiver, health insurance, stipend and research fund. The benefits seem desirable and the requirements seem reasonable. So why is there still a lack of PhD students in Emirati universities? The reasons might be as follows: the idea of tertiary education is rather new in the country's young, emerging economy; there is a lack of research infrastructure (including a low number of faculty members to supervise and support PhD programmes); there are certain cultural challenges as well as country-specific peculiarities (like the dominance of women in higher education); and a high number of faculty members are expatriates, and therefore very mobile.

THE ROLE OF DOCTORAL EDUCATION AND CURRENT CHALLENGES FOR PhD PROGRAMMES IN THE UAE

Government Support and the Special Role of Doctoral Education

There is no special focus on doctoral education in the Ministry of Education's Plan and Vision 2021. However, the UAE acknowledges the necessity of fostering home-grown leaders and talent. The government also understands the importance of providing first-rate education and equal opportunities to UAE citizens, and recognizes that it is impossible to build a sustainable, knowledge-based, productive economy without highly educated leaders (part of the UAE Vision 2021 and the Abu Dhabi Economic Vision 2030). Further, such capabilities are essential to the development of economic, social and human resources. For these reasons, providing first-rate education is one of the country's ultimate goals. Substantial effort has been put into building the basic education system, which turned out to be a benefit to the emerging economy. Enrolment rates have been 100 per cent for primary education and 95.6 per cent for secondary education. Youth between the ages of 15 and 24 have a literacy rate of 95.6 per cent (UNESCO 2015).

The Emiratization policy, briefly mentioned above, aims to increase Emirati participation in domestic employment, particularly at more senior levels. For this, the country needs highly qualified PhD holders in core positions at all educational and administrative organizations (Al-Ali 2008; Gonzalez et al. 2008; Smith 2008). A growing number of Emiratis are receiving graduate and postgraduate qualifications and are moving up organizational hierarchies (Samier 2014). To keep this process smooth and successful, there is a need for domestic PhD programmes to serve as the basis for building human resource capacities. Current policies are mainly aimed at sending talented youth to receive PhDs abroad, rather than establishing a strong doctoral degree system in the country. Thus, the next expected (and necessary) step for the UAE's top administration would be to focus on creating and developing doctoral education at home. Doctoral education is necessary for the development of a national identity. It is important to understand that doctoral programmes, unlike undergraduate studies, can only be sustained and developed through strong support from the government and through corporate investments (Hijazi et al. 2008; Muysken and Nour 2006).

Current Challenges for Doctoral Education in the UAE

As mentioned above, the number of expatriates in the UAE is very high. The migrant population is very diverse in terms of how long they stay in the country, their qualifications, education and family status. Most working migrants are men coming from rather poor countries for short periods of time. Their main goal is to earn money and remit their earnings to their families back home. As soon as their contracts finish, they return to their native countries. At the same time, there are expatriates who come to work in the UAE and bring their families with them. They tend to stay in the country for a longer time, raising families and often living in the UAE for 20–30 years.

As for university professors and lecturers, the expatriate turnover rate is rather high. This poses challenges in establishing doctoral programmes. Work contracts are usually for two to four years, with possible extensions, but without any possibility of tenure. Thus, organizational loyalty is very low among expatriates, who switch universities very easily, as they are not involved in tenure programmes or long-term university development strategies (Schoepp 2011). For these reasons, an adjustment was recently made to UAE immigration law. Scientists, researchers and university teachers are now eligible for ten-year working visas in the UAE. This is a marked change from the three-year visa of the past. However, no adjustments have been made with regard to contracts. Undoubtedly, the lack of job stability among faculty negatively affects the process of PhD supervision and the overall development of doctoral education in the country. There are simply no tenure-track professors available to invest their efforts, knowledge and expertise in either research or the students' long-term development.

Another problem related to the high number of expatriates is the dominance of the English language in the daily life of Emirati society. When applying to any higher education institution for bachelor's, master's or PhD programmes, students must pass the IELTS. Almost all undergraduate and postgraduate programmes (with the exceptions of Arabic language and law) are provided in English. Most of the faculty comes from different countries, and the language of instruction is English. Even though this trend is in line with the recent globalization and internationalization processes in education, it facilitates the usage of English in all spheres of life. The predominance of English over Arabic in the UAE represents a distinct cultural change.

The Role of Women in Doctoral Education in the UAE

Despite Western misperceptions of Arab women and gender discrimination, the UAE is an outstanding case study of equal opportunities in all fields (Samier 2014). Higher education has become a social and familial expectation for women in the UAE, and many families now expect their daughters to pursue higher education for better social and economic mobility (Abdulla 2007; Abdulla and Ridge 2010; Burden-Leahy 2009).

Since 2008, more than 70 per cent of Emiratis pursuing undergraduate degrees have been women (Fox 2008; Abdulla and Ridge 2010). This 'reverse' gender gap in higher education is discussed quite thoroughly in the literature (Abdulla 2007; Abdulla and Ridge 2010; Samier 2014). Beginning in secondary school, women usually outperform men. On average, women are more motivated, more dedicated and more committed to their studies and professional development. They often balance academic pursuits with their family duties, sometimes parenting several small children while completing demanding master's or doctoral studies (Samier 2015).

Despite the prevalence of women in postgraduate studies, there is a lack of family support policies in the degree-seeking process. Women are not entitled to any maternity or parental leave during their studies. If the government considers women potential members of the country's high-quality human resource pool, it needs to improve the balance between parenthood and academic careers for women pursuing master's and PhD degrees. The need for economic support, plentiful opportunities for higher education and the government's emphasis that all citizens should contribute to the economic development of the country have encouraged Emirati women to become highly qualified professionals (Burden-Leahy 2009; Samier 2014). Yet there is lack of social policies to support their contributions to academic research.

The lack of men in graduate and postgraduate studies is another issue for the country. High dropout rates among Emirati men at the high school level lead to low participation rates in higher and doctoral education (Abdulla and Ridge 2010). The predominance of women in higher education also tends to empower more women to pursue PhD degrees. As some scholars suggest, it is possible to talk about 'gendering' rather than 'regendering' the academy in the UAE, given the country's short history of higher education and the predominance of Emirati women in it (Samier 2015). The UAE government should provide more economic incentives for men to obtain doctoral degrees in order to keep them in research and academia.

Cost and Marketization of Postgraduate Education

The marketization of postgraduate education is another serious challenge in a globalized world, and even more so in the UAE, where the education system's core principles are imported from the United Kingdom and the United States (Ridge, Kippels, and Shami 2016). All master's programmes require tuition fees to be paid, irrespective of a student's citizenship. That means there are fewer entry opportunities for talented students to continue careers in academia. Master's degrees are usually seen as a path to obtaining better positions in the labour market, rather than as stepping stones for PhD degrees. Often, postgraduate education programmes are viewed by universities as merely another business, or as another way for a corporation to make a profit. The cost of these programmes might seem rather high compared with the almost free master's programmes in some European countries.

Only recently, universities have started introducing scholarships with free tuition for Emirati master's students who are involved in research activities. This is a very good development in building up an academic track for master's students who intend to pursue doctoral degrees in the future. Currently, most master's programmes provide only a basic professional degree, with no requirement for thesis submission. The challenge of enriching postgraduate education with academically oriented master's programmes, and thereby building a strong foundation for further doctoral education, is crucial for the tertiary education system in the UAE.

CONCLUDING REMARKS AND POLICY IMPLICATIONS

Doctoral education in the UAE is just emerging and the country is far from being considered a PhD factory (Gonzalez et al. 2008; Morgan 2017). The important social and economic roles of higher and doctoral education in the UAE include fostering highly qualified human resources, decreasing the country's dependence on foreign workers and speeding up the Emiratization of the labour market. These are crucial factors for the future of the UAE's economic growth and sustainable development strategy. Focusing on these factors will allow the country to shift from an oil-rich, resource-based economy to a technology and skill-based economy (Muysken and Nour 2006). Moreover, UAE leaders have set very ambitious goals for the country to become a regional research hub. This will not be possible without high-quality doctoral education. The UAE government has already taken steps to create a robust research infrastructure. This has been accomplished by building up academic cities and smart technology villages for the purpose of attracting more scientists and faculty to work in the country. Thus, it is reasonable to predict an increase in the number of PhD programmes and PhD students within the next decade.

Despite the increase in university graduates, the country still faces the challenges of expanding postgraduate and doctoral studies and improving the quality of existing PhD programmes. In this respect, the country should encourage both public and private universities to create more PhD programmes and to promote careers in academia. The establishment of new programmes is not possible without strong governmental support for a substantial number of tenure-track professors. Thus, it would be highly effective for the country's development if the UAE government could allocate enough funds to encourage local universities (on a competitive basis) to establish more master's and PhD programmes in different fields of study. Scholarships could be provided to qualified Emiratis seeking to pursue their postgraduate studies in the country's top universities. Moreover, selected outstanding expatriate students could be offered research scholarships as part of joining these master's/PhD programmes. In this way, the doctoral education system could achieve both diversity and high levels of competition among students.

During their doctoral studies, students should have opportunities and incentives to conduct their own research as well as being involved in ongoing research projects. More specifically, doctoral students need opportunities for part-time employment or full-time positions as research assistants and/or research fellows. This would provide them with a material incentive to stay in academia. This is a crucial undertaking for universities in order to retain the best research talent. Students are keenly aware that the alternative market costs of being in a doctoral degree programme are very high. Especially for young Emiratis, the amounts of money to be earned outside of academia are three to four times higher than within it.

Highly educated Emirati women may have great interest in pursuing academic careers. As they are more motivated and committed than their male counterparts, they could provide the human resource potential needed to build national research capacities. In this respect, it would be smart to create family-friendly environments, so that women can combine research and/or teaching jobs with family and parental responsibilities. Considering the limitations on Emirati women obtaining PhDs abroad, it is vital for the country to establish and develop its own doctoral education system, allowing women to receive doctoral degrees inside the country.

It may be possible to emulate knowledge and training exchange programmes such as ERASMUS Mundus and the Marie Skłodowska-Curie Actions, which support international education and career development inside Europe. Similar programmes could be established for Gulf countries, or for the entire Middle East and North Africa (MENA) region. Programmes like this could also link institutions in the Gulf with those in Europe. With government support, universities could establish associations and begin these initiatives, which could prove vital in internationalizing Emirati science and preparing doctoral graduates for work in international settings. Joint PhD programmes with established and reputable universities might be another attractive way to boost doctoral education in the UAE.

Yet another opportunity for the progress of doctoral education is for the UAE to become a receiving country for international PhD exchange programmes. Candidates could be hosted for 3–12 months at university research centres in the UAE. This could stimulate joint research projects and publication activity, and make use of data generated by Emirati scientists. It would provide universities with an opportunity to select potential faculty members and perhaps offer them positions after graduation. In order to attract large numbers of doctoral students from abroad, universities in the UAE will need clear research agendas, attractive research environments and incentives for prospective students (such as workshops on various research competencies, professional skills and intercultural competencies). A further step would be developing a system for inviting postdocs to work in Emirati universities for one or two years. With postdocs to help with teaching loads, young PhD graduates will have the opportunity to establish their research agendas and start their publishing activities.

Fostering support for the development of science among Emirati residents is essential. In order to strengthen doctoral education, it would be useful to develop programmes to connect science and research results with local communities. This has already been done successfully through such national initiatives as science festivals and hackathons.

Research outcomes should be translated from academic English into clearly articulated, simple Arabic terms that can be easily understood by Emirati citizens. The UAE's population is very advanced in using social media and new smart technologies. Thus, universities might also look for ways to transfer research knowledge to the population using social platforms, and to teach this competency within doctoral programmes.

REFERENCES

Abdulla, Fatma. 2007. 'Emirati Women: Conceptions of Education and Employment'. In *Soaring Beyond Boundaries: Women Breaking Educational Barriers in Traditional Societies*, edited by R. O. Mabokela, 73–112. Rotterdam: Sense Publishers.

Abdulla, F., and N Ridge. 2010. 'Where Are All the Men? Gender, Participation and Higher Education in the United Arab Emirates'. In *Towards an Arab Higher Education Space: International Challenges and Societal Responsibilities*, edited by B. Lamine, 125–136. Beirut: UNESCO Regional Bureau for Education in the Arab States.

Al-Ali, J. 2008. 'Emiratisation: Drawing UAE Nationals into Their Surging Economy'. *International Journal of Sociology and Social Policy* 28 (9/10): 365–379.

Al Farra, S. 2011. 'Education in the UAE: A Vision for the Future'. In *Education in the UAE: Current Status and Future Developments*, edited by the Emirates Center for Strategic Studies and Research, 219–237. Abu Dhabi: ECSSR.

Altbach, Philip. 2015. 'Higher Education and the WTO: Globalization Run Amok'. *International Higher Education* 23 (March). doi:10.6017/ihe.2001.23.6593.

Bennell, P., and T. Pearce. 2003. 'The Internationalisation of Higher Education: Exporting Education to Developing and Transitional Economies'. *International Journal of Educational Development* 23: 215–232.

Burden-Leahy, Sheila M. 2009. 'Globalisation and Education in the Postcolonial World: The Conundrum of the Higher Education System of the United Arab Emirates'. *Comparative Education* 45 (4): 525–544. doi:10.1080/03050060903391578.

Cyranoski, D., N. Gilbert, H. Ledford, A. Nayar, and M. Yahia. 2011. 'Education: The PhD Factory. The World Is Producing More PhDs than Ever before. Is It Time to Stop?' *Nature* 472: 276–279. doi:10.1038/472276a.

Donn, G., and Y. Al Manthri. 2010. *Globalisation and Higher Education in the Arab Gulf States*. Oxford: Symposium Books.

Eurostat. 2009. 'Statistics on PhD Holders'. http://appsso.eurostat.ec.europa.eu/nui/show.do?dataset=cdh_e_as&lang=en (accessed 25 May 2018).

FCSA (Federal Competitiveness and Statistical Authority). 2018. 'Online Statistics by Subject'. http://fcsa.gov.ae/en-us/Pages/Statistics/Statistics-by-Subject.aspx (accessed 25 May 2018).

Fox, W. 2008. 'The United Arab Emirates and Policy Priorities for Higher Education'. In *Higher Education in the Gulf States: Shaping Economies, Politics, and Culture*, edited by C. Davidson and P. M. Smith, 110–125. London: SAQI Press.

Gonzalez, G., L. A. Karoly, L. Constant, H. Salem, and C. A. Goldman. 2008. ' United Arab Emirates'. In *Facing Human Capital Challenges of the 21st Century: Education and Labor Market Initiatives in Lebanon, Oman, Qatar, and the United Arab Emirates*, 87–146. Santa Monica, CA: Rand Corporation Monograph Series.

Hijazi, R., T. Zoubeidi, I. Abdalla, M. Al-Waqfi, N. Harb. 2008. 'A Study of the UAE Higher Education Sector in Light of Dubai's Strategic Objectives'. *Journal of Economic and Administrative Sciences* 24 (1): 68–81. doi: 10.1108/10264116200800004.

Ibrahim, N. 2011. 'The UAE and Higher Education in the 21st Century'. In *Education in the UAE: Current Status and Future Developments*, 147–158. Abu Dhabi: ECSSR.

Jose, S., and J. Chacko. 2017. 'Building a Sustainable Higher Education Sector in the UAE'. *International Journal of Educational Management* 31 (6): 752–765. doi:10.1108/IJEM-05-2016-0102.

Lefrere, P. 2007. 'Competing Higher Education Futures in a Globalizing World'. *European Journal of Education* 42 (2): 201–212.

Morgan, Clara. 2017. 'The Spectacle of Global Tests in the Arabian Gulf: A Comparison of Qatar and the United Arab Emirates'. *Comparative Education*. doi:10.1080/03050068.2017.1348018.

Muysken, J., and Samia Nour. 2006. 'Deficiencies in Education and Poor Prospects for Economic Growth in the Gulf Countries: The Case of the UAE'. *The Journal of Development Studies* 42 (6): 957–980. doi:10.1080/00220380600774756.

Nerad M. 2010. 'The Internalization of Doctoral Education—a Two-Way Approach: Promoting Productive Educational Experiences for PhD Students'. In *Competition and Cooperation among Universities in the Age of Internalization*, edited by Kai Yu and Andrea Lynn Stith, 73–94. Shanghai: Shanghai Jiao Tong University Press.

OECD. 2016a. *Education at a Glance 2016: OECD Indicators*. Paris: OECD Publishing. doi: 10.187/eag-2016-en.

———. 2016b. *OECD Science, Technology and Innovation Outlook 2016*. Paris: OECD Publishing. doi:10.1787/sti_in_outlook-2016-en.

Ridge, N., S. Kippels, and S. Shami. 2016. 'Economy, Business, and First Class: The Implications of For-Profit Education Provision in the UAE'. In *World Yearbook of Education 2016: The Global Education Industry*, edited by Antoni Verger, Christopher Lubienski, and Gita Steiner-Khamsi. New York, NY: Routledge.

Samier, E. 2014. 'Western Doctoral Programmes as Public Service, Cultural Diplomacy or Intellectual Imperialism? Expatriate Educational Leadership Teaching in the United Arab Emirates'. In *Investing in Our Education: Leading,*

Learning, Researching and the Doctorate, edited by Alison Taysum and Stephen Rayner, 93–123. Vol. 13. Bingley: Emerald Group Publishing.

———. 2015. 'Emirati Women's Higher Educational Leadership Formation under Globalisation: Culture, Religion, Politics, and the Dialectics of Modernisation'. *Gender and Education* 27 (3): 239–254. doi:10.1080/09540253.2015.1028901.

Schoepp, K. W. 2011. 'The Path to Development: Expatriate Faculty Retention in the UAE'. *International Education* 40 (2): 58–75, 91.

Simadi, F., and M. Kamali. 2004. 'Assessing the Values Structure among United Arab Emirates University Students'. *Social Behavior and Personality* 32 1: 19–30.

Smith, P. M. 2008. 'Introduction'. In *Higher Education in the Gulf States: Shaping Economies, Politics and Culture*, edited by C. Davidson and P. M. Smith, 9–22. London: SAQI Press.

UNESCO. 2015. 'Participation Rate in Education: Literacy Rate'. http://uis. unesco.org/country/AE (accessed 25 May 2018).

———. 2016. http://uis.unesco.org/country/AE (accessed on 23 August 2018).

Wilkins, S. 2010. 'Higher Education in the United Arab Emirates: An Analysis of the Outcomes of Significant Increases in Supply and Competition'. *Journal of Higher Education Policy and Management* 32 (4): 389–400.

———. 2011. 'Who Benefits from Foreign Universities in the Arab Gulf States?' *Australian Universities Review* 53 (1): 73–83.

PART VIII

Conclusion

Chapter 19

Doctoral Education Worldwide
Key Trends and Realities

Maria Yudkevich, Philip G. Altbach, Hans de Wit and Victor Rudakov

Trends and Issues in Doctoral Education: A Global Perspective serves two simple yet complex purposes—to understand the current realities in doctoral education in key countries and to examine current and proposed reforms. Fourteen country case studies and one regional case study present a range of global practices and focus on key issues facing doctoral education worldwide. Together with the literature review and the analysis of changes in doctoral education around the world over the past three decades by Maresi Nerad, the case studies provide the basis for this concluding discussion of the broader issues and themes suggested by the previous chapters.

Doctoral education nurtures new scholars and thus is a key element for the successful future of academia. In recent years, the professional doctorate has also emerged as an important academic qualification in a number of fields. The future of the contemporary university and of the increasingly important research enterprise worldwide depends on effective, imaginative and relevant doctoral education. However, it faces challenges everywhere in the 21st century. In some lower-income countries, and even in some with middle-income economies, there is a dramatic underproduction of doctoral degree holders. Neither the demands created by rapidly growing post-secondary enrolments, nor those of the knowledge economy, are being met. In other countries— where enrolments are flat, or where enrolments in some disciplines and specializations are not in balance with requirements of the economy or of academe—we find an oversupply of doctoral graduates. And everywhere, there is discussion about the need for graduates to have transferable skills that would better prepare them for diverse labour market needs beyond academia.

Questions about the appropriate organization and purpose of the doctorate are common. Both the nature and the purpose of the doctorate are being challenged by critics who argue that doctoral training requires major reforms to face the realities of the labour market and the dramatic changes in knowledge production and research worldwide. As institutions have globalized and the borders between the university and non-university sectors have become fuzzier, many have argued that doctoral education needs to adjust to new realities. Despite these and other significant challenges, and the fact that there is great variety in the organization and practice of doctoral education among countries and universities around the world, there has been relatively little fundamental change in doctoral education. While universities have changed a lot in recent decades, doctoral education is perhaps the most rigid part of academe. Up to now, there has been little analysis of global trends and directions.

Some critics of doctoral education claim that traditional models are no longer relevant for the 21st century. Others point to long degree completion times, high dropout levels, a lack of interdisciplinarity and to the poor quality of training and research due, in part, to budget cuts. There are debates concerning the two main directions in educational training—the European model of the 'research doctorate', with little coursework and a high level of dependence on a single academic advisor or laboratory, versus the North American model, which features significant coursework combined with a dissertation and has a more collective advisory arrangement. At the same time, there has been scant discussion about how these models fit into the broader picture of the organization of academic systems in general, and academic labour markets in particular, and how rigid these systems may be when faced with new demands and realities. Further, 'professional doctorates' and other more vocationally oriented and often commercialized approaches to doctoral education have not been analysed. In other words, which system is more effective and which has better prospects to survive in the future?

Doctoral education may seem a small and limited topic, but it is of great importance for the future of universities and scientific research, for the knowledge economy and for the global scientific and academic workforce. While there are statistics on the total numbers of post-secondary students worldwide, there seem to be no easily available numbers for doctoral students, although national figures are available for many countries. It is clear that the large majority of doctorates come from the major research-producing countries in North America, Europe and Japan, although countries such as China are rapidly expanding their doctoral programmes. It is also clear that, in many countries, there are major variations in the production of doctorates and the national need for them, both in terms of specific disciplines and in overall numbers. In some cases, rapidly expanding post-secondary systems require larger numbers of doctoral degree holders than are being produced. Meanwhile, countries with stable enrolments are often producing too many doctorates for the traditional academic labour market.

As this book shows, there is no such a thing as a standard doctoral education model. The landscape of doctoral education across the world is considerably diverse and countries differ by institutional features and outcomes of their doctoral education systems. Currently, there are differences in programme length (although in general three to five years); in position (are doctoral candidates students or employees?); in funding (free, tuition based, with scholarships or loans, or with a salary); as well as in teaching responsibilities, supervision, requirements, and purpose and relevance. There are also differences in who awards degrees—the state or the universities themselves. There is discussion about the position of doctoral programmes with the university. Do they fall under the purview of the department or faculty, or are they part of one or more graduate schools within or between universities? Are they offered with master's programmes or without? There is discussion about academic versus professional doctoral programmes, as a growing number of doctoral graduates are not entering academia, but at the same time are not adequately prepared for the broader labour market. There are wide variations, by country, discipline and academic institution when it comes to jobs for young doctoral degree holders in academe, as well as to their career prospects in the non-university sector. Last but not least, doctoral education has become more internationalized. Our case studies show that student bodies are becoming more globally diverse, that doctoral students are much more mobile and that the international dissemination of research in publications and conferences is of increased importance.

Few analysts think that the current state of doctoral education is satisfactory. Yet traditional patterns of doctoral preparation have proved highly resilient and have, in general, produced well-prepared graduates. Nevertheless, all countries and systems may be classified in accordance with the main parameters of the doctoral education they offer. The diversity in the institutional structure of doctoral education across the world can be assessed along the following indicators:

1. Scale of the doctoral education system (share of PhD graduates in population, share of university faculty with doctoral degree, share of female students).
2. Internationalization of doctoral education (share of international students, language of dissertation).
3. Institutions and types of programmes available (public or private universities, universities or research institutes, forms of study, research- or course-based programmes).
4. Process of doctoral studies (number of levels, length of study, time before completion, obligation to pass comprehensive exam, PhD completion rate).
5. Types of PhDs, dissertations and supervision.
6. Financial organization of doctoral education and employment status of candidates (tuition, stipends, obligation to teach, salaries and benefits).

Judging by these parameters, the countries analysed in our study differ considerably. They can be classified into macro-regions: EU+ (France, Germany, Poland the United Kingdom); Commonwealth of Independent States or CIS (Kazakhstan, Russia); Asia (China, India, Japan, South Korea); Middle East (the UAE); Latin America (Brazil, Chile), North America (the United States) and Africa. However, within these macro-regions, there are also significant differences in terms of the models of doctoral education and in the main parameters of the system.

On the one hand, doctoral education is a sphere that attracts considerable attention. On the other hand, it suffers from a lack of relevant global statistics. Our analysis in this chapter is based on the indicators and parameters of doctoral education in the considered countries, which are presented in Table 19.1. We mainly used expert evaluations, as well as OECD and UNESCO statistics on doctoral education. We acquired a range of different indicators for the majority of countries.

Countries included in this analysis can be also classified by the historical formation of their doctoral education systems, which in turn affects institutional settings. There are countries with long histories of doctoral education and that were among the first in the world to establish doctoral programmes (France, Germany, the United Kingdom and the United States), some of which have long histories of colonization (France, Russia, the United Kingdom). These countries have had a considerable impact on the formation of doctoral education in other countries. At the same time, they are very attractive for international students, due to (perceived) high standards of doctoral education and future career prospects, and/or due to a high flow of students from former colonies or satellite countries. Another group includes relatively newly organized and expanding doctoral systems (Brazil, Chile, China, South Africa, the UAE). Some in this group used the models of countries with established doctoral programmes as benchmarks for the creation of their own systems, or adapted their systems to these older models (India, Poland).

For instance, doctoral education in China, Kazakhstan and Poland has some basic features in common with doctoral education in Russia, due to the significant influence of the Soviet education system and the role of the professorial elites in those countries. However, Russia itself looked earlier to Germany as a model. Russia also borrowed some features from the French, such as separating out the scientific sector from universities and concentrating research activities in research institutions affiliated with an academy of science rather than in universities.

More recently organized doctoral education systems tend to be oriented towards the American model, moving from a research-based to a course-based approach. The patterns and parameters of doctoral education depend considerably on the model that was chosen during the creation of the doctoral system and affect the current direction of reforms.

SCALE OF DOCTORAL EDUCATION SYSTEMS

Germany, the United Kingdom and the United States are the world leaders when it comes to the share of doctoral students in the overall population. Within the regions included in this book, France, Japan, Poland, Russia and South Korea are also among the leaders in the number of PhD students per 10,000 of the population. In Poland and Russia, the high share of PhD students in the population results in low PhD completion rates (below 30%). The two countries have common features in their doctoral education systems, which is a legacy of communist rule and the transition to a market economy that followed. In Poland and the Soviet Union during the communist era, the academic profession was prestigious, selective and reserved for the elite, with relatively well-paid jobs in the academic and research sectors. After the transition to a market economy, the higher education system, including doctoral education, experienced rapid massification. This was accompanied by relatively poor funding, and, consequently, a considerable decline in the prestige of the academic profession. In addition, entrance requirements for doctoral studies were lowered, along with stipends and other financial support. These factors, together with increasingly questionable prospects in terms of future careers in academic professions, led to very high dropout rates and low completion rates.

Although Polish and Russian doctoral education show very low completion rates (20–25%), in the majority of the other countries considered in this book completion rates exceed 50 per cent: from 55–70 per cent in Germany, the United Kingdom and the United States to more than 80 per cent in Brazil, Chile, Kazakhstan and South Korea. Higher completion rates seem to relate to the higher quality of education, as well as higher selectivity for entrance and adequate supervision during studies (as in France, Germany, the United Kingdom and the United States). Low completion rates, on the other hand, may indicate a lack of selectivity for admission to doctoral studies and relatively poor student support and/or prospects in the academic labour market (Poland, Russia). Very high completion rates—higher than 80 per cent—may indicate either that doctoral systems are working effectively or that there are low levels of selectivity or quality in the process of doctoral education and during the defence of the thesis.

In terms of the share of PhD holders among university faculty, there is a clear differentiation between countries with long histories of doctoral education and those with more recently created systems. Countries with long histories of doctoral education are among the leaders in the share of doctorates among university faculty. In Germany, Poland and the United Kingdom, the share exceeds 90 per cent. In Japan, it exceeds 80 per cent. It is also relatively high in Russia (72%) and France (62%). Other countries, which developed doctoral education more recently, have less than 40 per cent of faculty with doctoral degrees: 24–27 per cent in Chile and China, less than 30 per cent in Kazakhstan and 39 per cent in Brazil. The only exception is the UAE, which is a newly organized system and has 51 per cent of faculty with PhDs. This, however, is the result of attracting PhD holders from across the world to work in Emirati universities. Overall, in the majority of lower-middle income countries, the share of faculty with doctoral degrees is relatively low.

The issue of gender balance in doctoral studies reflects, to a significant extent, the following factors: the incidence of discrimination; the relative popularity of different fields (STEM, medicine, social sciences), which are traditionally different in gender structure; and economic prospects of the academic profession, demographic trends and cultural issues in each of these countries. In the majority of countries, the share of female doctoral students is below 50 per cent. The lowest share of female doctoral holders is in Japan (33%). To some extent, this indicates the country's heavy orientation towards STEM education, which traditionally attracts a higher share of male students, and also gender segregation in the Japanese labour market. In the Western world, the share of female students is between 45 and 48 per cent (France, Germany, the United Kingdom and the United States). However, in some countries there are trends towards the feminization of doctoral education (Poland, Kazakhstan and the UAE have 55%, 59% and up to 65% of female doctoral students, respectively). Kazakhstan and Poland are examples of countries where the feminization of doctoral education may reflect relatively modest opportunities and career prospects in academia, and the lack of financial support for doctorates, which make the academic profession less attractive for men. The UAE is a good example of how the feminization of doctoral education is connected to the considerable gender differences in the motivation to study. Women in the Emirates show higher motivation and better academic achievements than men, and frequently combine doctoral studies with childcare and family obligations.

THE INTERNATIONALIZATION OF DOCTORAL EDUCATION

Regarding the share of international students, countries that have both a rich history of doctoral education and a history as a colonizing power have the highest probability in attracting international students, the majority of whom come from former colonies undergoing massification of their higher education sector. The highest share of international students in doctoral education can be found in the United Kingdom, the United States and France (around 40%). Taking into consideration the scale of doctoral education systems, the United States is the main recipient of international doctoral students in terms of enrolments, but other countries (the United Kingdom, for instance) have a higher percentage of international students as part of the total number of doctoral students.

Japan and Germany also have considerable numbers of international students. Japan mainly attracts students from China, whereas Germany attracts students from across multiple European countries and Asia. Some countries (Chile, China, Russia) are regional powers in terms of higher education and mainly attract students from neighbouring countries. For instance, Russia (with 4% of international doctoral students) mainly gets students from the former Soviet republics and CIS countries. China, with a share of 5 per cent, attracts international students from neighbouring countries. Chile, with an 8 per cent share of international students, enrols doctoral students from less stable Spanish-speaking Latin American countries. India, Kazakhstan and Poland are currently not particularly attractive international destinations for doctoral students.

Among the factors that affect the international competitiveness of a country's doctoral education system is the language of dissertation. The United Kingdom and the United States have a considerable competitive advantage here, since English is the main language of international science in a majority of research fields. Countries that provide an option to write and defend dissertations in English along with the native language, usually benefit from an important competitive advantage and may increase their share of international students. Among the non-English speaking countries presented in our comparative study, Germany introduced the possibility of writing a PhD thesis in English. The same option is gradually being introduced in Brazil, Japan and the UAE, although the option usually depends on the field of study and/or the type of university. Russia is also gradually introducing the option of writing and defending theses in English, but only at some of the top, most selective universities. France, on the other hand, is an example of a major player in doctoral education where only the national language can be used for the dissertation. In the long run, this may negatively affect the internationalization and international competitiveness of French doctoral education. However, any negative effects are currently being compensated by the large number of doctoral candidates from former colonies, which are French speaking, and a few other Francophone countries. The problem of language is also relevant for Chinese doctoral education, which does not allow the thesis to be written in English, but only in the national language. Numerous students from Asia, and even from China itself, choose the United States, the United Kingdom, Europe or Japan as destinations for their studies because of a combination of language and reputation. Adding English as an option seems crucial for maintaining a country's global competitiveness in doctoral education.

Although not addressed as much in our case studies, there are other relevant internationalization factors in doctoral education that require attention. One is the possibility for students to attend international conferences and publish in international journals. In most countries, this has become an important requirement for the completion of their studies, and thus puts pressure on them to get papers accepted for international conferences and journals. As there is increased competition for access to quality international conferences and journals, many doctoral students are forced to turn to predatory conferences and journals. This is particularly true for students from low- and middle-income countries and from less prestigious universities. These students also face hurdles in finding funding to participate in international conferences and in getting support for editing and translating their articles.

International co-supervision and reader assessment of theses is an increasing trend, especially in smaller, low- and middle-income countries. Such international involvement is considered to be a reputational, quality and anti-inbreeding measure, but cost and quality control are challenges.

There is also a trend, still quite limited, to develop international joint and dual doctoral degrees. Online doctoral programmes targeting international students are emerging as well. However, issues such as costs, quality control and accreditation, joint supervision and other regulatory concerns restrict the prospects of such initiatives. It is more common for doctoral students to spend part of their research and study time at international partner institutions, in some cases with their international co-supervisor. National, regional (mainly from the European Union), and institutional fellowships stimulate such international stays, but costs and a lack of scholarships for students from low- and middle-income countries are also limitations here.

Another important issue is the relevance of doctoral education, not just for the local context, but also for the broader global knowledge society. The question here is finding a balance between the global and the local in a variety of aspects of doctoral education: research topics, labour market needs, education abroad, international supervision and funding are all challenges, in particular for low- and middle-income countries. Related to this is the relevance of doctoral education for local and national development, as well as for the United Nations Sustainable Development Goals.

WHAT TYPES OF INSTITUTIONS HAVE PhD PROGRAMMES?

An important issue in doctoral education across different countries concerns the type of institutions that prepare doctoral students. PhD programmes are offered in public universities in all countries, but in some places, they are also offered in private universities.

The main example of a country with doctoral education in private universities is the United States. In Brazil, Japan and the UAE, doctoral education in private universities is also quite common. In some countries, doctoral education in private universities appeared as an option after recent reforms and the transition from planned to market economies (Kazakhstan, Poland, Russia). In European countries with a long history of doctoral education (France, Germany, the United Kingdom) and in China, doctoral education is taught only in public universities, with a few exceptions in some fields and programmes.

Another difference is whether doctoral education is taught in research universities only or in research institutes as well. For instance, in Chile, France, Kazakhstan, the UAE and the United States, doctoral programmes are only offered in universities, while in China, Germany, Japan, Poland, South Korea, Russia and some other countries it is also possible to get a PhD in a non-university research institution. Also, in Germany and other European countries, universities of applied sciences are now putting pressure on governments for the right to offer doctoral degrees, although there is resistance from the research universities.

PROCESS OF DOCTORAL STUDIES

Globally, doctoral systems differ considerably in the process of study, reflecting the peculiarities of each country's institutions and traditions. One important indicator is the levels of doctoral education. Some of the European countries represented in our study (Germany, Poland, Russia) have two-level systems, or some elements of two-level systems: one level is the PhD and the other is the *habilitation* degree, which is awarded on the basis of a *habilitation* dissertation, a public lecture, the quality of publications and other factors. In other words, these countries essentially have a 'two doctoral degree' arrangement, and senior academics and researchers are, in general, expected to obtain both degrees over the course of their careers, with the *habilitation* coming later in their career. However, under the Bologna agreement, the *habilitation* degree is gradually disappearing. In the United States, there is a one-level system, but the length of the doctoral study is longer than in European countries.

With the exception of Kazakhstan, the vast majority of countries analysed in this book offer not only full-time doctoral programmes, but also part-time ones. Doctoral students also have an opportunity to pursue distance or online PhD programmes in France, Germany, Japan, the United Kingdom and the United States, while in other countries there are only full-time or part-time options. The introduction of distance learning requires a lot of technical sophistication and additional quality control.

In the majority of countries, the average length of study is three to four years, and the average time for completion is between four and five years, except in Chile and Poland, where six years to degree completion is the norm. In the United States, the average completion time for doctoral degrees varies considerably by field of study, but is usually between five and seven years. Another important factor, which speaks to the institutional settings of a country's doctoral education system, is the differences in a doctoral student's obligation to pass a comprehensive exam. In most of European countries (France, Germany, Poland and the United Kingdom) and in Brazil, students do not have an obligation to pass a comprehensive exam during their studies. They mostly focus on their (quite often, independent) research and work on their thesis. In other systems, students must pass a comprehensive exam during their doctoral studies as a prerequisite for working on the research part of the programme. In all of the countries included in this study, doctoral candidates must write and present a research-based dissertation to obtain a PhD degree, but defence procedures differ considerably, ranging from an oral, public defence to a presentation of text and/or research articles.

ACADEMIC AND PROFESSIONAL DOCTORATES

Doctoral degrees were originally created to prepare graduates for academic careers. In many countries—in particular those that still face rapid massification of their higher education systems—this is still the most important purpose, and is key for the enhancement of quality higher education and research. But overall, in particular in those countries with universal higher education, only a small proportion of the graduates are able or willing to pursue an academic career. In the countries involved in this study, we encountered several examples of mismatches between doctoral graduation rates and academic needs. We also found issues pertaining to the unemployment of doctoral graduates. Because the private sector can offer better salaries and benefits, there are labour market pressures on doctoral students to choose jobs outside of academia, perhaps even dissuading students from engaging at all in PhD studies.

We also see mismatches between the skills and competencies that doctoral graduates require and those that they receive. As Maresi Nerad states, doctoral students need professional competencies in addition to academic competencies. When the assumed market for doctoral graduates is academic, but the real market is more diverse, this should have implications for doctoral education. Although most countries are gradually becoming aware of this mismatch, there are few signs that substantive reform is taking place.

One response is the emergence of the professional doctorate in fields such as business, law and medicine. In Australia, the United Kingdom and the United States in particular, this trend is more apparent, although not in coherent and systematic ways. In other countries, there is an effort to include more transversal skills as part of the doctoral training, allowing students to prepare for alternative career options. One can say that doctoral education has still not been able to respond adequately to changes in the labour market. Nerad points to the risk that more focus on workforce preparation might happen at the expense of the need for intellectual risk-taking. To that danger, one can add the need for more attention to ethics in doctoral education.

DISSERTATION AND SUPERVISION TRENDS

Another trend one can observe is the change in dissertation requirements. Where the common practice has been that students have to deliver a research-based, monograph-type dissertation, one can now see a diversification in forms and requirements. Some graduates not only have to submit and successfully defend their dissertations, but now also have to publish a number of peer-reviewed articles before the defence. This has become more common, but the required number of articles differs widely, as does the required status of the article (submitted or accepted), the requirements of single authorship or co-authorship and the role of the (co)supervisor in the publication. A second, more recent trend is the option, or even the requirement, to complete the dissertation by published articles alone, thus dispensing with the traditional dissertation altogether. Again, there is no general agreement on the number, the status and the authorship of the articles, or what is needed as an introduction and conclusion of the article-based dissertation. There is also a discussion about the use of technology in delivering the dissertation, such as the use of visual content, in particular, but not exclusively, in the arts. And there is a debate about open access to research findings in cases of commissioned dissertations, which may be funded by external public and private entities.

The case studies in this book also show great variety in the ways the supervision and defence of dissertations is organized. Nerad mentions the shift from a single master–apprentice model to a model built around multiple supervisors accompanied by more programme and university quality assurance.

Whereas in the past, the doctoral student proposed a research project and looked for a supervisor, or the professor developed the research proposal and searched for a student to execute the proposal, doctoral research is now increasingly integrated and directed by the larger research plans and policies of research centres or graduate schools.

After completion of the dissertation and approval by the (co)supervisor(s), there are different models used for the formal approval and graduation. In general, there is a dissertation defence committee and/or external readers. Increasingly, a number of committee members or readers come from outside the department/school/centre. They may be from other universities, other countries and sometimes even from the private sector. But their number and their roles vary by country and within countries, by institution or even by schools. The number of cases in which a thesis is rejected after approval by the (co)supervisor(s) is, in general, extremely small, as this would not only disqualify the student but also the (co)supervisor(s). In most countries, the role of external readers and defence committee members is rather marginal. In the United States, the committee can and will ask only for minor revisions, while in the United Kingdom, the committee chooses between rejection, major revision, minor revision or approval. In nearly all cases, committees ask for minor or in some cases major revisions. In most other countries, their role is more ceremonial or limited to decisions about pass or pass cum laude. The trend is to have a more thorough supervision and approval process, but the variety of models is still quite substantial worldwide.

FINANCIAL ORGANIZATION OF DOCTORAL EDUCATION AND STUDENT EMPLOYMENT STATUS

Financial support during doctoral studies, as well as the employment status of doctoral students, are significant indicators of the opportunity costs of pursuing a PhD and of the economic conditions of doctoral studies. Incidence of strong financial support and employment security make the system more competitive and attractive to students, and contribute to the selection of the best students for doctoral education. Solid financial support increases the motivation of the student to dedicate all of his or her efforts to research and study, thereby increasing the PhD completion rate. Meanwhile, the lack of proper funding, together with uncertain career prospects, can lead to a considerable increase in the number of dropouts and force doctoral students to combine studies with outside jobs, decreasing the quality of education.

Among the countries covered in this book, only in Germany are the majority of doctoral students considered official employees of the university and paid based on this status. This is true in some other European countries as well, such as the Scandinavian countries and the Netherlands (not included in this study). In all other countries in this book, PhD candidates are considered students, although in some (Chile, Poland, Russia and the UAE) they may also have teaching responsibilities. Teaching by doctoral students is useful for university faculty, allowing them sometimes to reduce their teaching responsibilities. It is also cost-effective for universities. For their part, students get teaching experience, which is useful for future academic employment. In top doctoral destinations in the Western world (France, Germany, the United Kingdom and the United States), as well as in China and Japan, doctoral students do not have an official obligation to teach, but in Germany and the United States more than half of doctoral candidates are involved in teaching.

In terms of tuition for doctoral education, Brazil, Germany and the UAE are the only countries in our study that do not charge students for doctoral education. In Chile, Kazakhstan, Poland and Russia, some doctoral students pay tuition fees, whereas the majority do not pay and are provided funding from government sources. Moreover, tuition in these countries is relatively low. In France and India there are tuition fees, but the majority of students receive stipends. In other countries, including China, Japan, the United Kingdom and the United States, tuition costs are high and the availability of financial help depends on funding from programmes, research projects or from universities. In some cases, students pay for doctoral study themselves and can obtain loans from government or other sources. In the United States, doctoral students in many cases are provided graduate assistantships for teaching and/or research; these assistantships provide tuition remission, health insurance and a stipend. In Japan and the United Kingdom, students have few fellowship opportunities (in the United Kingdom, stipends are available only through research-funding bodies). Regarding financial opportunities and economic incentives for doctoral studies, the UAE seems to be an outstanding example. The Emirates offer free-of-charge doctoral studies and also very generous stipends that equal or even exceed the average salaries in the country. Among high-income countries, Germany provides students with the necessary support during their studies, making doctoral education there an attractive option for talented graduates from around the world. On the other end of the spectrum, Japan and South Korea, despite having high-quality doctoral programmes, seem to offer very limited funding opportunities for doctoral students. Due to an overproduction of doctorates, these countries also offer relatively modest labour market prospects.

CONCLUSION

Despite the numerous variations across countries discussed in this chapter, doctoral education has become a global system, complete with global flows of doctoral students and a globalized academic job market. Leading universities in different countries have common requirements for academic job candidates. There is also a tendency towards some convergence in doctoral education in terms of the process of studies, which has become more unified and internationalized. In order to successfully compete in the global competition for the best doctoral students and in the world university rankings race, higher education institutions are interested in unifying standards for doctoral education. They want to ensure that their programmes correspond with international standards, which are largely set up by global leaders in doctoral education training (the United Kingdom and the United States, for instance). This results in increased convergence of doctoral education around the world, especially within and among world-class universities in various countries. We can expect that in-country differences between leading universities and other institutions will continue to add significant variation to doctoral education, while cross-border differences between leading universities will be smoothed out.

While leading universities unify their approaches, other systems will continue to produce PhD candidates for local markets and may not experience any substantial changes in requirements, standards or programme routines. When it comes to doctoral education, each country will, to a large extent, continue to pursue its own national and even institutional models. More than striving for one global model—say, by copying the current dominant model of US doctoral education, or keeping to the traditional European 'dissertation only', highly individualized pattern—the way forward may be the development of common standards and values.

Universities with doctoral programmes have traditionally been research-intensive institutions, and in most countries, this is still the case. The fact that they have the infrastructure required for research—highly qualified professors who themselves hold doctorates, physical facilities such as laboratories and libraries, and an organizational and governance structure that fosters research—make these universities appropriate for doctoral education. Indeed, doctoral students contribute significantly to research productivity through their own work, as well as through their participation in laboratories and other university research. These universities are the ones that can be found at the top of the global rankings—the world-class universities. Indeed, all universities in the top 100 of any of the rankings are research-intensive institutions with strong and very selective doctoral programmes. (Of course, this is, in part, because rankings predominantly measure research productivity.)

The link between doctoral programmes and doctoral education, research universities and the world-class university movement is clear and inevitable. Efforts to build doctoral capacity at academic institutions that have little research focus will be unlikely to yield successful results. Even professional doctorates, which may not be aimed at providing qualifications to graduates who will enter academic or research careers, still require universities with an understanding of, and commitment to, research, in order to be offered successfully. It is clear from the research and analysis presented in this book that the link between doctoral education and research is close, and that doctoral education remains central to the mission and the success of universities and the research enterprise worldwide.

ANNEXURE

Table 19.1 Statistics on Institutional Settings of Doctoral Education in Analysed Countries[a]

Indicator	Korea	China	Japan	India	UAE	United Kingdom	France	Germany	Poland	Russia	Kazakhstan	Brazil	Chile	United States
Number of PhD students in 10K of population	74.3	5.71	12	1.2	—	—	8.46	—	11.3	7	2	5.4	3.12	—
Share of doctoral degree holders in population 25–64 (OECD 2017)						1.3%	0.9%	1.4%	0.5%	0.2%				1.8%
Share of PhD holders among faculty	85%	24%	>80%	—	51%	>90%	62%	93%	95%	72%	<30%	39%	9%	—
Number of levels	one	one	one	—	one	one–two	one–two	two	two	two	one	one	one	one

(Continued)

Table 19.1 (Continued)

Indicator	Korea	China	Japan	India	UAE	United Kingdom	France	Germany	Poland	Russia	Kazakhstan	Brazil	Chile	United States
Forms of study	full-time part-time	full-time part-time	full-time part-time distant online	full-time part-time distant online	full-time part-time online	full-time part-time distant online	full-time part-time distant online	full-time part-time distant online	full-time part-time	full-time part-time	full-time	full-time part-time	full-time part-time	full-time part-time distant online
Length of study	4 years	3–5 years max 8 years	3 years	3 years	3–4 years (full-time)	4 years (full-time) max 8 years (part-time)	3 years (full-time) max 6 years (part-time)	3–4 years	4 years	3–4 years (full-time) 4–5 years (part-time)	3 years	4 years	usually 4 years	varies by discipline and student
Average time for completion	5 years	4 years	4–5 years	—	—	4–6 years (full-time) 6–8 years (part-time)	4 years	3.5–4.5 years	6 years	4–5 years	3 years	4–5 years	6 years	5–7 years
Share of female PhD students	39%	38%	33%	42%	>65%	48%	45%	44%	55%	48%	59%	52%	45%	46%

Share of international PhD students enrolled (estimations from country reports and OECD 2016)	9%	5%	18%	—	43%	40%	9%	2%	4%	1%	2%	8%	40%
Tuition fees	yes	yes	yes	usually no (only for online PhD)	yes	yes	no	some of them	some of them	some of them (less than 1%)	no	some of them (small minority)	some of them
Stipend in public institutions	depend on programme and advisor	yes	depend on the personal case	usually no (most get fellowship); yes (mostly get a stipend)	yes (if externally funded by research funding body)	yes (for a majority of students)	depend on the programme, depend on the personal case	depend on the personal case	depend on the programme, depend on the personal case	yes	depend on availability	depend on the programme	depend on the programme and personal case
Presence of PhD programmes in research institutes	yes	yes	yes	yes	no	no	yes	yes	yes	no	yes	no	yes

(Continued)

Table 19.1 *(Continued)*

Indicator	Korea	China	Japan	India	UAE	United Kingdom	France	Germany	Poland	Russia	Kazakhstan	Brazil	Chile	United States
Presence of PhD programmes in private higher education Institutions	yes (but very few, limited to STEM field)	no (but will be approved in a few years in Westlake University)	yes	yes	yes	no (none in 'for profits' except University of Law)	no	not as a rule (only very few private higher education institutions)	yes	yes	yes	yes	yes	—
Share of PhD students enrolled in public and government dependent private institutions (OECD 2016)	38%	100%	75%	74%	—	100%	99%	100%	92%	100%	—	88%	89%	62%
Research-based versus course-based programme	strongly course work based	mainly research based	strongly course work based	mainly research based	mainly research based	both research based and 'research plus course work' based	mostly research based	mainly research based	usually research based	strongly course work based	mainly research based	programmes usually require 30–40% course work + research	both (taught phase of two years and research phase of two years)	combination of course work and research

Obligation to pass comprehensive exam	yes	yes	no	yes	no	no	no (only defence)	yes	yes	only in a few cases	yes (often in the form of a proposal defence)
Obligation of dissertation	yes	yes	yes	yes	yes	yes	yes	yes	yes	yes	yes
Language of dissertation	National or English	National	National/ regional or English	National or English	National = English	National (possible exceptions)	National or English	National or English	National (2 languages) sometimes English	National or Spanish or English	National = English
Obligation to teach	no	no	no	usually yes	no (except 'graduate teaching assistant + PhD' positions)	no (limited amount of teaching allowed)	no (but 67% of PhD students involved in teaching)	usually yes	usually no	usually no	usually yes

(Continued)

Table 19.1 (Continued)

Indicator	Korea	China	Japan	India	UAE	United Kingdom	France	Germany	Poland	Russia	Kazakhstan	Brazil	Chile	United States
Employment status of PhD candidates: Are doctoral students considered employees?	extremely few	none	none	none	none	none	yes for students who get a stipend	most of them (83%)	none	none	some of them	none	none	none, not usually
Completion rates	94%	high (no estimation)	90%	—	—	70%	75%	57%–67%	25%	20%–25%	90%	86%	83%	55% of all students and 70% of students who have completed coursework
Employment rate among PhD holders (OECD 2015)	—	—	—	—	—	88.3%	90.1%	93.3%	98.2%	88.9%	—	—	—	89.8%

Source: Country statistics are based on estimations from the country reports but in some cases, which are italicized, on OECD/UNESCO data.

Notes: [a] Data on South Africa is missing.

Sacro Cuore in Milan, Italy, and professor of Internationalization of Higher Education at the Amsterdam University of Applied Sciences. He is the founding editor of *The Journal of International Higher Education* and consulting editor of *Policy Reviews in Higher Education*.

CONTRIBUTORS

Ana Maria Fonseca de Almeida is associate professor at the School of Education, University of Campinas, Brazil. Her research focuses on education and inequality. She is the author of *As Escolas dos Dirigentes Paulistas* and co-editor of *A Escolarização das Elites* and *Circulação Internacional e Formação Intelectual das Elites Brasileiras*. Her publications have appeared in journals and books in Brazil, France, the United Kingdom and the United States. She has been a visiting professor at the École des Hautes Etudes en Sciences Sociales in Paris and at FLACSO in Buenos Aires, and a visiting scholar at the Stanford University Center for Latin American Studies.

Ann E. Austin is professor of higher, adult and lifelong education at Michigan State University, where she also serves as associate dean for research in the College of Education and assistant provost for Faculty Development—Career Paths. Her research publications focus on academic work, careers and professional development; organizational change in higher education; doctoral education and STEM in higher education. She recently co-authored *Faculty Development in the Age of Evidence: Current Practices, Future Imperatives*.

Andrés Bernasconi is an associate professor at the School of Education of the Pontificia Universidad Católica (PUC) de Chile, and director of its Center of Advanced Studies on Educational Justice. He has done research on Chilean and Latin American higher education, and has taught or carried out research/consulting work on higher education administration and policy in various countries in the Americas, Europe and Asia. He is currently interested in higher education law and regulation, university governance and organizational change in institutions of higher education. He holds degrees from the PUC, Harvard University and Boston University.

About the Editors and Contributors

EDITORS

Maria Yudkevich is vice-rector of the National Research University Higher School of Economics (HSE University) in Moscow, Russia. She also serves as associate professor in the Economics Department, and as director of the Center for Institutional Studies at HSE University. Her main area of interest and research is contract theory, with a special focus on faculty contracts, universities and markets for higher education. She has been a co-organizer of several international projects looking at the academic profession from comparative perspectives and other topics.

Philip G. Altbach is research professor and founding director of the Center for International Higher Education (CIHE) in the Lynch School of Education and Human Development at Boston College in the United States. He was the 2004–2006 distinguished scholar leader for the New Century Scholars initiative of the Fulbright programme, and has been a senior associate of the Carnegie Foundation for the Advancement of Teaching. His most recent book is *Global Perspectives on Higher Education*. He is a member of the Russian government's '5–100 Excellence Commission' and is on the advisory boards of the National Research University Higher School of Economics in Russia, the Lahore University of Management Science in Pakistan and the Graduate School of Education at Shanghai Jiao Tong University in China.

Hans de Wit is director of the CIHE in the Lynch School of Education and Human Development at Boston College, where he also serves as professor of the practice in international higher education. Before joining CIHE in 2015, he was the founding director of the Center for Higher Education Internationalisation (CHEI) at the Università Cattolica del

Julien Calmand is a senior researcher at Céreq (French Center for Research on Education, Training and Employment), and is also a PhD student at the Institute for Research in the Sociology and Economics of Education (IREDU, EA7318, Université de Bourgogne–Franche Comté) in Dijon, France. His research interests include the transition from school to work and changes in higher education systems.

Shuhua Chen is assistant professor at the Graduate School of Education, Shanghai Jiao Tong University, China. Her research interests include graduate students' learning experience and career preparation, doctoral examinations and researcher development. She is the principal investigator on multiple research projects about doctoral education in mainland China, including the one funded by China's Ministry of Education. Her most recent article, published in *Higher Education Research and Development*, looks at postdoctoral scholars' experience of preparing for their desired careers.

Thierry Chevaillier is professor emeritus of economics of education at the Institute for Research in Sociology and Economics of Education (IREDU) at the Université de Bourgogne–Franche Comté in Dijon, France. His research focuses on the funding, staffing, organization and evaluation of higher education institutions. He is a member of CHER (Consortium of Higher Education Researchers).

Rosemary Deem, OBE, is Doctoral School director (Quality, Enhancement and Inclusion) and professor of Higher Education Management at Royal Holloway, University of London, United Kingdom. An academician of the UK Academy of Social Sciences, she is a sociologist who has also worked at Loughborough, York, the Open and Lancaster Universities, as well as the former North Staffordshire Polytechnic. Since 2013, she has been a co-editor of the international journal *Higher Education*. In July 2015, she became the first woman to chair the UK Council for Graduate Education.

Shane Dowle is a postgraduate research student at Royal Holloway, University of London, United Kingdom. His research explores the factors that help or hinder the timely submission of PhD theses. His interest in this topic stems from his professional experience working as the manager of a doctoral college.

Mauricio Ernica is assistant professor at the School of Education at the University of Campinas, Brazil. While working in NGOs and after returning to academia, he has focused his research on education and inequality. His work has been published in journals and books in Brazil, Switzerland and the United States.

Jean-François Giret is professor of education at the Université de Bourgogne–Franche Comté, as well as director of the Institute for Research in the Sociology and Economics of Education (IREDU, EA7318, Université de Bourgogne-Franche Comté). His research interests include the transition from school to work and skills mismatch. He has published several books and scientific articles in the fields of economics and education.

Futao Huang is professor at the Research Institute for Higher Education, Hiroshima University, Japan. Before he came to Japan in 1999, he taught and conducted research at several Chinese universities. His main research interests include the internationalization of higher education, the academic profession and higher education in East Asia. He has published widely in Chinese, English and Japanese. He also served as a co-editor of *The Internationalization of the Academy: Changes, Realities and Prospects.*

Tatiana Karabchuk, PhD, is an assistant professor of sociology at United Arab Emirates University (UAEU). She also serves as coordinator of the Social Research Unit at UAEU, as well as vice-director for Eurasian Monitor. She was a visiting researcher at the Carolina Population Center, University of North Carolina–Chapel Hill (the United States), IOS Regensburg (Germany), GESIS EUROLAB (Germany) and Hitotsubashi University (Japan).

Barbara M. Kehm is a fellow at the Leibniz Research Center for Science and Society, University of Hannover, Germany. Her research focuses on internationalization in higher education, the Bologna

Process, changes in doctoral education and professionalization processes in higher education. Currently, she is the principal investigator of a research project about the future of the humanities. Her most recent publication (2018), edited with J. C. Shin and G. A. Jones, is *Doctoral Education for the Knowledge Society: Convergence or Divergence in National Approaches?*

Seung Jung Kim is a research fellow at Seoul National University. Her major research interests are doctoral education and higher education policy. Her doctoral dissertation focused on doctoral students' competency and academic socialization. She has published about 10 articles on doctoral education and education policy issues in academic journals.

Marcelo Knobel is rector and professor of physics at the University of Campinas (Unicamp) in Brazil. His research interests are nano-magnetism, the popularization of science and technology, and higher education. He has published several newspaper articles and more than 250 scientific papers, including, in 2013, 'International Collaborations between Research Universities: Experiences and Best Practices' in *Studies in Higher Education.*

Elena Kobzar is director of graduate studies at the National Research University Higher School of Economics in Moscow, Russia. Her areas of expertise are doctoral education management, higher education policy and doctoral education systems and institutions. As a consultant, she works with the Russian ministry of education and science on strategies for improving doctoral education.

Aliya Kuzhabekova is an associate professor at the Nazarbayev University Graduate School of Education, Kazakhstan. Her primary research interests include the internationalization of higher education (international faculty and student mobility, international research collaboration and the outcomes of international mobility); the research function of higher education (research capacity building in transitional economies, researcher socialization and experiences in countries with lower research capacities) and women in higher education.

Marek Kwiek is UNESCO Chair in Institutional Research and Higher Education Policy, University of Poznan, Poland. His research interests include quantitative studies of science, the internationalization of research and the academic profession. His most recent book is *Changing European Academics: A Comparative Study of Social Stratification, Work Patterns and Research Productivity*. He was a Fulbright New Century Scholar in 2007–2008, and is an editorial board member of *Higher Education Quarterly*, *European Educational Research Journal* and *British Educational Research Journal*.

HeeJin Lim is a research fellow at Seoul National University in South Korea. Her major research areas include doctoral education and the internationalization of higher education. She has published a number of articles and book chapters related to doctoral students' learning and research experiences, with a special focus on the Korean higher education context. She is currently exploring international doctoral students' academic socialization experiences in Korea. She has published a number of articles on doctoral education and education policy issues in academic journals.

Dara Melnyk is the head of the research group at SKOLKOVO Education Development Center, Moscow School of Management SKOLKOVO, Russia. Her professional and research interests are focused on university transformation. She has a bachelor's degree from the National University of Ostroh Academy in Ukraine, and a master's degree from Saint Petersburg State University in Russia. She also spent a year at the Lynch School of Education and Human Development at Boston College in the United States.

Emily R. Miller is associate vice-president for policy at the Association of American Universities. Her primary responsibilities are collaborating with member campuses on institutional policy efforts related to undergraduate and graduate education. She directs the association's Undergraduate STEM Education Initiative and PhD Education Initiative, and frequently works with other higher education policy organizations. She has published on organizational change in research universities, specifically as it relates to achieving systemic improvement of undergraduate education.

Ana Luisa Muñoz-Garcia is an assistant professor in the Faculty of Education at the Pontificia Universidad Católica of Chile. She has a PhD in educational culture, policy and society from SUNY Buffalo in the United States. She is currently leading one project on research policies in higher education, and another on issues of internationalization, knowledge and gender in academia. She is also the president of the Chilean Educational Research Network (RIECH).

Maresi Nerad is the founding director of the Center for Innovation and Research in Graduate Education (CIRGE) and professor emerita of higher education at the University of Washington (UW), Seattle, the United States. A native of Germany, she received her doctorate from the University of California, Berkeley. She has directed research on doctoral education at the Graduate Division of Berkeley as dean in residence at the Council of Graduate Schools in Washington, DC, and as associate dean of the UW central Graduate School. She is the author of *Towards a Global PhD?* and other books.

Sergey Roshchin is vice-rector of the National Research University Higher School of Economics in Moscow, Russia, where he also serves as associate professor in the Economics Department and as head of the Laboratory for Labour Market Studies. His major research interests are the interaction between labour and education markets, and labour market demand for skills.

Ksenia Rozhkova is a research assistant in the Laboratory for Labour Market Studies at the National Research University Higher School of Economics in Moscow, Russia. Her research interests include labour economics, investments in human capital and skills and academic labour markets.

Victor Rudakov is a research fellow at the Center for Institutional Studies and the Laboratory for Labour Market Studies at National Research University Higher School of Economics in Moscow, Russia. He is also a postdoctoral researcher at CIPES–Center for Research in Higher Education Policies at the University of Porto in Portugal. His main areas of research are labour economics and the economics of education.

Jung Cheol Shin is a professor at Seoul National University, South Korea. He served in the Korean ministry of education for about 20 years. His research interests are higher education policy, knowledge and social development, and the academic profession. He is co-editor-in-chief of the *International Encyclopedia of Higher Education* and a co-editor of the series *Knowledge Studies in Higher Education*. His recent book publications include *Doctoral Education for the Knowledge Society* and *Higher Education Governance in East Asia*.

Damtew Teferra is professor of higher education at the University of KwaZulu-Natal, South Africa. He is also the founding director of the International Network for Higher Education in Africa, which is closely associated with the Center for International Higher Education at Boston College, United States. He is founding editor-in-chief of the *International Journal of African Higher Education*. Teferra steers the Higher Education Cluster of the African Union's Continental Education Strategy for Africa. Most recently, he edited the book *Flagship Universities in Africa*.

N. V. Varghese is vice chancellor of the National University of Educational Planning and Administration, and director of the Centre for Policy Research in Higher Education (CPRHE), New Delhi, India. He holds a doctoral degree in economics with a specialization in educational planning. He served as head of governance and management in education at the International Institute for Educational Planning (IIEP/UNESCO) in Paris until October 2013, and ran the institute's training and education programmes from 2001 to 2006.

Ayenachew A. Woldegiyorgis is a research assistant and doctoral candidate of higher education at the Center for International Higher Education, Boston College, United States. His research interest broadly covers higher education in lower-middle income countries. Previously, he worked as a consultant for the World Bank, Washington, DC. In Ethiopia, he held teaching positions at Unity University and Addis Ababa University. He has also served as managing editor of the *International Journal of African Higher Education*.

Index

academia and industry
doctoral degree, 10–11
Academic Degrees Committee of the
State Council, 271
Advanced Human Capital Formation
Program, 420
African doctoral education
capacity gaps, 214
challenges, 227–231
colonial and postcolonial relationships, 214
enrolment, 213
history, 214–217
international collaborations,
222–224
new dawn, 217–219
prospects and future directions,
231–233
regional collaboration, 224–227
scholarly perceptions about knowledge, 216
variations, 219–222
African graduates, 252
American Association of Universities
(AAU), 182
assistantship, 15
At a 2012 conference, 214
At Cross Purposes, 196

bo-shi, 268
Bologna Process, 340
Brain Korea 21 Project, 365
Brazilian dilemmas in doctoral
education
Brazil today, 395–397

consolidation and expansion
programmes (1998–2016),
397–406
current challenges, 408–412
debates and policy changes,
406–407
expansion studies, 394–395
financing, 392–394
national graduate system, 390–392
recent developments, 406–407
British Council and German
Academic Exchange
(DAAD), 220

candidate of science, 271
career prospects, 275–276
chair holders, 85
Chile doctoral education
accreditation, 428–430
challenges and opportunities,
435–437
context and evolution, 416–420
distribution of enrolment, 420
doctoral studies abroad, 421–423
enrolments, 425–428
funding, 421
higher education system, 415
promotion policies
graduates, employment opportunities, 433–435
ministry of science and technology, 433
workforce, 432–433
promotion, policies, 430–431
results, 423–425

studies, 415
China Scholarship Council (CSC), 277
China's doctoral education, 268
China's strategic plan, 268
Chinese higher education system, 270
Chinese Ministry of Education (MOE), 283
Commonwealth of Independent States (CIS), 127
concerns and critiques of US doctoral education, 196–201
  alignment with career pathways, 197–198
  extent of student-centredness, 199–200
  length of time to degree and attrition, 198–199
  recruiting and retaining, 200
Council of University Rectors (CRUCH), 416

Destinations of Leavers from Higher Education (DLHE) surveys, 165
dissertation publication, 89
doctor of law degree (LLD), 244
doctoral candidates, 16
doctoral college, 59
doctoral contracts, 58
doctoral degree
  academia and industry, 10
  labour market value, 8–10
doctoral dissertations
  form and assessment, 13–14
doctoral education, 33, 267, 467
  academic and professional, 479–480
  access and registration, 61
  candidate status, 16–17
  career diversification and professionalization, 71–73
  centrality, 3–6
  challenges, 22–24

changing focus, 6
conflicts and contradictions, 144–145
countries, 471
dissertation and supervision trends, 480–481
duration of study, 62–63
European model, 468
evaluation, 149–150
expansion, 5
external changes and their impacts, 36–41
financial organization and student employment status, 481–483
France, 53–54
funding, 15–16
gender balance, 473
global challenges, 41–47
globalization and governmental innovation policies, 34–36
growing role of technology, 22
importance, 4
indicators, 470
international mobility, 6
internationalization, 474–477
  student mobility, 20–21
labour market conditions, 8–12
landscape, 469
low completion rates, 473
monetary incentives and quality, 41–42
networks and collaborations, 21
outlook, 47–48
part-time versus full-time study, 14–15
Phd programs
  types of institutions, 477
Polish and Russian, show, 473
present organization, 59–68
professional doctorate, 17–19
prospects, 24–25
prospects for future, 149–150
purpose, 6–8
quality, 12–13

ranking of universities, 141–142
reforms, 140–145
relevant themes, 33–34
results, 144–145
role and its challenges in society,
71–75
role of doctoral schools, 60–61
share of PhD holders, 473
STEM education, 474
studies, process, 478–479
subject selection, 62
system of PhD conferral, 142–144
traditional models, 468
transformation, 73–75
trends, 19–22
university–industry partnership, 21
variations, 13–19
work-based doctorate, 19
doctoral process, 278
American admissions model, 278
dissertation, 279
evaluation committee, 279
external examiners, 279
global versus local, 288–289
quality control, 287–288
reforms and trends, 281
application examination mechanism, 281–282
double-blind evaluation,
282–283
Double-World-Class (DWC)
Project, 284–285
government's quality check,
283
research universities, emergence, 285
State Council 2004, 278
stricter evaluation system, 279
time to completion, 278
top-down versus bottom-up
reforms, 286–287
traditional model, 278
doctoral programmes, 167
doctoral programmes in India

awarded, trends, 306–311
deeper analysis, 305
enrolment in research, 300
European approach, 301
fellowships, 302
higher education, 302
MPhil programmes, 303
NET, 302
open universities and distance
education programmes, 303
private universities, 302
UNESCO Institute for Statistics,
305
doctoral researchers, 84, 167
doctoral schools, 121
access and registration, 61
accreditation, 61
creation, 58–59
role in doctoral education,
60–61
subject selection, 62
doctoral students
France
preparing for various employment, 66
recruiting to the professoriate,
67
supervision, 63
doctoral studies, 296
completion, 63–66
duration of study, 62–63
France
creation of doctoral schools,
58–59
history, 54–56
funding, 64–66
Indian universities, 299
colleges and universities, 299
commissions and committees,
300
public policies, 300
Radhakrishnan Commission's,
300
scholars, 299

technological institutions,
300
doctoral supervisors, 277
doctoral training
funding, 139–140
doctorate, 119
career diversification and professionalization, 71–73
definition, 57
implementation, 122
types, 272

enrolments
patterns, 273–274
excellence and mediocrity, 256–257
external doctoral candidates, 84

FCSA 2016, 444
fellowship, 16
FONDECYT, 420
funding, 15–16, 274
assistantship, 15
doctoral studies, 64–66
doctoral training, 139–140
fellowship, 16

German Academic Exchange Service,
99
Germany
doctoral education, 86
historical roots, 79–81
international doctoral candidates,
99
magnitude of PhD production,
81–82
nature and magnitude of doctoral
education, 79–91
overproduction of PhDs, 98
procedures for awarding doctoral
degree, 88–89
recent reforms and new developments, 91–98
recruitment and status of doctoral
candidates, 82–85

relationship between doctoral
degree and habilitation,
89–91
role of doctoral education in and
for society, 98–101
supervisors and supervision, 85–88
governmental innovation policies
negative effect, 46
graduate education, 270
Graduate Record Examination
(GRE), 453
graduates
doctoral programmes, 4
gross enrolment ratio (GER), 298
growing role of technology, 21
Gulf Cooperation Council (GCC)
countries, 445

habilitation, 89
higher education in India, 297
autonomous colleges, 298
government colleges, 298
gross enrolment ratio (GER), 298
prestigious institutions, 297
private universities, 298
state universities, 297
university system, 297
higher education institutions (HEIs),
272, 295

implementation doctorate, 122
international students, 276
internationalization and student
mobility, 20–21

Japanese University Accreditation
Association, 319
Japan's doctoral education, 316
basic structure and scale, 320
organization, 324–326
quantitative trends, 322–324
categories of candidates, 318
colleges and graduate schools, 318
domestic students, 332–336

Education Act, 319
factors, 319
first four graduate schools, 319
graduate education and facilities,
320
Imperial University, 317
international students, 336–337
newly established universities, 319
recent policies and reforms,
326–330
society, 330
economic issues, 332
labour market and graduates,
330–332
training, 318

Kazakhstan doctoral education
comprehensive methodological
training, 348
coursework and dissertation, 347
dissertation writing and advising,
process, 348
European standards, 340
formal training programme, 346
numbers of students, 350–354
process of dissertation, 349
proliferation of publications, 348
publication requirement, 347
purchased dissertations, 346
reform in post-Soviet Kazakhstan,
343–346
restructuring system, 340
Soviet origins, 341–343
State Standards, 347
Korea Advanced Institute of Science
and Technology (KAIST),
365

labour market conditions
overeducation and job, 11–12
labour market value
doctoral degree, 8–10
liberalities, 65
Lisbon Convention in 1997, 340

Ministry of Education 2010, 276
modern challenges to Russian doctoral
education, 145–149
erosion of boundaries, 145–146
insufficient funding, 148–149
purpose, 146–147
quality, 147–148
research and science, 145–149
modern research-based doctorate, 80
modern Russia's doctoral education,
129–140
dynamics of awarding PhDs,
131–132
funding, 139–140
reforms, 140–145
rules of game, 134–138
Russian model of PhD, 138–139
universities versus. research institutes, 132–134

National Campaign for the
Advancement of High
Ranking Civil Servants
(CAPES), 392
National Center for Science and
Engineering Statistics
(NCSES), 188
National Council for Scientific and
Technological Development
(CNPq), 393
national degree, 57
National Eligibility Test (NET), 302
national research evaluation, 121
Nazarbayev University (NU) doctoral
education, 349
dissertation defense, 350
graduation requirements, 350
operates in partnership, 349
programmes, 350
networks and collaborations, 21
new dawn for doctoral education in
Africa, 217–219
capacity building, 218

growing focus on labour market, 219

impetus of knowledge economy, 217–218

massification, 218

overeducation and job, 11–12

overemphasis on workforce preparedness, 46–47

People's Republic of China, 267

performance-based doctorate, 157

PhD graduates

  career path studies, 43–45

  employment, 42

  equity of access and affordability, 45

  supervisor training, 45

PhD students

  competition with engineers and in R&D in France, 70–71

  employability and labour market perspectives, 66–68

  fostering employment tax credit scheme, 71

  high unemployment of in France, 68–70

Poland

  doctoral education

    funding, and internationalization, 109–112

    history, 103–105

    organization, 106–107

    procedures, 107–109

    society, 105–106

    structure, 113

Polish doctoral education, 123

  distribution of doctorates awarded, 113–119

  female-to-male (FM) ratio, 116

  implementation doctorate, 122

  international comparative perspective, 112–119

  reform debates, 120–123

Polish doctoral recipients, 113

Polish higher education reforms, 121

Postgraduate Research Experience Survey, 160

professional doctorate, 17–19

public investment and institutions, 296

Radhakrishnan Commission's, 300

Regulations on Academic Degrees of the People's Republic of China, 271, 278, 280

Regulations on Conferral of Scientific Degrees, 348

research units, 60

Russian doctoral education, 127, 128

  insufficient funding, 148–149

  modern challenges, 145–149

Russian doctoral programmes

  mobility and integration, 148

  quality, 147–148

Russian model of PhD, 138–139

sandwich model, 222

Savary Act, 56

Science Citation Index, 280

second doctorate, 89

Several government documents, 271

Sino-US diplomatic relations in 1979, 270

socialization process, 187

soft skills, 201

South African higher education institutions (HEIs), 238

South African higher education

  diversity in doctorate, 259

  doctoral marketplace, 257–258

  doctoral sector, 244–250

  drive and raison d'être of PhD programmes, 241–244

  excellence and mediocrity, 256–257

  funding dynamics, 254–256

  history, 239

increasing funding, 258
international collaboration, 260
international dimension, 254
key components, 248
managing throughput, 259–260
model, 250–251
overview, 240–241
promoting doctoral education,
258–260
public support, 259–260
three tiers, 240
South African Qualifications
Authority
database, 244
South Korea doctoral education
admissions requirements, 369
characteristics of degree granting
institutions, 371–372
critical educational problems, 364
development, 364–365
Education Law in 1975, 364
government programmes, 363
graduate education system,
365–366
graduation requirements, 369–371
issues and challenges
brain drain, 377–379
limited financial support,
379–380
project-based STEM, 380–382
student exploitation, problems,
376–377
supply and demand, 375–376
model, 368–369
policy efforts
world-class research universities and graduate education,
372–374
quality assurance, 374–375
student enrolment trends, 366–368
undergraduate enrolment, 364
Soviet system of training researchers
feature, 127
Soviet Union, 270

Standards of Establishment of
Graduate Schools, 320
state doctorate, 57
stewards of the discipline, 166
Success as a Knowledge Economy,
166
supervision, 274–275
supranational actors, 5
Survey of Earned Doctorates (SED),
188
system-level impacts, 36–38
São Paulo Research Foundation
(FAPESP), 393

teaching assistantships, 57
three-degree system, 122

UK Council for Graduate Education
(UKCGE), 161
UK doctorate, 152
completion and graduate destinations, 161–165
current debates about, 169–172
features, 158–161
history, 153–156
influenced by German, 166
outputs, 167
participation, 161–165
performance-based, 157
quality assurance of programmes,
160
role in society, 165–169
servant of academia to driving knowledge economy,
165–168
types, 156–158
underrepresented minorities (URM),
191
United Arab Emirates (UAE) doctoral
education, 444
emiratization, 450
expansion and diversity, 446
higher education, 445
international applicants, 453

OECD, 444
Phd programmes, 449
    challenges, 455–456
    cost and marketization, 457–458
    government support, 454–455
    role of women, 456–457
    postgraduate education, 448
    academic research, 444
    professional faculty, 451
United Arab Emirates University
    (UAEU), 445
university and programme-level
    changes, 38–41
University of Tokyo, 318
university–industry partnerships, 21
US doctoral education, 181
    approach to strengthening,
        203–204
    citizenship, race, and ethnicity of
        doctoral recipients, 191–193
    connections, 186
    creating student-centred learning
        environments, 202–203
    defining features, 184–188
    examples of reform efforts,
        204–206

feature, 191
function, 186
growth, 182
history, 182–184
location in academic departments,
    187–188
portrait, 188–196
programmatic changes, 201–202
recommendations and new direc-
    tions, 201–206
Second World War, 183
sex and age, 193–195
socialization process, 187
society concerns and critiques,
    196–201
US doctoral recipients
    data, 188
    primary sources of financial sup-
        port, 195
    sex and age, 193–195

Women In Science and Engineering
    (WISE), 163
work-based doctorate, 19